SET THEM FREE

SET THEM FREE

The Other Side of Exodus

Laurel A. Dykstra

ORBIS BOOKS

Maryknoll, New York 10545

Founded in 1970, Orbis Books endeavors to publish works that enlighten the mind, nourish the spirit, and challenge the conscience. The publishing arm of the Maryknoll Fathers and Brothers, Orbis seeks to explore the global dimensions of the Christian faith and mission, to invite dialogue with diverse cultures and religious traditions, and to serve the cause of reconciliation and peace. The books published reflect the views of their authors and do not represent the official position of the Maryknoll Society.

To learn more about Maryknoll and Orbis Books, please visit our website at www.maryknoll.org.

Library of Congress Cataloging-in-Publication Data

Dykstra, Laurel.
    Set them free : the other side of Exodus / Laurel Dykstra.
      p. cm.
    Includes bibliographical references and index.
    ISBN 1-57075-441-1 (pbk.)
    1. Bible. O.T. Exodus—Criticism, interpretation, etc. I. Title.
BS1245.2 .95 2002
222'.1206—dc21

                              2002004509

For Harriet and Myriam

And dedicated to the memory of

Ross Ackerly
Wendy Ackerman
Alex (a child)
Ali
Bill Amburgee
Don Babe
Angie's Baby
Arlene's baby daughter
Jesus "Chewie" Atalano
John August
Paoa "Toulie" Avaava
David Berlew
"Big Lee-lee"
Sherri Bishop
Maria Brassel
Scott Braiden
Homer "Buddy" Brown
Leo Brown
Larry Bunch
Dorothy Burr
Kenny Canley
Stanley "Junior" Chambers
Michael Cheney
Herbert "Spade" Coleman
Connie
"Cowboy" Russ
Fortino "Chaparro" Rojas
Cruz
"Dollar" Bill
Angie Dickinson
Larry Dilts
Susan Dugan
John Craig Draves
Earl
Michael Eddings
Gerald Edmonton
Connie Laforntaine Ellis
Mark Ewing
Judy Lynn Exum
Greg Fix
Matthew Gallagher
Bobby Glasser
Ed Goudmond

"Green Eyes"
Joseph Harns
Mike Harvey
James "Shakey" Hurd
Ed Henderson
Charles "One-Eye" Houts
Diana Lyn Hubbard
Barbara Hunsacker
Hunter
Danny Jackson
Reginald "Vegeta" Jennings
Jesse
Joey (Stormy's son)
Josephine
Stormy Kanoye
Kenny
"Killer"
Harold Kistler
Dave "Dewey" Laar
Steve Lawrence
Rick Lawty
James Lee
Pierre Lesvesque
Liz
"Lucky"
Mike Mares
Ernest Martin
Judy Matz
Michael Mays
Charles McCarver
Connie McDonough
Rick McGee
Melissa McLeod
"Jersey Joe" Metzner
Larry Middleton
Ray Middleton
Ross Miller
Daniel "Cardboard Man"
Rudy Miller
Terry Moore
"Nazi" Bob
"New York" Tony
Glen Otto

John Owens
Darren Panzer
Pasco
Patrick
Paul
Milton Pedraza
John Penny
Jim Perry
Myron Phillips
Ann Pirolo
"Kevin" Lloyd Putney
Bill Rogers
Ronald Ross
"Salt n Pepper"
"Sarge"
Roy Sawyer
Jimmie Schulz
Shirley
Simone (Lewis) Simm
Barbara Simms
Allen Simms
Mike "Little
Mikey" Skittlethorpe
Dale Smith
Ennis Smith
Michael Stephens
Sydney
Jerry T.
Tony
Virgil Tully
Jerry Turner
Chica W.
Wendel Wagner
Charles "Gurley" Walker
Stan Wayson
Jim West
Elaine Wilkinson
Grace Wilman
Alonzo Williams
John Wolfer
Crystal Wooster
James Worth

and all the others who have died homeless, alone,
and on the streets of Tacoma

CONTENTS

ACKNOWLEDGMENTS   x

INTRODUCTION   xi

PART ONE
READING EXODUS

1. History, Literature, and Story:
   An Introduction to Modern Biblical Criticism   3

   History and the Bible   4
   Who Wrote the Bible?   9
   The Bible as Literature   13
   The Bible as Sacred Story   19

2. Reading Exodus as Israel: Identification with Election   22

   Reading the Bible in English   22
   Introduction to Exodus   24
   Retelling Exodus   26
   Latin American Liberation Theology   31
   Latin American Readings of Exodus   32
   Black Theology   34
   Comparing Liberation Theologies   35
   Liberation Readings of Exodus   37

3. Prostitutes, Slaves, and Canaanites:
   Another Side of Exodus   38

   Liberation Readings Challenged   38
   Reading Exodus in the First World   50
   Reading the Text Wrong   52
   Reading for Our Lives   52

PART TWO
BEING READ BY EXODUS

4. Egypt as Empire   57

   Egypt in History   57
   Egypt in the Bible   58

Beginning to Read as Egypt   59
First World, Third World, and Biblical World   61
Empire, Past and Present   63
Violence of Exploitation   65
Slavery   68
Genocide   71
Lying and Deceit   75
Can We Change?   78

5. Egypt the Land   79

The Land of Egypt   79
Plague Narratives   82
Introduction to Ecofeminism   90
An Ecofeminist Reading of the Plague Narratives   91
Modern Parallels and Applications   97

6. Pharaoh: A Hardened Heart   105

The Pharaohs of Egypt   105
Pharaoh of the Prologue   106
The Building Blocks of Empire   110
First-World Hearts   119

7. Violence, Destruction, Hatred, and Judgment   128

Violence in Exodus   128
Chariots, A Symbol of Empire and Conquest   129
Midrash   132
Justification for God's Violence   133
Protesting a Violent God   134
Understanding the Violence in Exodus   137
Conclusion: Reading Violent Stories   144

8. Pharaoh's Daughter, Daughter of God   146

The Text   146
Context—Stepping out of the Text   151
Stepping Back into the Text   155
Conclusion   161

9. Shiphrah and Puah: The Power of Refusal   163

Midwives of the Hebrews   163
The Text   164
Civil Disobedience   172
Conclusion   178

10. Other Egyptians   179

    Moses the Egyptian   179
    Other Egyptians   183
    Conclusion   191

PART THREE
BEYOND EXODUS

11. Setting the People Free: A Commissioning   195
    A Review   196
    Where Do We Go from Here?   197
    In Closing   213

NOTES   214

BIBLIOGRAPHY   238

INDEX   249

ACKNOWLEDGMENTS

This book began as my master's thesis at the Episcopal Divinity School in Cambridge, Massachusetts.

I here express my sincere thanks

to Angela Bauer, my thesis advisor,

to Ched Myers, for early input and encouragement,

to Shay, Corey, Tara, and Kevin Glackin-Coley, on whose computer much of this book was written,

to Rosie Hyde and Michael Sterbick, who make cameo appearances,

to Wes Howard-Brook, for reading the manuscript and asking questions that sharpened my analysis,

to Nick Leider, for content suggestions and help editing,

to Susan Perry and Catherine Costello at Orbis, for their patience,

to Joy Phillips, my mother, for childcare and for always believing I was a writer,

to Bruce Triggs, for enthusiasm, editing, and for acting as my unpaid research assistant,

to the library staff at the Episcopal Divinity School, the Vancouver School of Theology, Regent College, Seattle University, and the Tacoma Public Library,

to the many communities where this book was written and where I encounter the poor: the Toronto Catholic Worker, the Open Door in Atlanta, the Cuernevaca Center for Intercultural Dialogue on Development, the Vancouver Catholic Worker, Nativity House, and, most of all, the Tacoma Catholic Worker.

Thank you all.

INTRODUCTION

MY CONTEXT

This is a book for people who want to read the Bible, who want to work for justice in the world, and who believe that these two things are connected.

I have always had a great love for the Bible. Before I could read, my own fierce desire for narrative was fed by my grandfather's endless supply of slanted, annotated Bible stories about trickster heroes. My "high Anglican" experience of church told me that the Bible was solemn, beautiful, exciting, and central. As a child I was deeply moved by the richness of my inherited tradition but quietly and terribly disappointed that I did not see anybody "doing what the Bible said": selling all they had and giving it to the poor. I knew that my questions would embarrass the adults and that their answers would embarrass me, so I did not ask.

Much later I had an experience that became one of the many tributaries of this book. When I was in my late teens and early twenties, a group of friends and I tried to do what we called "intelligent people's Bible study." Our arrogant title was our attempt to express what we did not want: conservative literalism and personalized readings without any context. We were hungry to bring our minds to scripture and to explore the ideas of justice that we half-knew were there, but we did not want to be told what to do or how to do it.

In time the group foundered and eventually stopped meeting; we did not know how to begin or where to look for resources. In retrospect we could have used a teacher, some simple commentaries, and an introduction to modern biblical scholarship. Unfortunately, while scholars have a great deal to say about the Bible, they mostly say it to one another. Resources for lay people who want some basic information and the tools to make their own judgments are still scarce. This book is an attempt to make some of the insights and tools of biblical scholarship accessible to groups like my own ill-fated little Bible study gathering.

One fundamental insight of modern biblical scholarship is that who we are influences how we read. Thus it is important for readers to disclose some of the context from which their interpretation arises. I offer the preceding story of my search for a place to read the Bible intelligently as an introduction to myself and my own social location. When I speak of how I am allied, whom I love, where I come from, and where I am going, it is not self-indulgence but rather a scholarly imperative. By grounding my work in my own context, I invite and even facilitate the critical engagement of others.

I am an able-bodied, white, North American, Christian woman with a university education. I am also a single mother from a working-class background, and I identify as queer. This inventory of privilege and marginalization influences my reading of the Bible but does not determine it. A woman with an almost identical profile might write a very different book. *How* I orient myself to the power structures in which I live is at least as important to my biblical reading as *where* I am located in them.

I have lived for most of my adult life in praxis-oriented, intentional Christian communities, mostly Catholic Worker houses. I am part of a movement dancing sometimes in and sometimes out of the peripheral vision of the church. These "radical discipleship" communities are characterized by work with the very poor, activism, community Bible study, civil disobedience, and simple living, and are made up for the most part of "white, middle-class persons struggling to respond to a context of inherited, socially constructed privilege."[1] In the radical discipleship movement I catch glimpses of a place where all aspects of myself and all of creation are valued. With this inclusive vision before me and with my community beside me, my writing and indeed my living are intended as cultural treason.[2] From a tradition of Christian activism and resistance, we are working for an end to straight, white-supremacist, capitalist patriarchy. Our agenda is transformative, *not* reformative, radical and in no way liberal. I cannot fully articulate this vision myself, as it is being carried out by many people in many ways, but it always has practical, political, and economic implications. This is the location from which I read the Bible.

Although I write mostly by myself and seek out the quiet of libraries and a neighbor's computer room, my scholarship comes from a context that is far from academic. Rough drafts of several chapters were hand-written on the back of old "Bad Date Sheets," a weekly bulletin that prostitutes use to let one another know about dangerous men. Women can pick up copies or fill out reports at our house. The other side of my biblical study and theological reflection features warnings like this:

White male, 35 years old, 5'8" 165 lbs. Brown hair in a pony-tail, blue Toyota truck. Picked worker up at McDonalds, asked for a blow-job. Drove to the railway tracks, raped worker, hit her repeatedly in the face, threw her out of the truck and drove off.

Carter Heyward says that theological reflection "provides dangerous deflection from the immediate business of taking humanity seriously on its own terms in order to effect justice in the world." This book has taken a period of years to write for that very reason. Any time that I choose to write, I am choosing not to attend to a host of other pressing realities. My writing has been interrupted for anti-globalization demonstrations, local organizing, finding blankets for homeless women, community meetings—and, most recently, diaper changes. One morning I got up from my desk and went upstairs to find that while I was writing about Exodus, a woman had come to take a shower, overdosed in our bathroom, and nearly died. Studying the Bible in this context is not a scholarly retreat or pious spiritualizing; it is a gritty encounter with the stuff of survival.

This book differs from the majority of biblical readings in the radical discipleship movement because of my feminist stance. The radical discipleship movement defines itself in opposition to popular culture but speaks of the authority of the Bible for our lives. The need for a suitably radical reading, or for traditional male heroes—Paul, Moses, Jesus, the prophets, God—to appear to support the communities' liberation agenda is often allowed to obscure the oppressive content of a text or to downplay the oppressive use to which it has been put. I take seriously Robert Allen Warrior's charge that "it is those who act on the basis of these texts who must take responsibility for the terror and violence they can and have engendered."[3] Rather than claiming that Christians are subject to a higher authority than others, I suggest that we in the radical discipleship movement admit that we are subject to *lower* authorities, the dubious and multiple authorities of the most oppressed speaking on their own behalf. I invite and challenge my community of faith and the readers of this book to the insecurity of struggling with me about issues of authority, accountability, and the deepest sources of our search for justice, while still living and defining ourselves in opposition to the surrounding imperial culture. I believe that our love of the Bible demands no less of us than that we say where and how it hurts us and others. So this reading does not avoid or try to explain away the violent and oppressive content of scripture.

READING THIS BOOK

Exodus is a beautiful and powerful book. A primary theme is that God sides with the oppressed and marginalized. But Exodus is a heritage from which people of privilege should not be cut off. *Set Them Free* is a liberation reading of the book of Exodus from a first-world perspective. This means that rather than identifying with the Israelites, I take stock of my own immense privilege under corporate capitalism and identify with the Egyptian oppressors. The first half of Exodus is set in Egypt, so more accurately what follows is a first-world reading of Exodus 1-15. This book is also a feminist project. It looks at the intersecting forms of domination at work in empire, particularly through the stories of women, known and hidden, in the text and in our modern context. To compare Exodus to our present situation, the book moves back and forth between close readings of the text and readings of the modern world.

While this book is about Exodus and the parallels between biblical

Egypt and our modern situation of global capitalism, it is also about narrative, reader response, and the function of story. Two major themes are identification and privilege. My engagement with these two concepts forms a web of questions that undergirds my writing. As a reader, how do I identify myself? When reading the text, with whom do I identify? With whom do other readers identify and how is that related to how they self-identify? For this reading I, a white, Christian, first-world, able-bodied reader am identifying with my material privilege. What impact does this have on my hermeneutical privilege? How do we identify a privilege? What are the consequences of privileging a text, as with Exodus in liberation theologies? How/Can oppressors read the texts of the oppressed? And how/can this serve the project of liberation? What does it mean to identify with privilege? With power? In terms of understanding the text, is my experience of oppression a strength? A privilege? How do power, shame, habit, safety, survival, economics, group, fear, and family relate to identification and privilege?

Set Them Free is a book about biblical Egypt, global capitalism, liberation and oppression, and reading the Bible in the first world. Here is a chapter-by-chapter overview to help the reader decide which parts of the book may be most useful to him or her.

The first part of the book, "Reading Exodus," provides an introduction to the ideas and tools used throughout the book. Chapter 1 introduces some of the tools of modern biblical scholarship using several passages from Exodus. It examines source theory, historical criticism, and literary criticism and then looks at the possibility of reading the Bible as sacred story, a valued heritage that we can encounter with our minds and our hearts. Chapter 2 introduces the book of Exodus, its structure and content, and the way that exodus themes have been used and abused through history. The second half of the chapter focuses on how Latin American and black liberation theologians have identified with Israel and used Exodus as a paradigmatic liberation text. Chapter 3 looks at three liberation writers who challenge the use of Exodus as paradigmatic based on their identification with characters other than male Israelites. In response to these challenges, I conclude that for first-world Christians to identify with Israel in Exodus is to read the text incorrectly.

One of the perils of these first three chapters is that they present introductory and background material. The reader who wishes to cut to the chase should begin with part 2, "Being Read by Exodus." The basic argument of the book—that in Exodus first-world readers have more in common with Egypt than with Israel—is presented in chapter 4 and substantiated in the remaining chapters.

Chapter 4 lays out the parallels between the Egyptian empire as portrayed by Israel in Exodus and our modern situation of global capitalism. We too participate in oppression, slavery, and genocide. Chapter 5 looks at the land of Egypt by focusing on the plague narratives. Using the biblical text and the tools of ecofeminism, it addresses current environmental issues. As in Exodus, exploitation and commodification of the environment in the present are linked to exploitation and commodification of humans. Chapter 6 examines the characters of the two pharaohs. We touch briefly on modern pharaohs and then use the passages about Pharaoh's heart as a way to talk about how ordinary people are captive to empire today. Chapter 7 is an exploration of the violence in the exodus story, particularly the violence of YHWH[4] against the Egyptians and how first-world readers might understand this violence.

After the hard truths of chapters 4-7, we move in a more hopeful direction, looking at the stories of Egyptians who seem to have furthered the project of liberation. Chapter 8 compares several feminist explorations of Pharaoh's daughter, the clearest biblical portrait of an Egyptian who acts on behalf of Israel despite her immense privilege. Chapter 9 examines the story of Shiphrah and Puah, assuming that these "midwives to the Hebrews" are Egyptian characters. The fact that these women enact the earliest recorded incident of civil disobedience provides us with an opportunity to talk about modern civil disobedience, direct action, and nonviolence. Chapter 10 looks at various other Egyptian characters who had some part in the exodus and how their stories might parallel our own stories of resistance and solidarity.

Part 3, the final chapter, addresses the question, Where do we go from here? It looks beyond the Exodus text and offers first-world Christians a new vocabulary and new ways of acting to resist the empire of corporate capitalism.

Although there are many reasons to read *Set Them Free* by oneself, the best use of this book would be by small groups working together. Each member of the group would read Exodus 1-15 and part 1 of the book individually as preparation. Then together the group would work through part 2 over the course of six to eight weeks, reading the book and the biblical texts together, and sharing insights. Ideally the culmination of the group's time together would involve concrete action that would be an embodiment of some of the principles and tools suggested in chapter 11.

CRITICAL EVALUATION

This book is not a definitive reading. It is one interpretation among many and is intended to complement the rich tradition of liberation readings of Exodus. I submit it to the community of readers with the commitment and expectation that it will receive critical scrutiny, not just by privileged first-world readers for whom the book is intended but also by readers from other liberation traditions. Mary Ann Tolbert suggests the following as categories for critical analysis: persuasiveness, dangerousness, subversiveness, insightfulness, and usefulness.[5] Additionally I invite evaluation of my reading's creativity, ferocity, rigor, honesty, and joy, and, from those for whom it is relevant and useful, some mention of God.

How this reading meets the criteria above will be determined over time, in dialogue, and, most important, through action. My goal in writing this book is to engage people of privilege, especially white, first-world, North American Christians, in concrete action to end injustice based on race, class, economics, sexuality, and gender. I do not intend to shame but rather to encourage, but neither do I want to underrepresent the absolute radicality such change represents. True liberation for the privileged is hard and it will feel like loss. Indeed it will be about loss, but it is loss of what was never ours.

Some years ago popular biblical educator Ched Myers and I talked about studying the Bible. Ched spoke about the difference between doing a critical literary analysis of a play with the intention of publishing an academic paper and doing a critical literary analysis in order to put on the play. Putting on the play is not my childhood notion of "doing what the Bible says," nor is it imitating thirteenth-century lives in the present. Putting on the play means concretely applying the spirit of liberation in the text to injustice today. This reading of Exodus is for first-world Christians who want, in community and critical conversation, to put on the play.

PART ONE
READING EXODUS

1

HISTORY, LITERATURE, AND STORY

An Introduction to Modern Biblical Criticism

Although many North Americans from Christian backgrounds have drifted quietly into post-Christianity, finding the church irrelevant and the Bible more so, the laws and codes of our countries are based on interpretations of Christian scripture. In popular culture, readings that accept or exaggerate negative aspects of the Bible—patriarchy, hierarchy, ageism, violence, racism, ableism, heterosexism, classism, and anti-Judaism—form and inform television, literature, film, education, advertising, and policy making. Whether we like it or not, the Bible is relevant to our lives; but most first-world Christians don't know how to read the Bible.

Christians from every denomination approach the Bible in an individualistic and spiritualized way. Whether we hear scripture in a worship setting or read it ourselves, the questions we most often bring to the Bible are, What is the message that this passage has for me? What is God telling me to do? This kind of reading has a long history.[1] At best it can be part of a deep spiritual and psychological growth; at worst it is a kind of holy fortune-telling. However much they contribute to one's personal life, spiritual readings of the Bible are limited because they take no account of the social and political realities that produced the Bible in the first place. The idea of scripture having a *personal message* would be completely alien to those who wrote the Bible. These kinds of readings tell us about ourselves, not the Bible.

Another kind of reading is less benign. Over the past ten years in North America, the swing to the political right has been linked with an increase in religious conservatism. An enormous amount of Bible reading takes place in a fundamentalist environment. This kind of reading transplants the narrowness and prejudice of another time and culture into modern lives. Under the guise of literalism or "biblical inerrancy," selective use is made of the Bible to reinforce a conservative political agenda that is pro-capitalist, anti-poor, anti-gay, anti-woman, and, despite its rhetoric, anti-family.

The Bible is a complex collection of writings from various times and perspectives. It contains internal arguments and contradictions; yet it has the status of scripture. How can modern Christians who seek justice and are turned off by literalism read the Bible with reverence, intelligence, and integrity?

Most justice seekers have taken one of two extremes when faced with the ambiguity of scripture. In a multifaith context, confronted with the harm that our tradition has caused, some withdraw from and disavow Christianity, refusing to support or be associated at all with institutions and traditions that have been so destructive. For their refusal, they pay the high price of being cut off from their roots. Others seek out and focus on the liberative aspects of scripture, making for themselves a canon within the canon. Either extreme grants some aspect of the tradition an elevated status, a response that is much too simple for the complex heritage that is the Bible. Dissociating from Christianity gives primacy to the harmful parts of the tradition while focusing solely on the liberative strands does not accurately reflect the content of scripture. Christians who seek justice do not need to surrender their heritage to those who use it for harm, nor are we obligated, because there are liberative, radical threads and voices within the Bible, to claim that the Bible is inherently and completely liberating. Yes, the Bible says, "do justice." It also says, "smash the heads of your enemies' children." When either right-wing Christians or left-wing Christians resort to proof-texting, we mistake something known and domesticated for the living word of God.

The Bible is not easy to read. In order to read the Bible with integrity and intelligence, with our hearts and our minds, people of faith require tools. The tools of modern biblical scholarship are available to lay readers. Using historical and literary criticism can help us to look at the Bible, in all its complexity, in a way that neither privatizes nor literalizes.

HISTORY AND THE BIBLE

ɣThe Bible is a historical document. As such it can teach us about the past, and it can be illuminated by studying the past. As Jon Levenson says, "History, the arena of public events (as opposed to private, mystical revelation and to philosophical speculation), and time are not illusions or distractions from essential reality. They are means to the knowledge of God."[2]

Ancient Egypt

This book is about ancient Egypt, empire, and a North American reading of Exodus; therefore the history of Egypt is of some concern to us. In the book of Genesis, Joseph, great-grandson of Sarah and Abraham, is sold by jealous brothers into slavery; he prospers in a time of famine and so repeats his ancestors' sojourn in the land of Egypt. The book of Exodus begins with Israel in Egypt under a pharaoh "who did not know Joseph"

(Exod. 1:8). What do we know about Egypt beyond the "theological screens surrounding these events"?[3]

Ancient Egypt was a powerful African society that white Western scholars have consistently sought to de-Africanize.[4] Over its two-thousand-year, multidimensional history, Egyptian influence extended well into Asia. For a significant portion of biblical history, Egypt either ruled or dominated Palestine through military occupation, a system of vassal kings, and forced tribute. Although there is no extrabiblical documentation of Israel's presence in Egypt, foreign migration to the Nile Delta was not uncommon, and Egyptian and Semitic languages show the other's influence.

Based on a comparison of historical data with the biblical text, some scholars date the events of the book of Exodus to approximately the thirteenth century B.C.E.[5] The second and third pharaohs of Egypt's empire period, Seti I (1305-1290 B.C.E.) and Ramses II (1290-1224 B.C.E.) bear some resemblance to the pharaohs of Exodus. They expanded the empire to great heights and inaugurated extensive building programs using forced labor. Much scholarly energy has been expended in the effort to match the biblical characters to historical figures, but in truth we do not know under which pharaohs the events of Exodus occurred. In Exodus the two successive pharaohs are nameless, in contrast to their "historically insignificant" antagonists Shiphrah and Puah, Moses and Aaron. In keeping with the literary and historical ambiguity of the text, I will not speculate further as to the identity of these unnamed rulers.

The text speaks of the structure of ancient Egyptian society. Repeatedly we encounter the formula, "Pharaoh, his officials, and all his people," which illustrates the stratified and hierarchical nature of the monarchical state. The Egyptian pharaoh was a god-king served by a small retainer class of priests, administrators, and military elite, all supported by the very poor majority in a centralized system directed toward the extraction of resources.

Ancient Israelites

Although in the popular mind archaeology is often thought to prove the Bible true (i.e., historical), this is seldom the case, and it is occasionally the opposite of the truth.

—Jon Levenson[6]

Egypt was an established world power by the thirteenth century B.C.E., but not so Israel. The oldest reference to Israel is recorded in Egyptian history and shows the relative status of the two nations. After a military campaign into Palestine in the late thirteenth century, Pharaoh Mernaptha, the son of Ramses II, erected a stele, a memorial stone, detailing his glorious exploits. Israel is mentioned among the many nations subdued. Ironically, "the earliest extant mention of Israel outside the Bible claims to be its last."[7]

The princes are prostrate, saying: "Mercy!"
Not one raises his head among the Nine Bows.
Desolation is for Tehenu; Hatti is pacified;
Plundered is the Canaan with every evil;
Carried off is Askelon; seized upon is Gezer;
Yanoam is made as that which does not exist;
Israel is laid waste, his seed is not;
Hurru is become a widow for Egypt!
All lands together, they are pacified;
Everyone who was restless, he has been bound
by the King of Upper and Lower Egypt.[8]

The inscription on the stele is the voice of empire. It relates the Egyptian regard for Israel. It also tells us that by 1220 B.C.E. there was a distinct nation or identifiable group called Israel dwelling between the Mediterranean Sea and the Arabian Desert. Of the nations described, only Israel features the hieroglyph for "a people"; the others are all designated as "lands."[9]

Although Egyptian history records expulsions of foreigners prior to the likely date of the exodus,[10] there is no extrabiblical record or evidence of Israel in Canaan before the end of the thirteenth century B.C.E. According to Exodus, more than 600,000 Israelites[11] marched out of slavery in Egypt, sojourned for forty years in the wilderness, then swept into the foreign land of Canaan (Syria-Palestine) in military conquest. Archaeological evidence suggests numerous difficulties with the biblical story of Israel's arrival in Canaan from Egypt:

1. Hebrew is the southern dialect of the Canaanite language;[12] Israelites did not come from somewhere else with a different language.

2. There is no Egyptian record of Israel in Egypt, nor of the departure of a large number of slaves, much less 600,000.

3. Many of the cities supposedly destroyed by Israel's invading army according to the Bible were in ruins centuries before Israel is said to have arrived in Canaan. The city of Jericho, which was never walled, is the most notable example.

Historians have put forward three theories of how Canaan came to be settled by Israel, and although each has some merit, the theories reveal as much about the situation and worldview of the theorists as they do about Israel.

Migratory Infiltration

This point of view is associated with German scholar Martin Noth. His hypothesis is that, over centuries, several groups of nomadic pastoralists settled the agricultural land of southern Palestine from various directions, first in the hills and later in the more fertile lowlands among the Canaanite farmers. Each nomadic group had distinct traditions and histories, but through immigration and infiltration they came together to form a tribal confederacy. This theory is supported by stories in Genesis of herding ancestors peacefully sojourning in Canaan, and by descriptions of Israel's gradual settlement in Canaan. Exodus 23:29-30 is one of the passages that explicitly supports the idea of Israel's gradual infiltration into Canaan: "I will not drive them out from before you in one year."[13] The hypothesis of migratory infiltration is not compatible with the picture of rapid, violent conquest in the book of Joshua. Gradual infiltration is further supported by the fact that the Israelites were a heterogeneous but indigenous Canaanite population. Moreover, archaeological evidence of a massive conquest is lacking.

External Attack

American scholars John Bright, William Foxwell Albright, and G. Ernest Wright follow the story of the book of Joshua for their reconstruction of how Israel came to be in Palestine. Those who left Egypt formed an army in the wilderness, under the military leadership of Joshua. They had already developed a tribal structure and recognized YHWH[14] as their god. This army was joined by sympathetic groups from the Canaanite hill country and swept into the lowlands, destroying cities in a sudden conquest. In addition to the support of the biblical text, there is archaeological evidence of violent destruction of some Canaanite cites such as Bethel.

Internal Uprising

George Mendenhall and Norman Gottwald propose a scenario that in some ways reconciles the two previous theories. Disenfranchised resistance groups and individuals in Canaan, such as the prostitute Rahab and her family, were joined by a group of fugitive slaves with a story of a delivering god. This catalyzed a rebellion among both farmers and herders against the city-states that exploited them. The alienated Canaanites are identified with the 'apiru or habiru, a word used in ancient Egyptian documents to designate noncitizen outlaws and troublemakers. Proponents of the hypothesis of internal uprising say that the habiru became the Hebrews and formed a social system of "retribalization." In conscious contrast to the centralized city-states of Canaan, they returned to smaller kin-based tribal organization. Their governmental and economic structures were comparatively egalitarian, and they linked this political system to worship of their god, YHWH.

A review of these three hypotheses tells us more about what we can't know than about what is certain; but it is clear that Israel is a hybrid nation, not very distinct from its Canaanite neighbors.

A Short, Short History of Biblical Israel

Later in this chapter we will look at the history of the composition of the book of Exodus and the rest of the Bible. Exodus was composed long after the events it records. Although Exodus portrays the very early part of Israel's history, parts of the Exodus text date from hundreds of years later. It is therefore important to have at least a sense of the later history of this people and how their experiences and perspectives might have influenced the telling of their earliest stories.

Whether the Israelites arrived in Palestine through conquest, gradual infiltration, or as catalysts of a peasant uprising, earliest Israel was a heterogeneous kin-based society similar in language and culture to their Canaanite neighbors. Their livelihood was based on intensive subsistence farming in the hill country. Throughout the time of scriptural composition, rural agricultural life probably remained fairly constant with the extended-family household as the basic societal unit.[15] These early Israelites had no temple, no city, and no king.

Through the tenth century B.C.E., Israel became increasingly centralized, economically and politically. Israelites came down from the hills. Regional conquests and power alliances led to an emerging nation-state, which by the late eleventh century was united under the leadership of Saul to counter the threat of the Philistines, a group of Sea Peoples from the south coast. Saul was succeeded by his champion and rival David, and David by his son Solomon, the temple builder. In terms of wealth, territory, prestige, and relative calm, this was Israel's zenith, at least for the elite. David and his dynasty were looked to ever after as the golden age in Israel's history. After Solomon's death the kingdom was split between the northern tribes, descended from Rachel, and the southern tribes, descended from Leah. Samaria-centered Israel in the north and Jerusalem-centered Judah in the south continued for hundreds of years. The period of the monarchies was characterized by urbanization and its attendant bureaucracy and taxation, increased use of writing for communication, a coordinated and professional military, and more developed trade. These changes were most profound for the 10 percent of the population living in the urban centers.

In 722 B.C.E., Israel, the northern kingdom, fell to Assyrian expansion. Most of the ruling class of Israel was deported; foreigners were brought in to occupy the land, and it was carved up into various Assyrian administrative provinces. For the next 135 years Judah, the southern kingdom, retained its independence. As the Babylonian empire began to rise in power and push west toward Egypt, Assyria began to wane. In 587 B.C.E., Jerusalem was taken by Babylon. The city's walls were pulled down, and the temple and the palace burned to the ground. The elite of Jerusalem were taken off to exile in Babylon, where they eventually settled and established a home. Seventy years later the Babylonian empire fell to the Persians, and the Jerusalem elite were permitted to return. Some returned to Jerusalem and, backed by money from the Babylonian exile community, rebuilt the temple and the city walls. But Israel was no longer an independent nation; it was a Persian outpost.

Throughout this history, groups and factions within Israel recorded and compiled their experiences, perspectives, songs, stories, and laws. These writings have become our sacred scriptures.

WHO WROTE THE BIBLE?

Unlike most books we know, the Bible was not written by one author at one time. Indeed it was not first written at all. According to tradition, the Torah (or the Pentateuch, which means the five books, Genesis, Exodus, Leviticus, Numbers, and Deuteronomy) was written, in its entirety, by Moses. From as early as the time of Jesus, readers have pointed out difficulties with this idea, not the least of which is this passage:

> Then Moses, the servant of the LORD, died there in the land of Moab, at the LORD's command. He was buried in a valley in the land of Moab, opposite Beth-peor, but no one knows his burial place to this day. Moses was one hundred twenty years old when he died: his sight was unimpaired and his vigor had not abated. The Israelites wept for Moses in the plains of Moab thirty days; then the period of mourning for Moses was ended. (Deut. 34:5-8)

The biblical author describes Moses' death and burial, making Mosaic authorship, at least of the final verses of Deuteronomy, unlikely. There are also internal inconsistencies in the Pentateuch. Moses' father-in-law is called Jethro in some passages and Ruel in others. There are two creation stories and two versions of the Ten Commandments. The name of the sacred mountain upon which the deity appears is alternately Sinai and Horeb.

In the Bible, the God of Israel has not one name but several. *Elohim* is a generic Hebrew term for god/gods/goddess/goddesses,[16] derived from *El*, the proper name of a Canaanite deity. YHWH, the sacred tetragrammaton or four-letter name of God, is a form of the verb "to be." Because of the prohibition against speaking the name of God, in Hebrew texts the consonants for YHWH were written with the vowels (which were represented by dots under the consonants) for the word *adonay*, meaning "lord." Jews knew by convention to substitute the word *adonay* for YHWH when reading aloud. Late medieval Christian translators were unaware of this practice and pronounced the consonants of YHWH with the vowels of *adonay*, creating a new name—Jehovah—in error. A combination of the proper name and the generic term, YHWH *Elohim*, is usually translated LORD God, with LORD in capitals to indicate that the Hebrew text has YHWH rather than *adonay*. *El Shaddai* is another name used in the Hebrew Bible. Usually translated "God Almighty," it also has to do with mountains and can be understood as "the God with Breasts."[17]

Source Criticism

The contradictions, repetitions, and parallels that appear in the Bible, as well as striking differences in vocabulary, style, theology, and emphasis, were examined by scholars as early as the eighteenth century. In 1878, German biblicist Julius Wellhausen, building on the work of others, presented what became known as the Documentary Hypothesis: a marshaling of evidence that the first five books of the Bible were assembled over time from a number of separate and previously existing documents. Scholars tend now to speak of strands and layers rather than "documents" but Wellhausen's work continues to be a reference point for either disagreement or agreement.

Source critics recognize four sources, commonly referred to by the initials J, E, D, and P. These four sources can be characterized most simply in two ways: by origin and content, coming from either northern or southern Israel and having either narrative or legislative/cultic material. The sources are dated according to the latest events they record and by comparing them to one another and to documents whose ages we know.

The Jahwist Source—J (960-930 B.C.E.), named for the German spelling of YHWH, is the southern narrative believed to have been composed in the courts of King Solomon. The J authors combined existing material from the tribal history of Israel to form a broad and detailed national epic for the existing monarchy. J focuses on nationhood, and Israel's success is explained in terms of God's promise and fidelity. The divine name YHWH is used frequently from the beginning of the narrative, and this god is near, accessible, and human—walking in the garden in the evening. J material, found in Genesis–Numbers, is pro-monarchy and pro-south (Judah); the Davidic empire is portrayed as the fulfillment of God's promise to Abraham. In J, Moses' father-in-law is Ruel; natives of Palestine are called Canaanites; and the holy mountain is Sinai.

The Elohist Source—E (900-850 B.C.E.) is the northern national epic, composed after Israel split into separate northern and southern kingdoms in 922 B.C.E. The generic term *elohim* is used for God until after the revelation of the name YHWH in Exodus 3:14. This god is more distant, powerful, and transcendent than the god of J, communicating in a mediated way through dreams or angels. Fear, reverence, and obedience are the proper responses to this god. The E authors downplayed monarchy and emphasized the older stories of Moses and the covenant community. In E, Jethro is Moses' father-in-law; the natives of Palestine are Amorites; and

Horeb is the holy mountain. E material appears in Genesis–Numbers and is the "source" scholars most often question as an independently existing history.

The Priestly Source—P (550-450 B.C.E.), named because it represents the interests of the priesthood, consists largely of legislative materials from the south. Prominent in Leviticus, Numbers, and the latter half of Exodus, P material comprises more than half the Pentateuch. These writings were produced by priestly groups associated with the Jerusalem Temple late in the Babylonian Exile, when Israel was no longer a politically independent nation. Consequently, P focuses on "religious" identity, Israel's distinction from Babylon, and family and temple rather than nation. Most of P material is law, genealogy, chronologies, itineraries, lists, and the details of ritual practice. Numbers and dates have liturgical significance. The narrative portions of P form a unifying editorial layer in Genesis–Numbers, reorienting the J and E narratives to explain Israel's exile. In P material, God is a creator even more transcendent than in the earlier E material. The Priestly authors, as the latest editors, are largely responsible for the present form of the Pentateuch.

The Deuteronomist Source (D) is a comparatively isolated unit. Second Kings 22 tells the story of a scroll found during temple repairs in 621 B.C.E. On the basis of this law text, King Josiah initiated an era of reform, the critical element of which was centralization of worship of YHWH in Jerusalem. The scroll is identified, at least in part, with the book of Deuteronomy. This northern material emphasizes fidelity to the law and consists largely of laws and theological ideas. The tone is urgent, characterized by the words "you," "now," and "today." Deuteronomy, the last book of the Pentateuch, prefaces Joshua–Kings, which continue Israel's history according to a "Deuteronomistic" perspective. D is not a significant source in Exodus.

Over time these four traditions were woven together by various editors. Often the catalyst for preservation and compilation was a historical crisis such as the formation of the monarchy or the destruction of Jerusalem. These repetitions, grafts, and editing make it difficult for modern people to read the Bible, or even one book, from start to finish.

Absent Sources

Each of the four sources may contain material that dates from earlier than the tribal confederacy of approximately 1200 B.C.E. Miriam's song, one of the oldest examples of Hebrew poetry, is believed to date from the thirteenth century B.C.E.[18]

I will sing to Yahweh, the glorious one,
horse and rider he has thrown into the sea. (Exod. 15:1b, CCB)[19]

The text attributes this first stanza of the song to Miriam and the remaining seventeen verses to Moses. But even before the advent of feminist biblical criticism, scholars deduced that this song of victory was originally Miriam's and that as Moses grew in importance it was attributed to him. In light of the relative absence of women in the Bible it is important to realize that some of the oldest material in our sacred scriptures is music attributed to women[20] and that women's contributions have been attributed to men.

Biblical authors from various times drew from a pool of older material, such as Miriam's song, interpreting not for history's own sake, but in the light of and in the service of their current situation. Thus the emphasis, meaning, and function of a particular song, saying, law, or story were not static. For the present work, the most important insight of source criticism is that the identity and agenda of writers shape what is written, what is included, and what is left out. The following poem by Merle Feld illustrates this point and speaks of the missing stories of women in the Torah.

WE ALL STOOD TOGETHER

My Brother and I were at Sinai
He kept a journal
of what he saw
of what he heard
of what it all meant to him

I wish I had such a record
of what happened to me there

It seems like every time I want to write
I can't
I'm always holding a baby
one of my own
or one for a friend
always holding a baby
so my hands are never free
to write things down

And then as time passes
the particulars
the hard data
the who what when where why
slip away from me
and all I'm left with is
the feeling

But feelings are just sounds
the vowel barking of a mute

My brother is so sure of what he heard
after all he's got a record of it
consonant after consonant after consonant

If we remembered it together
we could re-create holy time
sparks flying[21]

Limits of Source Criticism

One of problems with the source theory and the Documentary Hypothesis is that their proponents often disagree and assign the same passages to different sources. Another problem is that it is possible deliberately to write in the style of a past era. Indeed, while at one extreme there are scholars who still maintain that each source represents a distinct, clearly identifiable document, others assert that the whole of the Pentateuch is the work of a single Hellenistic author and can tell us only about that one worldview and time.

Current proponents of source theory seem to concur that E is not an autonomous tradition at all. Many scholars question the traditional view that a unified and distinct P document is identifiable, and some assert that there are "Deuteronomistic" elements throughout Genesis–Numbers. As Everett Fox points out, "the nature of biblical texts militates against recovering the exact process by which the Bible came into being."[22] I have not introduced source theory on one page to dismiss it on the next, but to show that the Bible is complex, that there is no single right answer. As we read Exodus we will bear with us the insights of source criticism, but we will also attend to the wholeness and integrity of the text as it stands.

THE BIBLE AS LITERATURE

Literary criticism is nothing more than applying the same tools to the Bible that we would to any other piece of literature. When we read a passage from the Bible, we can observe its genre, characterization, pace, and other literary qualities. We can also pay attention to how it affects us as a reader. Below are six very different passages, each about ten verses long, all from the book of Exodus. Read through each of them carefully.

Now a man from the house of Levi went and married a Levite woman. The woman conceived and bore a son; and when she saw that he was a fine baby, she hid him three months. When she could hide him no longer she got a papyrus basket for him, and plastered it with bitumen and pitch; she put the child in it and placed it among the reeds on the bank of the river. His sister stood at a distance, to see what would happen to him.

The daughter of Pharaoh came down to bathe at the river, while her attendants walked beside the river. She saw the basket among the reeds and sent her maid to bring it. When she opened it, she saw the child. He was crying, and she took pity on him, "This must be one of the Hebrews' children," she said. Then his sister said to Pharaoh's daughter, "Shall I go and get you a nurse from the Hebrew women to nurse the child for you?" Pharaoh's daughter said to her, "Yes." So the girl went and called the child's mother. Pharaoh's daughter said to her, "Take this child and nurse it for me, and I will give you your wages." So the woman took the child and nursed it. When the child grew up, she brought him to Pharaoh's daughter, and she took him as her son. She named him Moses, "because," she said, "I drew him out of the water." (Exod. 2:1-10)

The following are the heads of their ancestral houses: the sons of Reuben, the firstborn of Israel: Hanoch, Pallu, Hezron, and Carmi; these are the families of Reuben. The sons of Simeon: Jemuel, Jamin, Ohad, Jachin, Zohar, and Shaul, the son of a Canaanite woman; these are the families of Simeon. The following are the names of the sons of Levi according to their genealogies: Gershon, Kohath, and Merari, and the length of Levi's life was one hundred thirty-seven years. The sons of Gershon: Libni and Shimei, by their families. The sons of Kohath: Amram, Izhar, Hebron, and Uzziel, and the length of Kohath's life was one hundred thirty-three years. The sons of Merari: Mahli and Mushi. These are the families of the Levites according to their genealogies. Amram married Jochebed his father's sister and she bore him Aaron and Moses, and the length of Amram's life was one hundred thirty-seven years. The sons of Izhar: Korah, Nepheg, and Zichri. The sons of Uzziel: Mishael, Elzaphan, and Sithri. Aaron married Elisheba, daughter of Amminadab and sister of Nahshon, and she bore him Nadab, Abihu, Eleazar, and Ithamar. The sons of Korah: Assir, Elkanah and Abiasaph; these are the families of the Korahites, Aaron's son Eleazar married one of the daughters of Putiel, and she bore him Phinehas. These are the heads of the ancestral houses of the Levites by their families.

It was this same Aaron and Moses to whom the LORD said, "Bring the Israelites out of the land of Egypt, company by company." It was they who spoke to Pharaoh king of Egypt to bring the Israelites out of Egypt, the same Moses and Aaron. (Exod. 6:14-27)

This month shall mark for you the beginning of months; it shall be the first month of the year for you. Tell the whole congregation of Israel that on the tenth of this month they are to take a lamb for each family, a lamb for each household. If a household is too small for a whole lamb it shall join its closest neighbor in obtaining one; the lamb shall be divided in proportion to the number of people who eat of it. Your lamb shall be without blemish, a year-old male; you may take it from the sheep or from the goats. You shall keep it until the fourteenth day of this month; then the whole assembled congregation of Israel shall slaughter it at twilight. They shall take some of the blood and put it on the two doorposts and the lintel of the houses in which they eat it. They shall eat the lamb that same night; they shall eat it roasted over the fire with unleavened bread and bitter herbs. Do not eat any of it raw or boiled in water, but roasted over the fire, with its head, legs, and inner organs. You shall let none of it remain until the morning; anything that remains until the morning you shall burn. This is how you shall eat it: your loins girded, your sandals on your feet, and your staff in your hand; you shall eat it hurriedly. It is the passover of the LORD. (Exod. 12:2-11)

> I will sing to the LORD, for he has triumphed gloriously;
>   horse and rider he has thrown into the sea.
> The LORD is my strength and my might,
>   and he has become my salvation;
> this is my God and I will praise him,
>   my father's God and I will exalt him.
> The LORD is a warrior;
>   the LORD is his name.
>
> Pharaoh's chariots and his army he cast into the sea;
>   his picked officers were sunk in the Red Sea.
> The floods covered them;
>   they went down into the depths like a stone.
> Your right hand, O LORD, glorious in power—
>   your right hand O LORD shattered the enemy.
> In the greatness of your majesty you overthrew your
>   adversaries;
>   you sent out your fury, it consumed them like
>   stubble.
> At the blast of your nostrils the waters piled up,
>   the floods stood up in a heap;
>   the deeps congealed in the heart of the sea.
> The enemy said, "I will pursue, I will overtake
>   I will divide the spoil, my desire shall have its fill of
>   them.
>   I will draw my sword, my hand shall destroy them."
> You blew with your wind, the sea covered them;
>   they sank like lead in the mighty waters.
>
>   (Exod. 15:1b-10)

When you buy a male Hebrew slave, he shall serve six years, but in the seventh he shall go out a free person, without debt. If he comes in single, he shall go out single; if he comes in married, then his wife shall go out with him. If his master gives him a wife and she bears him sons or daughters, the wife and her children shall be her master's and he shall go out alone. But if the slave declares, "I love my master, my wife, and my children; I will not go out a free person," then his master shall bring him before God. He shall be brought to the door or the doorpost; and his master shall pierce his ear with an awl; and he shall serve him for life.

When a man sells his daughter as a slave, she shall not go out as the male slaves do. If she does not please her master, who designated her for himself, then he shall let her be redeemed; he shall have no right to sell her to a foreign people, since he has dealt unfairly with her. If he designates her for his son, he shall deal with her as with a daughter. If he takes another wife to himself, he shall not diminish the food, clothing, or marital rights of the first wife. And if he does not do these three things for her, she shall go out without debt, without payment of money. (Exod. 21:2-11)

You shall make a lampstand of pure gold. The base and the shaft of the lampstand shall be made of hammered work; its cups, its calyxes, and its petals shall be of one piece with it; and there shall be six branches going out of its sides, three branches of the lampstand out of one side of it and three branches of the lampstand out of the other side of it; three cups shaped like almond blossoms, each with calyx and petals, on one branch, and three cups shaped like almond blossoms, each with calyx and petals on the other branch—so for the six branches going out of the lampstand. On the lampstand itself there shall be four cups shaped like almond blossoms, each with its calyxes and petals. There shall be a calyx of one piece with it under the first pair of branches, a calyx of one piece with it under the next pair of branches, and a calyx of one piece with it under the last pair of branches—so for the six branches that go out of the lampstand. Their calyxes and their branches shall be of one piece with it, the whole of it one hammered piece of pure gold. You shall make the seven lamps for it; and the lamps shall be set up so as to give light on the space in front of it. Its snuffers and trays shall be of pure gold. It, and all these utensils, shall be made from a talent of pure gold. And see that you make them according to the pattern for them, which is being shown you on the mountain. (Exod. 25:31-40)

Certainly it is not possible glibly to assign each of these readings to one of the four sources described above. At the same time, observations and distinctions can be made that require no technical expertise. Each passage is quite different in terms of style, content, form, use of language, intent, theme, structure, and feeling. Exodus 2:1-10, the baby in the basket, and

Exodus 15:1b-10, the battle at sea, are narrative material; each tells a story, but one is prose, and the other poetry. The remaining four examples are legislative or cultic material, but each is quite distinct in terms of content: Exodus 6:14-27 is a genealogy; Exodus 12:2-11 gives instructions for a ritual sacrifice and meal; Exodus 21:2-11 is an example of case law; and Exodus 25:31-40 is a detailed description of a fixture of the tabernacle.

Literary Details

Reading these texts as literature, we can direct our attention in two ways, either to the details of the particular passage or to how the text is related to surrounding materials. Looking at the details of the passage means noticing things like how many times a particular word is used, if there is an abrupt change in style, to whom the passage is addressed, and so on. We can observe that Exodus 6:14-27, the genealogy of Moses and Aaron, includes the names of forty men and mentions only four women, two of whom are unnamed. In the case law example, Exodus 21:2-11, notice that the text is addressed to adult male slave owners. Whether he is addressed in the second person or described in the third person, the subject is always the male head of household. Sentences do not begin "when you are sold into slavery . . ." or "when a woman takes a husband. . . ." In the case where a male slave remains enslaved, love of his wife and children is not distinguished from love of his master.

Here is a more complex exploration of detail from Exodus 2:1-10, the story of Pharaoh's daughter. The entire passage is a pattern of words, ideas, and word order focused on the women surrounding a particular child. This kind of biblical literary structure is called a *chiasm*—a series of parallel phrases in a sandwich-like structure that emphasize a central point.

A   A woman bears a *son* (2:2)

  B   *Mother* puts child in river (2:3)

    C   Child's *sister* watches to know what will happen (2:4)

      D   Pharaoh's *daughter* sees the basket (2:5)

        E   Pharaoh's daughter recognizes *the child* (2:6a)

      D'   Pharaoh's *daughter* has compassion (2:6b)

    C'   Infant's *sister* offers a plan (2:7-8)

  B'   *Mother* gets child back to nurse (2:9)

A'   Pharaoh's daughter adopts and names the *son* (2:10)

The word *child* appears seven times, and in Hebrew the entire passage is 141 words long with seventy words appearing before and after "the child" (a single word in Hebrew). The number 7 is a very important number in

Israelite numerology, a "complete number"; so too is 70, which is ten times 7.[23] The biblical authors used structures and word order to convey the importance of the women and child. We will look at this particular passage in greater detail in chapter 8 of this book.

Surrounding Material

In addition to focusing on the details of a particular passage, we can also consider the text in terms of its relationship to the material surrounding it: the rest of Exodus, the Bible as a whole, and the cultures of the ancient Near East.

Returning again to the first example, Exodus 2:1-10, the word for the basket in which the baby is placed on the waters (*tebah*) appears twenty-eight times in the Hebrew Bible: twice in this passage and twenty-six times in Genesis referring to Noah's boat. The story of the baby in the basket suggests another time when the survival hope of the people was vulnerable and afloat in dangerous waters. The story of Moses' infancy parallels the story of his people. He is miraculously delivered from watery danger.

This story appears in between the list of names of Jacob's sons who came to Egypt and the story of Moses' contest with Pharaoh. The transition between the two stories is not smooth, and the prologue, as it is called, seems to be a later addition.

The final example above, Exodus 25:31-40, gives detailed instructions from God to Moses for the construction of a golden lampstand to appear in the tabernacle, an elaborate tent that will be God's dwelling. Later, Exodus 37:17-24 is an almost identical passage in the past tense, describing the lampstand that the artisan Bezalel made according to the instructions of God and Moses. The lampstand described is in the shape of a small tree or shrub. The shape of the lampstand is significant because in Exodus 3, YHWH appears to Moses in a bush that burns but is not consumed by fire.[24]

Miriam's Song of the Sea (Exod. 15:1b-10) describes Israel's miraculous deliverance. This theme is repeated throughout Exodus in the various intermingled tellings of the going out from Egypt. The prophets reiterate this theme; it appears in the Psalms and in the Christian Bible as well. In the next chapters we look at how the exodus theme has been used for good and for harm throughout history. Similarly, the theme of God as warrior runs through the Bible and through history. We examine the history and use of this violent imagery in chapter 7.

Some of these topics are more than surface observations and require more than a neophyte's familiarity with a variety of resources and tools. In addition, there are many other observations to be made about these passages. Some aspects of modern biblical criticism are not open to the casual lay reader. We are not able to look closely at the differences between the various ancient translations of the Bible. We cannot do statistical analysis of the frequency with which certain words and phrases appear. We cannot compare the language and subject matter of the Bible to that of other ancient Near Eastern literature. Most of us have neither the time nor the inclination to do so, although through computers and libraries the tools are increasingly accessible. As we look at parts of Exodus, we will draw on some of these tools and on the work of various scholars to bring more information and other voices to our conversation.

If you are struck by a particular passage, idea, or theme and want to go further, I recommend you acquaint yourself with commentaries, concordances, Bible dictionaries and atlases, and other literature. Consult a variety of sources and compare them; expect them to disagree.

Each type of biblical criticism has its uses and limitations. Are the patterns we see deliberate or accidental, merely pleasing or suffused with theological meaning? These questions can never be answered with certainty. In the following reading of Exodus we will make use of various traditions and tools. We will proceed with caution and humility, knowing that what the text offers us are hints, not certainties.

THE BIBLE AS SACRED STORY

But the interpretation of Holy scripture does not find expression only in preaching and doctrine, and certainly not primarily in commentaries, but also in doing and suffering.

—Roland Murphy[25]

Historical and literary criticism are two modern avenues to biblical study. Perhaps it is more accurate to say they are the modern and postmodern avenues, respectively. Often they are presented in a kind of binary opposition to each other. Historical criticism is characterized as understanding the text as a window to the past, a transparent opening to an era important to the reader. Literary criticism is described as understanding the text as a mirror, an artifact that reflects back what is projected onto it. Both of these kinds of academic readings are not usually practiced by lay people or related much to the world of "doing and suffering." I propose another kind of reading, which functions as a third strand in our braided examination of text. I suggest we read the Bible as sacred story.

At its various layers of composition and redaction, biblical authors, collectors, singers, compilers, and composers were not in the modern sense producing either literature or history, nor were they promoting an idea or philosophy. Rather, "Israel began to infer and to affirm her identity by telling a story."[26] As we discussed earlier, this affirmation of identity was produced in turbulent situations. "Often poetry, stories, and literature especially of the earliest periods, had the specific purpose of supporting and furthering the struggle for liberation."[27] In other words Israel's story-making was an active part of Israel's struggle for identity and liberation. Such stories need to be read as an active part of *our* struggle for identity and liberation.

> *Oh, I could tell you stories that would darken the sky and stop the blood. The stories I could tell no one would believe. I would have to pour blood on the floor to convince anyone that every word I say is true. And then? Whose blood would speak for me?*
>
> —Dorothy Allison[28]

To read the Bible as story is in no way less serious than reading it as history or literature. Whether the events related happened or not, they are profoundly true in the sense of myth. Modern people tend to dismiss myth as falsehood rather than recognizing it as something that is powerfully true, indeed fundamental to survival. "[A] myth is not an idle tale but an ideological force. Myths of origin serve to legitimize property claims, distinctions in rank, and the dominance of a particular clan."[29] We have lost the tribal knowledge that says stories are "all we have to fight off illness and death. You don't have anything if you don't have stories."[30] First-world Christians are perilously close to having no stories to sustain us.

The Bible is a heritage that is deep, old, dark, and rich. The words of scripture are thousands of years old, and the cultures they grew out of, older still. The Bible contains our ancestors' wisdom about what it means to live, the power and sanctity of the earth, encounters with the divine, and how to be a community. It tells with profound honesty the human struggle. The Bible was written by people, but because God is in the struggle and ambiguity, the word of God lives in it. In the Bible we encounter archetypes, heroes, and unique personalities. Tricksters and kings, poetry and economics, sex and violence, honor and betrayal, resistance and love are all part of this sacred inheritance. Our scriptures tell the depths and heights of human nature. We can bring our full selves to *this* Bible, including our intelligence, our doubting, and our own stories.

The Bible is a rich inheritance and a sacred trust, but it is *not* an instruction manual for living. Bishop Ruíz of Chiapas has an important insight when he compares the Word of God to a light shone on social reality. "The light does not tell me what to do," Ruíz says, "but it shows me what is there so that I can decide what to do."[31] We are not obliged to espouse particular values simply because they are "biblical." Nor do we need to ignore that which disturbs us—indeed we must not.

The Bible may, as liberation theologians tell us, be the historical memory of the poor, but it is the memory of only some poor, recorded and rerecorded with very specific intent. As Judith Plaskow has it, the Torah is a "partial record of the 'Godwrestling' of part of the Jewish people."[32] The forces and sources that have preserved in the Bible a small and particular portion of the history of God have abused and distorted it as well. The

Bible has no single theme: it is a document of patriarchy and a document of liberation, a story of yearning for God and of alienation from God, a "strange mix of great good and frightening evil."[33] Liberation, economic justice, freedom, right relationship, and God's consistent siding with the oppressed in history are all prominent biblical themes. At the same time, because "the writings of the Bible are profoundly androcentric and hierarchical and deeply imbued with patriarchal values, they cannot be read simply as authoritative or normative visions of life as it should be."[34]

As we have seen, the Bible is a collection of voices from different times and perspectives; it is not inherently anything except perhaps *ours* and thus something we must grapple with. We are faced with an exceptionally difficult task because we are seeking to integrate a tribal heritage into the fiercely antitribal world of modern global capitalism. In this context, to hold fast to the stories we love and hate and do not always understand presents a profound challenge to the modern world which prizes sameness and rewards conformity.

To read the Bible as sacred, living story is an approach that is both newer and older than historical and literary criticism. It looks past the postmodern paralysis which keeps us from saying much of anything, lost in a maze of objectivity where every reading is equally valid. It recognizes the Bible as a living thing. Reading the Bible as story, we look back to the production of the texts in a particular history. We appreciate their complexity as literature, but we treat them as a dynamic heritage that can help us live our own stories.

I take seriously the idea that reading, hearing, and telling our stories is the stuff of survival. Through the middle chapters of this book I move back and forth between the stories of Exodus and the stories of our present lives. The traditional *Passover Haggadah,* the order of service for celebrating the feast, says, "praise is due to the person who adds unto the story."[35] The rest of this book will attempt to do just that: to bring our own sacred stories of living in the first world at the turn of the millennium to the stories we have inherited, specifically the story of the exodus.

2

READING EXODUS AS ISRAEL

Identification with Election

READING THE BIBLE IN ENGLISH

Exodus is the second book of the Pentateuch. The names of the books in the Christian Bible come from their designations in the third-century B.C.E. translations of the Torah from Hebrew to Greek. These names reflect the books' contents. The names of the books in the Jewish Bible are the first words of the books in Hebrew. Thus, for Christians, the second book is "Exodus," which refers to the Israelites' departure from Egypt; for Jews, the Hebrew name for this book is translated as "these are the names." "These are the names of the sons of Israel who came to Egypt with Jacob, each with his household" (Exod. 1:1a).

Throughout this book, whenever possible, I have included the full printed text of the passages from Exodus. I consider myself to be a person of average conscientiousness as well as a Bible nerd, but if I see a chapter-and-verse citation in the middle of a sentence, I don't very often get out my bedside Bible to check the text. If the passage is there in front of me I am much more likely to read it.

For most passages I use the New Revised Standard Version (NRSV) of the Bible. The NRSV is a Christian Bible produced by an ecumenical committee and copyrighted in 1989. It is an updated translation of the Revised Standard Version of 1952, which is authorized for use by many major Christian churches (Protestant, Roman Catholic, Anglican, and Eastern Orthodox). The NRSV incorporates new advances in translation and recent discoveries and corrects for the masculine bias in the English language. It is essentially a literal translation, which means that each word is translated rather than attempting to convey the "sense" or "poetry" of the text. Paraphrasing is used rarely and most often to compensate for a lack in English.

I sometimes include the following alternate modern translations, each of which has its own strengths and weaknesses. The Tanakh is the standard modern Jewish translation of the Bible,[1] begun in 1955. The Torah section,

22

which includes Exodus, was published in 1962. The Tanakh is a literal translation, like the NRSV, and was produced by a committee of the Jewish Publication Society. A more recent translation by Everett Fox is quite different. His English is not flowing and familiar, but his translation emphasizes the structure and word order of the Hebrew.[2] The Christian Community Bible (CCB), published by the Claretian Order, is easy to read, nontechnical, and emphasizes liberation themes. Finally I include the King James Version (KJV), published in 1611, because it is the most widely known and influential translation of the Bible in the English language.

The oldest versions of the Bible that we have date from hundreds of years after the time we assume the books were first circulating as a complete unit. In the third century B.C.E., the Torah was translated from Hebrew into Greek for the Hellenized Jews of Alexandria, Egypt.[3] In the first century C.E., the early church adopted this Greek translation, the Septuagint, as its Bible. In the last centuries of the millennium, Hebrew ceased to be the spoken language of the Jews and the Bible was also translated into Aramaic and Syriac. As Latin became the common language of the Roman Empire, Jerome (340-420), one of the church fathers, produced the Vulgate, a Latin translation of the Bible based on Jewish tradition. From the sixth to the ninth century, Jewish scholars known as the Masoretes standardized the traditional Hebrew text, which dated from the early part of the millennium, by adding vowel points. In written Hebrew, consonants are large blockish letters, and vowels are smaller dot-like characters written below or above the consonants. In the earliest Hebrew texts, only the consonants were written. Merle Feld's poem that was quoted in the preceding chapter illustrates this aspect of the Hebrew language.

> as time passes
> the particulars
> the hard data
> the who what when where why
> slip away from me
> and all I'm left with is
> the feeling
>
> But feelings are just sounds
> the vowel barking of a mute
>
> My brother is so sure of what he heard
> after all he's got a record of it
> consonant after consonant after consonant[4]

Occasionally the unpointed consonants suggest an interpretation other than that in the Masoretic Text, and often there are differences between ancient versions, just as there are between modern translations.

The kind of reading we are doing requires us to examine and evaluate differences in both ancient and modern translations. Translators consider both what is traditional and what makes sense; but real people translated these texts and translation is by no means a value-neutral activity. Randall Bailey says, "That which is conceivable within the ideology of the translator is what gets translated."[5] He illustrates this point using chapter 1 verse 5 from the Song of Songs, "I am black (conjunction) beautiful." Black *and* beautiful is the accurate translation given the context, but the passage has consistently been translated into English as "black *but* beautiful," because the translators' ideology assumed black to be incompatible with beauty.

Before we delve into Exodus itself, there is one more point that perhaps has been left too long and may be so obvious it does not need saying. In reading the Bible it makes a difference who the reader is. In the first chapter of this book we looked briefly at source theory, the idea that the Bible is made up from sources that represent different times and perspectives in Israel's history. A central concept of this theory is that who you are and how you live influence how and what you write. A fundamental principle of *this* chapter is that who you are and how you live also influence how you *read.* People of color read differently from white people. Children read differently from adults. Women read differently from men. Disabled people read differently from the currently able. Poor people read differently from the rich. The same texts and stories can mean different things to different people at different times.

INTRODUCTION TO EXODUS

The basic plot of Exodus is as follows. Through their own action, the work of God, and the action of their leader, Moses, the Israelites leave slavery in Egypt. They cross the Sea of Reeds[6] and travel through the wilderness to Sinai, where God self-reveals to the whole people and makes a covenant with them. The covenant includes practical details of what it means for Israel to be God's people.

The major themes and subjects of Exodus are birth, liberation, revelation of YHWH, covenant, YHWH's kingship, and the tabernacle. Exodus is a critical book in the Hebrew scriptures; it contains the narrative traditions fundamental to the origins of ancient Israel. Exodus bridges the gap between myth and history, between family and nation. For modern readers, the Exodus stories of a mother who hides her baby, God on a mountain, and an army drowned in the sea are vaguely familiar to some and paradigmatic for others.

In terms of content, Exodus can be separated into two parts of roughly equal length. Chapters 1-18 are predominantly narrative material, and chapters 19-40 are mainly legislative. Below I have further divided the narrative material by setting, so that there are three sections: what happens in Egypt, what happens at Sinai, and what happens in between.[7] The boundaries of the in-between section are a little vague, as it is debatable precisely when and where the departure, *the exodus*, begins.

EGYPT	1:1-2:10	Egyptian Oppression of the Hebrews
	2:11-7:7	YHWH Commissions Moses
	7:8-13:16	Plagues on Egypt/Hardening of Pharaoh's Heart
	13:17-15:21	Destruction of Pharaoh's Army
WILDERNESS	15:22-18:27	Turbulent Journey to Sinai
SINAI	19:1-24	Theophany and Covenant
	25:1-31	Instructions for Building and Maintenance of Tabernacle
	32:1-34	Golden Calf, Renewal of Covenant
	35:1-40	Tabernacle Built

This book is about Egypt so our focus is Exodus 1:1-15:21, which is set in Egypt. I have highlighted those sections which we will spend time on later.

1:1-2:10	Egyptian Oppression of the Hebrews
1:1-7	Israel's Children Grow Strong in Egypt
1:8-14	**Pharaoh's Campaign of Forced Labor**
1:15-20	**Midwives vs. Pharaoh's Campaign of Genocide**
2:1-10	**Women Conspire to Save the Infant Moses**
2:11-7:7	YHWH Commissions Moses
2:11-22	Moses Kills an Egyptian, Flees, then Settles in Midian
2:32-25	Cries of Israelites Come up to God
3:1-4:17	Call of Moses/Burning Bush
4:18-29	Moses Returns to Egypt with Zipporah of Midian and Their Son
4:21-26	Zipporah Circumcises Her Son
4:27-31	Aaron and Elders Recruited
5:1-6:1	First Meeting with Pharaoh Escalates Forced Labor Campaign
6:2-13	Call of Moses
6:14-27	Genealogy of Moses and Aaron
6:28-7:7	Call of Moses

7:8-13:16	Plagues on Egypt/Hardening of Pharaoh's Heart
7:8-14	A Contest with Pharaoh's Magicians
7:14-20	Water Is Turned to Blood
7:25-8:15	Frogs
8:16-19	Insects
8:20-32	Insects
9:1-7	Death of Egyptian Livestock
9:8-12	Boils on Humans and Animals
9:13-35	Destructive Fire and Hail from Heaven
10:1-20	Locusts
10:21-29	Darkness
11:1-13:16	Death of Egyptian Firstborn and Passover Rituals

13:7-15:21	Destruction of Pharaoh's Army
13:17-14:31	Israelites Cross Sea, Pharaoh's Army Drowned
15:1-21	Miriam's Song of the Sea

As you read through the outline, notice the repetitions: the call of Moses and the plagues of insects. Notice which stories are familiar to you, what you remember, and what you feel. How do *you* read these stories?

The story of Israel's sojourn in Egypt begins with Israel already in Egypt because of the political and economic maneuverings of their ancestor Joseph. As Israel increases, a pharaoh who does not know Joseph responds with an escalating campaign of harassment, forced labor, and infanticide. Under the threat of genocide, a handful of Israelite and Egyptian women conspire to save the infant Moses. As an adult, Moses kills an Egyptian and flees. In response to the cries of the suffering Israelites, YHWH calls Moses to lead the Israelites out of Egypt. Moses returns to Egypt and recruits Aaron and the elders of Israel. In a series of contests involving natural phenomena, YHWH defeats the new pharaoh, and the Israelites march out of Egypt. Pharaoh pursues with his army, and the fleeing Israelites are trapped between the advancing army and the sea. Moses parts the Sea of Reeds, and the Israelites walk through on dry land. The waters return, drowning Pharaoh's army, and the Israelites celebrate on the far shore.

RETELLING EXODUS

Exodus in Jewish History

The Exodus story has been read and reread, used and reused throughout history by many different people. If we posit a sort of minimum historical exodus—that is, if we affirm that at least some small pre-Israel group left Egypt and brought with them the seeds of the story of their escape—then this "exodus event" is our starting point. The oldest reference to this event, Miriam's song of late twelfth or early eleventh century B.C.E., seems to describe a sea battle in which Egyptian troops, perhaps in ships, are sunk.[8] This version makes no reference to crossing the sea on dry land.

> Pharaoh's chariots and his army he cast into the sea;
>   his picked officers were sunk in the Red Sea.
> The floods covered them;
>   they went down into the depths like a stone. (Exod. 15:4-5)

Preceding Miriam's song is a prose description of the dramatic events at sea (Exod. 14). These passages are a weaving together of the Priestly version of the story, which emphasizes the power of God, and the Jahwist version, with its more human scale.[9] "One strand highlights the human perspective (Pharaoh's plans, Israel's fear) while another features the divine (divine word spoken and fulfilled). One strand presents a miraculous occurrence (waters like walls) whereas another describes an act of nature (a strong east wind)."[10]

Yet another version of *an* exodus is evidenced by scattered references to fleeing slaves plundering their Egyptian enslavers.

> The Israelites had done as Moses told them; they had asked the Egyptians for jewelry of silver and gold, and for clothing, and the LORD had given the people favor in the sight of the Egyptians, so that they let them have what they asked. And so they plundered the Egyptians. (Exod. 12:35-36; see also Exod. 3:21-22; 11:2-3; Ps. 105:37)

Was it a triumphant marching out or a covert sneaking away? Whatever happened at the sea, this event and its telling and retelling have reverberated through time.

Beyond the book of Exodus, the exodus theme appears throughout the Hebrew Bible as what Marcus Borg calls a macro-story, one of the fundamental ways in which Israel's religious life is imagined.[11] Much of the legislative material of the Pentateuch is grounded in the memory of enslavement in Egypt. YHWH's deliverance is Israel's impetus for keeping the law. The prophets assert that the exodus was not an isolated episode and that YHWH remains in solidarity with Israel and continues to act for justice. Psalms celebrate the mighty warrior god, protector, and deliverer of Israel. Israel's exodus from Egypt was told and retold by priests, storytellers, musicians, and lawyers to meet their changing world. But the retelling of the exodus is not limited to the stories that became the Bible.

Throughout history, different groups have read Exodus and acted according to their identification with the enslaved Israelites. Between approximately 200 B.C.E. and 100 C.E. there were "no fewer than 62 Jewish revolts, rebellions, attempts at revolution and resistance movements" against Roman occupation. They took as their inspiration the exodus edict

that Israel be slave to none but YHWH.[12] Even after the destruction of the
Second Temple in 70 C.E., there were several armed Jewish uprisings
against the "heathen yoke" of foreign occupation. From 115 to 117 C.E.
there was a Jewish revolt against the emperor Trajan, and again in 351
Jews revolted against Constantine. In 614, Jews revolted yet again, this
time united with Persians. In each of these struggles, Jews took their inspiration from Exodus and the understanding that God desires human liberation.[13]

Certainly the most consistent rereading of Exodus is found in the most
widely celebrated of Jewish holidays, Passover. For thirty centuries of Jewish history "families have gathered together not to memorialize the Exodus
from Egypt but to relive it"[14] through this ritual meal. The following texts
come from a traditional order of service and a modern feminist *haggadah*
respectively.

> We celebrate tonight because we were Pharaoh's bondmen in Egypt, and
> the Lord our God delivered us with a mighty hand. Had not the Holy
> One, blessed be He, redeemed our fathers from Egypt, we, our children,
> and our children's children would have remained slaves. Therefore even
> if all of us were wise and well-versed in the Torah, it would still be our
> duty from year to year, to tell the story of the deliverance from Egypt.
> Indeed to dwell at length on it, is accounted praiseworthy.[15]

> We were slaves to Pharaoh in Egypt. A wind came out of the wilderness
> bearing the divine aroma of freedom, and the spirit of the people rose
> up to meet it. They put down the trowels that they used to lay bricks for
> Pharaoh's storehouses, they abandoned their ovens and stewpots. And if
> our ancestors had not possessed the courage to walk away from the
> familiar, to cross the Sinai desert in the dark of night, we and our chil-
> dren and grandchildren would still be slaves in Egypt.
>   We went out of Egypt but after a few generations the Assyrians came
> down and conquered us, and then the Greeks and then the Romans. We
> were torn on the racks of the Inquisition, beaten in the Czar's army,
> worked without a sabbath in the textile mills of America. We became the
> ashes of slaves in the Führer's ovens. Yet each time the legend of our
> deliverance sustained us and gave us the courage to fight our oppressors.
> Therefore, it is incumbent on us to tell our children the story of each
> Exodus, to guide them when they embark on their own journeys. And
> whoever teaches her children the truth of her own struggle, withholding
> nothing, that woman is worthy of praise.[16]

Through this ritual enactment, Israel's central story is truly re-membered,
not just verbally, but through the body.[17] Generations have made the liber-

ation experience of the exodus their own, remembering, "that despite all the overwhelming obstacles, there is a Force of Healing and Transformation that makes it possible to overcome the evil and cruelty in the world."[18]

Exodus in Christian History

The documents of one particular Jewish resistance movement evidence ample reconfiguration and incorporation of exodus liberation traditions. In Christian scriptures, Jesus is portrayed as the new Moses: Moses escapes Pharaoh's campaign of infanticide, Jesus escapes Herod's campaign; Israel spends forty years in the wilderness, Jesus forty days; Moses parts the sea, Jesus walks on water; Moses feeds with manna, Jesus multiplies bread; Moses is rejected, Jesus is rejected. The passion narratives focus particularly on aspects of the Passover, and throughout the Christian Bible the vocabulary of redemption, liberation, and salvation recalls the exodus.[19] In the Epistles, Pauline and other, the history of Israel is looked to as both an example and a warning. Finally, in Revelation "there can be detected John's conviction concerning the continuing meaning of the Exodus: God remains his people's redeemer, the judge of their oppressors, the guarantor of their eternal inheritance."[20]

The history of Christianity contains numerous episodes of groups and individuals acting out their identification with Israel. The church father St. Augustine (d. 430) developed from Exodus 32 his justification for the persecution of heretical Christians by the Roman state and the basis of the theory of holy war.[21] Medieval debates about the legitimacy of the Crusades refer to Exodus, as does literature of the European peasant revolts. The most radical proposals of the Protestant Reformation of the 1500s were undergirded by exodus theology. From my own cultural history, Dutch nationalist literature of the late sixteenth and early seventeenth centuries likened the Netherlands to Israel fighting for independence from Egypt-like Spain. During the 1800s, Lutheran Prussians and several self-described "Exodus communities" of northern Europe appropriated the exodus story to describe their own situations of exile and religious persecution. In North America, New England Puritans looked at the Americas as the New Canaan, which they were called to enter and conquer, a belief that contributed to the near extinction of Native people on the continent.[22] Enslaved Africans in North America, Latin America, and the Caribbean found in their captors' religion a god who acts for slaves against enslavers. The great Underground Railroad conductor Harriet Tubman was called Black Moses. In the antebellum South, slave spirituals were often code songs expressing the yearning for deliverance from slavery, but also signaling the moment for action to achieve it.[23] An early design for the great American symbol the Liberty Bell showed the drowning of Pharaoh's army.

Christian Anti-Judaism

Christianity began as one of many Jewish resistance movements during the time of the late Second Temple but eventually and ironically became the religion sanctioned by the Roman state. What began as an intrafaith conflict within Judaism, became an interfaith conflict between Judaism and a new religion, Christianity. As Christianity came into ascendancy, the balance of power shifted significantly. Christians, who like Jews had been persecuted for their refusal to participate in emperor worship, became aligned with the power of empire and became oppressors of the Jews. Herein lies the central question of this book: What happens when a powerful people take an oppressed people's story, produced in a context of oppression, and read it as their own?

The importance of the theme of misappropriation and the horror that has resulted from Christian anti-Judaism[24] are ample justification to interrupt this review of the influence of the book of Exodus on history to delve into the issue more deeply. Christian anti-Judaism has its roots in the Gospels with John's tirades against the Judeans[25] and its apex in the Holocaust, but it continues today. For liberal Christians, this prejudice manifests itself in subtle ways. People who would never make an overtly anti-Jewish remark glibly imply that Christianity is the culmination and intended end point of Judaism; or they contrast the "punishing Old Testament God" with the "forgiving God of the New Testament." Feminist Christians mistakenly compare the open, "Christian" Jesus with the rigid laws of Judaism. In reality Jesus was an open, justice-seeking Jew. Post-Christian feminists blame Judaism for the end of prepatriarchal goddess religion.

Is it possible for modern Christians to read Exodus or any story from the Hebrew scriptures outside of its historical Jewish context and not perpetuate the history of Christian anti-Judaism? While there are those like Jon Levenson who are adamant that the exodus paradigm is not transferable,[26] the Christian history of appropriating Exodus is already two thousand years old. As we explore Exodus in this book, we will deliberately avoid the patterns of Christian anti-Judaism. As Christians who seek justice, we must respect modern Judaism as independent, living, and nuanced.[27] Many Christians tend to behave as if Judaism went into a state of suspended animation with the death of Jesus of Nazareth. We need to be in active solidarity and dialogue with Jewish scholars and activists. We must be open to criticism and aware that we are not the best judges of our capacity to harm with our assumptions. But we can still claim Exodus as our heritage and look honestly at how Christians have used and abused this sacred story.

Exodus in Modern History

In modern history, uses and abuses of the exodus story have continued. In the late 1800s and early 1900s Boer Nationalists in South Africa saw themselves as Israel and the British as Egypt.[28] Later in a sort of hideous irony, the German Christian Movement of the early 1930s cast themselves in the role of the children of Israel while denying the canonicity of the Hebrew Bible.[29] The Warsaw uprising in the Polish ghetto in 1943 took inspiration from Exodus. After World War II, both Jewish and Christian understandings of Exodus were among the many factors that contributed to the formation of the state of Israel. During the civil rights movement in the United States, Martin Luther King Jr. spoke the language of Exodus, his legacy from the slave churches. Today, Exodus International is an umbrella organization for seventy-five "Christian ex-gay ministries" dedicated to "leading homosexuals out of bondage into liberating union with God."[30]

Michael Walzer claims that "wherever people know the Bible and experience oppression, the Exodus has sustained their spirits and (sometimes) inspired their resistance."[31] While this may be true, it is not all that is true. There is a parallel history of dangerous misappropriation of the exodus story, often unintentional but causing immense harm nonetheless. As we have seen, the history of reading Exodus and identifying with Israel is long, complex, and sometimes abusive.

In the past fifty years, some of the most intensive, persuasive, and, in the best sense of the word, subversive[32] readings of Exodus have come from Latin American theologians and black theologians in the United States. Although other liberation theologies (black South African, Korean *minjung*) are also persuasive for the oppressed and dangerous to those who benefit from power structures, I am focusing on Latin American and black theologies because they have longer histories and are more relevant to the context of the Americas. Black and Latin American theologians have brought to the Christian community powerful insights into the exodus tradition, and they claim that Exodus is the story from which their liberation theologies are derived. The following is by no means a historical review of these theologies; it is simply a quick look at how two different groups read Exodus by grounding themselves in their own experiences.

LATIN AMERICAN LIBERATION THEOLOGY

The Bible is read quite differently in Latin American liberation churches than it is in middle-class North American churches. Latin American liberation readings of Exodus are formed in *base communities* that study the Bible together in a spiral of action-reflection-action, based in their daily lives.

Base communities are a less hierarchical model of church in which poor people meet weekly in groups of five to 150 to pray, read the Bible, and apply concretely what they read to their own lives. They *see* their own situations of impoverishment, racism, classism, sexism, and so on, *judge* those situations in light of what they have read in the Bible, and then *act* to better their situation. As Bishop Ruíz of Chiapas said, the Bible shines a light on social reality so that we can see what is there and decide what to do.[33] When the poor read the Bible in a way that is grounded in their everyday realities, they see how the current system of global economics furthers their impoverishment by treating them as commodities and resources. They judge this system to be oppressive and immoral, and they act to change it.

Members of base communities, many of whom are new to the Bible and even new to reading, are involved in struggles for clean water, education, sewers, health clinics, and, above all, land. Because of the threat that an organized, empowered, and conscientized poor presents to unchallenged authority, these communities, since the early 1960s, have known repression, arrest, torture, and martyrdom in their villages and towns. "In nearly every country of Latin America, under highly repressive military governments, hundreds of laity and religious, as well as a goodly number of priests, have been expelled from their countries, tortured and murdered. Not even bishops have been spared."[34]

The poor of Latin America read Exodus and identify with Israel, because, like Israel, they suffer imposed social and economic violence. Their experiences resemble the experiences of Israel in Egypt, and thus they have particular insight when reading the text. This idea, that poor Latin Americans, because of their experience of oppression, have a special understanding of biblical texts, is called "the hermeneutical privilege of the poor." Hermeneutics means simply the way that we come to understand something. Another key phrase in liberation theology is "the hermeneutics of suspicion." It means simply that for those of us who have not been well served by the Bible, one of the ways in which we come to know it better, is by regarding it with suspicion, by asking difficult questions. By asking questions about power and politics in the Bible and in the world, liberation theologians have found much in Exodus to challenge and sustain them.

LATIN AMERICAN READINGS OF EXODUS

Exodus is a fundamental text in Latin American liberation theology. In the words of Margaret Guider:

> Those who have followed the evolution of Latin American liberation theology during the course of the past twenty-five years know the extent to which the Exodus narrative has been foundational in its origins and development both in terms of theological speculation and pastoral practice.[35]

With regard to Exodus, Latin American liberation theologians are adamant, even extravagant, in their statements about its depth and relevance. Gustavo Gutiérrez claims that Exodus has "inexhaustible subversive meaning." José Severino Croatto says that the exodus paradigm is permanently relevant; he calls it "a focal point of the first magnitude and an inexhaustible light." Leonardo Boff says, "Exodus is the journey of the whole of humanity and of creation toward the resurrection of all flesh and the renewal of heaven and earth."[36]

The first main point the Latin American liberation theologians make in reading Exodus is that God knows about the suffering of the oppressed— *Blessed be the Lord* God hears their cry.

> After a long time the king of Egypt died. The Israelites groaned under their slavery, and cried out. Out of the slavery their cry for help rose up to God. God heard their groaning, and God remembered his covenant with Abraham, Isaac, and Jacob. God looked upon the Israelites, and God took notice of them. (Exod. 2:23-25)

"The liberation of Exodus started because God listens to the cry of the oppressed."[37] In the text God's response to the suffering of the oppressed is to side with them against their oppressors and bring about political change.[38]

> Then the LORD said, "I have observed the misery of my people who are in Egypt; I have heard their cry on account of their taskmasters. Indeed I know their sufferings, and I have come down to deliver them from the Egyptians, and to bring them up out of that land to a good and broad land, a land flowing with milk and honey, to the country of the Canaanites, the Hittites, the Amorites, the Perizzites, the Hivites, and the Jebusites. The cry of the Israelites has now come to me; I have also seen how the Egyptians oppress them. So come, I will send you to Pharaoh to bring my people, the Israelites, out of Egypt." (Exod. 3:7-10)

Thus liberation theologians affirm that God *acts in history*. "The God of life could not remain neutral in a situation of death: he [*sic*] had to commit himself."[39] These paired observations—that God hears the cry of the poor and acts on their behalf in history—constitute God's *preferential option for the poor*, the heart of Latin American readings of Exodus.

Liberation theologians also assert that in Exodus both God and Israel are defined. Somehow God is known through leaving oppression, struggling in wilderness, and coming to a new land. God's name is revealed in Exodus (3:13–14) and throughout the Hebrew Bible God is identified as "the one who brought you out of the land of Egypt." Israel is formed by the exodus, through the concrete involvement of the people in the project of liberation.

Further, Latin American liberation theologians claim that liberation and the story of the exodus are not about privatized spirituality; they are instead the experiences of a people and a community and thus can only be truly understood in community. Liberation theologians conclude that the exodus story demands of its readers some action in the present. For the relatively privileged theologian this means acts of solidarity with the oppressed. Gustavo Gutiérrez says:

> [The theologian] will be engaged where nations, social classes, people struggle to free themselves from domination and oppression by other nations, classes and people. In the last analysis, the true interpretation of the meaning revealed by theology is achieved only in historical praxis.[40]

The articulators of these liberation readings to the world community have mostly been European-educated men—priests of at least some position in the Roman Catholic hierarchy. Even those born in poverty, educated, and returned to serve their people have experienced some privilege. Thus there has been some inconsistency between this "perspective of the poor," typically imaged as the male *campesino*, and the theologians who articulate it. Leonardo Boff addresses this inconsistency by pointing out that theology is carried out at various levels by popular, pastoral, and professional theologians.[41] This is not in any way to belittle these professional theologians, their work, or their praxis. People have been and continue to be silenced, harassed, and even killed for preaching and acting out the theology of liberation in Latin America.[42] Recently at the prompting of women, indigenous people, and Latin Americans of African heritage, some theologians have begun to acknowledge their biases and have tried to include categories of race and gender in their analyses.

BLACK THEOLOGY

In the Exodus-Sinai tradition Yahweh is disclosed as the God of history, whose revelation is identical with his power to liberate the oppressed. There is no knowledge of Yahweh except through his political activity on behalf of the weak and helpless of the land.

—James Cone[43]

Black liberation theology, which takes black history and experience as the source for theological expression, emerged formally out of the turmoil and violence of the late 1960s.[44] Its roots, however, lie in the faith of black slaves in the Americas, transmitted over centuries in the black church through songs, preaching, and storytelling. Black slaves in the United States identified with the Hebrew slaves in Egypt; they had parallel experiences. "The record shows clearly that black slaves believed that just as God delivered Moses and the Israelites from Egyptian bondage, he also will deliver black people from American slavery."[45]

> Dey kin fo'ge yo' chains an' shackles
> F'om de mountains to de sea;
> But de Lawd will sen' some Moses
> Fu' to set his chillun free.[46]

For black theologians, Exodus is *the* paradigmatic text because it was the paradigmatic text for their slave ancestors. Thus, identification with Israel is an inherited tradition relevant in the present to the systemic racism that all black people in the United States experience and to the economic injustice that many know. African Americans read Exodus differently than white people and other North Americans because of their particular experience of oppression.

If reading the Bible in base communities can be characterized by the idea of community, then reading in the black church might be characterized by the word "tradition." "We do not begin as if black people have just started reading the Bible. There is already a tradition. What can we learn from your grandfather and my aunt about what the Bible means?"[47] Black theology has a rich and creative understanding of the word of God drawn from a resistance-heritage of spirituals, slave narratives, and testimonies, as well as the traditional canon.

> When Israel was in Egypt's land
>   Let my people go;
> Oppressed so hard they could not stand,
>   Let my people go;

CHORUS: Go down Moses
>   Way down in Egypt land
>   Tell old Pharaoh
>   Let my people go!

> We need not always weep and moan
>   Let my people go;
> And wear these slavery chains forlorn
>   Let my people go![48]

COMPARING LIBERATION THEOLOGIES

Black theologians espouse a race-based theology, and Latin American liberation theology is economically and class based. Still, readings of black theologians such as James Cone and James Deotis Roberts, based in the experience of black America, are very similar to those of Latin American liberation theologians, who have a very different context. Black theologians, like Latin American liberation theologians, identify with Israel; they assert that God hears the oppressed and sides with them, acting for their political liberation on earth. God is in relationship with *a people*, and theology demands political involvement of that people. "God is a God of history. He adopted Israel and entered into her life"[49]

> Black theology focuses on black history as a source for its theological interpretation of God's work in the world because divine activity is inseparable from the history of black people. There can be no comprehension of Black theology without realizing that its existence comes from a community which looks back on its unique past, visualizes the reality of the future, and then makes decisions about possibilities in the present.[50]

Compared to Latin American liberation theologians, black theologians focus more on the revelatory nature of Exodus. "The Exodus of Israel from Egypt was a revelation-liberation event. In this revelatory event Israel came to know God as the liberator of the oppressed."[51] Black theologians also have a somewhat stronger emphasis on God's destruction of oppressors, which we will discuss further in chapter 7. Historically, liberation theology in Latin America has been associated with the Catholic Church while black liberation theology has Protestant roots and remains largely a Protestant phenomenon. While the Catholic Church has responded to the radicalness of liberation theology by harassing and silencing Latin American liberation theologians, the white hierarchies of Protestant denominations have for a long time simply ignored the work of black theologians.

Black liberation readings of Exodus are much more Jesus-focused, more christological, than Latin American readings. "The exodus provides a central category for interpreting not only the Old Testament but the work of Jesus."[52] The God of Exodus is the God of Jesus; the God of liberation is the God of resurrection.

> One of these morning, five o' clock
> Dis ole world gonna reel and rock
> Pharaoh's army got drownded,
> Oh Mary don't you weep.[53]

The four lines of this song capture three fundamental aspects of black liberation theology: political change in this world; God's destruction of the oppressors; and the continuity between the god of liberation (Pharaoh's army got drownded) and the god of resurrection (Mary don't you weep).

For black theologians in the United States, where racism and white supremacy are deeply ingrained, the expression of what Latin American liberation theologians call the preferential option for the poor is the assertion that "Exodus has confirmed that God has chosen blackness over whiteness in the same way that God elected the enslaved progeny of Jacob over imperial Egypt."[54]

Black theologians differ significantly from Latin American theologians in their willingness to disagree publicly with one another.[55] Black theology exists in a state of "productive critical exchange and confrontation."[56] The ongoing debate between James Cone and James Deotis Roberts about reconciliation and violence in black–white race relations in the United States is an example.[57] More recently, and over the past ten years especially, womanist theologians such as Katie Cannon, Renita Weems, Delores Williams, and many others have added their voices and challenges to black theology. Delores Williams's call for dialogue between womanist and black theologians about issues of gender and other forms of marginalization will be examined in the next chapter.

LIBERATION READINGS OF EXODUS

Black and Latin American liberation readers ground their readings of Exodus in their own histories and in their everyday lives. Reading the biblical texts, they identify with the characters whose situations most resemble their own. The impoverishment, repression, violence, and racism experienced by blacks in North America and by poor Latin Americans mirror the experiences of Israel in Egypt. Despite the fact that for centuries diverse groups and individuals have identified with Israel when they read Exodus, the insights of liberation readers are fresh and startling.

- God acts in history for human liberation.
- God sides with the oppressed against oppressors.
- Salvation is a community rather than an individual concern.
- Humans must take an active role in God's liberation project.

These insights are not new, but because churches have allied themselves with political power, their readings of Exodus have focused instead on individual salvation and the power of God. It has been difficult for churches to say that God sides with the powerless when they themselves side with the powerful, but black and Latin American liberation theologians have opened up the book of Exodus for the world. They have given us a new understanding of a God who liberates and of people who struggle for justice.

3

PROSTITUTES, SLAVES, AND CANAANITES

Another Side of Exodus

LIBERATION READINGS CHALLENGED

There are numerous critiques of liberation theologians' use of Exodus. Some critics are simply opposed to liberation theology; some hold that the exodus story cannot be generalized and appropriated beyond its very specific Jewish context; and others fault the quality of liberation theologians' biblical scholarship.[1] The three critics we will discuss in this chapter, Margaret Guider, Delores Williams, and Robert Warrior, support the principles of liberation but take issue with the way liberation theologians use the exodus story as a paradigm or a model for how liberation should be. They disagree with liberation theologians' complete identification with the people of Israel.

Despite the fact that for centuries individuals and communities have read Exodus, identifying "naturally" with Israel and comparing their struggles to Israel's, recent biblical scholarship has raised the idea that identification is a complex issue. Reading across a gap of thousands of years, all modern readers differ in time and culture from the biblical characters they encounter, and they may differ in class, race, age, gender, ability, and social status as well. Furthermore, whether the biblical personalities in question are historical figures or characters in an allegory or parable, we encounter them as literary portraits, which are necessarily limited. Sometimes our biblical imaginations and a universal theme can bridge the distance between reader and text, but on other occasions, "what is an essentially simple act of identification . . . becomes a tangle of contradictions."[2]

Guider, Williams, and Warrior are three very different writers who recognize the contradictions in identifying with Israel. They look at Exodus from the perspective of other characters. I have chosen to focus on these three non-Israelite readings because they address the history and present situation of racism, sexism, and colonialism in the Americas and because they speak from places of active suffering. In keeping with the theme of reading the Bible as story, each section begins with a story or poem to illustrate the human relevance of the more academic critique.

Margaret Guider—Prostitutes

Foolish men who accuse
women unreasonably
you blame yet never see
you cause what you abuse.
        —Sor Juana Inez de la Cruz,
                Mexican nun (1651-1695)[3]

It kind of kills you, but it's over fast.
        —A streetwalker talking about prostitution[4]

Margaret Guider is a Franciscan sister who spent several years in the 1970s as a lay missioner in the rural interior of Brazil. Her book *Daughters of Rahab: Prostitution and the Church of Liberation in Brazil* is a history of the Pastoral Project for Marginalized Women, originally a church-sponsored, national forum for prostitutes and church leaders to meet. *Daughters of Rahab* begins with an exploration of Latin American liberation theologians' foundational use of the exodus story. Guider frames her careful examination with an important observation. In Latin America both the literal survival of individuals and the survival of a transformative vision have been threatened by "military regimes, multinational corporations, the mass media, the International Monetary Fund, the Vatican, the Congregation for the Doctrine of the Faith and natural disasters."[5] In this context, liberation theologians' negative reaction against any criticism of Exodus as a liberation paradigm is not an exercise in academic freedom; it is a strategy for survival.[6]

Nevertheless Guider challenges the use of Exodus as paradigm. Despite her stated allegiance to Latin American liberation theology, Guider deliberately exercises a hermeneutic of suspicion with regard to the liberation church's *selection* of texts. She points out that, although Exodus is bracketed by stories of women who act for survival, liberation theologians focus instead on men, liberation, and conquest. As her biblical starting point for theological reflection on prostitution, Guider examines the often-neglected story of Rahab, the prostitute of Jericho. The story, found in the book of Joshua (chap. 2), takes place at the end of the exodus event. Because Rahab's story specifically, and the few biblical women's stories in general, tend to be further marginalized by liturgical and scholarly neglect, I include Rahab's story here in its entirety.

The story begins with Joshua, Moses' military successor, on the verge of entry into Canaan.

Then Joshua son of Nun sent two men secretly from Shittim as spies, saying, "Go, view the land, especially Jericho." So they went, and entered the house of a prostitute whose name was Rahab, and spent the night there. The king of Jericho was told, "Some Israelites have come here tonight to search out the land." Then the king of Jericho sent orders to Rahab, "Bring out the men who have come to you, who entered your house, for they have come only to search out the whole land." But the woman took the two men and hid them. Then she said, "True, the men came to me, but I did not know where they came from. And when it was time to close the gate at dark the men went out. Where the men went I do not know. Pursue them quickly, for you can overtake them." She had, however, brought them up to the roof and hidden them with the stalks of flax that she had laid out on the roof. So the men pursued them on the way to the Jordan as far as the fords. As soon as the pursuers had gone out, the gate was shut.

Before they went to sleep, she came up to them on the roof and said to the men: "I know that the LORD has given you the land, and that dread of you has fallen on us, and that all the inhabitants of the land melt in fear before you. For we have heard how the LORD dried up the water of the Red Sea before you when you came out of Egypt, and what you did to the two kings of the Amorites that were beyond the Jordan, to Sihon and Og, whom you utterly destroyed. As soon as we heard it, our hearts melted, and there was no courage left in any of us because of you. The LORD your God is indeed God in heaven above and on earth below. Now then, since I have dealt kindly with you, swear to me by the LORD that you in turn will deal kindly with my family. Give me a sign of good faith that you will spare my father and mother, my brothers and sisters, and all who belong to them, and deliver our lives from death." The men said to her, "Our life for yours! If you do not tell this business of ours, then we will deal kindly and faithfully with you when the LORD gives us the land."

Then she let them down by a rope through the window, for her house was on the outer side of the city wall and she resided within the wall itself. She said to them, "Go toward the hill country, so that the pursuers may not come upon you. Hide yourselves there three days, until the pursuers have returned; then afterward you may go your way." The man said to her, "We will be released from this oath that you have made us swear to you if we invade the land and you do not tie this crimson cord in the window through which you let us down, and you do not gather into your house your father and mother, your brothers and all your family. If any of you go out of the doors of your house into the street, they shall be responsible for their own death, and we shall be innocent; but if a hand is laid upon any who are with you in the house, we shall bear the responsibility for their death. But if you tell this business of ours, then we shall be released from this oath that you made us swear to you." She said, "According to your words, so be it." She sent them away and they departed. Then she tied the crimson cord in the window. (Josh. 2:1-21)

Joshua said to the two men who had spied out the land, "Go into the prostitute's house, and bring the woman out of it and all who belong to her, as you swore to her." So the young men who had been spies went in and brought Rahab out, along with her father, her mother, her brothers, and all who belonged to her—they brought all her kindred out—and set them outside the camp of Israel. They burned down the city, and everything in it; only the silver and gold, and the vessels of bronze and iron, they put into the treasury of the house of the LORD. But Rahab the prostitute, with her family and all who belonged to her, Joshua spared. Her family has lived in Israel ever since. For she hid the messengers whom Joshua sent to spy out Jericho. (Josh. 6:22-25)

Rahab is a fascinating character in a story of boundaries, inclusion, and seeming contradictions. As a Canaanite, Rahab is outside of Israel, yet she is a prostitute and thus an outsider in Canaan. Joshua's spies are sent to view the land, but instead they enter Rahab's house, a house that emphasizes Rahab's marginality, as it is literally within the city wall. Doors, windows, going in, and going out are all heavy with significance and innuendo. Somehow Rahab, sexualized, female, foreigner, and in every way an outsider, knows that YHWH has given the land to Israel. She acts decisively, betraying her city but trading the lives of Joshua's spies for the lives of her family. Rahab, the Canaanite prostitute, saves her family and becomes part of Israel. She is a powerful survivor; indeed she is referred to as the head of her household.

In her reading of Rahab's story, Guider attempts "to underscore the centrality of women as agents of resistance and solidarity in the life project called survival."[7] She focuses on women's faith and on Rahab's loyalty to her family. From her reading of Rahab, her study of liberation theology, and her work with the marginalized women's project, Guider concludes that history has revealed certain inadequacies and limitations of the exodus paradigm that are not acknowledged by liberation theologians. The exodus paradigm does not address the situation of exploited women, and it justifies violent conquest.

The themes of captivity and slavery are central to the Exodus narrative. Reflections on these themes by ostracised unwed mothers, sexually exploited domestics, and actual prostitutes provide very different interpretative correlations with reality from those of landless farm labourers or underpaid factory workers. Given the particular circumstances of each group, the category of the oppressor shifts from the beneficiaries of imperialism and classism to the beneficiaries of machismo and racism.[8]

If there is one fatal flaw in the analogical use of the Exodus, it is the justification of slaughter and conquest in which the Christian tradition grounds itself and from which none of us associated with the tradition can extricate ourselves.[9]

Based on the radical premise that prostitutes might have something to teach the church, Guider calls for the liberation church to acknowledge the limits of the exodus paradigm, particularly its failure to address the suffering of marginalized women. Ultimately she concludes that a savior/liberator model of church is inadequate on its own and must be partnered with a "theology of incarnate presence," where the church is a companion to the oppressed and itself the subject of transformation. In some cases, the church can only *be with* those who are suffering, resisting, and surviving. Rather than saving the poor, the church must open itself to being changed by them. In her commitment to liberation theology, Guider considers this a broadening of the exodus paradigm, not a departure from it.

Delores Williams—Slaves

When I was eleven years old, I went to working out. My mother was working for some people, and she got sick, and I had to go in her place. I was eleven years old. And I've worked ever since. But I've had enough domestic work. The bad point is when you resent the person you're working for, for being, I guess you would call it prejudiced and cruel and wanting to be superior to you. Just because you're working for 'em as an individual, they don't see that they're not any more than you are. They treat you like some kind of animal instead of a person.
—Aletha Vaughn, black domestic worker[10]

Delores Williams is a womanist theologian. For those not familiar with the term, "womanist" was coined by African American novelist Alice Walker. In *In Search of Our Mothers' Gardens*, a book subtitled "Womanist Prose," Walker gives an extensive definition of her term, which includes the following aspects:

1. A black feminist or feminist of color. From the black folk expression of mothers to female children, "You actin womanish," i.e., like a woman. Usually referring to outrageous, audacious, courageous or *willful* behavior.
2. A woman who loves other women, sexually and/or nonsexually. Appreciates and prefers women's culture, women's emotional flexibility (values tears as natural counter-balance of laughter), and women's strength. Sometimes loves individual men, sexually and/or nonsexually. Committed to survival and wholeness of entire people, male and female.

3. Loves herself. *Regardless.*

4. Womanist is to feminist as purple to lavender.[11]

In *Sisters in the Wilderness: The Challenge of Womanist God-Talk,*
Williams articulates a Christian theology from her own perspective as an
African American woman using the story of Hagar from Genesis.[12] Hagar
is an Egyptian slave who, by the matriarch Sarah's design, bears Abraham
a son and is then driven out of the camp. Her story appears in Genesis
16:1-16 and 21:8-21, in a form that represents either two consecutive
episodes or two parallel versions.

Now Sarai, Abram's wife, bore him no children. She had an Egyptian
slave-girl whose name was Hagar, and Sarai said to Abram, "You see
that the LORD has prevented me from bearing children; go in to my
slave-girl; it may be that I shall obtain children by her." And Abram listened to the voice of Sarai. So, after Abram had lived ten years in the
land of Canaan, Sarai, Abram's wife, took Hagar the Egyptian, her
slave-girl, and gave her to her husband Abram as a wife. He went in to
Hagar, and she conceived; and when she saw that she had conceived, she
looked with contempt on her mistress. Then Sarai said to Abram, "May
the wrong done to me be on you! I gave my slave-girl to your embrace,
and when she saw that she had conceived, she looked on me with contempt. May the LORD judge between you and me!" But Abram said to
Sarai, "Your slave-girl is in your power; do to her as you please." Then
Sarai dealt harshly with her, and she ran away from her.

The angel of the LORD found her by a spring of water in the wilderness, the spring was on the way to Shur. And he said, "Hagar, slave-girl
of Sarai, where have you come from and where are you going?" She
said, "I am running away from my mistress Sarai." The angel of the
LORD said to her, "Return to your mistress, and submit to her." The
angel of the LORD also said to her, "I will so greatly multiply your offspring that they cannot be counted for multitude." And the angel of the
LORD said to her,

> "Now you have conceived and shall bear a son;
> you shall call him Ishmael,
> for the LORD has given heed to your affliction.
> He shall be a wild ass of a man,
> with his hand against everyone,
> and everyone's hand against him;
> and he shall live at odds with all his kin."

So she named the LORD who spoke to her, "You are El-roi"; for she
said, "Have I really seen God and remained alive after seeing him?"
Therefore the well was called Beer-lahai-roi; it lies between Kadesh and
Bered.

Hagar bore Abram a son; and Abram named his son, whom Hagar bore, Ishmael. Abram was eighty-six years old when Hagar bore him Ishmael. (Gen. 16:1-16)

. . . Abraham made a great feast on the day that Isaac was weaned. But Sarah saw the son of Hagar the Egyptian, whom she had borne to Abraham, playing with her son Isaac. So she said to Abraham, "Cast out this slave woman with her son; for the son of this slave woman shall not inherit along with my son Isaac." The matter was very disturbing to Abraham on account of his son. But God said to Abraham, "Do not be distressed because of the boy and because of your slave woman; whatever Sarah says to you, do as she tells you, for it is through Isaac that offspring shall be named for you. As for the son of the slave woman, I will make a nation of him also, because he is your offspring." So Abraham rose early in the morning, and took bread and a skin of water, and gave it to Hagar, putting it on her shoulder, along with the child, and sent her away. And she departed, and wandered about in the wilderness of Beer-sheba.

When the water in the skin was gone she cast the child under one of the bushes. Then she went and sat down opposite him a good way off, about the distance of a bowshot; for she said, "Do not let me look on the death of the child." And as she sat opposite him, she lifted up her voice and wept. And God heard the voice of the boy; and the angel of God called to Hagar from heaven, and said to her, "What troubles you, Hagar? Do not be afraid; for God has heard the voice of the boy where he is. Come, lift up the boy and hold him fast with your hand, for I will make a great nation of him." Then God opened her eyes and she saw a well of water. She went, and filled the skin with water, and gave the boy a drink.

God was with the boy, and he grew up; he lived in the wilderness, and became an expert with the bow. He lived in the wilderness of Paran; and his mother got a wife for him from the land of Egypt. (Gen. 21:8-21)

This is another woman's story that has been neglected by most biblical scholars. Although the story of Hagar takes place generations before the exodus, it is relevant to Exodus and to this reading because it presents a counter story, a story where an Egyptian is enslaved by a Hebrew. Hagar's "predicament involved slavery, poverty, ethnicity, sexual and economic exploitation, surrogacy, rape, domestic violence, homelessness, motherhood, single parenting and radical encounters with God."[13] For these reasons the story of Hagar has been adopted and studied intensively by African American women.

Even if it is not our individual story, it is a story we have read in our mothers' eyes those afternoons when we greeted them at the front door after a hard day of work as a domestic. And if not our mothers' story, then it is certainly most of our grandmothers' story.[14]

Through Hagar's story, which is congruent with many present-day African American women's lives, Williams recounts the history of African American women's theologizing and its critical intersections, dialogues, and conflicts today. Williams applies a hermeneutic of suspicion to the story of Hagar. She observes that Hagar's sojourn in Canaan parallels that of Israel in Egypt. Like Israel, Hagar serves, is afflicted, flees, dwells in the wilderness, and meets God. But unlike Israel, God sends her back to slavery! In high contrast to "Black Liberation Theology's normative claim of God's liberating activity on behalf of *all* the oppressed,"[15] God does not liberate Hagar; she must liberate herself. In light of this contradiction, Williams calls black liberation theologians to dialogue with her and other womanists on the use of the Bible, particularly the paradigmatic use of the exodus story.

Williams and other womanist readers observe that "the abused do not always experience God's liberating power. If one reads the Bible identifying with non-Hebrews who are female and male slaves ('the oppressed of the oppressed') one quickly discerns a non-liberative thread running through the Bible." Williams points out the relative privilege of free male Israelites in Exodus. She condemns the violence and genocide sanctioned by or attributed directly to God in Egypt, Jericho, Makkedeh, Libnah, and Canaan. In conclusion she declares that "womanist theologians, especially those who take their slave heritage seriously, are therefore led to question James Cone's assumption that the African American theologian can today make *paradigmatic* use of the Hebrew's exodus and election experience recorded in the Bible."[16]

Williams invites dialogue between two traditions of African American biblical appropriation: the *liberation* tradition articulated by black liberation theologians such as James Cone, James Deotis Roberts, and Cecil Wayne Cone, and the *survival/quality-of-life* tradition articulated by womanist theologians. This *survival/quality-of-life* tradition is exemplified by the understanding that God's response to Hagar is not liberation but participation in her survival and the survival of her child. On the basis of this understanding Williams believes that black liberation theologians must ask themselves hard questions:

Have they, in the use of the Bible, identified so thoroughly with the theme of Israel's election that they have not seen the oppressed of the oppressed in scripture? Have they identified so completely with Israel's liberation that they have been blind to the awful reality of victims making victims in the Bible? Does this kind of blindness with regard to non-Hebrew victims in the scripture also make it easy for black male theologians and biblical scholars to ignore the figures in the Bible whose experience is analogous to that of black women?[17]

She encourages black theologians to adopt a womanist hermeneutic of *identification-ascertainment*, exploring how they identify subjectively, communally, and objectively with events and individuals in scripture in order to see where they need to be critical of their own and the community's use of the text. Williams calls black theologians to be critical of the text itself "in those instances where the text supports oppression, exclusion and even death of innocent people."[18]

Williams claims that "identifying with God *solely* through the exodus of the Hebrews . . . belongs to the black historical period of American slavery." Such an identification does not include black women and the most oppressed and impoverished people living in the United States today. It limits both God and humans by denying "the possibility of change with regard to the people's experience of God and with regard to the possibility of God changing in relation to the community."[19]

Just as we read scriptures as sacred story, Williams suggests approaching the exodus as a *holistic story*, with liberative and nonliberative elements, rather than seeing it as a paradigmatic event. Both Delores Williams and Margaret Guider challenge their communities to move beyond the liberation paradigm to a more complex reading of Exodus, a more complex portrait of God and a more complex understanding of God's people.

Robert Allen Warrior—Indians

In the plains of Moab by the Jordan at Jericho, the LORD spoke to Moses, saying: Speak to the Israelites and say to them: When you cross over the Jordan into the land of Canaan, you shall drive out all the inhabitants of the land from before you, destroy all their figured stones, destroy all their cast images, and demolish all their high places. You shall take possession of the land and settle in it, for I have given you the land to possess. You shall apportion the land by lot according to your clans; to a large one you shall give a large inheritance, and to a small one you shall give a small inheritance; the inheritance shall belong to the person on whom the lot falls; according to your ancestral tribes you shall inherit. (Num. 33:50-54)

> We have watched with great
> sadness for a very long time
> while strangers came
> and desecrated this sacred land
> and its people.
> It seems that they followed

the ways of a god who was a stranger
to us.

But the strangers came
and they divided things:
They divided the land
and they divided the people,
they divided everything
from everything else
so that now everything
is broken.
—Arthụr Solomon, Ojibway[20]

In response to the encouragement of "Christians who are breaking away from their liberal moorings and looking for more effective means of social and political engagement," Robert Allen Warrior, a member of the Osage Nation, addresses the idea of a Native American theology of liberation.[21] Warrior admits the advantages that an alliance with left-wing Christians would have for Indian activists: financial, political, and institutional resources and support from non-Indians. He also points to the dangers: Native Americans have "different modes of leadership, different ways of making decisions, different ways of viewing relationships between politics and religion" and historically Christians have imposed *their* ways on indigenous people. "The idea that Indians might know best how to address their own problems is seemingly lost on these well-meaning folks."[22] But the chief obstacle that Warrior sees to a Native American theology of liberation is *the use of the exodus story as the fundamental model* in other liberation theologies—because of the Canaanites.

Warrior reads the exodus story from his own perspective as the descendant of a people who were already in the land when strangers came and took it as their own. His people were decimated, and their religion was outlawed and nearly destroyed. He reads Exodus and identifies with the people of Canaan. From settings as diverse as Taiwan and Australia, indigenous people identify with the Canaanites in the story of the "Promised Land's" conquest.[23] According to Warrior, for indigenous people and for Christians who would do activism with them, the story of the Canaanites presents both a narrative and a historical problem. The narrative problem, the problem expressed at the story level, is greater, for, as Warrior so succinctly puts it, "History is no longer with us. The narrative remains."[24] The narrative problem is that God commands the Israelites to annihilate mercilessly the indigenous population of the Promised Land.

When my angel goes in front of you, and brings you to the Amorites, the Hittites, the Perizzites, the Canaanites, the Hivites, and the Jebusites,

and I blot them out, you shall not bow down to their gods, or worship
them, or follow their practices, but you shall utterly demolish them and
break their pillars in pieces. You shall worship the LORD your God, and
I will bless your bread and your water; and I will take sickness away
from among you. No one shall miscarry or be barren in your land; I will
fulfill the number of your days. I will send my terror in front of you, and
you will throw into confusion all the people against whom you shall
come, and I will make all your enemies turn their backs to you. And I
will send the pestilence in front of you, which shall drive out the Hivites,
the Canaanites, and the Hittites from before you. I will not drive them
out from before you in one year, or the land would become desolate and
the wild animals would multiply against you. Little by little I will drive
them out from before you, until you have increased and possess the land.
I will set your borders from the Red Sea to the sea of the Philistines, and
from the wilderness to the Euphrates; for I will hand over to you the
inhabitants of the land, and you shall drive them out before you. You
shall make no covenant with them and their gods. They shall not live in
your land, or they will make you sin against me; for if you worship their
gods, it will surely be a snare to you. (Exod 23:23-33)

The LORD said to me, "See, I have begun to give Sihon and his land over
to you. Begin now to take possession of his land." So when Sihon came
out against us, he and all his people for battle at Jahaz, the LORD our
God gave him over to us; and we struck him down, along with his offspring and all his people. At that time we captured all his towns, and in
each town we utterly destroyed men, women, and children. We left not
✓ a single survivor. (Deut. 2:31-34)

These passages have been used repeatedly and violently throughout history
by those who imagined themselves to be a "chosen people": Boers in South
Africa and Puritans in "New England." The story is "ready to be picked up
and believed by anyone wondering what to do about the people who
already live in their promised land."[25]

We touched on Warrior's historical problem in chapter 1. Scholars agree
that the Canaanites were not systematically annihilated and in fact made
up a large proportion of the new nation of Israel. Despite the fact that the
Canaanites were an integral part of Israel, their story, the indigenous people's story of oppression was "revised out of the new nation's history of salvation. They were assimilated into another people's identity and the history
of their ancestors came to be regarded as suspect and a danger to the safety
of Israel. In short they were betrayed."[26]

Warrior points out that in Exodus there are two parts to the covenant—
deliverance and conquest—and that, when an oppressed community or
indeed anyone reads the narratives and not the history behind them, there
is no guarantee that they will differentiate between the "liberating god and

the god of conquest." Warrior insists that the Canaanites be at the center of Native and non-Native Christian theological reflection and political action in order that when the powerless come to power they do not perpetuate a cycle of oppression and domination. He calls Christians to read *all* our scriptures, not just the parts that inspire us and justify our actions; for it is "those who know these texts who must speak the truth about what they contain." Warrior calls Natives and non-Natives both to know how the exodus story was used in the genocide of Native people in the Americas. He concludes by asking "the indigenous people of this hemisphere [who] have endured a subjugation now a hundred years longer than the sojourn of Israel in Egypt," if they will choose again to listen to the gods of strangers promising liberation and deliverance, or if they will listen this time to themselves.[27]

Guider, Williams, and Warrior as Guides to Reading Exodus

Well, you gotta know how to recognise
Your story when you hear it
From just the other side of the railroad tracks
Or an ocean away from here.
                              —John McCutcheon[28]

Williams is a womanist theologian; Guider identifies as documentor of a shift within liberation theology; and Warrior sees himself as completely outside liberation theology and indeed outside Christianity. Yet all three are producing theological work and critiquing liberation theology by its own standards. Each of these writers has a vision of justice, survival, good life, and self-determination for the people they love and for the communities they come from. Each of them questions the use of Exodus as a paradigmatic liberation story, particularly because of the violence commanded by and attributed to God. We will take up this discussion of violence, especially divine violence, in chapter 7.

Despite their rigorous critiques of liberation theologians' use of Exodus, Williams, Guider, and Warrior all restate a fundamental liberation insight: the preferential option for the poor. In fact they each call for a reexamination of this principle and an expanded definition of "the poor."

I began to raise new questions about who was to be included in the "Church of the poor" or rather who was to be excluded—and why.[29]

Include black women and speak on behalf of the most oppressed black people today—the poor homeless, jobless, economically "enslaved" women, men and children sleeping on American streets, in bus stations, parks and alleys.[30]

First, the Canaanites should be at the center of Christian theological reflection and political action. They are the last remaining ignored voice in the text, except perhaps for the land itself.[31]

These three writers are all from the United States, but they come from very different backgrounds and social locations. As they attend to their own situations and the communities of active suffering and struggle that they represent, each is unable or unwilling to identify with election. They do not read Exodus from the perspective of Israel. Although, like black and Latin American liberation theologians, Guider, Williams, and Warrior represent oppressed groups, they do not find the exodus story universally liberating. The work of these writers is so striking because through them we read the text with new eyes. By taking seriously characters to whom most readers accord the status of props, Guider, Williams, and Warrior open up new layers of meaning in a story that is so familiar as to be considered safe. Prostitutes, foreign slaves, and indigenous Canaanites each experienced a different exodus, and so too do the communities who identify with them today.

READING EXODUS IN THE FIRST WORLD

In reading Guider, Williams, Warrior, and other writers like them, it became clear to me that if I was going to learn anything new or authentic about Exodus, it would be by attending to my own situation and reading from the perspective of those in the text whom I most resemble.

It seems to be inadequate even presumptuous simply to transpose this theology, wrung from suffering into the "First World." It is inadequate because we of the "First World" live in a different socio-economic context and liberation theology rightly insists that theology must be contextual.[32]

Liberation theologian Jon Sobrino says, "the fundamental division in humankind is that between life and death, between those who die because of oppression and those who live because of it."[33] When put in these stark terms, it is clear to me that as a white, first-world, North American,[34] able-bodied, Protestant Christian, I am among those who live because of oppression. My access to food, clothing, shelter, education, and employment, all of which I have expended some effort for,[35] is predicated upon violent systems of extraction and exploitation. The simple luxuries of my daily living—a computer, a sweatshirt, fresh fruit—are available to me *because* twelve-year-olds work in free-trade-zone factories, garment workers earn starvation wages, and agricultural workers are exposed to pesticides. In Exodus it is the Israelites who die because of oppression and the Egyptians who live because of it. Following the examples of Guider, Williams, and Warrior, if I am to bring my own experience to Exodus, then I must identify with the Egyptians, the villains of the story. I must explore their traits and qualities.

Perhaps some readers will object that I am identifying only with my privilege. It is true that as a low-income, queer woman, and a single parent in a culture that punishes poverty, difference, and femaleness, I am among those who die because of oppression. I am no different from the young women who were massacred at the Polytechnique in Montreal;[36] in 1989 I also was an undergraduate science student at a Canadian university. I am no different from Rebecca Wright, Brandon Teena, or Matthew Shepard, who were murdered because they were lesbian, transgender, and gay.[37] In my home and on the streets, I am no different from the women, children, gays, lesbians, bisexuals, and transgender people who are beaten, raped, stabbed, shot, and killed in escalating numbers every day.[38] Like everyone I know, I have experiences of privilege and experiences of oppression; but "privilege on one power axis does not negate oppression on another."[39]

In the past twenty years postmodern thinkers, particularly women of color, like Audre Lorde and Gloria Anzaldua, have challenged the notion of a single unified self.[40] They affirm that each person has multiple identities, we live in a pluralistic world, and texts may have more than one truth. The acceptance of these insights has made biblical readings from marginal perspectives, like those of Guider, Williams, and Warrior, possible. Where once texts were thought to have a single, fixed, and known meaning, now there is the possibility for a rich exchange of perspectives.

With this opening to new voices and perspectives has come a disturbing backlash to which white academics are particularly prone. The argument goes something like this: since concepts such as truth, meaning, or justice are not grounded in any reality that applies across culture and language, any move to evaluate a reading in terms of accuracy, rigor, or liberative potential is an illegitimate attempt to assert a new universalism or impose some false authority.[41] The insidious result is that nothing changes; with their sheer volume and familiarity, the old, white, patriarchal readings maintain their place of privilege by default. I think of this phenomenon as post modern paralysis.

> When I think no thing is like any other thing
> I become speechless, cold, my body turns silver
> and water runs off me. There I am
> ten feet from myself, possessor of nothing,
> uncomprehending of even the smallest piece of dust.
> —James Tate[42]

READING THE TEXT WRONG

Postmodern paralysis keeps us from acting. Energy that could bring about social change is channeled into "the analysis and critique of culture without any real sense of human agency capable of altering that construction."[43] Furthermore, it is sloppy thinking, "an escape into the transient pleasures of irony, or a flight into cynicism and more history as usual."[44] Openness to diverse voices and rejecting a fixed interpretation do "*not* mean that all perspectives are applicable at all times to all readers."[45] Although it is something of a postmodern heresy, I believe it is possible to read a text wrong. Here are some examples of what I mean.

1. Genesis 19, the story of Sodom and Gomorrah, is primarily about the failure to attend to the ancient obligation of hospitality. Two messengers of God come to the city, and, rather than receiving food and shelter, they are set upon by a gang and threatened with rape. As a consequence God destroys the city. Whenever the incident is referred to again in the Bible, it is used as an example of the punishment for those who refuse to provide hospitality. Ironically, in recent history, the story has been used persistently as an excuse to deny hospitality. Interpreting the text as a condemnation of homosexuality, churches have used the text to exclude gays, lesbians, bisexuals, and transgender people.[46]

2. In the 1980s, during the cold war, many politically conservative Americans, including then president Ronald Reagan, read the book of Revelation as though it were a prediction of events in the near future. The European Economic Community and the United Nations were both described as the ten-headed beast. Soviet leader Mikail Gorbachev's port-wine birthmark was the mark of the beast. The Russians were poised to enter and desecrate Jerusalem, and nuclear war was the inevitable end that would hasten Christ's return.

3. First-world Christians read Exodus and identify with the enslaved Israelites. As Marcus Borg says, Exodus "provocatively images the human condition as bondage, an image with both cultural-political and psychological-spiritual dimensions of meaning and it invites us to ask, 'to what am I in bondage and to what are we in bondage?'"[47] These are not the most appropriate questions for first-world North Americans to ask, and certainly not the only questions. Exodus is about the political bondage of the poor, *not* the spiritual bondage of the rich. More appropriate questions might be, To whom am I oppressor and how can I stop oppressing?

READING FOR OUR LIVES

I believe that each of us, in the Exodus story, is *both* Israel and Egypt. We are called to go out from the land of bondage *and* to let the oppressed go free. Thus, for the remainder of this book I will focus on the similarities between Egyptians in Exodus and privileged first-world Christians. This is not an exercise in white liberal guilt; it is an accurate reflection of our situation. I identify with our privilege because, in a global context it is immense. Further, as a starting point for biblical reflection, to clearly identify our own context is a requirement of good scholarship. Finally, I identify with Egypt because for first-world Christians it is the best possible reading. It reflects our situation, accounts for power dynamics, and may even help us to participate in the work of justice.

For the duration of this book, I will maintain the assumption that first-world readers resemble the Egyptians, as an exercise in what Mary Ann Tolbert calls "protesting our privilege."[48] This means not behaving as if our position on the high side of a huge material divide were natural or accidental but drawing attention to the divide and the fact that, however comfortable, it is neither just nor deserved. I invite the reader to join with me in this challenging exploration of Exodus. Looking at how we resemble the villains in this story may not be comfortable or flattering; it may teach us things about ourselves that we would rather not know. My intention is not to blame or to create bad feelings. It is to unmask destructive systems in which we participate, so that we can begin to dismantle the culture of domination in which we live. Knowing what we do, what is destructive and what is constructive, can help us to change the patterns of our behavior so that despite our privilege we may be a part of God's liberation project.

Am I ready to turn the page? Can I hear what I am about to read about myself + my privileged position? As a woman, I know discrimination, but, come on now, how much discrimination have I really borne given I am a well-educated, white woman of above average means?

Today, Lord, give me the grace I need to hear these words + let them touch me -- deeply enough to get my attention + call me to action that I can take -- where I am, as I am.

amen,

PART TWO

BEING READ BY EXODUS

4

EGYPT AS EMPIRE

*It is pretty clear that where we fit in the exodus story is among the func-
tionaries in Pharaoh's court rather than among the workers in slave
labor camps. We don't make the big political decisions, but we acquiesce
in them; we don't torture people, but our tax money supports the train-
ing of torturers; we don't force dictators on the Chileans, but we are
complicit in our government's decision to do so. We end up, almost by
default, among the oppressors.*

—Robert McAfee Brown[1]

EGYPT IN HISTORY

Egypt is the setting for the first thirteen chapters of Exodus. To begin
our "Egyptian" reading of Exodus let us briefly review a historical sketch
of ancient Egypt. During the time of the pharaohs, Egypt was a powerful
and complex empire spanning two millennia and influencing North Africa,
the Mediterranean, and parts of Asia. The Egyptian pharaohs were god-
kings served by a small retainer class of priests, administrators, and military officers. Beneath the pharaoh, the major powers in Egypt were the
court and the priesthood. The country had an extensive but centralized
bureaucracy; local administrators were responsible directly to the pharaoh.
Craftspeople, scribes, traders, and artisans formed a small middle class,
and there was a large professional army—but the bulk of the population
were peasants. This 80 percent of the population produced all the food in
Egypt, paid the majority of the taxes, and provided almost all the nation's
labor. Slaves made up a small proportion of the population, and their social
status varied from that of forced laborers to wealthy administrators.[2] The
Egyptian empire functioned through the extraction of resources and wealth
as tribute from occupied territories and client states. As liberation theologian Juan Alfaro says, "Israel was a Third World country, while Egypt,
Assyria, Babylonia, Persia and others took their turns as First World powers."[3]

The great empires that succeeded Egypt in ruling over the ancient Near East all operated by domination, extraction of resources, and exploitation of labor. Egypt was not a particularly cruel or horrible example. We concern ourselves with Egypt because it was the superpower at the time of Israel's emergence. The portrayal of Egypt that we are engaging is Israel's, and historically Israel as such was probably never in Egypt. Israel, however, lived most of its ancient history under the shadow of some exterior superpower and defined itself in relation to these surrounding empires. For those strands of Israelite society that sought to live deliberately counter to empire, Egypt served as a foil, a symbol of empire.

EGYPT IN THE BIBLE

The importance of Egypt as a foil for Israel is illustrated by the term Jews use to speak of the Exodus, *yetsi'at mitsraim,* the "going out from Egypt." The place that is left is as significant as the leaving. Egypt, the place that was left, became shorthand for everything that was rejected and should be left. As Michael Walzer says, "The Exodus is not a lucky escape from misfortune. Rather, the misfortune has a moral character and the escape has a world-historical meaning. Egypt is not just left behind; it is judged and condemned."[4]

The Hebrew word for Egypt is *mitsraim,* a proper noun that designates both the land and the people. The consonants of the word for Egypt are the same as the consonants for the word *metsarim,* which means "hardships, straights, or narrow places," and can suggest a situation of oppression,[5] Egypt's narrow fertile corridor, and even the birth canal.[6] Thus, whenever one reads the word "Egypt" in Hebrew, there is always the suggestion of a hard and watery place where something is born. The nature of Israel's sojourn and oppression is encoded in the very word.

African American biblical scholar Randall Bailey has categorized the ways in which African nations are depicted in the Hebrew Bible. In the narrative and poetry of several centuries, Egypt was a standard for various measures of prestige. Egypt and Cush were the nations that signified the farthest point south, the very edge of the world. Egypt was acknowledged as a great military power, and both Israel and Judah actually looked to Egypt as a military protector. Egypt was described in terms of wealth and as the source of luxury items. The wisdom of Egypt was highly regarded, and there is a strong resemblance between the wisdom literature of Egypt and that of Israel.[7] In general, until the time of the exile, mention of Egypt was an indicator of status and value.[8]

Because of Egypt's power and success as an empire, Egypt was highly regarded by some early biblical writers. Later, because of the same power and success, the prophets targeted Egypt in their tirades against worldly wisdom, military might, political power, and wealth rather than dependence on YHWH and YHWH's justice. Thus the biblical portrait of Egypt is ambiguous, reflecting both Israel's desire for and rejection of empire.

In Exodus, Israel's ambiguity toward Egypt is evident as the portrait of Egypt as empire is elaborated. Although the greatness of Egypt is grudgingly acknowledged, the violent, oppressive, and capricious aspects of Egyptian life are emphasized. The two consecutive pharaohs who appear in the text personify various negative qualities of empire. They are arrogant, dominating, abusive, and self-serving. In Exodus, Egypt is "a massive and burdensome regime where state and culture are presented as colluding in the perpetuation of slavery and degradation."[9]

> Now a new king arose over Egypt, who did not know Joseph. He said to his people, "Look, the Israelite people are more numerous and powerful than we. Come, let us deal shrewdly with them, or they will increase and, in the event of war, join our enemies and fight against us and escape from the land." Therefore they set taskmasters over them to oppress them with forced labor. They built supply cities, Pithom and Rameses, for Pharaoh. But the more they were oppressed, the more they multiplied and spread, so that the Egyptians came to dread the Israelites. The Egyptians became ruthless in imposing tasks on the Israelites, and made their lives bitter with hard service in mortar and brick and in every kind of field labor. They were ruthless in all the tasks that they imposed on them.
>
> The king of Egypt said to the Hebrew midwives, one of whom was named Shiphrah and the other Puah, "When you act as midwives to the Hebrew women, and see them on the birthstool, if it is a boy, kill him; but if it is a girl, she shall live." (Exod. 1:8-16)

Egypt was a "patriarchal, hierarchical and socially stratified society,"[10] the site of forced labor, religious oppression, and the execution of children. For the Israelites in this life-and-death situation, Egypt unequivocally represented death.

BEGINNING TO READ AS EGYPT

Earlier in this book we laid out two fundamental ways in which we will read Exodus: (1) by reading it as sacred story, and (2) by identifying with Egypt. But what in practical terms does this mean? How do we read as sacred story? How do we identify with Egypt?

In corporate-controlled, North American culture, where consumption serves as a substitute for any kind of spiritual engagement, reading the Bible as sacred story is an act of resistance. It means we take seriously the notion that our scriptures are something to be approached with reverence. They are a gift from our ancestors that has endured because they contain something of lasting value. They are worth our time. Reverence does not mean we must make excuses for our heritage or attend to it with only one aspect of ourselves. Reverence means we engage with our hearts, minds, spirits, and bodies.

Today most Christians encounter the Bible in isolated segments heard in a worship setting. Some of us have participated in different kinds of Bible study, and the most devout or avid among us read the Bible alone. Reading as sacred story does not preclude any of these ways of encountering the text, but it demands more than each of them alone. Contrary to what most of us have been taught, the Bible is not fundamentally about personal morality; it is about collective experience and social and economic justice. Reading the texts by ourselves may provide comfort and spiritual satisfaction, but it is of limited use in the work of true liberation. To read these stories well we must share them together, in groups and out loud.

Reading aloud together is essential. Before these stories were written, they were told. When they were finally written, the intention was that they would be shared aloud with others, not consumed silently in isolation. When we read together, even in groups that do not seem very diverse, each of us can add to and question the others' interpretations. As a text is read aloud we can experience it with three of our five senses, hearing the words as we and others read them, seeing the words on the page, and feeling the words with our bodies as we speak them. The more of ourselves we bring to the text, the more avenues we have for understanding and knowing the story. Hearing the text a number of times in different translations and then telling the stories to one another in our own words helps to make the stories our own. Although this book can be read on its own, the arguments and research herein will be of the most use to groups reading Exodus together as sacred story.

What does it mean to identify with Egypt? In this book, what it means is that we will look at Egypt the empire, Egypt the land, the Egyptian people, and specific Egyptian characters that appear in Exodus. People of privilege are not the target audience for Exodus; we do not resemble the Israelites, and so we must work harder, looking at the characters we do resemble. We will examine the behaviors, traits, and qualities of the Egyptians and compare them to our own lives and stories. This kind of unfamiliar reading is an invitation to insecurity. Acknowledging our resemblance to Egypt makes us vulnerable, something we are not used to because security is one of the marks of privilege. If these comparisons with Egypt are painful or threatening, I encourage the reader not to be too quick to say, "This doesn't fit, this isn't me." As readers of our culture, through television and film, we first-world people identify on a daily basis with characters who resemble us far less than the Egyptians in Exodus. This is one of many possible ways to read Exodus. If we try it on for a while, it may prove useful or even transformative.

Victor Porter, a popular educator in the field of theater, once said, "It is a great gift of love to portray the oppressor."[11] This is my hope for first-world readers in identifying with Egypt: if we have the courage to see in ourselves the traits of the oppressor, and if we are willing to be open about that, then we offer the world a great gift of love simply by telling that truth. We may even encounter the possibility of our own conversion.

To make the ideas of sacred story, identification with Egypt, and reading together less abstract, I present an account of one group's experience practicing these skills.[12]

FIRST WORLD, THIRD WORLD, AND BIBLICAL WORLD

A few years ago, I was a program leader for a mostly white, liberal church group from Ontario, Canada, which came to Cuernavaca, Mexico. For many this was their first exposure to one-room homes, open sewers, and abject poverty. For most it was the first time they had spoken to people who lived in these conditions. After the eighteen Canadians had spent five days visiting squatter settlements, base communities, teachers, labor leaders, medical clinics, and wealthy neighborhoods, we met to reflect on their experiences and on Exodus.

We began by simply sharing anything we remembered from the book of Exodus. People were familiar with the story and pretty soon we had a basic outline of the plot. I gave a review of some of the information covered in the first chapters of this book (for example, the word *Egypt* in Hebrew and Exodus in Latin American liberation theology); then we got right to the texts.

We read a variety of passages from the first chapters of Exodus that describe the escalating Egyptian campaign against Israel: forced labor, propaganda, impossible quotas, and infanticide.

That same day Pharaoh commanded the taskmasters of the people, as well as their supervisors, "You shall no longer give the people straw to make bricks, as before; let them go and gather straw for themselves. But you shall require of them the same quantity of bricks as they have made previously; do not diminish it, for they are lazy; that is why they cry, 'Let us go and offer sacrifice to our God.' Let heavier work be laid on them; then they will labor at it and pay no attention to deceptive words."

So the taskmasters and the supervisors of the people went out and said to the people, "Thus says Pharaoh, 'I will not give you straw. Go and get straw yourselves, wherever you can find it; but your work will not be lessened in the least.'" So the people scattered throughout the land of Egypt, to gather stubble for straw. The taskmasters were urgent, saying, "Complete your work, the same daily assignment as when you were given straw." And the supervisors of the Israelites, whom Pharaoh's taskmasters had set over them, were beaten, and were asked, "Why did you not finish the required quantity of bricks yesterday and today, as you did before?" (Exod. 5:6-14)

While the rest of our group listened, each of us took a turn reading aloud in different translations, several passages like the one above. Then, closing our Bibles, we told the story ourselves, each relating the word, passage, or idea that struck us most. Next I asked the group to focus on the Egyptians in the passages we had just read. What do they do? What are their, "traits, qualities, and behaviors?" This is the list they produced:

Egyptians are/Egyptians do:

Afraid
Genocide
Racist/prejudice
Lying/deceitful
Ruthless
Efficient
Production oriented
Cruel
Target males/treat men, women differently
Slave-based
Exploiting
Powerful
Controlling
Intolerant
Stereotyping
Violent
Dominating

After reading over the list I asked the group, "Does this, or how does this resemble our own North American first-world situation, in relation to the poor, people of color, immigrants, the developing world, and the people you have met here in Mexico?" There was a long, uncomfortable silence, and then a young father said, "We are just like that." A middle-aged medical technician disagreed, and others quickly jumped in offering examples of how we are like Egypt: "What about *maquilas* and sweatshops?" "Look at how many black men are in prison. The way black men are targeted in the U.S. is just like Egypt." "What about Natives in jail in Canada?" "Being production-oriented isn't necessarily bad." "The pollution of the air and water could be like the plagues."

After some discussion, debate, and time to work out their defensiveness, the group agreed that they had a great deal in common with the Egyptians in the text and that not all Egyptian qualities were bad. For the rest of their time in Mexico these insights gave the group a way to talk about their experiences. Is the premier of Ontario really like Pharaoh? Is it possible to live in the first world and *not* benefit from the exploitation of others? How can we stop being Egyptians if we live in Egypt? While we may not like what we find, modern readers, through collective reading, can readily identify ourselves, or the people like us, in Exodus.

Many of the insights of this book have come from groups such as the one described above, reading the text together and reflecting on their own experience. Such readings can be a powerful catalyst for change. As feminist biblical scholar Phyllis Trible says, "reflections themselves neither mandate nor manufacture change; yet by enabling insight, they may inspire repentance."[13] My hope in writing this book is that more first-world people will be encouraged to read this way and be inspired to change.

EMPIRE, PAST AND PRESENT

The list of "Egyptian" traits that the Ontario group produced is strikingly similar to what Stanley Rothman identifies as the values driving Western society today: profit, personal comfort, exploitation, control, individualism, and dominance.[14] While individualism is a modern phenomenon, there are striking convergences between Egypt of 1200 B.C.E. and North America at the dawn of the twenty-first century, most notably exploitation, control, and dominance. This convergence is based in similar structures of empire. Wes Howard-Brook and Anthony Gwyther describe the hallmarks of empire as "slave labor, demonization, genocide, and displacement of indigenous people; colonization of distant lands . . . ; cultural arrogance; and global military power."[15] I would add that empire has an economy based on the extraction and import of wealth and resources from subject states. The most fundamental similarity between the Egyptians in Exodus and privileged North American readers is that we benefit from empire.

The ancient Egyptian empire operated on the classical colonial model:

Classical colonialism occurs when: "metropolitan nations incorporate new territories or peoples through processes that are essentially involuntary, such as war, conquest, capture, and other forms of force or manipulation (Blauner 1987, 150)." Classical colonialism is distinguished by economic exploitation, forced entry, and cultural imperialism through the imposition of new institutions and ways of thought.[16]

Euro-colonialism of the fifteenth to early twentieth centuries was classical colonialism's successor, operating on basically the same model, with western European nations colonizing Africa, the Americas, and the Pacific islands. North America has been both the subject of colonization and, with the rise of the United States as a neocolonial power, a center of empire. From the time of ancient Egypt's centuries of dominion and into the last century, the nation-state was the critical unit of imperialism; but with the recent rise of global capitalism, the role of the nation-state in colonization has changed.[17] Corporations have eclipsed countries in their power and influence. More than half the world's largest economies are corporations not countries.[18] Rather than nations being the center of empire, transnational corporations are now the controlling entities. They use the state to

maintain the conditions of accumulation and competitiveness in various ways, including direct subsidies and rescue operations at taxpayers' expense (Mexico, the Asian Tigers). They need the sate to preserve labor discipline and social order in the face of austerity and "flexibility" and to enhance the mobility of capital while blocking the mobility of labor.[19]

The proponents of corporate globalization claim that it is an engine of prosperity, spreading democracy and decreasing poverty, but just the opposite is true. Democracy is being replaced with corporate rule. The rights of groups and individuals are being eroded while the privileges of corporations increase. Jane Anne Morris, corporate anthropologist, says, "one of the signs of our being colonized is that we personify corporations."[20] Under globalization the gap between rich and poor is increasing, and the poor are not getting richer.

The past quarter-century of globalization has seen not a reduction but a vast increase in poverty. According to the 1999 UN *Human Development Report*, more than 80 countries have per capita incomes lower than they were a decade or more ago. James Wolfensohn, president of the World Bank, says that, rather than improving, "global poverty is getting worse. Some 1.2 billion people now live in extreme poverty." Global unemployment is approaching 1 billion.[21]

Whether they hide behind the guise of nation or of corporation, a few—kings, presidents, CEOs—have always benefited enormously by exploiting the many—slaves, serfs, peasants, indigenous people, laborers. In changing proportions through time there have been those necessary to the smooth running of empire who benefit to lesser degrees from empire's accumulation: government functionaries, scribes, lawyers, overseers, managers, military officers. Because of the extreme disparity of wealth between nations due to the recent manifestations of colonialism, most middle-income people in the first world, whether they come from the middle or working class, benefit from empire. The wealth of our countries comes from our colonial past. The land we live on was stolen from indigenous people. The products we buy are subsidized by the cheap labor of those who produce them.

Throughout the rest of this chapter we will move back and forth between the biblical text and the modern manifestations of empire, comparing Egypt of Exodus with our situation of global capitalism. We will do so by focusing on four overlapping "Egyptian" traits observed by the Ontario group: violence, slavery, genocide, and deceit.

VIOLENCE OF EXPLOITATION

The Egyptians became ruthless in imposing tasks on the Israelites, and made their lives bitter with hard service in mortar and brick and in every kind of field labor. They were ruthless in all the tasks that they imposed on them. (Exod. 1:13-14)

In Exodus the Israelites were forced to produce bricks for Pharaoh's construction projects. They were given impossible quotas that prevented them from attending to their own livelihood. When they failed to meet these quotas, Israelite supervisors were beaten and humiliated. This was a situation of violence at many levels. The nature of the work itself and the stress of impossible tasks were a violence to their bodies. Failure to meet quotas brought both the threat and reality of physical assault. Israelites suffered the economic violence of impoverishment because making bricks kept them from providing for their own subsistence. Egypt's social order was purposefully structured to maintain this relationship of exploitation of the Israelites and other groups on the bottom. Further, the supply cities they built were a means of preparing Egypt for continued war and conquest.[22] Israel's experience in Egypt was one of ingrained, systemic violence from which Egyptians of all but the peasant class benefited.

Similarly North American acquisition culture and our obsession with possessions violently affect those who "service our needs."

Growing food crops for North American supermarkets is negatively affecting the availability of basic foods for native people. In Mexico in the 1970s, the rate of deaths from malnutrition in early childhood increased 70 percent while acreages of wheat, corn, beans, and rice declined 25 percent. The change in production priorities has made the cost of even the lowly rice and bean diet a luxury that many of the poor cannot afford. It is an added irony that 65 percent of the fruits and vegetables raised in Latin American countries are dumped or used for animal feeding because they do not meet the beauty standards of American consumers.[23]

Unless one shops incredibly carefully, the products that North Americans, from the wealthiest to the most impoverished, consume are produced in situations that range from moderately exploitative to virtual slave labor.

> Dorka Diaz, a twenty-year-old textile worker who formerly produced clothing in Honduras for Leslie Fay, a U.S.-based transnational, testified before the Subcommittee on Labor-Management Relation of the U.S. House of Representatives that she worked for Leslie Fay in Honduras alongside twelve and thirteen-year-old girls locked inside a factory where the temperature often hit 100 degrees and there was no clean drinking water. For a fifty-four hour week, she was paid a little over $20. She and her three-year-old son lived at the edge of starvation. In April 1994, she was fired for trying to organize a union.[24]

Conditions like these are no longer confined to plantations, mines, and factories beyond the borders of "developed" nations. On August 3, 1995, forty-five Thai women were discovered imprisoned in three small apartments in a building complex in El Monte, California. The women had been brought to the United States illegally several years before. They were working from dawn until midnight, seven days a week, in a makeshift factory producing shirts and dresses for sale in American fashion outlets. Working for one dollar per hour, the women were indentured for years paying off their passage, food, and cramped accommodations at hugely inflated rates. Sweatshops like this exist and are mostly ignored in large cities all over North America. When they are discovered, it is the workers who are penalized, imprisoned, and deported. The companies who exploit them receive token penalties.[25]

Violence and exploitation in the food and garment industries as well as in the production of luxury items is so pervasive as to be almost impossible to escape. But for most of us trying to get along, finding a bargain does not seem like an act of violence. Similarly, when Reverend Martin Luther King Jr.'s freedom marches were attacked by white middle-class leaders for bringing violence to previously peaceful communities, King's response was that they were not causing violence but revealing the violence that already existed in those communities—the violence of racism and inequity. "We do not seek to precipitate violence. However, we are aware that the existence of injustice in society is the existence of violence, latent violence."[26] Most of the violence that first-world Christians and biblical Egyptians participate in is this kind of hidden violence.

The latent or institutionalized violence in biblical Egypt is easily recognized over the distance of centuries. Theirs was a slave or forced-labor based economy. After several decades and from the safe distance of the North or another nation altogether, the violence of the segregated southern United States that King challenged is also evident.[27] However, when it comes to the violence of our own time and culture, the benefiting classes of the first world persist in the myth that ours is a benign, even benevolent situation, that the worst off are at least better off than they used to be.

> One of the greatest difficulties in American Culture is that the dominant white cultural self-image is of a peace-loving democratic people who live in the land of opportunity, not in a land in which oppressed groups of poor whites, African slaves, Asian and Hispanic and European immigrants and Native Americans were repeatedly set against each other by ruling elites to protect their self-interests.[28]

One need not be white to ascribe to this cultural self-image, but the further one lives from the privileged center in terms of race, class, gender, and so on, the more the image clashes with lived reality. Persons of privilege are for the most part not unaware of violence, but we are able to distance ourselves from it or to project it onto others. For the least regarded, however, violence is most overt:

> Prostitutes are potential victims of virtually everyone with whom they are in contact. Violence may come from a brothel manager, a pimp, a law enforcement officer or a customer. Murder of prostitutes is not uncommon and death is a constant threat for those who work in the industry. . . . In a study of the street walkers in the Waikiki area, who . . . are among the most elite members of the sex industry in Hawaii, Pam Vessels discovered that women experienced an average of fifty-seven assaults and nineteen rapes a year from pimps and johns.[29]

> Among black males, firearm injuries were the leading cause of death among children 10-14 through adults 25-34 years of age. For children 10-14 years, firearms were responsible for 30 percent more deaths than motor vehicle injuries. For black males 15-19 through 20-24 years, firearm homicide was the single leading cause of death.[30]

> [In prisons] the claiming of the woman's body and mind begins with admission to the system. Women's prisons operate based on the threat of sexual assault, and dehumanizing invasion of privacy. Invasive "pat searches" of women by male guards is a constant reminder of her powerlessness: she cannot even defend her own body. Prisons are small totalitarian societies of agony.[31]

Like the Israelites in Exodus, prostitutes, youth and children of color, prisoners, and others are intimately acquainted with the violence that undergirds empire. As Rap Brown says, "violence is American as cherry pie."[32] First-world Christians participate in this violence by ignoring it and by refusing to question all that comes to us at the price of others' suffering.

SLAVERY

The Israelites groaned under their slavery, and cried out. Out of the slavery their cry for help rose up to God. (Exod. 2:23)

Although the Bible tells us that the Israelites were slaves in Egypt, we do not know what this entailed. Some scholars do not distinguish the experience from chattel slavery, where individuals are bought and sold. Others describe it as a form of feudal obligation involving only the men. Descriptions in Exodus of Egyptians and Israelites as neighbors seem to indicate that Israelites did not live in Egyptian homes. The Israelites were members of large, anonymous labor gangs who had no rights and received no compensation for their work, and so their situation was probably worse than that of household slaves.[33] Whatever the practicalities, the Israelites' experience in Egypt involved cruelty, repression, humiliation, and alienating work.[34]

For those of us reading as Egypt, benefiting from slavery seems to be one of the few Egyptian traits we are not guilty of. This is not so. If reluctantly, most white North Americans will acknowledge that slavery is part of our collective past.[35] Few of us, however, are aware of the extent to which slavery and all forms of forced labor function today.

In 1903, forty years after emancipation in the United States, W. E. B. DuBois observed how the penal system was being used as a substitute for slavery to extract labor from the black population.

And here, too is the high white washed fence of the "stockade," as the county prison is called; the white folks say it is ever full of black criminals, the black folks say that only colored boys are sent to jail, and they not because they are guilty, but because the State needs criminals to eke out its income by their forced labor.[36]

Today, the pattern continues; African Americans make up more than 55 percent of the incarcerated population in the United States and people of color consistently receive harsher sentences for the same crimes as white people.[37] Even more insidious, the most disenfranchised descendants of slaves find themselves in circumstances almost as dire as those of their ancestors. "When the reality of being *free* means homelessness, hunger, street violence, no healthcare, unemployment and racism, many may find prison as an alternative to death."[38] The enslavement of men and women of African and indigenous heritage within the prison industrial complex,[39] where they are disproportionately represented, is a direct and indirect continuation of the enslavement of Africans and indigenous people by Europeans which began in the Americas in the early 1500s.

> Among urban African Americans, imprisonment is so extensive and deeply ingrained that it may be viewed as the modern equivalent of slavery. Like slavery, prison represents a profound influence on black culture, black identity, black social and political status, the black family, and race relations.[40]

> Prisoners are increasingly used as a source of labor for private industry. For private business, prison labor is like a pot of gold. No strikes. No union organizing. No unemployment insurance or workers' compensation to pay. No language problem, as in a foreign country. New leviathan prisons are being built with thousands of eerie acres of factories inside the walls. Prisoners do data entry for Chevron, make telephone reservations for TWA, raise hogs, shovel manure, make circuit boards, limousines, waterbeds and lingerie for Victoria's Secret. All at a fraction of the cost of "free labor."[41]

Although the Thirteenth Amendment to the U.S. Constitution outlawed slavery, prisoners are specifically excluded from emancipation and can be forced to work for pennies a day.

Forced labor of prisoners in the United States is a limited example, but all forms of slavery are increasing around the world. By slavery I mean any situation in which an individual or organization owns another human being or, as is increasingly the case, owns their labor.

Within the United States and other developed nations, situations like that of the Thai women imprisoned in California are increasingly common. Foreign nationals are brought into a country having been kidnapped, bought outright, or lied to. They are held captive without passports and forced to work in factories producing textiles and other consumer goods, or in fields doing agricultural work. Women, teenagers, and girls as young as eight and ten are held prisoner and used as prostitutes in London, Los Angeles, Tokyo, Paris, and New York. Isolated in private homes in wealthy countries, young women and children are forced to cook, clean, and care for children. They are often beaten and underfed. It is estimated that there are three thousand household slaves in Paris and one thousand in London.[42]

Although slavery is illegal in virtually every country in the world, there are at least twenty-seven million people enslaved today, more than all the people stolen from Africa during the transatlantic slave trade.[43] In South Asia several million debt slaves work the land and labor in factories. In South America slaves are charcoal harvesters and agricultural workers.

Slaves harvest sugar cane in the Caribbean, and chattel slaves serve families in western Africa. Many modern slaves are children; some work with their families, but many others are sold, kidnapped, or otherwise taken from their homes. Child slaves are prostitutes, factory workers, carpet weavers, soldiers, and household laborers.

The enslavement of children and adults is carried out with the knowledge and tacit consent of national governments in the name of profit. Thailand is one of a number of countries where slave-based prostitution and sex tourism are part of their official development strategy.[44] Slavery is illegal in Mauritania, northwest Africa, but the courts uphold the ownership of one individual by another. In India debt bondage has existed for thousands of years and persists today. The immigration laws of many "developed" nations allow the import of slaves, provided their "employers" can produce employment contracts, which are nothing more than a legal fiction. With the globalization of capital under various trade agreements, industry moves to where labor is cheapest. Unpaid labor is the cheapest of all; so, increasingly it is transnational corporations that benefit from slave labor. "Large international corporations, acting through subsidiaries in the developing world, take advantage of slave labor to improve their bottom line and increase the dividends to their shareholders."[45]

Despite being nearly invisible to us in the privileged first world, slavery impacts our lives.

> Slaves in Pakistan may have made the shoes you are wearing and the carpet you stand on. Slaves in the Caribbean may have put sugar in your kitchen and toys in the hands of your children. In India they may have sewn the shirt on your back and polished the ring on your finger. They are paid nothing.
>
> Slaves touch your life indirectly as well. They made the bricks for the factory that made the TV you watch. In Brazil slaves made the charcoal that tempered the steel that made the springs in your car and the blade on your lawn mower. Slaves grew the rice that fed the woman that wove the lovely cloth you've put up as curtains. Your investment portfolio and your mutual fund pension own stock in companies using slave labor in the developing world. Slaves keep your costs low and returns on your investments high.[46]

First-world Christians resemble Egyptians in Exodus because, like them, our lifestyles are supported by slavery.

> If we have not participated in slavery through investment we almost certainly have through consumption. Slave produced goods and services flow into the global market, making up a tiny but significant part of what we buy. But the sheer volume of our consumption overwhelms our ability to make responsible choices.[47]

GENOCIDE

Then Pharaoh commanded all his people, "Every boy that is born to the Hebrews you shall throw into the Nile." (Exod. 1:22)

When the Israelites "multiplied and spread" despite their forced labor, Pharaoh ordered the midwives to the Hebrews to kill every boy baby born to the Hebrews. The midwives disobeyed and lied to Pharaoh, who then commanded *all his people* to throw every male Hebrew infant into the Nile. Egypt was home to a campaign of genocide, and all Egyptians were commanded to take part.

The United Nations has defined genocide as:

1. Killing members of a group;
2. Causing serious bodily or mental harm to members of the group;
3. Deliberately inflicting on the group conditions of life calculated to bring about its physical destruction in whole or in part;
4. Imposing measures intended to prevent births within the group;
5. Forcibly transferring children of the group to another group.[48]

Considering this definition, one must conclude that genocide has been integral to the history of North America. The two most obvious cases are the genocide of indigenous peoples and the genocide of Africans and African Americans in slavery.

From the time of their first contact with Europeans, First Nations people in the Americas have been hunted, exterminated, driven from their land, enslaved, deliberately infected with disease, and had their religious practices outlawed. Native children have been forcibly removed from their families to residential schools and European caregivers, where they were forbidden to speak their own language and prevented from participating in their culture. When European trade in African slaves was grafted to the Americas in the early 1500s, Africans were captured, sold, and shipped like cargo.[49] Vast numbers died in transit. They were prevented from speaking their language and were deliberately separated from members of their own cultural groups. They were forbidden to practice African religions. Women were subject to systematic rape and children were intentionally separated from their parents.

These facts clearly match the United Nations' definition of genocide, but what is less obvious, even to those who are its targets, is that this genocide continues today. After slavery was outlawed, thousands of African American men were lynched by whites. This horrific practice continued into the 1920s and 1930s; it is not ancient history.[50] In the past one hundred years people of color have been subjected to forced sterilization programs, with

Canadian programs focusing on First Nations and Metis people, and U.S. policies on blacks, Native people, and Latinos.[51] Although Canada has excellent laws regarding the removal of children from their families, they are not applied consistently. Native children are taken from their homes at a much higher rate than any other group.

As we noted earlier, both Natives and African Americans are disproportionately represented in prison populations and receive consistently harsher sentences than whites accused of the same crimes. At the same time the perpetrators of racist hate crimes are consistently sentenced to shorter terms. Execution in the United States is a blatantly racist practice. Blacks make up 12 percent of the American population, more than 44 percent of the jail and prison population, and 40 percent of inmates on death row.[52]

All nuclear disposal sites are on Native land, and race is the single greatest factor in predicting who will live near toxic waste.[53] This is environmental racism. Corporations and governments that cooperate in targeting poor black and Native American communities as disposal sites for all kinds of environmental poisons participate in a slow form of genocide.

African Americans and Native people are among the poorest people in North America today.[54] Whether the agent is addiction, street violence, lack of medical care, stress, suicide, prison and police violence, malnutrition, homelessness, or environmental poisoning, targeted and abandoned sectors of the North American population are literally dying of poverty.

In 1996 the infant mortality rate for African American infants was 14.7 per 1,000 live births, compared with 6.1 for whites. African-American infants face the same risk of death as infants in much poorer countries, such as Bulgaria and Costa Rica.[55]

Some inner-city neighborhoods have infant mortality rates as high as 30 per 1,000. Poor prenatal care, related to lack of health insurance coverage, accounts for much of the problem. The increasing ratio of black to white infant deaths also reflects the general increase in income inequality and poverty.[56]

Many Native health problems, such as malnutrition, violence and substance abuse, can be traced to the effects of poverty combined with the legacy of mass murder, land theft, cultural attacks, disenfranchisement and dependence.[57]

In the United States the life expectancies for African Americans and Native Americans is significantly lower than for whites.[58]

Delores Williams says:

Attempting to destroy the cultural identity of black Americans: destroying the language of African slaves; attacking African-American leaders;

preventing the formation of institutions in the community; trying to destroy the national feelings of African Americans; destroying the economic existence of the group—all this amounts to weakening the viability of the black American community. This aspect of the definition (of genocide) brings to light the fact that black people have experienced genocide during every phase of their history in America. And this kind of genocide has been caused or indirectly condoned by the State.[59]

Her observations are equally true of Native people and are not limited to the United States. In North America genocide is part of our past and our present.

Probably no one who has bothered to read this book is actively involved in the more overt forms of genocide. Likely no one reading this belongs to an organized hate group, but overt violence and hate mongering are merely the most obvious ways that genocide operates. As June Jordan says:

There is a powerful hatred loose in the world. And the most powerful practitioners of this hatred do not deploy a hateful rhetoric. They do not declare, "I hate Blackfolks," or "I hate women," or "I hate Jews," or "I hate Muslims," or "I hate homosexuals." They make "civil" pronouncements.[60]

Genocide is the destruction of a people, but not all peoples are characterized by race. Consider the two following examples.

Some people with mental illness are fortunate to have family support, adequate income, and meaningful employment; however, the vast majority of North Americans living with mental illness live in poverty. For several reasons, "being diagnosed with a mental illness is now a predicting factor for a premature death."[61] The medical system focuses on people with mental illness solely as "mental patients" and ignores or dismisses their physical symptoms. Psychiatric programs reward "good behavior" with unhealthy sweets and cigarettes. It is nearly impossible to eat well at soup kitchens and on the food portion of disability income. The social stigma of being mentally ill is deeply stressful, which has a further impact on physical health. People with mental illness are disproportionately represented in the homeless population. They are frequently victims of violence, and crimes against people with mental illness often go unreported or uninvestigated because the victim is a "mental case." All these factors contribute to the often harrowing and short lives of people with mental illness in our society.

Lesbian, gay, bisexual, and transgender youth attempt suicide at two to three times the rate of their straight peers, and they account for 30 percent of completed teen suicides.[62] Queer youth are much more likely than their heterosexual peers to be forced into homelessness as a result of rejection by their families, abuse and harassment at school, or a combination of the two. Forty to 50 percent of street youth cite the attitude of others toward their sexual orientation as a reason for their homelessness.[63] While services for street kids are inadequate everywhere, the few shelters that exist are rarely safe places for queer youth. Gay and transgender males have a particularly difficult time, and prostitution is often the only employment available to them. The streets are violent and dangerous for anybody, but these most vulnerable kids are particularly targeted for assault, rape, and even murder. Male-to-female transgender sex workers are especially vulnerable to violence, and crimes against them are seldom investigated seriously. The disregard for their lives by law enforcement reflects the disregard for them in the culture at large.

People of color, queer people, people with mental illness, drug addicts, prostitutes, people with developmental and physical disabilities, and people with more than one of these strikes against them die in shocking numbers because in our economy it is not worth the price for them to live. Genocide is the deliberate destruction of a people. In the cases above, killing people may not be the goal, but deliberate choices have been made for other priorities and against these most marginalized people. During the post–cold war era, a time when the United States had no identifiable enemy, the country's military expenditures were almost double those of France, Germany, and the United Kingdom combined, and more than ten times those of Syria, Iran, Iraq and North Korea combined. Cuts in military spending and increases in social programs would not have imperiled national security, but they threatened the industries and congressional districts that had come to depend on that spending.[64] Now, to fund their "war on terrorism," the United States president, government, and people have abandoned their most vulnerable citizens to the terror of structurally created poverty and violence at home. In the United States, ordinary citizens acquiesce in decisions to put military spending before vulnerable people. What is more, we can comfortably hear this litany of genocide because part of our cultural pathology is to blame the victims for their fate.

Beyond the United States and Canada, genocide is sometimes more blatant and sometimes just easier for us to identify from a distance. In places like Iraq; Chiapas, Mexico; and the rainforest of Colombia, there are strong links between economics and genocide. It is cheaper for governments and corporations to have intermediaries "deal with" people through terror, repression, starvation, and murder than to acknowledge people's rights to the resource-rich lands where they live. As people of privilege we participate in this genocide, knowingly or not, through our economic and political choices. We support institutions like the U.S. Army School of the Americas (now Western Hemispheric Institute for International Security Co-operation [WHISC]), which train the soldiers involved in political killings.[65] We don't ask where the gas for our cars comes from and who is affected by that extraction. We invest in the companies that orchestrate repression and we expect to make a profit.

EGYPT AS EMPIRE 75

As in Rwanda, Bosnia, and Somalia, genocide often involves a long history of racial, ethnic, and religious animosity as well as complex economic issues. When people of privilege are confronted with these situations, we recognize them as genocide. We respond with horror, but with little concrete action and almost no analysis. If the situations involve Africans or religions other than Christianity, we invoke a kind of willful ignorance and refuse to look deeply into what are admittedly complex situations. First-world Christians are like the Egyptians in Exodus. At worst we participate in genocide, and at best we stand by and allow others to carry it out.

LYING AND DECEIT

You can call me Cleopatra
because I'm the Queen of Denial[66]

Despite the facts chronicled in the preceding pages, it is difficult for people of privilege to believe that words like *slavery* and *genocide* have anything to do with us. We know that slavery and genocide are wrong, so wrong that they have attained a symbolic status such that it is impossible for most of us to imagine that we would not recognize and reject such evil. Poet and essayist June Jordan expresses her childhood experience of this collective mental block.

> I used to wonder what it must have felt like to be a grown-up living in Germany or in the United States during World War II. How did anybody hear about the Nazis? Did everyone believe the news? Did anybody care?
> I always wanted to imagine that only bad people could choose to ignore or else accommodate to evil.[67]

The atrocities against Africans, Native people, Jews, and others could not have happened without the mute acquiescence of hundreds of thousands of good people. The reality is that good people did and still do accommodate to evil. We face dueling stories. On the one hand white, middle-income, liberal Christians see ourselves as, for the most part, good people. At the same time, we have ample evidence that we participate in the oppression, enslavement, and even genocide of others. The simple fact is that, like Pharaoh, we lie.

> So Pharaoh said, "I will let you go to sacrifice to the LORD your God in the wilderness, provided you do not go very far away. Pray for me." Then Moses said, "As soon as I leave you, I will pray to the LORD that the swarms of flies may depart tomorrow from Pharaoh, from his offi-

cials, and from his people; only do not let Pharaoh again deal falsely by not letting the people go to sacrifice to the LORD."

So Moses went out from Pharaoh and prayed to the LORD. And the LORD did as Moses asked: he removed the swarms of flies from Pharaoh, from his officials, and from his people; not one remained. But Pharaoh hardened his heart this time also, and would not let the people go. (Exod. 8:28-32)

We are addicted to lying. We cannot openly face the knowledge that the entangled and ingrown systems that support us deal death to others, so we must deceive ourselves. Daily we lie; we lie to keep on in the face of death. Like Pharaoh, we lie to preserve our power, control, and precarious comfort. As African American essayist and educator bell hooks said, "a culture of domination necessarily promotes addiction to lying and denial,"[68] and North America is certainly a culture of domination.

> It's a fib that this nation [the U.S.] is a democracy. But such lies often assume lives of their own, become obstacles to change. This lie of "democracy achieved" warps thinking and organizing by encouraging people to believe that if enough of us bring enough accurate information to enough elected officials, they will set things straight.
>
> This lie camouflages continuing efforts of the wealthy few to govern, for example, by redefining Earth's genes as *their* property; by enacting corporate property rights agreements masqueraded as trade agreements; by extending constitutional powers to corporations.[69]

In the United States, official narratives speak of freedom, liberty, and democracy while the government supports dictators, squashes peoples' movements for autonomy, and goes to war for the control of natural resources. Neo-liberal economists in various countries tout the glories of the free market and unimpeded international trade, never addressing the fact that what they call growth results in the increasing impoverishment of the most poor. Corporations form "citizen" groups to further their interests. Consumer Alert fights product safety regulations; National Wetlands Coalition combats legislation that protects wetlands from pavement and oil wells; and Keep America Beautiful tries to quash mandatory recycling legislation.[70] Although we hear lies from the mouths of economists, corporate executives, and politicians, the mechanisms for empire's deceitful self-promotion are much more sophisticated than mere speechmaking.

Through television, magazines, billboards, and radio, we face a daily onslaught of information, entertainment, and advertisement. Most of us are sophisticated enough to realize that Pepsi will not make us sexy and that quality is not actually Ford's top priority, but the lies go deeper than the advertising message. With the rise of infomercials, product placement in films, paid advertisements that masquerade as news stories, and sensationalist "infotainment," the lines between fact, fiction, and commerce are blurred at best. When we consider that the vast majority of the international media is owned or controlled by a small corporate elite with clear interest in promoting a neo-liberal economic agenda, it becomes clear that the "reality" presented to us is deliberately shaped.

[L]ying takes the presumably innocent form of many white people (and even some black folks) suggesting that racism does not exist anymore. . . . Lying takes the form of mass media creating the myth that the feminist movement has completely transformed society, so much so that the politics of patriarchal men, just like emasculated black men, have become the victims of dominating women. . . . Add to this the widely held assumption that blacks, other minorities, and white women are taking jobs from white men, and that people are poor and unemployed because they want to be, and it becomes most evident that part of our contemporary crisis is created by a lack of meaningful access to truth. That is to say, individuals are not just presented untruths, but are told them in a manner that enables most effective communication.[71]

What we are not told is as significant as what we are told. Indian physicist, ecologist, and activist Vandana Shiva gives the following example.

[I]n a remote area of India, 300,000 village and small town youth joined hands to lock out a Pepsi plant, to say we don't want this for our future. No national paper carried it—only Hindi papers. BBC and CNN didn't carry it either. But 300,000 people! That's much larger than the protests in Seattle. It was a very large mobilization against the destruction of our food culture and the corporate takeover of our economy. And it's no surprise that 300,000 youth in the streets are not news. That's the point of globalization—that millions do not matter. Millions can be rendered invisible and voiceless. That is the violence of globalization.[72]

The lying that pervades our culture causes the most harm to the most vulnerable. Rachel, a street kid from Vancouver, eloquently describes the impact of a culture that ignores her reality of homelessness, poverty, and abuse, and in fact blames her for it.

The world becomes a strange and unrecognizable place when something that is so obviously wrong and destructive to you is constantly ignored and minimalised by society for the most part. You inevitably begin to disassociate yourself. That's what real loneliness is to me. Being constantly surrounded by people and a way of life that you can't relate to or respect, and realizing that you aren't prepared to compromise your ideals for money or acceptance like so many other "lobotomized robots" that overpopulate the capitalist world.[73]

Those of us who live lives of relative privilege lack the courage to hear Rachel's truth. We harden our hearts and we make our lives into lies. The lies that we are told and the lies we tell keep us dazzled by the spectacle of empire so that we cannot imagine anything else. Held in the thrall of corporate culture, we are powerless to resist, even though its fruits are violence, slavery, and genocide. Like the Egyptians in Exodus, we acquiesce to the lies.

> Instead of staying awake to structures of racism at home or displays of militarism abroad, our eyes grow heavy, sedated by the mediated reality of the Dream Factories. Our credulity nurtures a willful ignorance of the complexities of modern capitalism, a benumbed apathy, a preoccupation with the trivial and a fascination with spectacle.[74]

CAN WE CHANGE?

The Egyptians became ruthless in imposing tasks on the Israelites, and made their lives bitter with hard service. (Exod. 1:13-14)

First-world Christians have much in common with the Egyptians in Exodus. Just as they played a part in the empire that enslaved the children of Israel, we in our daily living quietly uphold the empire of global capitalism, which oppresses God's children all over the world. Because we have lied and been lied to for so long, it is important to take time to acknowledge this truth.

The Pan African Healing Foundation, an organization of Africans in Britain, points out that liberal people of privilege, church people, and white people lack credibility with the oppressed because, "when you carry a past without acknowledging it, everything you take on in the future is cast in doubt."[75] They raise the question, "Are people of privilege capable of change?" There is an old African American proverb that says "it is easier to get the people out of Egypt than to get Egypt out of the people." It refers to the responsibilities of freedom. But for people of privilege, for whom Egypt and empire have offered not only security and comfort but everything we have known, leaving Egypt and ridding ourselves of egyptian[76] ways and habits will be slow and hard. Acknowledging our role in empire is a first step in the long, slow journey out of it.

Although we are not harmed in the same way or on the same scale as those we oppress, it is not possible to exist in a situation of violence and denial and not be harmed deeply. At some level we are aware of the destruction that we are a party to and it eats away at our souls. We are not, however, powerless.

5

EGYPT THE LAND

*I used to admire everything in Egypt. But the palms and the plains ain't
scenery to me no more. They just look like suffering to me now.*
                                                    —Zora Neale Hurston[1]

THE LAND OF EGYPT

The previous chapter addressed Egypt as a nation and an imperial
power. The following chapters explore the traits and actions of specific
Egyptian characters in Exodus. This chapter focuses on the land of Egypt,
the soil, the plants, the animals, and elements—those parts of the world
that in our time are referred to as the environment. Robert Warrior calls
the land the last unheard voice in scripture.[2] This chapter provides a chance
to listen to that voice while learning more about Egypt and delving deeper
into Exodus.

In modern-day Egypt, 95 percent of the vegetation on the Nile is non-
indigenous; the once ubiquitous papyrus is found only in botanical gardens, and many of the creatures worshiped in the ancient pantheon are
either endangered, threatened, or presumed extinct. The loss of bird species
has been particularly devastating. A current travel guide reads: "The most
common critters are house mice, black and brown rats and bats. Besides
these, you'll be lucky to see anything other than camels, donkeys, and to a
lesser extent domesticated horses and buffalo."[3] Yet the inscriptions and
paintings of antiquity attest to human interaction with a number of rich
and distinct ecologies.

The desert, or Red Land, as the ancient Egyptians called it, was not an
empty expanse of sand with the occasional camel; it was home to delicate
but tenacious ecosystems. Gravel wadis made a foothold for gnarled trees
and scrub; in the sandy soil, seeds lay dormant for years awaiting the
storms that might come only ten times in a hundred years. Beyond the
usual desert dwellers—mice, scorpions, foxes, lizards, and vipers—the Red
Land was home to a startling array of large mammals: ibex, cheetahs, leop-

ards, gazelles, wild goats. Egyptian hunters accompanied by dogs went into the desert in search of these creatures; but, except in times of very low food production, hunting was not a necessity but a pastime for the wealthy.

Grass and papyrus wetlands in the delta were home to frogs, hippopotamus, fish, crocodiles, and numerous species of water birds. Although hippos and crocodiles were dangerous and feared, human venture into the marshlands was quite extensive. Elite parties hunting for sport pursued hippo, speared fish, or used a boomerang to catch birds. Peasant workers employed more utilitarian methods, netting both fish and birds. Cattle grazed in pastureland attended by herders, while other workers harvested papyrus and various reeds for paper, weaving, building, and food.[4] Although there were fish in the Mediterranean and abundant reef ecosystems in the Red Sea, there is no evidence that the Egyptians ventured far into these waters.

Egypt has been described as "the gift of the Nile,"[5] for throughout its history, human activity in this region of northeast Africa has centered on this life-giving river. The ancient Egyptians called the Nile's fertile corridor where they dwelt "the Black Land." Two ancient kingdoms, Upper and Lower Egypt, represent two aspects of the Nile's geography. Upper Egypt was the Nile Valley, approximately fifteen kilometers wide and hundreds of kilometers in length. Geographically the valley has changed very little over the centuries. Lower Egypt was the wedge-shaped fertile delta stretching from modern-day Cairo, the point where the river first branches, to the Mediterranean. At one time there may have been as many as twelve branches fanning out through marshy wetlands to the sea. Years of silt deposits have filled some of the river branches and made solid land of the marshes. Since the time of the pharaohs, the delta has migrated westward and the coastline has moved north.[6]

The Nile brings water to the desert. Most of Egypt receives little or no rain. None of the Nile's tributaries originate in Egypt, and the maximum rainfall is a scant twenty centimeters per year in the delta area. But annual flooding of the river from July to September rejuvenates the land with water and deposits of rich alluvial soil, bringing abundance to a land bordered by desert and sea. For millennia the banks of the Nile have been the site of intensive, highly organized agriculture. Complex irrigation canals brought the Nile's inundation to normally dry land, and when the waters receded, immense fields were planted in flax and grains. After these crops had been harvested, legumes and vegetables were planted, and the great estates had gardens, orchards and vineyards. Fish were harvested from the Nile and from irrigation canals. Livestock, goats, sheep, cattle, and pigs provided food and hide, but with the advent of intensive agriculture, donkeys and oxen became increasingly important as draft animals, as attested to in this work song.[7]

Thresh for yourselves, thresh for yourselves, oxen!
thresh for yourselves, thresh for yourselves!

Straw to eat and barley for your masters;
    give yourselves no rest, it is cool today![8]

Ducks and geese were domesticated, as were cats and dogs. Depictions of court scenes show tame gazelles, baboons, herons, monkeys, and hyenas. The horse was introduced into Egypt around 1600 B.C.E., which changed the nature of warfare and hunting, at least for the elite. Domestic animals and creatures from the desert, the delta, and the Nile featured in the Egyptian pantheon.

Egyptian cosmology was rooted in the natural world. The fertile Black land was understood by its inhabitants to be in perpetual conflict with the chaotic forces of the desert or Red Land and with the peoples who emerged from it. The Nile protected Egypt from the severity of drought and famine to which neighboring countries were subject, and in times of crisis Egypt was a reluctant destination for refugees.

Now there was a famine in the land. So Abram went down to Egypt to reside there as an alien, for the famine was severe in the land. (Gen. 12:10)

When Jacob learned that there was grain in Egypt, he said to his sons, "Why do you keep looking at one another? I have heard," he said, "that there is grain in Egypt: go down and buy grain for us there, that we may live and not die." (Gen. 42:1-2)

In Egypt the precarious annual miracle of the river's flooding became a central religious symbol for the cycle of return: birth, death, and rebirth.

The Black Land's fertility provided the agricultural basis for an economy that grew to encompass trade, industry, cities, and complex power relations. Although pharaonic Egypt spanned nearly three millennia, geographic isolation and the stability of the Nile environment contributed to a remarkable continuity of political rule and religious expression such that Egyptian civilization and culture were already ancient by the time of the patriarchs.

According to Walter Brueggemann, "land is a central, if not the central theme of biblical faith."[9] For Israel, a nation born in the wilderness, land belongs to YHWH and is YHWH's gift and promise. But land is a dangerous gift. With land people become subject to the management of land and not to YHWH. There is an underlying tension in scripture between obligation to the land and freedom to leave, between farmers and herders. Throughout the Bible good land is depicted as agriculturally productive, domesticated, and controlled. Parallel to the themes about the land are concerns about the productivity and fertility of women.

How was the naturally abundant, ancient, and socially stratified land of Egypt portrayed in Exodus? In Exodus, the land of Egypt serves a complex symbolic function. Recall that *mitsraim,* the Hebrew word for Egypt, suggests hardship and birth: Israel's experiences in Egypt. The prologue and early chapters of Exodus, where Pharaoh makes decrees of genocide against the Hebrews and stores up Egypt's wealth on their forced labor, depict Egypt as, "a house of bondage." There human relationships are grossly distorted by oppression, and wealth is accumulated, not shared. From the vantage point of the wilderness and imminent death, however, the goodness and abundance of Egypt are praised: "we remember the fish we used to eat in Egypt for nothing, the cucumbers, the melons, the leeks, the onions and the garlic" (Num. 11:5).

The biblical authors brilliantly present the facts of life according to empire: as distasteful as slavery is, the wilderness seems to offer only death —there is no alternative but Egypt. In Exodus, Israel sought to define itself against Egypt but at the same time vividly portrayed the seemingly inescapable nature of empire. This message is deeply compelling for first-world readers who seek an alternative to the empires of slavery and abundance that surround us. From our entrenchment in the system of global capitalism, it is difficult to find "the imagination to believe that our salvation is not in the storehouses of Egypt or the vaults of Chase Manhattan."[10]

Within Exodus, the most extensive portrait of the land of Egypt—terrain, vegetation, species diversity, weather—appears in the plague narratives, which are deeply rooted in the nonhuman order.

PLAGUE NARRATIVES

Chapters 7-10 of Exodus relate in great detail an epic battle between opposing gods, leaders, cosmologies, and political realities. In this contest, soil, water, air, sky, plants, and animals become battlefield and ammunition. The engagement takes the form of a series of interactions that follow a roughly similar pattern and include some of the following elements:

- God instructs Moses, with or without Aaron, to go to Pharaoh demanding Israel's release and threatening some environmental sign.
- Moses encounters with Pharaoh.
- Pharaoh refuses, either directly or by inaction, to release the people.
- Sign is described.
- Pharaoh summons Moses, asks for intercession, and negotiates Israel's release.
- Sign is removed.
- Pharaoh reneges.
- The state of Pharaoh's heart is described.

Some of these accounts are detailed and elaborate; others almost terse. The *Passover Haggadah* lists ten plagues: blood, frogs, lice, wild beasts,

blight, boils, hail, locusts, darkness, and the slaying of the firstborn. But the
ten plagues, or wonders, like the Ten Commandments and the twelve tribes
of Israel, are notoriously difficult to number. Nine of the episodes listed in
the *Haggadah* follow the pattern outlined above, but the account of the
tenth, the slaying of the firstborn, seems to be of a different magnitude and
is interrupted by detailed instructions for avoiding this fate, instructions for
the Passover ritual. These ten central wonders are bracketed by several
other supernormal environmental events. Before sending him to Egypt,
God gives Moses instructions and skills involving the control of snakes and
skin disease. Moses uses these signs to establish his credibility with both
Israel and Pharaoh. The description of Moses' display of power is similar
to the plague pattern above. Following the sequence of ten wonders are
more miraculous events: the Israelites leave Egypt and the Reed Sea mysteriously parts for them but closes in on the Egyptians. At this point the signs
and "natural" wonders seem to number fourteen: snakes, skin disease,
blood, frogs, bugs, bugs, cattle disease, boils, hail, locusts, darkness, firstborn, sea crossing, and drowning.

To add to the confusion there are several independent traditions of the
wonders in Egypt. Two of the psalms describe plagues against Egypt, but
each has a slightly different list.

> He turned their rivers to blood,
>   so that they could not drink of their streams.
> He sent among them swarms of flies, which devoured them,
>   and frogs, which destroyed them.
> He gave their crops to the caterpillar,
>   and the fruit of their labor to the locust.
> He destroyed their vines with hail,
>   and their sycamores with frost.
> He gave over their cattle to the hail,
>   and their flocks to thunderbolts.
> He let loose on them his fierce anger,
>   wrath, indignation, and distress,
>   a company of destroying angels.
> He made a path for his anger;
>   he did not spare them from death,
>   but gave their lives over to the plague.
> He struck all the firstborn in Egypt,
>   the first issue of their strength in the tents
>   of Ham. (Ps. 78:44-51)

> He sent darkness, and made the land dark;
>   they rebelled against his words.
> He turned their waters into blood,
>   and caused their fish to die.

Their land swarmed with frogs,
> even in the chambers of their kings.
He spoke, and there came swarms of flies,
> and gnats throughout their country.
He gave them hail for rain,
> and lightning that flashed through their land.
He struck their vines and fig trees,
> and shattered the trees of their country.
He spoke, and the locusts came,
> and young locusts without number;
they devoured all the vegetation their land,
> and ate up the fruit of their ground.
He struck down all the firstborn in their land,
> the first issue of all their strength. (Ps. 105:28-36)

The confusion turns to absurdity when we focus on the fate of one group of plague victims, Egyptian cattle. Cattle (*miqneh*), is a broad term that covers animals ranging from goats to camels. Along with the rest of the population of Egypt, animal and human, cattle endure polluted water, frogs, and two kinds of insect inundation. Then, perhaps mercifully, all Egyptian cattle are killed in an epidemic striking flocks, herds, and transport animals. Dead, they escape the boils, but when the hail comes, Egyptian cattle in the fields are again struck dead. In the final blow, the angel of death kills all the firstborn of Egypt, including cattle! A short time later there are horses to pull Pharaoh's chariots.[11] What is going on in the recounting of the plagues?

Clearly in the plague narratives we have evidence of multiple traditions. Some scholars identify as many as three sources in the text. They identify patterns of repetition, word use, and themes that they attribute to the agenda and concerns of particular times and factions in Israel's history. Although a few scholars identify Elohist passages and themes, we will limit ourselves to some basic generalizations on the two major sources: J and P. The Jahwist material emphasizes the plagues as a means for Pharaoh, Egypt, and Israel to know YHWH. The God of this account is one who distinguishes between Israel and Egypt. Priestly material is characterized by the appearance of cultic figures: Aaron and Pharaoh's magicians. In P material, God controls all aspects of the contest, and all changes in the natural world are designed to bring glory to God through Pharaoh's defeat.

In describing the plagues, scholars contradict one another with incredibly detailed observations and arguments. The plagues are grouped in pairs, in sevens, and in three parallel groups of three with "*yet one more.*" They are divided according to location, agent, characters, and the state of Pharaoh's heart. Some scholars consider the pattern to consist of carefully controlled variations, while others describe a haphazard collection. It is not necessary for our purposes to judge these arguments; what we can say with assurance is that the text contains a number of variant traditions and the description of each follows a somewhat similar pattern. For this reason, although the plagues read as a single story, I have used the plural, "plague narratives" in order to indicate the various layers and traditions.

Another kind of detailed examination of the plagues may be more familiar to lay readers. Certain writers whose concern is to prove that biblical wonders represent scientifically and historically identifiable events have treated the plague narratives as a basically accurate description of a series of linked, unusual but natural phenomena. Their "historical" explanations go something like this: a bloom of red algae killed massive numbers of fish in the Nile, driving contaminated frogs onto the land where they died; this attracted swarms of insects which in turn carried disease to animals and humans. Greta Hort is the author of the most intricate and well-researched example of this kind of writing. She posits a historical kernel for the narratives, asserting that in the course of one unusual year nine of the events could have taken place, in the stated order, through a causal sequence of events. Further, she supports Israel's exemption from some of the events with the contention that Goshen, where the Hebrews lived, was climatically and geographically distinct from the rest of Egypt.[12]

Such rationalist explanations couple a refusal to believe in miracles with the assertion that all events recorded in the Bible are historical and are meant to be understood literally. Furthermore, trying to account for the plagues in terms of unusual but explicable events denies the very meaning of the passage. None of these events is *normal*, and ten or fourteen of them together are certainly not normal. The point of the story is that something outside the ordinary is going on. A clue to what is going on is found in the words themselves. We tend to speak of these events as plagues, which means "blows," but the text rarely uses the verb "to smite" (*negeph*). More common are the words "sign" (*oth*) sign and "wonder" (*mopeth*).[13] These words indicate that although the signs punish in the present, they do not only punish, nor are they spectacle for its own sake, but rather they point in some direction. Before we look at what the signs might point to, let us review the events in sequence, examining each sign individually in terms of historical and literary meaning and how it helps us to understand Egypt. It would be helpful at this point to put down this book and to read Exodus 7-15 as the passages are too long to quote here in full.

Plague by Plague

Snakes (Exodus 7:8-13)

Snakes are a source of fascination in every culture. Often dangerous, they are sticks that move and they posses the amazing ability to unhinge their jaws and swallow objects wider than their own girth. There are thirty-four species of snakes in modern Egypt.[14] A snake appears often in pharaonic iconography, and the cobra is depicted on Pharaoh's crown. Perhaps the snakes produced by Pharaoh's magicians represent Pharaoh himself. The word for snakes in this passage (*tannin*) refers not to the common garden variety but to particularly large snakes or reptiles. There is an Egyptian story about a wax crocodile that comes to life to swallow its master's enemy, and the Egyptian king is described in the Bible and elsewhere as a basking reptile.[15] Yet a crocodile that becomes a rod is not as physically tidy as a snake. In many cultures, snakes are a symbol of wisdom and power, and here Pharaoh's wise men are defeated by the greater wisdom of YHWH's servant. The fate of the magicians' serpents, swallowed by Aaron's staff-turned-serpent, prefigures the fate of Egypt. The next time the verb "to swallow" (*bala*) is used, the Egyptians are swallowed beneath the sea.[16]

Blood (Exodus 7:14-25)

Of all the plagues, this is most often attributed by scholars to the memory of an actual event. Every year rain in the upper Nile region brings red silt-bearing water into the delta. Accounts of this phenomenon could have been known in Israel, and the idea of the bloody Nile may have influenced the story of infant genocide in the prologue. On the other hand, bloody water as an omen or curse is a theme in the mythology of many nations. The second aspect of this sign is that all the fish die, decay, and stink. Although freshwater fish were a significant contribution to the Egyptian diet, water, not food, is the focus of this incident. It is not clear whether it is the blood or the fish that make the water undrinkable, but, curiously, this state of complete and prolonged water pollution is not treated as a great calamity. The Egyptians dig for drinking water along the Nile, and Pharaoh returns to his palace—his heart hardened.

Frogs (Exodus 8:1-15)

As in the previous plague, not just the Nile but every conceivable water source is affected. All water is teeming with frogs. William Propp calls this the most original plague of the sequence, for although the Nile has a significant frog population that makes a noisy annual sojourn onto land to mate, no other culture has myths of frog inundation.[17] Even in the numbers described, frogs are only incredibly annoying, not a threat to life or health. Yet this is the first assault described as *negeph*, a blow to Pharaoh.[18] He cannot shut himself off in the palace, there are frogs in his bed. This plague touches the royal person.

The invasion of frogs has always been my favorite plague. I relish its comic appeal and absurdity. How could frogs possibly have "destroyed" Egypt? But I am also coming to understand it better. I work in a street shelter where people die daily from AIDS, despair, violence, and addiction, but more often than not it is the plagues of small creatures—mice, rats, and insects—that threaten my equilibrium. As Psalm 78 says, the little things destroy me.

Insects (Exodus 8:16-19, 20-32)

The next two inundations appear to be alternate renditions of the same story. Biting insects are quite common in Egypt and insect swarms are a stereotypical curse in the ancient Near East.[19] In the first version, the noun for these agents of persuasion, *kinnam*, refers to a specific but unknown biting insect. The word has been translated as "gnats," "lice," "mosquitoes," and "sand fleas." Although the wording is quite terse, featuring neither Moses' warning nor Pharaoh's concession, this event represents escalation in the campaign against Egypt. This plague is an assault on the bodies of the Egyptians, and for the first time Pharaoh's magicians cannot duplicate the wonder.

In the second rendition (Exod. 8:20-32) the perpetrators of the inundation are *arab,* an obscure word that indicates a mixture but does not specify its content.[20] As the *Passover Haggadah* shows, there is an old tradition that the mixture is beasts of prey, but modern scholars favor the alternate tradition and translate *arab* as insects. For the first time the Israelites in Goshen are specifically exempted from a plague. Much longer than the first, this version includes elaborate negotiations regarding the demand to go and worship. "The sacrifices we offer to the LORD our God are offensive to the Egyptians" (Exod. 8:26). This may reflect differences between animal worshipers and animal sacrificers, or it may be a tactical maneuver on the part of Moses.

Cattle Epidemic (Exodus 9:1-7)

Cattle disease is not especially prevalent in Egypt, so this sign might be transplanted from a Canaanite context or it might be symbolic. As a symbol, the curse on cattle may represent an economic attack on Egyptian wealth and accumulation. It might also be a cosmological assault on an Egyptian deity represented by a cow or bull.[21] All Egyptian cattle die, and all Israelite cattle are spared.

Skin Disease (Exodus 9:8-12)

This short description of a skin disease of "blossoming boils"[22] is the final episode involving Pharaoh's increasingly ridiculous magicians. Not only do they fail to produce such a plague; they cannot protect themselves from it and will not show their afflicted bodies in public. The ability to manipulate skin disease appears as a sign of power during the commissioning of Moses (Exod. 4:6-8),[23] and threat of affliction is a typical covenant curse. It is also featured in nationalist name-calling; in ancient writing from both Egypt and Israel, the other nation is defamed and warned against as a carrier of skin disease.[24] The use of ashes to transmit the boils may refer to the memory of a volcanic eruption or it may indicate some early notion of disease borne in particles on the air.

Hail and Fire from the Sky (Exodus 9:13-35)

For the first time Egyptians other than Pharaoh have agency. They are given the opportunity to escape the plague: Egyptians who fear YHWH can save their slaves and (mysteriously resurrected) cattle from the devastating onslaught of hail and fire from the sky. Other Egyptians are also indicted at the close of the passage; Pharaoh *and his servants* harden their hearts. Hail in Egypt is not unheard of but is far more common in Canaan. Further, where YHWH is associated with the power of storms, there are frequent references to hail. The plague is probably to be traced to Canaanite origins of YHWH as a storm and warrior god transplanted to the Egyptian context. Fire is often described with hail, whether as naturally occurring lightning or an awe-inspiring pairing of opposites. The account of hail is particularly lengthy and includes a note on crop succession which explains how, after the total devastation of plant life, the locusts have something to eat.

Locusts (Exodus 10:1-20)

This account is based on a frequently occurring and greatly feared phenomenon in North Africa. Swarms of locusts today can number up to ten billion individual insects and can completely devastate hundreds of hectares of vegetation.[25] The notion of such an occurrence as divine punishment figures in many traditions. In this lengthy narrative, Egyptians other than Pharaoh again have a role; they call on Pharaoh to relent. Negotiations too take up a significant part of the description. Pharaoh is being worn down. When he finally calls for help, Pharaoh describes the insects as "this death," and when the locusts are dispatched, it is into the Sea of Reeds. Thus Egypt's fate is foreshadowed.

Darkness (Exodus 10:21-29)

Darkness or blotting out the sun is an ubiquitous curse, perhaps based on a solar eclipse. Some commentators posit that desert sandstorms or clouds of volcanic ash could be the practical explanation for a darkness that is felt and that impedes movement, but both Egypt and Israel would certainly have had accurate vocabulary to describe darkness resulting from particles in the air. Further, the emphasis on light in Hebrew homes (Exod. 10:23) shows that this plague is about the absence, not the masking, of light. After this sign, all negotiations break down; Pharaoh concedes freedom; but Israelite cattle must remain. Moses refuses to accept this compromise. Pharaoh will not let Israel go, and Moses cannot let them stay. The account ends in deadlock and threats.

Death of the Firstborn (Exodus 11:1-10; 12:29-32)

The contest in Egypt culminates in *"yet one more plague."* If this sign has a counterpart in historical reality, it would be a sudden epidemic of a fatal childhood disease. However, there is no natural phenomenon that could cause a pattern of mortality that distinguishes birth order; neither is it a stereotypical curse, so we must look to the symbolic order for explanation. This plague is connected to the Passover and an understanding that YHWH has a special claim on the firstborn. It is paralleled by the Egyptians' attack on Israelite infants in the prologue. As we noted earlier, the typical plague pattern is interrupted by detailed instructions for the Passover rite, but it remains essentially the same: instructions from God, threat of the plague, description of the plague, concession, YHWH hardens Pharaoh's heart, and Pharaoh reneges.

Drowning (Exodus 14:21-31; 15:1-12)

As with the sign of the insects, there are multiple versions of this blow, both side by side and conflated. Miriam's song, Exodus 15:1b-18, describes the Egyptians sinking at sea and drowning. Exodus 14 describes a miraculous, or at least an unlikely, crossing and drowning that features both natural and supernatural events. Numerous rationalist explanations for the crossing have been offered —tides, comets, and the idea that the sea was not a sea—but as with the other signs and wonders, the intent of the authors is to show the might of YHWH and the election of Israel.

In the plague narratives, every manifestation of YHWH's power involves control of the natural world. How are modern readers to understand this? Some biblical scholars offer an ecological reading of the text. According to Terence Fretheim, Egypt's anti-life acts against Israel are in fact acts against all creation. When Pharaoh tries to subvert the creational promise of fruitfulness, that is, when Pharaoh tries to control Israel's population through forced labor and genocide, the ethical order is breached. This impacts the cosmic order and threatens to return the earth to its pre-creation chaos. The fact that the only previous use of *choshek*, this particular form of the word darkness, is in Genesis 1, supports this creational reading of the plagues. The plagues can be seen as a deliberate inversion of creation. As Pharaoh and the Egyptians break the law of justice, creation breaks the bounds of createdness, becoming both victim and aggressor.

Modern ecological readings like Fretheim's focus on the environmental aspects of the plague narratives, but they neglect the political narrative and fail to address the presence of women in the text at all. For our Egyptian reading, which focuses on questions of empire, economics, and justice, this approach is not sufficient.

INTRODUCTION TO ECOFEMINISM

The ecofeminst issue is born of the lack of municipal garbage collection, of the multiplication of rats, cockroaches, and mosquitos, and of the sores on children's skin. This is true because it is usually women who have to deal with daily survival issues. . . .

—Ivone Gebara[26]

Over the past twenty years and increasingly over the last ten, women from a number of traditions and disciplines have explored the connections between the material conditions of women in a culture and how the earth is treated and understood in that culture. Over time these discussions have developed from a fairly simple focus on gender and environment to nuanced and complex explorations which take into account economics, race, class, and culture.

Ecofeminist theology is the application of ecofeminist understandings to traditional theological questions, sometimes resulting in very nontraditional answers. Ten to fifteen years ago ecofeminist theology was largely a project of white academics. There was a significant focus on the culpability of organized Western religion, mainly Christianity, in promoting a nature- and woman-hating worldview. A disturbing aspect of this work was that the focus on an earth- and woman-positive past led to the anti-Semitic implication that this golden past was destroyed by the rise of Judaism or, as Judith Plaskow has it, that "the Jews killed the goddess."[27] A secondary focus of early ecofeminist theology was on the recovering of woman- and creation-positive aspects of the Christian and Jewish traditions. Over the past decade the study of ecofeminist theology has become more diverse, more sophisticated, and more concerned with the realities of everyday people. Ecofeminist principles are derived from women's experience.

There are many ecofeminst theologies born of numerous contexts and concerns, but those with which I choose to align myself share some of the following principles. Humans are not the center of God's creation, and God is not separate from creation. Economics, race, and class are vital to understanding gender and environmental justice. All faith traditions can learn from one another. The land and all creatures are sacred. The earth is fragile. The logic of domination and the promotion of suffering must be opposed. Humans are at home on the earth and dependent on it; the earth is not our enemy. Humans have power for healing and creativity. Everyone has the right to meaningful work. Bodies are important: the earth's body, human bodies, the bodies of all living creatures. The lives of women and children, especially the poor and people of color, are important. The earth, the lives of women, and the connections between them are not to be romanticized. Theological work must support grass-roots political movements.

A Christian ecofeminist approach to reading the Bible keeps these principles in the foreground as well as asking some specific questions. How are women portrayed? How is the nonhuman world portrayed? How is the divine understood in relation to women and the nonhuman world? How are other faith traditions and cosmologies portrayed? By asking these questions ecofeminist theology offers new insights into the plague narratives.

AN ECOFEMINIST READING
OF THE PLAGUE NARRATIVES

Women

Women are largely absent from Exodus. The daring actions of the women of the prologue—Shiphrah, Puah, Jochebed (Moses' mother), Moses' sister, Pharaoh's daughter, Zipporah—and the strong leadership of Miriam in the wilderness stand in stark contrast to the revelation at Sinai. As the Hebrews prepare to enter into covenant with YHWH, Moses addresses "all the people." "So Moses went down from the mountain to the people. He consecrated the people, and they washed their clothes. And he said to the people, 'Prepare for the third day; do not go near a woman'" (Exod. 19:14). Clearly in this passage women are not included among the people.

Within the whole of the plague narratives (Exod. 7-12) there are only three direct references to women and one theme that, while focused on men, implies the existence of women. All three direct references appear toward the end of the cycle. As Moses negotiates with Pharaoh for who may go into the wilderness to worship YHWH, he is adamant that women be included, "we will go with our young and old; we will go with our sons and daughters" (Exod. 10:9). Anticipating the final sign, the death of the firstborn, YHWH instructs Moses, "Tell the people that every man is to ask his neighbor and every woman is to ask her neighbor for objects of silver and gold" (Exod. 11:2). Here, in contrast to Exodus 19:15, women seem to be included in "the people." This injunction refers obliquely to Egyptian women as well, for why would women of one household have different neighbors than the men of that household. The suggestion is that men have male neighbors and women have female neighbors (we will explore this passage further in chapter 10 below).

The third mention of women is the only direct reference to Egyptian women in the plague narratives, and it refers as well to the classed nature of Egyptian society. Threatening the pervasiveness of the final plague, Moses says, "Every firstborn in the land of Egypt shall die, from the first-born of Pharaoh who sits on his throne to the firstborn of the female slave who is behind the handmill" (Exod. 11:5). This short mention indicates that not every Egyptian benefited equally from the nation's wealth and abundance. The issue of the firstborn raises other questions about gender. First, birth itself points to the presence and importance of women. In the instructions for Passover this is emphasized by the expression, "the first to open the womb" (Exod. 13:2; 13:12). If there are wombs, there must be women. In the case of Israel, those firstborn consecrated to YHWH and sub-sequently to be redeemed are definitely male. In the case of the firstborn of Egypt it is not clear whether those killed are firstborn, firstborn male, first-born juveniles.[28] In this situation exclusion from their people may be an advantage for Egyptian women.

These three references to women indicate the ambiguity with which women were regarded by biblical authors. Clearly women were present in both Israel and Egypt in numbers at least equal to those of men, and they occupied a variety of different stations with varying degrees of autonomy and agency. In the Bible, women are often referred to in a way that acknowledges their status both as human and as an economic asset. Like slaves and children, they were a kind of sentient property. In two of the three plague-narrative references to women, they appear in a hierarchical sequence, where they are listed after men and before cattle. All the refer-ences are brief and utilitarian and give no voice to women's experience.

Here is one of the great ironies of the exodus story. While it is the par-adigmatic liberation story in which the oppressed Israelites cry out, and in which God acts in history for their salvation, nowhere in the text do we hear the cry of oppressed women, Israelite or Egyptian. This absence is par-ticularly glaring when we consider how intimately women's lives are con-cerned with the earthly manifestations of this contest between gods. Latin American ecofeminist Ivone Gebara points out that it is women who deal with daily survival issues: rats, roaches, mosquitoes, and sores on children's skin. Her list of "survival issues" bears striking resemblance to a number of the plagues: wild beasts, different kinds of insects, and skin disease. In Egypt women would have been most profoundly impacted by these events. Women and children must find and carry clean water for families; women prepare food and must account for its absence; and women do basic nurs-ing and respond to small-scale health crises. The plagues in Exodus relate a story that has been repeated in country after country throughout history and into the present: powerful men mess up while women and the poor are left to clean up.

Consider the industrial disaster in Bhopal. On December 3, 1984, toxic methyl isocyanide leaked from Union Carbide's pesticide factory into the slums of Bhopal, India, killing thousands and seriously affecting 240,000 more. The majority of those affected were the poorest of the poor, and the majority of those were children, women in their reproductive years, and elderly women.[29] As of the year 2000 the American-owned company has paid only a fraction of the agreed settlement to victims and their families,[30] and Union Carbide refuses to disclose the chemical makeup of its lethal gas, which prevents the survivors from receiving the best possible treatment. Neither American nor Indian courts have successfully prosecuted Union Carbide, which demonstrates that multinational corporations are beyond the law.[31]

An ecofeminst reading of the plague narratives must draw attention to the story that is not told. When gods, men, and corporations fight, women and children are hurt; and when the land, crops, and animals are harmed, the lives of women are disproportionately impacted.

The Non-Human World

The plague narratives provide the modern reader with evidence of how the biblical authors regarded the nonhuman world. There is no singular biblical perspective on the environment, but, in general, creation was regarded with more familiarity, less sentimentality, and a greater sense of dependence than most modern city-dwellers have. Creation in Egypt is not portrayed as a generic category; rather, the nonhuman realm is divided into creatures that serve humans, chiefly cattle and crops, and those which do not. The aspects of creation that do not serve humans or are not completely domesticated include elements—water, storm, disease, death, darkness, fire—and particular phyla—snakes, insects, frogs. These untamed entities are the agents of Egypt's tribulation, but their victims are not only human. The whole of the human-allied world suffers, or more accurately, the whole of the Egypt-allied world.

The assault on Egyptian crops and cattle is reasonably congruent with Egyptian cosmology. Any attack on Egypt, land or animal, constituted an attack on the person of Pharaoh, the god-king. The division of the world into wild and domesticated parallels the struggle between the Black Land and the Red Land. But, as we observed earlier, in Exodus, Egypt stands for empire and Egyptian content tends to set the scene more than it communicates cross-cultural understanding. The composite portrait of the natural world in Exodus was produced by various groups in Palestine over several centuries. Their understandings of animals, plants, and land differed from one another, from Egyptians' understandings, and significantly from the understandings of first-world readers. Throughout the Bible's legal books there are commandments and examples of case law that depict land and animals as subject to the same laws as humans. They too are included in the covenant between YHWH and Israel. Cultivated land and domestic animals especially are entitled to justice and are deserving of punishment. An ox that gores a man or a woman is to be stoned (Exod. 21:28); fields are to enjoy periodic rest (Lev. 25:5); enemy cattle are to be slaughtered and

not eaten (Deut. 14:15-16); and firstborn humans and animals are consecrated to God (Exod. 13:2). When Moses negotiates for Israel's release, he
includes cattle among those who constitute Israel. We will go with our
young and our old; we will go with ours sons and daughters and with our
flocks and herds (Exod. 10:9). Not a hoof shall be left behind (Exod.
10:26).

Biblical authors were necessarily aware of their dependence on agriculture and domesticated animals, but this does not mean that humans and
animals were regarded as equals. Although the early tribal alliance was
designed to keep power decentralized, tribal life had rigid rules and the
extended family functioned hierarchically under the male head of household. Repeatedly throughout the legal texts, animals are included in the
formulaic listing of household members in relative order of importance.
The most familiar example is probably Exodus 20:17: "You shall not covet
your neighbor's house, you shall not covet your neighbor's wife, or male or
female slave, or ox or donkey, or anything that belongs to your neighbor."
Wives, slaves, oxen, and donkeys are all members of the household; they
are at the same time property and possession. In fact the Hebrew word for
cattle (*miqneh*) also means possessions.[32]

When Moses negotiates for the release of the cattle, it is as members of
the community of Israel; but the direct context is that of sacrifice. "But
Moses said, 'You must also let us have sacrifices and burnt offerings to sacrifice to the LORD our God. Our livestock also must go with us; not a hoof
shall be left behind, for we must choose some of them for the worship of
the LORD our God, and we will not know what to use to worship the LORD
until we arrive there'" (Exod. 10:25-26). This constant awareness of the
reality of sacrifice and slaughter, in tension with the sense of all living
things as participants in divine covenant, stands in stark contrast to the
modern industrial use of fields and cattle as raw materials to be exploited
for maximum profit while the reality of their lives is kept invisible.

Reading the text from an ecofeminst perspective we must be careful not
to project our cosmology onto it. The biblical regard for creation and its
inclusion in Israel's covenant with YHWH cannot be equated with modern
earth-based spiritualities' regard for *all* life. Earth-based spiritualities make
use of a scientific metaphor. Ecosystems are depicted as an interconnected
web of life. The household formula—wife, slave, ox, donkey—shows that,
for biblical authors, the relative value and power of humans and animals
were understood as a chain or a pyramid with a definite top and bottom.
These are two very distinct ways of imaging the nonhuman world.

Ecofeminism and earth-based spiritualities emphasize the positive qualities of *the wild*, but in Egypt, wild things are the threat. There are hints in
the plague narratives of simple awe for the integrity and terrifying power
of creation, but these are intertwined with descriptions of YHWH's absolute
control over these forces. Ecofeminism honors creation and sees its fundamental integrity; in the plague narratives for the most part, creation is
respected and honored only in as much as it serves humans.

The Divine

In Exodus, God is almost entirely absent from the stories where women appear. In the plague narratives YHWH is a main player but women are almost entirely absent. While human liberation and the integrity of creation are certainly themes in the plague narratives, they are secondary to the contest between YHWH and Pharaoh. The text is fundamentally God-centered. Even the heroic Moses and the entire people of Israel are little more than supporting actors. The plot of the plague narratives is basically as follows. YHWH, through a messenger, Moses, engages with Pharaoh in a contest over the release of the Hebrews from their forced labor. YHWH strikes at Egypt with a series of hypernatural occurrences, and Pharaoh counters with stubborn refusal. YHWH's victory is decisive, and Moses leads the Hebrews out of Egypt. In the several chapters that comprise the plague narratives, there is only one incident where the existence of women is even acknowledged by YHWH (Exod. 11:5).

The relationship between YHWH and the nonhuman world in the plague narratives shows evidence of layers of composition. At the oldest level of the text are hints of a fierce primal deity whose appearance is accompanied by thunder and storm. In the later Priestly version of the plagues, YHWH exercises complete control over creation, turning locust swarms, darkness, and even death on and off like a switch. A modern interpretation of these events is that YHWH simply turns Pharaoh over to the destructive consequences of his own actions against creation. That is, God lets nature take its course. By either of the latter interpretations, YHWH is outside of creation.

In the plague narratives, YHWH is distant from women and manipulates nature, not a very flattering portrait from a perspective that values women and respects the sanctity of creation. Nevertheless, ordinary women from various times and traditions—enslaved women, women from base communities, women of the black church, and others—have related strongly to the god of Exodus. To understand why disenfranchised women recognize this god, ecofeminist readings must attend to power dynamics and economic issues in the text. The plagues are clearly an attack on Egypt's economic base; like the fat and lean cows and ears of grain in the Joseph story (Gen. 41:1-7), cattle and crops were the basis of Egypt's wealth. Crops directly, and cattle through trade, translated into the stored wealth which allowed Egypt to flourish. In Exodus 1:11, where Israel's slave labor builds Pharaoh's supply cities, stored wealth is explicitly linked with exploitation. Thus when YHWH uses elements of creation to attack Egyptian fields and livestock, the biblical authors are attacking the ideology of accumulation. Further, fields and livestock were not singled out for attack; YHWH lays siege to all of Egypt: babies and slaves, houses and water. Thus it is not simply the economic life of Egypt that is rejected but something more pervasive, something that taints every aspect of Egyptian existence.

The plague narratives communicate YHWH's condemnation of an Egypt that worships only itself. God rejects the hubris of empire. For women who carry water, raise children, grow crops, and work in factories, women who are exploited by the wealthy and by empire, the message of the plague narratives is that God, however distant, condemns their oppressors and is on their side. This is sobering news for first-world readers who take part in their oppression.

Egyptian Religion

The portrait of Egyptian cosmology in Exodus serves two functions, neither of which has much to do with the reality of religion in ancient Egypt.

Firstly, Egyptian religion is attacked as an expression of Egypt's political status. The Moses group, in rejecting both the physical and psychic bondage of the Egyptian socio-political and economic system, had also abandoned the religious ideology that legitimated and reinforced that system. In replacing the Egyptian gods, whose son the pharaoh claimed to be, they chose, or claim to have been chosen by Yahweh, the god of the oppressed, a god who stands by the poor and frees those enslaved.[33]

Despite later editing, some of the older traditions in the plague narratives preserve anti-empire sentiments. While the Elohist material is overtly suspicious of kings and centralized power, the pro-monarchy Jahwist material preserves the history in a manner similar to Americans' pride in their "revolutionary" history despite the present status of the United States as an imperial power. To the groups that became Israel, Egypt represented empire with all its attributes: arrogance, accumulation, exploitation, centralization of power, and decadence. Egypt's behavior toward the oppressed was read by Israel as fundamental to Egypt's cosmology. The spiritual life of Egypt was depicted as upholding such values, particularly through the character of the man-god Pharaoh. In short, Egyptian religion was rejected because it was the religion of Egypt.

Egyptian cosmology was further denigrated because it is not YHWH religion. This is particularly so in Priestly material. The forces behind P were concerned with Israel's identity as a religious community, and they explained the Babylonian Exile as the result of unfaithfulness to YHWH. Priestly material features Pharaoh's magicians and Aaron as cultic representatives. The mocking portrayal of the Egyptian religious functionaries, the formulaic reference to idols,[34] and control of the animal representatives of Egyptian deities are all examples of religious polemic. They assert that YHWH is a greater god than Pharaoh and the whole of the Egyptian pantheon, but say nothing about the content of YHWH religion.

The plague traditions denigrate Egyptian religion, yet these traditions evolved in Palestine, not Egypt. Some hallmarks of Egyptian cosmology are acknowledged and symbolically defeated. The sun is extinguished, the life-giving Nile turns to blood, and most importantly, Pharaoh is humiliated. However, evidence for a deeper understanding of the basic precepts of Egyptian religion, such as the cycle of life or the roles of various deities, is scant. Egyptian content sets the scene—this happened in Egypt—rather than conveying religious truths.

For modern ecofeminist readers who do not wish to perpetuate the history of Christian religious intolerance and racism, the biblical portrayal of Egyptian cosmology is problematic. It is a wholesale condemnation of an African religion without knowledge of its content. Ancient Egyptian religion was neither limited to nor chiefly concerned with conquest and accumulation. Further, certain aspects of Egyptian cosmology, the cycle of the year, the sacred qualities of living creatures, lend themselves to respectful dealings with creation, at least as much as aspects of Christianity and Judaism.

Woven through the text, however, is a thread that justice seekers can embrace. The plague narratives can be read as an indictment of *any* religion that does not attend to the reality of the oppressed. Whatever the Egyptians *believed*, they are condemned for what they *do*. For modern readers, the disturbing message is, no matter its precepts, your faith sanctifies domination if slaves made your shirt and you do nothing about it.

MODERN PARALLELS AND APPLICATIONS

Maybe old Egypt was lucky after all
so what if the Nile stank of blood for a week?
year after year our rivers
run excrement, effluent, profit and poison

the Egyptians scratched lice
and slapped at gnats
and when locusts devoured the crops
they netted the critters and
fried 'em for dinner
we're fool enough to poison the bugs
the birds that eat them
and our wheat as well

their cattle died and frogs overran
the land: our cattle overgraze and
we burn down the forests to feed them
we've developed chemicals that eat the sky and kill
all the pretty little amphibians
our frogs are rarer than princes

they had boils and we have AIDS
they had hailstorms but
everyone gets some bad weather

we could bear the blows of heaven and earth
even endure a child's death
bear all evils but the two
that cause most misery;
human greed
and human cruelty.
—Martha Shelley[35]

Can the lessons of Egypt and the application of ecofeminist principles to Exodus help first-world Christians to read our own stories? Let us look at the parallels between the plague narratives and our modern situations.

Where Are the Women?

The greatest lie of the plague narratives is that women are absent. But the inadvertent truth is that in much of the world's decision making, women are invisible.

Consider Tendai, a young girl in the Lowveld, in Zimbabwe. Her day starts at 4 A.M., when, to fetch water, she carries a thirty-litre tin to a borehole about eleven kilometers from her home. She walks barefoot and is home by 9 A.M. She eats a little and proceeds to fetch firewood until midday. She cleans the utensils from the family's morning meal and sits preparing a lunch of sadza for the family. After lunch and the cleaning of the dishes, she wanders in the hot sun until early evening, fetching wild vegetables for supper before making the evening trip for water. Her day ends at 9 P.M., after she has prepared supper and put her younger brothers and sisters to sleep. Tendai is considered unproductive, unoccupied, and economically inactive. According to the international economic system, Tendai does not work and is not part of the labor force.[36]

To legislators and policy makers this young woman is invisible. Since the early 1980s, international communication and cooperation between women on women's issues has increased so that today awareness of different women's struggles around the world is as widespread as it has ever been. Western feminists have become aware of women like Tendai and in some cases she of them. Unfortunately, while this awareness has translated into concerns about gender and development, it does not for the most part address recent changes in the global economy and international division of labor.

In recent years "industrialized" nations have experienced the loss of domestic industry as corporations move jobs to wherever labor is cheapest. Because of their supposed compliance, women are specifically recruited as workers in the so-called free trade zones.[37] Increasing numbers of third-world women are displaced from their traditional agricultural work and forced by poverty to service the reproductive needs of the North.

> These services include: working as domestics and home support workers, providing babies for adoption and the traffic in children, surrogate motherhood, working in the sex-tourist industry, becoming mail-order brides, and working as domestic labor in the global tourist industry.[38]

Most North American consumers do not want to know that the woman who sewed our shirt was locked into an unsafe factory for twelve hours a day. We do not want to know that poor mothers' children are sold for adoption and sex trade with the knowledge and consent of national governments. In the empire where we live, by design and by our own collusion in that design, women are invisible even to one another.

Human-Made Plague

Until his army is destroyed and the Israelites are completely outside his grasp, Pharaoh is stubborn and seemingly impervious to the escalating campaign against him. When the Nile runs with blood, Pharaoh returns unperturbed to his palace where the rabbis say he drank wine.[39] As the assaults mount, his heart remains hard. The land and the people are devastated, but when his courtiers beg Pharaoh to let Israel go he remains obdurate. Even the death of his firstborn child breaks through Pharaoh's obstinacy only temporarily. Although Pharaoh is YHWH's opponent in this campaign of destruction, if he is killed, his death is not recorded. So the land and the people of Egypt are devastated because Israel's god is at war with Egypt's king. This situation is disturbingly similar to the great invisible genocide of the 1990s, the U.S.-backed military violence and economic sanctions against Iraq. The two campaigns resemble one another because they were intended to devastate completely: morally, socially, and economically.

In Egypt, the water turned to blood. In Iraq, sewage treatment systems are nonfunctioning. Lakes of raw sewage lie in city streets and contaminate drinking water, but chlorine to clean the water is banned. In Egypt, insects covered the land and the people. In Iraq, swarms of disease-carrying flies and mosquitoes breed in the open water, but pesticides are illegal. In Egypt, cattle died from disease and hail. In Iraq during the war, cattle were strafed

from planes. Now there is insufficient food or medicine for livestock, and
dairy animals are too malnourished to produce. The Egyptians suffered
skin disease. In Iraq, hospitals and medical suppliers were bombed during
the war. Medicine is unavailable for asthma, diabetes, and heart disease.
Polluted water transmits typhoid, hepatitis, meningitis, and diarrhea.
Many Iraqis show the cancerous effects of radiation from U.S. weapons,
and everywhere are the diseases of malnutrition: kwashiorkor, marasmus,
and stunting. Egypt's crops were destroyed by locusts and hail. In Iraq during the war, irrigation systems were destroyed and even after the cease-fire,
fields were burned and bombed. Seeds, fertilizers, pesticides, herbicides,
and parts for equipment cannot be obtained, so there is not enough food.
Egypt was in darkness for three days. When Iraq was left for months without electrical power, thousands of people died, as did hundreds of thousands of domesticated animals. The campaign against Egypt lasted at most
a period of months; the campaign against Iraq has lasted for nearly a
decade.[40] In Egypt the firstborn of every household was killed. In Iraq it is
the same. People, especially children and the elderly, are dying from treat-
able diseases and starvation. From a population of 20 million, 1.2 to 1.5
million people, at least 500,000 children under five years of age, have died
as a direct cause of sanctions.[41] "There was not a house without someone
dead" (Exod. 12:30).

This is perhaps the most disturbing reading in this book. First of all it is
disturbing because Iraqi children are still dying as I write. It is also disturbing because while the parallels between the civilian populations of
Egypt and Iraq are striking, comparisons between Pharaoh and the straw-
man Hussein sit less easily. The third pair in the allegory—YHWH and the
United States—is even more troubling. Are they vengeful superpowers or
defenders of liberation? From a justice perspective, neither interpretation is
satisfying. In the text, YHWH is the violent destroyer of innocent children.
In the present, the U.S.-backed military and economic campaign against
Iraq is not surprising if one accepts such a violent image of God. A comparison between God and the United States is especially disturbing when
those who support this America-authored genocide are confident that the
United States has a special role to play in God's plan.

Although the parallels between ancient story and modern atrocity are
striking, the differences are striking as well. The exodus is a fundamental
story for Israel, but it is a story. In the long history of pharaonic Egypt there
is no mention of the devastation and emigration detailed in Exodus. The
historical exodus may in fact have been a small clandestine escape which
barely ruffled the surface of Egyptian life. But in story, the convictions of
Israel are conveyed: that God is deeply opposed to oppression and that no
matter how powerful empire is, God is more powerful. The assault on Iraq
is not a story; it is a U.S.-driven, United Nations policy to secure access to
the world's major petroleum reserves, at the cost of the lives of children. In

Exodus, God acts against the Egyptians on behalf of enslaved Israel, as a judgment on empire. In Iraq, the United States acts against the Iraqis to expand and secure empire.

As modern readers of Exodus we can and should assert that God does not orchestrate or approve of the destruction of innocents. But to do so credibly we must oppose, by our actions, the destruction of innocents in the real world by governments and nations who try to act like gods.

The Human–Environment Connection

In the plague narratives, Pharaoh's acts of injustice and oppression against the Israelites have devastating environmental consequences. For the biblical authors this was because the human moral order and the cosmic creational order were fundamentally connected; a breach in one caused a breach in the other. Modern readers do not need to posit a mysterious or cosmological connection between human injustice and environmental destruction in the present to say that the two are linked. The connections are simple, practical, and blatant.

Worldwide, the dominant ideology is one of growth, profit, and consumption. This resource-exploitation model regards everything—animal, vegetable, mineral, and human—in terms of its dollar value. Thus Tendai's work for her family, or oil in the ground on U'Wa indigenous land in Colombia[42] have no value; they are wasted. To this ideology, the world— human and nonhuman—is made up of resources to be turned into profit, and unrealized profit has no value.

The factory farming of poultry in the United States is a single example of how human–human and human–creature relationships are distorted by the resource-exploitation mentality.

> In the broiler business producers aim to grow the biggest bird in the shortest time for the lowest cost. That is business. But in factory-farm systems . . . the lowest cost to the producer is usually the greatest cost to the animals in terms of pain, suffering, and deprivation.[43]

Tens of thousands of chickens live crowded together on factory floors, each in a space smaller than the cover of this book. With a hot knife that cuts through bone, their beaks are burned off to reduce the number of pecking deaths caused by overcrowding. The birds are drugged copiously against the high incidence of avian flu, cancer, and respiratory disease caused by their crowded and unclean living conditions. Drug residues remain in their meat.

Workers are treated little better than the birds.

On September 3 [1991], fire broke out at the Imperial Food Products chicken-processing plant in Hamlet, a small town in south-central North

Carolina. As the flames spread throughout the factory, workers rushed to the exits only to find six of the nine doors shut tight, most padlocked by the owner to prevent employees from stealing his chickens. Trapped in the burning building, twenty-five people died and more than fifty were injured.[44]

Since the Imperial Food plant fire, the situation in the poultry industry in the United States has only worsened.

Amid clouds of ammonia and fecal matter carrying salmonella and other harmful bacteria, workers called "catchers" wade into 100-degree holding pens crowded with angry fowl. Braving sharp beaks and claws, they grasp birds by their feet and hurl them into containers bound on trucks for the processing plant. A catcher generally handles 8,000 birds a day, many of which urinate on him. At the plant, "hangers" fasten the feet of up to 50 birds a minute (more than 20,000 a day) into metal shackles so that the dangling heads may most efficiently be lopped off by the razor-sharp wire just down the line. A typical plant can in one eight hour shift turn 144,000 chickens into packages of ready-to-eat meat, but the human cost even early on in the process is high: rotator-cuff and other repetitive-motion injuries abound among hangers; catchers are prey to cuts, eye infections, and respiratory ailments.[45]

Workers in chicken plants are usually poor, undereducated, and people of color. As more workers refuse these conditions for wages of $6.50 an hour and less, the meat processing industry is working with governments to promote programs that force welfare recipients and coerce desperate internationals to work in chicken and hog factories.[46] Abuse of humans and animals is simply a means to profit.

Poverty is not the only factor in the human–environmental connection. In the United States, the single greatest factor that determines how likely you are to live near dangerous pollutants is race.[47] All nuclear test sites in the continental United States are on Native American land.[48] Communities of color are targeted by multinational corporations as sites for hazardous waste. Dangerous pollutants are forced upon those whom our culture least regards and who are least able to protest. "Children are the most vulnerable, from the underage fruit pickers in the California strawberry fields breathing in methyl bromide, to the kids of Altgeld Gardens in Chicago, who have nowhere to play but toxic waste dumps."[49] In North America disregard for the earth is clearly linked to disregard for people of color.

Meeting labor laws, minimum wages, safety codes, and environmental standards reduces a company's profits. With the increasing globalization of capital and the expansion of free trade zones, mega-corporations can move operations to the most "favorable" site in terms of low wages and few environmental restrictions. Lawrence Summers, chief economist of the World

Bank, argued that it is most *economically efficient* for rich countries to dispose of their toxic wastes in poor countries, because people in these countries have shorter life spans and less earning potential. In reporting this, *The Economist* argued that it is the moral obligation of rich countries to export their pollution because this provides poor countries with economic opportunity.[50]

Under the terms of the North American Free Trade Agreement (NAFTA) and the impending Free Trade Agreement of the Americas (FTAA), corporations can sue countries and provinces if their environmental or labor laws "present an unfair barrier to trade." This bargaining away of national sovereignty pits debt-impoverished countries against one another in a race to the bottom and leads to situations where the shacks of industry workers are clustered around contaminated effluent streams flowing from the factory.

> *I've seen the lands beyond these borders, where the corporations rule,*
> *And they spin their lies, and they globalize and the workingman's*
>   *their tool*
> *And the streams are so polluted that their banks are bleak and bare,*
> *And the babies all are born deformed, and the smog is everywhere.*
>   —Desert Rat[51]

Where resources have particularly high cash value, like timber, fish, or oil, entities of lesser value, like rainforests, indigenous traditions, ocean ecosystems, and the children of Iraq, are destroyed mercilessly. As in the story of the plagues, modern human exploitation is fundamentally connected to environmental destruction.

Sign of the Times

The Hebrew word *oth*, meaning "sign," is used repeatedly to describe the events in Exodus 7-10. What does this mean? How can a swarm of insects or a change in the water be a sign? First of all, the signs indicate that something is drastically wrong. In Exodus, nature is not behaving as it should. More specifically, the signs point to the fate of Egypt. The Nile is filled with blood just as the Reed Sea will be filled with dead Egyptians. Locusts are swept into the Reed Sea in the same way that the army will be destroyed. Can what is obviously a literary device have any relevance for those of us who would read the signs of our own times?

Terence Fretheim calls the plagues in Egypt "ecological signs of historical disaster." They function in a way not unlike certain damaging ecological events do today, portents of unmitigated historical disaster.[52] Fretheim suggests that the ecological crises of our time—global climate change, extinction of species of plants and animals—are like the plagues, a sign, not in a metaphoric way but in terms of simple logical consequence. They point back to the causes of such disasters—deforestation, burning fossil fuels, and consumption—and they point forward to the fate of the whole planet if these excesses go unchecked. "Nothing green was left, no tree, no plant in the field, in all the land . . ." (Exod. 10:15b).

Martha Shelley's poem earlier in this chapter is an eloquent modern reading of the plagues. In it she refers to one of the most widely recognized modern signs of our perilous ecological state. It is the reverse of what happened beside the Nile and, upon consideration, more chilling.

> We've developed chemicals that eat the sky and kill
> All the pretty little amphibians
> Our frogs are rarer than princes.

In the late 1980s biologists from Nova Scotia, Canada, to South India began to report that species of frogs were quietly disappearing all over the world. These delicate creatures have dual habitats and are exposed to water-based, land-based, and air-borne contaminants. Their permeable skin interacts with water, air, and dirt. They lay exposed eggs in the water and their lack of hair or feathers makes them especially vulnerable to changes in ultraviolet radiation. This combination of factors makes frogs and all amphibians sensitive to environmental stresses.[53] Whether their absence is caused by the destruction of habitats, acid rain, global warming, new pathogens, increased ultraviolet radiation, or some combination of these factors, the disappearance of one of the earth's oldest creatures from a diversity of habitats is a sign that something is desperately wrong. Their fate points to our own if nothing changes.

There is a great hope in the plague narratives for those of us living under empire. A sign presupposes a reader. The signs, and the Egyptians who read these signs, indicate that there was the possibility for change in Egypt. For modern Christians living under the imperial rule of corporate culture, global capitalism, and its consequent environmental destruction, there is still possibility for change, as long as there are still signs. We do not need to follow the amphibians into extinction; we can act for true democracy, community, autonomy, and the web of life on the planet.

6

PHARAOH

A Hardened Heart

Sure. You all talk like somebody else made these laws and Pharaoh don't
know nothin about 'em. He makes 'em his own self and he's glad when
we come tell him they hurt. Why that's a whole lot of pleasure to him,
to be making up laws all the time and to have a crowd like us around
hand to pass all his mean ones on. Why, he's got a law about everything
under the sun! Next thing you know he'll be saying cats can't have kit-
tens. He figures that it makes a big man out of him to be passing and
passing laws and rules. He thinks that makes him look more like a king.
Long time ago he done passed all the laws that could do anybody good.
So now he sits up and studies up laws to do hurt and harm, and we're
the only folks in Egypt he got the nerve to put 'em on. He aims to keep
us down so he'll always have somebody to wipe his feet on.

—Zora Neale Hurston[1]

THE PHARAOHS OF EGYPT

The Egyptian word *pharaoh*, is a combination of two words meaning
"great" and "house." The word referred originally to the royal palace and
its court.[2] By the fifteenth century B.C.E. the term began to be used to designate the person of the monarch in the same way that we might use "City
Hall" or the "White House" to refer to the mayor or the president. Although
it is something of an anachronism for rulers prior to the fifteenth century,
in modern usage the word has come to refer to all the monarchs of ancient
Egypt.

Egypt was ruled by kings and occasionally by queens for nearly thirty
centuries.[3] The role of the pharaoh changed as Egypt's political role
changed, but for the most part the pharaoh operated within fairly rigid con-
fines, and the position was not much swayed by the personality of a par-

ticular king. Even the most original rulers brought personal innovation to a very tight model. Artistic renditions of the pharaoh exemplify this rigidity. The king was represented by a stereotyped figure—young, strong, and several times the stature of his subjects and enemies.[4]

The pharaoh served a political and a religious function in Egypt. He was both head of state and semidivine. As a political ruler he carried out economic, diplomatic, and military functions. Religiously he was both the representative of the chief god and the people's intermediary to the gods. A pharaoh's clothing, emblems, and attributes all pointed to the divine realm. The integrity of the pharaoh's physical body represented Egypt's fertility and prosperity. This text from the Middle Kingdom (approximately 2000-1500 B.C.E.) attests to the cosmic qualities Egyptians attributed to their pharaoh.

> His eyes probe every being. . . . He illuminated the Two Lands more than the sun disk. . . . He makes green more than a great inundation. He fills the Two Lands with strength and life. Noses grow cold when he falls into a rage; when he is calmed one breathes the air. He ensures the sustenance of those who follow him. . . . His enemy will be impoverished.[5]

The pharaoh was human yet completely unlike any other human.

The pharaoh of Exodus—or rather the first pharaoh of Exodus, for there are two—employs the Israelites building "supply cities, Pithom and Rameses" (Exod. 1:11). Rameses can be identified with the Egyptian capital city of Pi-Ramesse established by Pharaoh Seti I and completed by and named for his successor Ramses II.[6] Ramses II was known as an ambitious builder, especially in the Nile Delta, which had a significant Semitic population, and he preferred to use conscripted foreign labor for his building projects.[7] For those who would connect the exodus to a particular time period, the reign of Ramses II or those of his predecessor and successor, Seti I and Mernaptha respectively, are very appealing. Biblical and historical scholars have expended much energy on the question of the pharaohs' identities but I will honor the wisdom of the text in this matter and inquire no further. The biblical text names numerous politically insignificant individuals—slaves, mothers, and midwives—but the god-kings of Egypt are unnamed and the father is virtually indistinguishable from the son. The account of the exodus with its nameless pharaohs is a deliberate counter-story to empire's unchallenged self-description.

PHARAOH OF THE PROLOGUE

In Exodus the first pharaoh does not have much of a story. He appears in all of eleven verses.

Now a new king arose over Egypt, who did not know Joseph. He said to his people, "Look, the Israelite people are more numerous and powerful than we. Come, let us deal shrewdly with them, or they will increase and, in the event of war, join our enemies and fight against us and escape from the land." Therefore they set taskmasters over them to oppress them with forced labor. They built supply cities, Pithom and Rameses, for Pharaoh. (Exod. 1:8-11)

The king of Egypt said to the Hebrew midwives, one of whom was named Shiphrah and the other Puah, "When you act as midwives to the Hebrew women, and see them on the birthstool, if it is a boy, kill him; but if it is a girl, she shall live. But the midwives feared God: they did not do as the king of Egypt commanded them, but they let the boys live. So the king of Egypt summoned the midwives and said to them, "Why have you done this, and allowed the boys to live?" (Exod. 1:15-18)

Then Pharaoh commanded all his people, "Every boy that is born to the Hebrews you shall throw into the Nile, but you shall let every girl live." (Exod. 1:22)

Immediately following Pharaoh's genocidal command a group of Israelite and Egyptian women conspire together to save the infant Moses. He is raised in Pharaoh's court; then as an adult Moses kills an Egyptian. At this point Pharaoh reappears.

When Pharaoh heard of it, he sought to kill Moses. (Exod. 2:15)

After a long time the king of Egypt died. (Exod. 2:23a)

Let us look at these eleven verses more closely.

Who Did Not Know Joseph

A ruler great in his newness and new in his greatness had arisen in Egypt.
—Zora Neale Hurston[8]

The first things we learn about this pharaoh are that he is new and he does not know Joseph. To be new is relatively neutral but, according to Nahum Sarna, the choice of the verb "arose" (*qum*) indicates that this is not a simple change of monarchs but the beginning of a whole new era.[9] Zora Neale Hurston's quotation above captures the arrogance and folly of this pharaoh's newness. The new pharaoh does not *know* Joseph. This is the first use of *yada*, "to know," a verb that is thematic in Exodus. The word means much more than to be aware of or acquainted with.

In the biblical conception, knowledge is not essentially or even primarily rooted in the intellect and mental activity. Rather, it is more experiential and is embedded in the emotions, so that it may encompass such qualities as contact, intimacy, concern, relatedness, and mutuality. Conversely, not to know is synonymous with dissociation, indifference, alienation, and estrangement; it culminates in callous disregard to another's humanity.[10]

So, the author of a new era disregards Joseph. What does this mean? Joseph was the great-grandson of Abraham and Sarah; through him Israel was preserved and came into Egypt. Joseph's council resulted in Egypt's weathering a severe famine, and as a ruler Joseph was second in Egypt only to Pharaoh. The biblical portrayal of Joseph is ambiguous, as he rises to power and saves his family by currying favor with a king. During a time of famine he exploits the Egyptians' desperation, buying them, their land, and their livestock for the king, in exchange for food (Gen. 47:13-26). Pharaoh, in not knowing Joseph, dissociates himself from the people who are this story's protagonists but also from a people who have significantly benefited his empire and his personal wealth. Pharaoh's knowing or his refusal to know, lead to his actions. Pharaoh has already disregarded the humanity of Joseph's descendants. To oppress and treat them as a resource is a logical conclusion.

Pharaoh's Wisdom

The narrator makes note of Pharaoh's alienation from Joseph's descendants, "Now a new king arose over Egypt, who did not know Joseph" (Exod. 1:8). Pharaoh substantiates this with a public speech differentiating us (Egyptians) from them (Hebrews).[11] He enjoins his people to deal shrewdly, or as the King James Version has it, *wisely* with the Israelites. But what does Pharaoh's wisdom entail? Is he in fact wise?

Pharaoh is something of a stock character, the ruler who believes himself to be wise but is instead foolish. Pharaoh undertakes a campaign designed to eliminate the very workers he needs for his building projects. He seeks to destroy a population by killing only infant males. He is defeated by a group of ordinary women. His chosen executioners disobey him. He is ignorant of childbirth. He neglects to exclude his own people from his campaign of genocide.[12] His own daughter raises a Hebrew child under his nose. Joseph is not all that Pharaoh does not know; the wise pharaoh is a fool.

Because we know how the story ends and who the hero is, it is easy to see Pharaoh as ludicrous. To some extent this is the function of the narrative; but because the text communicates Pharaoh's foolishness so well, the content of his speech—foreigners are a threat; they should be happy just to have a job; growth is good, and poor people have too many babies—is seldom examined. The fact that such views are held by many good people, Christians among them, is the cause of much suffering today. As in Exodus, the refusal to know the strangers in our midst is often the beginning of violence against them.

Pharaoh's wisdom, which blames and fears the vulnerable, is the wisdom of empire. He was not unintelligent; he believed what many people believe: that the way of life of the privileged and powerful is, in moral and practical terms, the best possible way to live. Pharaoh believed, as many of us do, that the elite have earned and are entitled to a lifestyle that is endangered by the supposed crimes and threats of immigrants, the impoverished, the disabled, and people of color. The content of Pharaoh's polemic calls for evaluation both in his time and in our own.

Pharaoh calls on his people to oppress the Israelites. "He said to his people, 'Look, the Israelite people are more numerous than we. Come, let us deal shrewdly with them, or they will increase and, in the event of war, join our enemies and fight against us and escape from the land'" (Exod. 1:9-10). The form of Pharaoh's invitation to his people offers a clue to its end. The formula, "come let us do *this* or *that* will happen" appears in only one other place in the Pentateuch.[13] In Genesis 11:3-4 settlers propose a construction project using a similar phrase. They begin to build a city with an enormous tower—Babel—to guard against being scattered abroad over the earth. When Babel is destroyed because it is a monument to human arrogance and centralized power, the result is precisely what the people had set out to avoid. "They are scattered abroad on the face of the earth" (Gen. 11:8). The use of the same linguistic formula suggests that Pharaoh's project, too, is doomed to failure.

The consequence that Pharaoh fears, or that he uses to frighten his people, is nothing but an elaborate rationalization for oppression. He bases his campaigns of genocide and forced labor on a shaky tower of four increasingly unlikely possibilities: the Israelites *might* increase further, there *might* be a war, Israel *might* join Egypt's enemies and fight against Egypt, then Israel *might* escape. Nothing suggests such a scenario is likely, yet Pharaoh's fear, indeed his paranoia, sets his nation on a course so counter to justice that it ends only when YHWH has become Pharaoh's enemy and the king's delusion is fulfilled. Israel joins YHWH, fights against Egypt, and escapes the land. It is ironic that the Pharaoh's greatest "wisdom" is predicting his own defeat.

Pharaoh's venomous speechmaking is translated into policy, and the Israelites are forced to build supply cities for Pharaoh. These storage cities, according to Walter Brueggemann, served both a practical and a symbolic function much as contemporary missile systems do today.[14] Practically, they stored food to be used in case of war or, as in the days of Joseph, famine. Symbolically, however, they pointed to the glory, power, and efficiency of Egypt and by extension to the glory, power, and efficiency of Pharaoh. With Israelites maintaining and producing them under forced labor conditions, supply cities, which the Egyptians intended as sustainers of life, became instruments of death.[15] Israel's condemnation of Pharaoh's cities of stored wealth is illustrated in Exodus 16 by YHWH's gift of manna in the wilderness, which cannot even be stored overnight.

While the Egyptians carried out a forced labor campaign against the Israelites, Pharaoh initiated a campaign of genocide.[16] In the final two references to this pharaoh, he is associated again with killing and death. "When Pharaoh heard of it, he sought to kill Moses" (Exod. 2:15). "After a long time the king of Egypt died" (Exod. 2:23a).

His successor is also a tyrant. Many commentators and parts of the text itself do not differentiate between the two pharaohs. Although we will look at this first pharaoh again in the chapters on the midwives and Pharaoh's daughter, here we will follow the lead of history, text, and tradition and make little of the distinction between the two. Bear in mind as we look at the second pharaoh of the exodus, that the qualities of one blend into the other. The story of this first pharaoh is actually a later composition, and thus his personality traits and characteristics reflect the older story, the story that follows.

THE BUILDING BLOCKS OF EMPIRE

In the matter of a few verses Moses, the infant hero of the prologue grows up, kills an Egyptian, flees to Midian, settles, and marries. The death of the first pharaoh, who did not know Joseph, triggers a series of events inside and outside the land of Egypt. In Egypt under the new pharaoh, the people cry out, and God hears and remembers the covenant with their ancestors. In Midian, Moses encounters God and is commissioned to bring the Israelites out of Egypt. Moses and his brother Aaron return to Egypt, prove themselves to the people, and go to Pharaoh with God's message of liberation. Pharaoh responds promptly with an assault on all Israelite workers:

That same day Pharaoh commanded the taskmasters of the people, as well as their supervisors, "You shall no longer give the people straw to make bricks, as before; let them go and gather straw for themselves. But you shall require of them the same quantity of bricks as they have made previously; do not diminish it, for they are lazy; that is why they cry, 'Let us go and offer sacrifice to our God.' Let heavier work be laid on them; then they will labor at it and pay no attention to deceptive words."
So the taskmasters and the supervisors of the people went out and said to the people, "Thus says Pharaoh, 'I will not give you straw. Go and get straw yourselves, wherever you can find it; but your work will not be lessened in the least.'" So the people scattered throughout the land of

Egypt to gather stubble for straw. The taskmasters were urgent saying, "Complete your work, the same daily assignment as when you were given straw." (Exod. 5:6-13)

Although the great monuments and pyramids of Egypt are marvels of cut stone, the structures of everyday life—homes, walls, supply houses—were made from bricks. Wall drawings and papyrus inscriptions indicate that mud-brick making was carried out on a massive scale in the ancient world in much the same fashion as it is in many parts of the world today. Brickworks are located near a water source where water, clay, and straw are worked together in a specific ratio. The mixture is then formed into bricks and dried in the sun on both sides.[17] As in Exodus, in some parts of the world bricks are still made by slaves today. In Pakistan, much of the brick making is carried out by two hundred thousand families of debt slaves.[18]

The practice of assigning quotas for brick makers is well attested. A scroll from the reign of Ramses II records that the daily quotas of two thousand were rarely made, while a modern Egyptian brick maker who is very skillful might produce about three thousand bricks a day.[19] The "shop-floor" power dynamics described in the text, with Egyptian overseers, Hebrew foremen, and finally Hebrew brick makers, correspond to ancient paintings of brick production.

Brick making is hard physical labor; an ancient document, the "Satire on the Trades," describes the conditions of brick makers and builders in Egypt.

He is dirtier than vines or pigs from treading under his mud. His clothes are stiff with clay; his leather belt is going to ruin. Entering into the wind, he is miserable. . . . His sides ache, since he must be outside in a treacherous wind. . . . His arms are destroyed with technical work. . . . What he eats is the bread of his fingers, and he washes himself only once a season. He is simply wretched through and through. . . .[20]

Straw is an essential ingredient in the process, not simply a binder. When the straw decays, acid is produced making the bricks stronger and more flexible. Bricks made without straw shrink, become brittle and crack; so Pharaoh's refusal to supply straw was not trivial. In practical terms, to increase the brick makers' burden by requiring them to provide their own straw, and to do so without reducing their quota, effectively made a difficult task impossible.

Outside of Exodus 5, the word *lebenah*, derived from the word for "white,"[21] is used to indicate bricks in only one other place in the Pentateuch. In Genesis 11:3, the word appears in the story of the city and tower of Babel. Recall that in Exodus 1:9 the first pharaoh was associated with Babel. These two linguistic pointers invite a closer examination of the

Babel story. Babel is a critical episode in a theme that runs through the Bible. From Cain, the first city builder, to the great city of Revelation, cities are regarded with deep suspicion because of their arrogance, concentration of power, and accumulation of wealth. The account of the construction and abandonment of Babel appears in the middle of a list of Noah's male descendants (Gen. 11-12). Noah's heirs are city builders, and the list is essentially a genealogy of empire.[22] The list of cities and nations is interrupted by the story of one city, Babel.

The abrupt start to the story draws attention to its content. The people settle near Shinar and without reason or provocation suddenly say, "'Come let us make bricks and burn them thoroughly,' and they had bricks for stone and bitumen for mortar" (Gen. 11:3).

This verse and the entire passage are filled with wordplay and rhyme that scream, "Pay attention!" My somewhat frivolous translation of v. 3 retains some of the assonance and alliteration; read it aloud for the full effect.

> Come let us brick bricks and burn (them) burning," and they had bricks for rocks and [more] tar for mortar.

The seemingly innocent, "come let us brick bricks," turns quickly to the arrogant, "come let us build a city, and a tower with its top in the heavens, and let us make a name for ourselves" (Gen. 11:4). The city is effectively a world where God is not needed and bricks are literally the building blocks of empire. The people's initiative, "come let us build," is paralleled by YHWH's response, "come let us go down" (Gen. 11:7) and subsequent confusion of the building project. This same pattern echoes in the first pharaoh's call to Egypt: *Come let us deal shrewdly* (Exod. 1:9). Thus by use of language and symbol from the story of the first skyscraper, both pharaohs are confirmed as builders of empire who have set themselves against YHWH.

The short episode of the bricks is Israel's first encounter with the new pharaoh. He is shown to be decisive, deliberate, and shrewd. Hundreds of years ago Jewish scholars recognized the inhumanity of Pharaoh's actions and emphasized it with the following story:

> And he put before them a measure of bricks, according to the number they were to make day by day, and whenever any deficiency was discovered in the measure of their daily bricks, the taskmasters of Pharaoh would go to the women of the children of Israel, and take their infants from them, as many as the number of bricks lacking in the measure, and these babes they put into the building instead of the missing bricks. The taskmasters forced each man of the Israelites to put his own child in the building. The father would place his son in the wall, and cover him over with mortar, all the while weeping, his tears running down upon his child.[23]

In more recent history, liberation theologians brought class analysis to the same passage and characterized it in the following way.

The pharaoh's reaction to the workers' demands follows an oft repeated pattern in history. First, he seeks to disparage the leaders who have attempted to organize the workers. Secondly he uses his control over working conditions to "teach the workers a lesson": teach them that the consequences of seeking relief will be heavier labor. The workers must be brought to see that their lot depends on the good will of the pharaoh, and that his good will is compromised when he is forced to deal with petitions and demands. Thirdly for getting the burdensome tasks done he selects gang leaders from among the workers themselves, thus dividing the people.[24]

But Pharaoh himself acted according to the logic of production. If the Israelites had time to formulate a plan and send representatives to Pharaoh, they must not be working hard enough. In Exodus, the weight of increased labor crushes the people's unity, and they turn against Moses and Aaron. This same scene has been played out over and over again in factories, mines, and fields. But as with any labor struggle that is successful, the workers in Exodus continue their campaign. The conflict over the bricks sets the stage for the plague narratives, where the negotiations between Moses and Pharaoh continue.

Pharaoh of the Plagues

The plagues communicate the triumph of YHWH, Israel's champion, over Pharaoh, the personification of Egypt. The plagues against the land are also a personal attack on Pharaoh, who is identified with the land. Each successive episode increases Pharaoh's humiliation. When the fundamentals of Egyptian life are attacked—water, crops, cattle, and even the bodies of the Egyptians themselves—Pharaoh's empire is paralyzed, politically, economically, and socially. YHWH's victory is complete and decisive. The language of the plagues is pure hyperbole, with the word "all" (*kol*) used more than fifty times:[25] all the water, all the dust, all the land, every plant, every tree, all the Egyptians, not one remaining. Every aspect of Egyptian life is devastated by the power of YHWH.

The plagues do not only relate a struggle between YHWH and Pharaoh the king; they are also a literary assault on the entire Egyptian cosmology, a "judgment of the gods of Egypt" (Exod. 12:12). The portrait of the Egyptian priests is deliberately mocking.[26] The frog, sun, cobra, cow, and the Nile are all deities in the Egyptian pantheon, yet each is distorted or defeated by the superior power of YHWH. The priest's serpents are consumed by Aaron's serpent. Frogs cover the land in grotesque numbers, then die and decay. The sun is darkened; cattle are struck with disease and hail; and the Nile is turned to blood. The reference to blood, which appears even in wood and stone containers (7:19), is also a derogatory reference to Egyptian deities, as the pairing of wood and stone is a formula used to denote idols.[27] The blood, skin disease, and countless corpses render Egypt ritually unclean according to Jewish law. The decay and disease are metaphors for the corruption and decadence of an empire built on slave labor and extraction. The use of curse motifs communicates that Egypt is cursed in Israel's eyes. Through the plagues, Egypt is denigrated in every conceivable way; Pharaoh is defeated both as a king and as a god.

Pharaoh as Vassal

Biblical theologian Walter Brueggemann brings a different perspective to the contest between Pharaoh and YHWH. He asserts that the plague narratives portray Pharoah as a recalcitrant vassal to YHWH.[28] A vassal is a client ruler who owes tribute and obedience to a suzerain or overlord. While a suzerain has many vassals, a vassal may serve only one suzerain. The small nations bordering the Davidic kingdom at its political zenith (Israel of 1000 to 922 B.C.E.) were vassals of Israel, and Israel, through its less illustrious history, was often a client state, so the biblical theme is rooted in political reality. Egypt, however, was a huge and powerful empire, and to describe Egypt as vassal, even metaphorically, would have been a bold claim. According to Brueggemann's analogy, YHWH's actions against Egypt are neither the aggressive tactics of an upstart nor the wanton violence of a tyrant but rather the deliberate actions of sovereign authority commanding, correcting, and finally replacing Pharoah as lord over Israel.

The theme of service is central to the events in Egypt. In the prologue the Israelites served (*abad*) Pharaoh, but in the plague narratives, Moses demands that the people be released to worship (*abad*) YHWH. The verb is the same. Service to YHWH means release from forced labor (service to Pharaoh). According to Brueggemann, Pharaoh and YHWH "are practitioners and embodiments of social policy."[29] Pharaoh represents tyranny, empire, and decadence, while YHWH's rule strives toward liberation.

Comparisons

In the text, what little we know about Pharaoh is communicated through his actions and in contrast to other characters. In one scene the pharaoh of the plagues is contrasted subtly with the daughter of the previous pharaoh. Both encounter Moses while walking by the river. Pharaoh's daughter has compassion, while Pharaoh's heart is hardened. She saves Moses' life, and he threatens it. She encounters Hebrews as humans, he as slaves. And in the final reckoning Pharoah loses a son and his land is devastated, but Pharaoh's daughter gains a son and, according to the Midrash, gains the Promised Land as well.

The parallel between Moses and Pharaoh is extensive and overt.

Although they are pitted against each other, Pharoah and Moses are not unalike. Both are stubborn and unrelenting negotiators. Both are leaders whose people do not obey them unquestioningly. Pharaoh, however, rules alone while Moses is supported by Aaron, Jethro, Miriam, and others. Pharoah rules both the political and religious realm of Egypt; he is the son of a god and divine himself. Moses, on the other hand, is flawed and mortal, requiring a spokesperson and a cultic representative. Pharaoh is rich, Moses is poor. Pharaoh is arrogant, Moses is humble—or so says the text.[30] For the most part Pharaoh is Moses' better in those qualities esteemed by Egypt. Yet Moses bests Pharaoh, either because YHWH is glorified by doing great things with the lowly, or because YHWH genuinely values Moses' seeming liabilities: poverty, powerlessness, outsider status, and lack of social station.

Although in popular film and literary renditions the plague narratives are depicted as a struggle between the two men, Moses and Pharaoh, in the text YHWH is the central player, overshadowing both. In this play, God has all the lines. But as YHWH is described, we come to know Pharaoh. YHWH listens to the cries of the Israelites and responds; Pharaoh hears the same cries and his heart is hardened. YHWH chooses a people and promises to be with them. Pharaoh is isolated and cut off even from his own people. As Zora Neale Hurston says, "Pharaoh was locked up in his own palace and inside himself."[31] YHWH is all-powerful and in control of the situation, while Pharaoh is increasingly out of control. YHWH is invisible yet powerful and Pharaoh is visible but increasingly impotent. YHWH insists on being known; Pharaoh refuses to know YHWH. Ultimately YHWH is victorious and Pharaoh is defeated, but as Brueggemann points out, it is the nature of each one's reign that matters to Israel. YHWH's victory means liberation and Pharaoh's defeat ends slavery.

In the Hebrew Bible beyond Exodus, Pharaoh is a symbol for all the various faults of Egypt and of empire. He is the prototype for foreign rulers who defy YHWH, and his fate a warning for those who would do likewise. In Kings and Chronicles, Solomon "the wise," who centralized Israel's power and built cities, is portrayed as another Pharaoh. In Ezekiel, the oracles against Pharaoh shame him for his arrogance and false authority and promise terrible devastation for Egypt. Samuel's warning on the nature of kings hearkens back to Egypt and Pharaoh's oppression. In Jewish literature, Pharaoh is known as the first of the tyrants.[32]

The Portrait of Pharaoh

By contrast with other characters and through his own actions, Pharaoh is revealed to be greedy, lying, arrogant, usurping, exploitative, and stubborn, not a very redeemable character and not a very well-rounded one. The Bible does not spare a lot of words for character development. As we have observed earlier, the pharaoh of the prologue is virtually indistinguishable from the pharaoh of the plagues. He has no name, no link with a historical time period, and for the most part, no discernible personality traits. He is a stock villain who seeks with all his means to thwart Israel at every turn. What then can such a cardboard cutout offer to our first-world reading?

First of all, Pharaoh is the personification of empire according to a group profoundly exploited by empire. Empire is not very personable, and those blessed by empire are not well liked by those who are not. The story of Pharaoh tells us that it is public deeds that are important; personality and private virtue of the powerful carry little weight with the oppressed. This portrait can help first-world Christians to understand how we are seen by those we exploit, or those whose exploitation benefits us. It is important for people of privilege to know that the distinctions we make and the rationalizations we hold dear are often meaningless to the poor and oppressed. As a Canadian, I was baffled and embarrassed to learn that my careful differentiation, "I come from Canada, I'm not an American," made no difference at all to many of the workers and villagers I met in Latin America. I was still a *gringa*.

Recall that in the midrash on the bricks Pharaoh was a baby-killing monster. This understanding was obviously useful for the rabbis in their context, but I think it is a mistake and potentially dangerous for people of privilege to view Pharaoh this way. To understand Pharaoh as a monster is an interpretation that lets us off the hook, allows us to distance ourselves, and reassures us that we are nothing like him. Just as it is currently popular to portray Nazis as psychotic because it absolves us from examining or resisting modern manifestations of genocide,[33] making Pharaoh a monster excuses us from taking seriously the modern corporate empires that hold us in thrall and others enslaved. For readers of privilege I suggest a more useful interpretation: Pharaoh was operating reasonably and logically from a system that did not value Israelite lives, the logic of empire. The logic of empire says that no impediment, human or environmental, may be allowed to limit growth and expansion. Empire is an ever-increasing, ever-consuming monument to itself.

Modern Pharaohs

Today those few who live in palaces and preside over empires supported by peasants and slaves are mostly white or Japanese men from northern industrialized nations. Michael Eisner, chairman of the Walt Disney Company, receives an annual compensation package of over a hundred million dollars,[34] while teenage girls earn starvation wages in Philippine factories sewing Mickey Mouse pajamas. When Robert Goizueta, chairman and CEO of Coca-Cola Corporation, died in 1997, his eulogist proclaimed, "he was marketing more than a product, he was marketing a way of life."[35] This may be so, but it is a way of life that has devastated the traditional food cultures of countless countries and turns a blind eye to the kidnapping and murder of trade unionists at Coke bottling plants in Colombia.[36]

In 1998 the assets of the three richest men in the world totaled more than the combined GNP of the world's least developed countries and their six hundred million people.[37] These are our modern-day pharaohs. The super-rich receive hundreds of times the income of those who are merely rich: and they are completely insulated from the daily realities of those whose lives they control. They do not owe loyalty to any government or nation. They have common interests only with one another. While Egypt's pharaohs ruled North Africa, today's pharaohs carve up the world to share among themselves. No slave leader could gain access to *these* god-kings.

Pharaoh's Heart

We will return now to the Pharaoh of the plagues. From the burning bush to the Reed Sea there are nineteen references to this pharaoh's heart. A recurring change in Pharaoh's heart triggers cycle after cycle of disaster and negotiation. In half of the incidents, YHWH is the causal agent: "the LORD hardened Pharaoh's heart." Because of Christianity's emphasis on individual sin and repentance, Pharaoh's heart has become a biblical springboard for discussions of theodicy (God's use of evil for good), and human sin. Did God cause Pharaoh to sin? Some commentators have answered this question by suggesting that responsibility shifts from Pharaoh to YHWH. They say that Pharaoh began by hardening his own heart; in time he could not do otherwise and by the time God hardened his heart it was already inevitable. This explanation attributes agency to Pharaoh in those passages in passive voice, "Pharaoh's heart was hardened." Other readers see the hand of God in every passage and grant Pharaoh no agency at all.

What these interpretations reflect is the tension between different sources. The Bible does not present a single clear position on human freedom and divine control. In J material, God is an entity who demands to be known. The signs and wonders are designed so that Pharaoh and Israel may know YHWH. But as each sign is removed, Pharaoh deliberately chooses not to see God; he hardens his own heart. In P material, YHWH hardens Pharaoh's heart prior to each plague rendering him insensible to it. Thus the plagues are multiplied and YHWH's eventual victory is all the more glorious. The god of these passages is distant but very much in control. So to the question, Did God cause Pharaoh to sin?, the Priestly answer is yes. The J and P perspectives overlap and intertwine in the text as it stands. The Priestly perspective dominates because theirs was the later edition.

The problem of a hard heart, which appears nowhere else in the Pentateuch,[38] is further obscured by issues in translation. Biblical Hebrew is an embodied language; emotions and ideas are expressed in bodily metaphors that are not always translated into English. Consider the following examples.

Exodus 5:21   For making us loathsome to Pharaoh (Tanakh)
              For having made our smell reek in the eyes of Pharaoh
              (Fox)[39]

Exodus 6:12   How should Pharaoh heed me,
              a man of impeded speech? (Tanakh)
              How will Pharaoh hearken to me?
              I am of foreskinned lips (Fox)

Exodus 14:8   the Israelites were departing defiantly, boldly (Tanakh)
              the children of Israel were going out with hand
              upraised (Fox)

Exodus 20:3   You shall have no other gods before me (NRSV)
              You shall have no other gods besides Me (Tanakh)[40]
              You are not to have any other gods on my face (Fox)

The decision whether to translate a metaphor literally or to paraphrase involves trading off different kinds of depth and clarity.

"I will bring you into the land which I lifted up my hand to give to Abraham" (Fox). "I will bring you into the land which I swore to give Abraham" (Tanakh). Both of the above translations for Exodus 6:8 are reasonable. The first emphasizes the physicality of the divine—YHWH has a hand—but downplays or assumes knowledge of the legal and covenental significance of raising one's hand. The second translation accurately represents the meaning of the action, but eliminates its earthly physicality; YHWH loses a hand.

In the case of Pharaoh's heart, the metaphor is most often translated literally into English, only occasionally do translators refer to "Pharaoh's resolve." Indeed in English we have a bias toward translating this metaphor literally because the heart is a symbolic organ in our language and culture as well. When the changes to Pharaoh's heart occur, we observe that it becomes insensible to the workings of God, but we interpret this as an affirmation of what we already know about Pharaoh as oppressor: he was cruel and unmoved by Israel's suffering.

In English the heart is an organ with many associations; hearts sing, bleed, break, weep, dance. They can be warm, cold, soft, hard, empty, full, troubled, easy. In the Bible, the Hebrew noun *leb*, which means heart, can also be translated as: "seat of vitality, inner self, mind, character, disposition, loyalty, concern, determination, courage, morale, intention, purpose, attention, consideration, understanding, self, interior, middle, life, or person."[41]

In English, the heart is the seat of compassion, love, and affection, a role that Hebrew reserves for the womb, kidneys, or bowels. In Hebrew, the heart is the seat of courage, resolve, and intention, more like guts or mind in English. The assumption that a hard heart means cruelty is therefore an artifact of language.[42] In English a hard heart is cruel; Pharaoh has a hard heart and we already know Pharaoh to be cruel, so readers of English mistakenly assume cruelty to be the meaning of the Hebrew metaphor. This illustrates what a delicate and complex process translation is. The expression "lost in translation" does not apply here so much as the reverse; in translation, something is added. This linguistic bias affects how the rest of the metaphor is translated as well.

There are two verbs to which Pharaoh's heart is the object, *kabed* and *chazaq*; for the most part, J material favors *kabed* and P/E *chazaq*. The verbs are synonyms, subtly different, but close enough that most Christian translators feel comfortable rendering both as "hardened." The Tanakh, the Jewish Bible, does not use the word hardened at all; *chazaq* is translated as stiffened, and the verb *kabed* and the noun *leb* are incorporated into a paraphrase, "became stubborn."[43] In general, translations of *kabed* emphasize stubbornness, but translations of *chazaq* emphasize strengthening, on the whole a positive action. In English a strong heart is very different from a hard heart. Pharaoh becomes less a stock villain, and perhaps easier for first-world readers to relate to, when what appears to be senseless cruelty is understood as the distortion of an essentially good or neutral trait. This is important for our first-world, Egypt-identified reading. Under pressure, Pharaoh does not increase in cruelty; he strengthens his commitment to the values of his culture and class. First-world Christians have little in common with a genocidal tyrant, but much to learn from a threatened man deeply entrenched in a death-dealing ideology and way of life.

FIRST-WORLD HEARTS

Few of us have reason to identify with the absolute power that Pharaoh wields. Nevertheless, we can use the theme of Pharaoh's strengthened heart to explore how even the most ordinary of us get stuck in first-world privilege and how that keeps us insensible to the wonders of creation and the urgings of God's prophets. What are the values of *our* culture and class that prevent us from doing justice? What is it that keeps our first-world hearts from functioning as they should?

Rather than rehashing a familiar metaphor by talking about hearts and hardening, let us look at other possible translations and paraphrases. Remember the various translations for heart (*leb*): "seat of vitality, inner self, mind, character, disposition, loyalty, concern, determination, courage, morale, intention, purpose, attention, consideration, understanding, self, interior, middle, life, person." The most frequent translations for the verb *chazaq* are: "be strong, become strong, strengthen, be firm, be severe, be hard, support." The most frequent translations for the verb *kabed* are: "weigh heavily, be honored, honor, be heavy, be dull, harden, increase."[44]

Using these translations, there are many possible and enlightening paraphrases for what happened to Pharaoh's heart. Pharaoh dulled his mind. He rigidified his understanding. I will make him stubborn. He honored his inner self. Pharaoh's character was strengthened. He made his heart heavy. YHWH increased his courage. Pharaoh firmed his loyalty. His resolve grew strong. YHWH supported his determination. I will use four of these paraphrases as starting points for exploring first-world dysfunction.

First-World Despair

And Pharaoh made heavy his heart.

We do not know anything about the state of Pharaoh's mind, we are twenty-some hundred years from the texts' final editors, who were themselves six hundred years from the events they recorded. The ancient world was far more concerned with spiritual than psychological realities. Mental health is a recent and culturally specific preoccupation. However, the notion that Pharaoh's heavy heart and dull disposition lead to his failure to act for justice and to his eventual downfall, rings true. In the United States, one in ten adults is diagnosed with depression.[45]

> The people of the United States on the whole are not a joyful people. We are not spiritually at peace. We are a troubled, turbulent people, breeding addiction, abuse and poverty among ourselves . . . there is little real joy these days in the United States and a great deal of suffering and shame.[46]

In Canada, northern Europe, and Australia the situation is much the same. When we consider the globalization of poverty, the rate of environmental devastation, and the increasing precariousness of the lives of all but the mega-rich and their retainers, that is not surprising. Depression is perhaps the most healthy reaction to the state of the planet.

For many people of privilege, however, this necessary and human grieving turns into despair, and that is where perceptions become distorted. People with access to telephones, photocopiers, the Internet, automobiles, frequent-flier miles, video cameras, and more habitually perceive themselves as unable to effect change.[47]

> I'm only one person, what can I do?
> The problems are so huge it depresses me to think about them.
> You can't fight city hall.
> Who am I to impose my version of reality.

It makes me sad but I can't do anything about it.

Me? I'm just a middle-aged woman: a housewife and mother. I'm a nobody.[48]

Rabbi Michael Lerner describes this social and spiritual pathology as *surplus powerlessness*.[49]

Rather than being galvanized to action by our sadness, we take a kind of voluptuous pleasure in our despair, reveling in the comfort of our own discomfort. Or else we medicate ourselves against it and in so doing become both accomplices and victims of the voracious mental health industry where drug companies control safety testing and hospitals prescribe medication to manage more clients with fewer staff, all in the name of greater profit from suffering. This does not mean you should not take medicine if you are sick, but if all of us are sick and we pay the same people for medicine, it is time to ask some questions.

In our despair, we perceive not only that we are unable to act, but that we are excused from acting: "I'm already depressed, I can't possibly deal with some horrible justice issue on top of that." Any action that would affirm our own capacity for change and claim some of our own authority becomes a chore or a punishment. Unable to act, neither do we respond to the demands of those who do act. God's prophets—unwashed tree-sitters, angry young black men, illegal aliens, transgender warriors, domestic political prisoners, and all their sisters and brothers—come to us like Moses came to Pharaoh. Like Moses they seem to us wild, arrogant, and irrelevant; they don't say please and refuse to follow proper channels. We do not know them or their gods, and through the haze of our despair they are easy to disregard.

Every increase in the weight of Pharaoh's heart brought him closer to death. For the very vulnerable, the impoverished, the homeless, the poor of the third and fourth worlds,[50] the connection between despair and death is swift and clear. But the affluent are cushioned from this as from every reality. The deaths that result from our despair and consequent inaction are either slow, or removed from us. A dead lake still looks pretty, an extinct species is merely absent, and it is not *our* children who are shot in the streets. So we sink deeper into despair.

German theologian Dorothee Sölle says that despair is a luxury we cannot afford.[51] It seems clear that we cannot afford despair, but from our disposable diapers to our recreational vehicles, most middle-income North Americans have lived all our lives beyond our means in terms of what the earth will bear. We know no other way to live. This connection between the state of our hearts and the state of the environment is highlighted in a different way by feminist theologian Rosemary Radford Ruether. Ruether points to a deep wounding of our spirits. She contends that human creativity is diminished significantly by our impoverishment in terms of interactions with other species. Engaging with creation is a spiritual act, but for most of us our contact with nonhuman life consists mainly of the purchase and consumption of factory farmed, chemically and genetically altered, hyper-processed plants and animals. Most North Americans recognize one thousand corporate logos and fewer than ten species of plants.[52] We are becoming as isolated as Pharaoh behind his palace walls. The less contact we have with other forms of life, Ruether says, the less able we are to see, think, and use our imaginations.[53] The less able we are to act.

Dumbing Down

Pharaoh dulled his mind, he hardened his understanding.

The second Pharaoh's deliberate refusal to know YHWH, and his predecessor's denial of Joseph, have modern parallels.

> We First World Christians . . . see and hear more information about more things than any people in history, we are the most educated, economically powerful, and socially mobile people in the world, yet most of us experience a profound sense of confusion and paralysis when it comes to how power is distributed in the real world. This is the most crucial contradiction of imperial culture. The more US hegemony is unrestrained, the more citizens feel impotent to change the world. Instead of staying awake to structures of racism at home or displays of militarism abroad, our eyes grow heavy, sedated by the mediated reality of the Dream Factories. Our credulity nurtures a willful ignorance of the complexities of modern capitalism, a benumbed apathy, a preoccupation with the trivial and a fascination with spectacle. This vicious spiral of dependence, delusion, and denial has led to near-complete loss of vision: We see the world neither the way it is nor the way it could be.[54]

Intelligent people with a wealth of resources believe that issues such as global economics are beyond our capacity to understand, have sound-bite attention spans, and are increasingly disinclined to critique or question the constructed nature of the "information" we receive through the corporate-owned media.

This final point was driven painfully home for me in November of 1999. After the Seattle protests against the World Trade Organization, I returned to my community, only forty miles from Seattle, to describe my fairly typical experiences: dance, cultural work, remarkably diverse participation, peaceful protest, good analysis, creative negotiations, angry encounters with WTO delegates, standoffs with police in riot gear, some violence (overwhelmingly on the part of the police), and rock solid jail solidarity. Good, intelligent people who know and trust me were convinced that the televised riot they had seen in their living rooms was the sum total of what had happened in Seattle. They would not or could not believe my personal account.

A phenomenal amount of first-world mental energy is spent on not thinking. One of the most disturbing examples of our dumbing down is the way that we talk about racism in North America. Racism is the systematic disadvantaging of people of color in all measures of what constitutes the good life—housing, income, safety, respect, leisure, meaningful work, and so on. In public at least, the vast majority of people will say that racism is a bad thing and that they are opposed to it. School systems, corporations, and governments produce and promote festivals, posters, and campaigns focused on tolerance. Almost without exception they portray racism as personal prejudice based on skin color, independent of any political power or economic structure. Intolerance is the problem; tolerance, then, is the solution. This model completely fails to address the historical roots of racism in North America: conquest, slavery, colonialism, immigration, and nationalism. Neither does it address current economic and social inequities. Nearly one-third of all African Americans and Latin Americans in the United States live below the poverty line.[55] Discussion of racism, and in fact all ethical discourse, is kept at an individual level so that the moral imperative is to be tolerant, or nice, not to seek societal change.

The way that we persist in racism by denying its existence is perhaps the most blatant and pervasive example of our dulled attention, but we are equally fatuous in dealing with issues of class, disability, gender, sexuality, and so on. In Exodus, one-third of the time Pharaoh's heart is simply hardened, not through divine intervention, nor through his own action. "Pharaoh's heart was hardened." This passive-voice hardening is an apt metaphor for the benumbed first-world refusal to acknowledge our participation in the structures of injustice like racism, ableism, classism, and homophobia. We perceive them as things that "just happen." "That's just the way things are, you can't change it."

Privatized Spirituality

Pharaoh honored his inner self, he strengthened his spirit.

Pharaoh was so full of a sense of his own rightness that there was no room for self-doubt. When *kabed* is translated as "to bring honor," it suggests that Pharaoh was glorifying and enriching some part of himself. When first-world people "honor our inner selves" with a rich interior life of prayer and spirituality, our personal relationship with the divine can actually keep us from the work of justice.

Recently in North America there has been a resurgence of interest in all things "spiritual." This hunger is born of the alienation and destruction of communities imposed by corporate culture. But capitalism swiftly co-opted spiritualists' legitimate critique of materialism and sold it back to them and their followers in the form of overpriced feathers, crystals, meditation tapes, magic, yoga classes, and incense, most of which are fast-food versions of other cultures' most sacred wisdom.

As North Americans we are also vulnerable to the Western cult of the individual and the myth of the meritocracy. From this perspective, prayer, knowledge of the divine, and personal insight can and must be individual achievements. We honor our inner selves. Privatistic piety is shaped by economic individualism so that somehow personal salvation and worship can seem completely separate from the corporations we work for, the plight of the homeless, or the destruction of forests and indigenous people.

This kind of spiritual triumphalism, in which prayer is divorced from action, is not limited to Christians nor even to the overtly "religious," but Christianity is more prone than some religions because we have come to emphasize belief over identity or practice. This is particularly ironic in light of the fact that many of Christianity's central texts—the Prophets, the Gospels, Revelation, as well as Exodus—are profoundly political, economic, and social in nature. Our scriptures demand action, yet most liberal Christians are politically and socially indistinguishable from their non-Christian neighbors. Indeed, in the United States and Canada, most Christians whose faith does impact their politics, promote a right-wing agenda profoundly at odds with the radically inclusive, morally loose, anti-empire texts they claim to follow. This similarity to liberal Jews, atheists, and others can offer a certain satisfaction to liberal Christians: we have more in common with them than with the fundamentalist or literalist members of our respective traditions. But when being indistinguishable from our neighbors means that all of us are cutting a deal with empire and exploitation by ignoring the justice-making aspects of our traditions, then sameness is neither good nor even benign.

This false separation of spiritual and political is maintained in Christianity by reducing our history's and scriptures' systemic and pervasive demands for justice to the practice of charity. Charity is the opposite of justice; it diminishes the oppressed by defining them as passive recipients and honors the already privileged, describing them as generous and benevolent. Indeed, charity without concrete action to change the conditions that make it necessary is nothing but the exercise and maintenance of control.

A more secular example of spirituality that substitutes for any kind of praxis is the phenomenon of "issue entertainment." Hundreds of thousands of us pay to see lavish spectacles of human suffering like *Angels in America* or *Schindler's List*. With our ticket price each one receives the right to leave the theater feeling like a "better" person. We have neither lived the reality nor acted to change it, but somehow the thought, "I'm doing something about the issue, I saw the movie," doesn't sound as ludicrous as it should. Vicarious feeling substitutes for real-world action.

One evening on Granville Street in Vancouver I watched people leaving the theater. The performance was *Rent*, a musical about the difficulty of making ends meet. Affluent theater-goers streamed out into the night past the upturned palms and empty baseball caps of homeless street kids. For the price of a pair of tickets a kid could have spent a month in one of the residential hotels across the street.

People are hungry for meaningful spiritual engagement, and spiritual practice is important and necessary. I have watched committed activists burn out, burn up, and go home because they do not have a spiritual base or they do not know how to pray. Movements for social change have been incredibly harmed by leaders who have no way to deal with the damage they have experienced and so reproduce it. As one often guilty of forgetting contemplation for action, I call activists to reclaim prayer with me, but I think that ours is the more uncommon failing. When a rich interior life excludes or substitutes for a rich political life, when liberation is a personal phenomenon and "political" is a dismissal, then this is the religion of legitimation. We honor ourselves like Pharaoh, and it keeps us from knowing God.

Traditional Values

Pharaoh's resolve was strengthened, he firmed his loyalty.

As YHWH's immanent victory and Pharaoh's eventual defeat become increasingly evident, Pharaoh digs in and becomes ever more obstinate. He strengthens his commitment to the old order. As in Exodus, the lifestyles of the affluent and indeed all of us are threatened by the deteriorating state of the planet. One response has been a shift to the right, a return to so-called traditional values in many areas of North American life: economics, sexual morality, education, and so on.

For those who most resemble Pharaoh in terms of wealth and power, the return to "traditional values" has global implications. The influence of the super-rich in North America does not stop at national borders. For these modern-day pharaohs, strengthening their resolve or hardening their hearts takes the form of neo-liberal economics or savage capitalism. This perversion of the liberal economics envisioned by Adam Smith removed all checks and balances; the competition of the free market is replaced with monopoly capitalism in the form of mega-corporations that have no longer to answer even to nations. Through the for-profit international lending institutions of the World Bank and the International Monetary Fund, wealthy individuals and corporations imposed structural adjustment programs on indebted nations. Each structural adjustment package called for sweeping economic policy reforms intended to channel more of the adjusted country's resources and productive activity toward repayment of debt, to privatize public assets and services, and to open further national economies to the global economy. Restrictions and tariffs on both imports and exports were reduced, and subsidies were offered to attract foreign investors.[56] The effect of these changes is to override local government authority and make any form of economic organization other than corporate capitalism illegal. It is one thing to believe your system is better, but to outlaw any alternatives is quite another.

And Pharaoh summoned wise men and sorcerers (Exod. 7:11). Like Pharaoh, the super-rich consult wise men and sorcerers. Milton Freedman and Alan Greenspan are oracles of globalization. Paid brains in high-powered think tanks like the Heritage Foundation are the authors of soulless policies that translate into misery for the already struggling. With a terrible arrogance they assume that the interests of white male business can determine and implement the wants and needs of the diversity of the world's nations and peoples.

Those of us who are not of Pharaoh's status find ourselves in some middle level of the Egyptian power structure. "It is pretty clear where we fit in the exodus story is among the functionaries in Pharaoh's court rather than among the workers in the slave labor camps."[57]

For us, hardening of our hearts manifests itself in a simplification and idealization of the past. Every sound bite for decency and old-fashioned values is newspeak for crushing those who already cry out. Cleaning up the streets means open season on the homeless; getting tough on crime criminalizes youth of color; back to basics in education spells gross funding cuts, especially to kids with disabilities; family values promote hate crimes, book burning, and the alarming suicide rate of queer youth; welfare reform is nothing but punishment for poverty.

In the Catholic Worker house where I live, I bore witness recently to one of the bitter ironies of this traditionalist backlash. I heard a homeless grandmother argue vehemently that "the United States may have its problems but it is still the best country in the world to live in. In other countries their governments tell them what to do." This woman has been living on the streets and in inadequate shelters for a period of years, and every day her country tells her what to do: shut-up, go away, and disappear.

A Story to Conclude

In the way of most diseases, the problems with our first-world hearts are due to either underfunctioning or overfunctioning. The underfunctioning heart fails to perform as it should: the despairing heart fails to hope; the dumbed down heart fails to think. On the other hand, the overfunctioning heart persists in a single activity in an exaggerated manner to the neglect of all else. Privatized spirituality substitutes for political engagement, and those who have strengthened their loyalty to traditional values consider it a weakness to acknowledge criticism. Each of these patterns reinforces another. Despair at the state of the world and an exaggerated sense of powerlessness cause us to retreat into willful ignorance about the workings of the world in which we live. Both neo-liberalism and apolitical spirituality depend on this deliberate refusal to see and know the world around us. Then we use individualistic piety and aggressive faith in the salvific power of old ideas—biblical literalism, capitalism, family values—as an antidote to our despair, filling up our emptiness with imagined glory. And so we first-world Christians are caught swinging back and forth between grandiosity and despair,[58] becoming more and more entrenched in patterns that harm ourselves and others.

But the cycle can be broken. We will end this chapter with a counter-story to Pharaoh's heart—a story of first-world Christians who came together and defied each of the four manifestations of heart trouble that plague us. They were hopeful, thinking, active, and looked clearly at past and present.

The year 1999/2000 saw new hope in North American activism. People all over the continent were galvanized by a series of giant protests, in the United States and around the world, aimed at interfering with and drawing attention to structures of global capitalism: the World Bank, the International Monetary Fund, and the World Trade Organization. Faith-based activists were among the thousands bringing an adamantly this-world spirituality of action to the streets. For months beforehand we schooled ourselves and others in nonviolent direct action, jail solidarity, legal issues, radical puppetry, street medicine, consensus decision making, and the meaning and elaborate workings of the structures we opposed. On the days of action, blocking streets, staring down tear gas, singing in jail, and kneeling before buses, we proved ourselves powerful and effective beyond our dreams.

7

VIOLENCE, DESTRUCTION, HATRED
AND JUDGMENT

*Savageness belongs to the core claims of YHWH. Violence belongs to
the very fabric of this faith.*

—Walter Brueggemann[1]

At midnight the LORD struck down all the firstborn in the land of Egypt,
from the firstborn of Pharaoh who sat on his throne to the firstborn of
the prisoner who was in the dungeon, and all the firstborn of the livestock. Pharaoh arose in the night, he and all his officials and all the
Egyptians; and there was a loud cry in Egypt, for there was not a house
without someone dead. (Exod. 12:29-30)

Then the LORD said to Moses, "Stretch out your hand over the sea, so
that the water may come back upon the Egyptians, upon their chariots
and chariot drivers. So Moses stretched out his hand over the sea, and
at dawn the sea returned to its normal depth. As the Egyptians fled
before it, the LORD tossed the Egyptians into the sea. The waters
returned and covered the chariots and the chariot drivers, the entire
army of Pharaoh that had followed them into the sea; not one of them
remained. But the Israelites walked on dry ground through the sea, the
waters forming a wall for them on their right and on their left.

   Thus the LORD saved Israel that day from the Egyptians; and Israel
saw the Egyptians dead on the seashore. Israel saw the great work that
the LORD did against the Egyptians. So the people feared the LORD and
believed in the LORD and in his servant Moses. (Exod. 14:26-31)

VIOLENCE IN EXODUS

Exodus is a story fraught with violence: it begins in genocide and slavery and ends in conquest. The fulfillment of God's promise to Abraham and
Sarah in Genesis does not bring about peace for their descendants, who
number as the stars. The exodus begins with the institutionalized violence

128

of the first pharaoh's military regime and his escalating campaign of repression, murder, and genocide. Moses is born in violence. Israel is born in violence. Egypt is a violent setting, and birth is a pain-filled metaphor.

Pharaoh and YHWH are the great perpetrators of violence. Two nations are assaulted in a battle between these gods and the ideologies they represent. The Egyptians are pummeled by YHWH's plagues. The Israelites face Pharaoh's violence at every level of their existence: a public hate campaign, exploitation, genocide, forced labor, and production quotas that make even subsistence impossible. Despite the later addition of the story of infants drowned in the Nile (Exod. 1:15-2:10), the enduring image of Pharaoh's doomed commitment to violence is his headlong pursuit of Israel to the sea.

> When the king of Egypt was told that the people had fled, the minds of Pharaoh and his officials were changed toward the people, and they said, "What have we done, letting Israel leave our service?" So he had his chariot made ready, and took his army with him; he took six hundred picked chariots and all the other chariots of Egypt with officers over all of them. The LORD hardened the heart of Pharaoh king of Egypt and he pursued the Israelites, who were going out boldly. The Egyptians pursued them, all Pharaoh's horses and chariots, his chariot drivers and his army; they overtook them camped by the sea, by Pi-hahiroth, in front of Baal-zephon. (Exod. 14:5-9)

This translation of Exodus 14:6, "he had his chariot made ready, and took his army with him," does not reflect the actual Hebrew, which says (asar) he hitched, implying that Pharaoh's haste in pursuing Israel was such that he himself attended to the task of preparing his chariot.[2] Pharaoh threw himself and his whole army into the violent pursuit of the escaping slaves. The phrase "every horse" appears twelve times in chapters 14 and 15, "every chariot" fourteen times.

CHARIOTS, A SYMBOL OF EMPIRE AND CONQUEST

Chariots are light, two-wheeled vehicles drawn by horses. The earliest extant Egyptian chariots date from the Eighteenth Dynasty (sixteenth to thirteenth century B.C.E.), and by that time the design was quite sophisticated. Egyptian depictions show chariots used for battle, hunting, transportation, and on state occasions. In the Bible, chariots are associated with war and power.

As a military vehicle the chariot was usually drawn by two horses and carried either two or three persons: a driver, a warrior, and sometimes a shield bearer.[3] In battle, chariots provided a fast, mobile platform and were used most effectively in flanking maneuvers on relatively flat land. During the conquest and infiltration of Canaan, Israel fought against chariot forces; but because they were of no use in the rough terrain of the highlands, tribal Israel did not use chariots. Not until Israel had a standing army under King David (eleventh century B.C.E.) were chariots a feature of Israelite warfare.

Chariot warfare was a military innovation that required skilled professional warriors, not conscripted soldiers with a day job to return to. Charioteers were an elite force and had considerable prestige. This relates to the second function of chariots; chariots were a symbol of power, rank, and honor. Nonfighting chariots were lavishly decorated and were preceded by runners. As a sign of his power in Egypt, the pharaoh in Genesis honored Joseph by giving him his second chariot (Gen. 41:43). In Egyptian art the pharaoh is frequently shown in a chariot; one depiction of Ramses III shows him as a mighty warrior, calm and majestic, doing battle alone in a chariot, reins tied to his waist, dominating the scene.[4] In courtly settings the chariot communicated the monarch's power and served to depict him on a higher level than his subjects; indeed he was only shown on physically equal footing with the gods.[5]

In the Bible, chariots appear as symbols of both military might and imperial power. Tribal Israel viewed chariots negatively, as signs of the oppressive power of the Canaanite city-states: "And the LORD said to Joshua, 'Do not be afraid of them, for tomorrow at this time I will hand over all of them, slain, to Israel; you shall hamstring their horses, and burn their chariots with fire'" (Josh. 11:6). But by the time of the early monarchy, chariots were portrayed positively as a sign of Israel's own military power and economic prosperity.

> Solomon had four thousand stalls for horses and chariots, and twelve thousand horses, which he stationed in the chariot cities and with the king in Jerusalem. He ruled over all the kings from the Euphrates to the land of the Philistines, and to the border of Egypt. The king made silver as common in Jerusalem as stone, and cedar as plentiful as the sycamore of the Shephelah. Horses were imported for Solomon from Egypt and from all lands. (2 Chron. 9:25-28)[6]

These contrasting portrayals reflect Israel's own ambivalence toward military power and empire.

YHWH Is a Man of War

> YHWH is a man of war
> YHWH is his name. (Exod. 15:3, Fox)[7]

The notion of God as dominating Other finds quintessential expression in the image of the holy warrior who punishes the wicked with destruction and death.[8]

Chariots in the Bible are associated with worldly power but also with the might and power of YHWH. Perhaps the most violent character in Exodus is God. As William Propp has observed, "in most of the Hebrew Bible God plays the role later Judaism reserves for Satan."[9] YHWH subjects Egypt to an increasingly devastating onslaught culminating in the death of all firstborn, drowns the entire Egyptian army in the sea, then orders a campaign of slaughter and conquest in Canaan. The God who hears the cries of the suffering children of Israel responds by killing the children of Egypt for the sins of their parents. This God is by turns distant, compassionate, volatile, accessible, relentless, cruel, liberating, and exacting. As Terence Fretheim points out, "Israel does not offer a finished portrayal of God."[10]

The god we encounter in scripture is a composite portrait, bearing elements of other African and Near Eastern deities. Over time, as YHWH became *the* God and not simply a god, qualities of other deities, even contradictory qualities, were selectively added to Israelite innovations. YHWH exhibits attributes of the indigenous Canaanite deities Baal, the storm god and warrior, and Ashera, a mother goddess associated with high places and the tree of life.[11] Yet some strands of the Bible forbid the worship of these same deities and attribute Israel's misfortunes to such worship.

> Then the Israelites did what was evil in the sight of the LORD and worshiped the Baals; and they abandoned the LORD, the God of their ancestors, who had brought them out of the land of Egypt; they followed other gods, from among the gods of the peoples who were all around them, and bowed down to them; and they provoked the LORD to anger. They abandoned the LORD, and worshiped Baal and the Astartes. So the anger of the LORD was kindled against Israel, and he gave them over to plunderers who plundered them, and he sold them into the power of their enemies all around, so that they could no longer withstand their enemies. (Judg. 2:11-14)

"Within monotheistic Yahwism the figure of Yahweh absorbed some of the features of other deities without acceptance of their separate reality."[12]

One aspect of YHWH's multifaceted nature is that of a tribal warrior god or divine warrior king: a god who goes to war for one people and whose presence is evidenced by thunder, earthquakes, and a trembling of creation. "One of the central Old Testament images for the nature and activity of God is that of divine warrior."[13] YHWH *tsebaoth* is one of the divine names. In the NRSV it is translated "LORD of hosts," and whether these hosts are heavenly or earthly, the name means YHWH of armies. As a warrior, YHWH is associated with the tools of war, including chariots.

> With mighty chariotry, twice ten thousand,
>   thousands upon thousands,
>   the LORD came from Sinai into the holy place.

> You ascended the high mount,
>   leading captives in your train
>   and receiving gifts from people,
>   even from those who rebel against the LORD God's
>   abiding there. (Ps. 68:17-18)

Another and perhaps the best known biblical association of God with chariots appears in 2 Kings, when a fiery chariot appears and carries the prophet Elijah away to heaven.

> As they continued walking and talking, a chariot of fire and horses of fire separated the two of them, and Elijah ascended in a whirlwind into heaven. Elisha kept watching and crying out, "Father, father! The chariots of Israel and its horsemen!" But when he could no longer see him, he grasped his own clothes and tore them in two pieces. (2 Kgs. 2:11-12)

This is not only a warrior image; the god in a burning chariot represents another face of our composite deity—the sun-god who rides a fiery chariot across the sky. The passage above is one of the few places where we can detect a solar deity in the biblical portrayal of God.[14]

Whether riding a fiery chariot, brandishing a mighty arm, commanding armies, or making all creation tremble, images of God as war maker pervade our scriptures. However we choose to understand it, violence is a significant part of the biblical portrait of God, and those of us who claim this story as a heritage must deal in some way with this disturbing fact.

MIDRASH

In the centuries after the destruction of the Second Temple in 70 C.E., Jewish scholars began producing commentary on their scriptures. In this midrash they fleshed out the bare bones of the biblical texts, moving between verses. "These added on stories were sometimes invented by scholars in the heat of discussion, sometimes gleaned from legends and embellished with more comment."[15] These stories form a vast corpus that is reverent, passionate, and sometimes witty. The rabbis recognized a fundamental contradiction in Exodus, that God's extension of goodness toward the Hebrews involves God's violence toward the "other" peoples along the way who do not know or live according to God's commandments.[16] They protested this depiction of God as merciless with the following stories.

At the Reed Sea, God's angels—and by extension any who would rejoice at an enemy's death—are rebuked. "God's ministering angels sought to chant in jubilation after the Israelites had crossed the Red Sea. Their song, however, is stayed by God. 'The work of my hands has drowned in the sea and shall you chant songs?'"[17]

As to the killing of innocent children, the following midrash is quite beautiful. Children who were killed for the sins of their parents confront God, win from God a change of heart, and even redeem their parents.

> The children of the wicked who had to die in infancy on account of the sins of their fathers will be found among the just, while their fathers will be ranged on the other side. The babes will implore their fathers to come to them, but God will not permit it. Then Elijah will go to the little ones, and teach them how to plead on behalf of their fathers. They will stand before God and say: "Is not the measure of good the mercy of God, larger than the measure of chastisements? If then we died for the sins of our fathers, should they not now for our sakes be granted the good and be permitted to join us in Paradise?" God will give assent to their pleadings, and Elijah will have fulfilled the work of the prophet Malachi: "Lo, I will send you the prophet Elijah before the great and terrible day of the LORD comes. He will turn the hearts of parents to their children and the hearts of children to their parents." (Mal. 4:5)[18]

JUSTIFICATION FOR GOD'S VIOLENCE

Justice is a radical good that demands of love a violent action. This is a truth so limpid that it shocks us because we have disfigured the image of love.

—J. Severino Croatto[19]

The rabbis guarded against celebrating God's destruction of the Egyptian army, but some modern liberation theologians come dangerously close to doing just that. There are Latin American and black liberation theologians who justify and even embrace the violence of God in Exodus. They are adamant in their understanding of the significance and the meaning of YHWH's violence against Egypt for their theologies and for their people. African American theologian Josiah Young says, "the drowning of Pharaoh's army is *the central liberating event* of Exodus." It is here that God liberates the oppressed and afflicts the oppressor.[20] Here God's sensitivity to the oppressed and destruction of the oppressor are most clearly revealed.[21] Womanist theologian Renita Weems concurs: "in the scene at the Sea of Reeds the right to determine Hebrew destiny based on the sheer strength of the Egyptian Military (14:7-8) is finally exposed for the fraudulent claim that it is."[22] J. Severino Croatto of Argentina is even able to justify the killing of the firstborn, "if oppression is carried to the extreme of repression, then liberating action is necessarily violent. . . . God is violent because oppression is never justifiable even when peaceful means are exhausted."[23]

Liberation theologians explain God's violence in Exodus in a number of ways. Croatto condones the destruction of the Egyptian army as "necessary violence," but he holds Egypt and Egypt's repressive regime responsible for making violence necessary. Some theologians observe that in the story of the exodus, the violence comes from God, not Israel; they conclude that violence is therefore the prerogative only of the divine and not of humans.[24] Others maintain that the violence is not an act of God but the natural consequence of Egypt's unjust action. Many liberation readers find a key to the identity of God in an event where people of privilege are destroyed.

Even Martin Luther King Jr., a champion of nonviolence, considers the drowning of the Egyptian army a central liberating text. He said we should not rejoice over the drowning of the Egyptians, but he called the event "the death of evil upon the seashore."[25]

PROTESTING A VIOLENT GOD

There are modern readers who, like the rabbis, are profoundly unsatisfied with a portrait of the divine as violent, wrathful, and capricious. Our guides from chapter 3 of this book, Margaret Guider, Delores Williams, and Robert Warrior, find violence one of the most significant problems with Exodus as a model for liberation. Guider says:

> If there is one fatal flaw in the analogical use of the Exodus, it is the justification of slaughter and conquest in which the Christian tradition grounds itself and from which none of us associated with the tradition can extricate ourselves.[26]

Delores Williams decries the violent acts of God and the violent acts sanctioned by God, concluding that "the end result of the biblical exodus event, begun in the book of Exodus, was the violent destruction of a whole nation of people."[27]

Warrior concerns himself specifically with this people, the Canaanites:

> It is the Canaanite side of the story that has been overlooked by those seeking to articulate theologies of liberation. Especially ignored are those parts on the story that describe Yahweh's command to mercilessly annihilate the indigenous population.[28]

Warrior, an indigenous man who is not Christian, rejects the violence against the Canaanites; but he accepts that the Christian God is violent by nature. Guider and Williams, both Christians, claim that violent images of God misrepresent the divine.

In the portion of Exodus that concerns us, chapters 1-15, YHWH's violent acts against Egypt are the plagues, which culminate in the killing of the firstborn and the drowning of Pharaoh's army. Theologians who condone God's violence in Exodus focus primarily on the violence at the sea, where professional soldiers are killed at war. They tend to gloss over the plague against Egypt where children are killed in their homes, a disturbing parallel to the million Iraqi children dead of malnutrition and preventable disease since the imposition of sanctions in 1990. In the plague on the firstborn, YHWH's violence is not focused on the perpetrators of injustice but is almost entirely indiscriminate: "At midnight the LORD struck down all the firstborn in the land of Egypt, from the firstborn of Pharaoh who sat on the throne to the firstborn of the captive who was in the dungeon" (Exod. 12:29).

Many readers, women and feminists especially, agree with Williams and Guider and reject the depiction of God as a destroyer of innocent children. Some are concerned about the representation of the divine, others are concerned about harm in the real world.

Although Croatto accepts divine violence as necessary, he refuses to accept that God is tyrannical. He calls descriptions of God playing with human lives "projecting onto God the shadow of the oppressor."[29] Thus, he maintains, it is human oppression that has produced this distorted portrayal of God. Delores Williams calls the wrathful punisher an "awful model of god."[30] Some feminists challenge passages like Exodus 12:29 with radically different biblical images of God such as a nursing mother (Num. 11:12-13; Isa. 49:15) or a mother bird (Ruth 2:12; Exod. 19:4; Deut. 32:11; Pss. 17:8; 57:2; 61:5; 91:4).[31] Feminist liberation theologians from all over the world, but particularly women of color, look to the sacred texts of women's lives and describe God as healing, loving, and sustaining.[32] Some Christian feminists find the idea that God condones any suffering, including the suffering of Jesus, alien to their experience of God.[33]

Scholars such as Mary Daly, Judith Plaskow, Rita Nakashima Brock, Joanne Carlson Brown, and Carol Bohn claim that portraying God as violent sanctions and promotes violence and abuse. They observe that the violent images of God are also male images of God. The notion of a violent, male god is dangerous, especially when in every culture, women and children are overwhelmingly the recipients of violence and men are almost exclusively the perpetrators, whether that violence comes through fists, tax systems, war, corporate poor-bashing, rape, or starvation.[34] When God is violent or sanctions violence, then the violent are godlike. When God is a warrior, war making is glorified. Judith Plaskow writes: "The God who hears the groaning of his people in Egypt is a fighter more powerful than all the armies of Pharaoh, a God whose arm can destroy the Egyptians, drowning them in the sea (Exod. 15)."[35]

> If the image of God as male provides religious support for male domi-nance in society, the image of God as supreme Other would seem to legitimate dominance of any kind. God as ruler and king of the universe is the pinnacle of a vast hierarchy that extends from God "himself" to angels/men/women/children/animals and finally the earth. As hierarchi-cal ruler, God is a model for the many schemes of dominance that human beings create for themselves.[36]

Rita Nakashima Brock puts it very simply: "Because we have believed in a divine being capable of such destructive power, we have made ourselves in that image."[37]

Some Christian readers, troubled by the violence of God in scripture, seek to escape the problem by asserting that it is only the god of the Old Testament who is wrathful and violent and that, in the New Testament, Jesus and his followers offer the world a kinder gentler vision of God. However, as Phyllis Trible says, "to contrast an Old Testament God of wrath with a New Testament God of love is fallacious. The God of Israel is the God of Jesus, and in both testaments resides tension between divine wrath and divine love."[38] The divine warrior imagery inherited from Canaanite religion and used in the Hebrew Bible is further adapted to describe Jesus in the Gospels.[39] The God of the Christian scriptures is also a wrathful God.

> And in anger his lord handed him over to be tortured until he would pay his entire debt. So my heavenly Father will also do to every one of you, if you do not forgive your brother or sister from your heart. (Matt. 18:34-35)

Furthermore, there are Jewish scholars like Judith Plaskow, Michael Lerner, and Norma Rosen who also protest and reject violent images of God. The idea that a loving Christian God replaces an angry Jewish God is nothing but Christian anti-Judaism. It is neither accurate nor is it just; and it fails to account for the tremendous amount of violence done by Chris-tians in the name of Christianity.

For a number of reasons, legitimate and less so, first-world Christians are uncomfortable with violent images of God. In the first half of Exodus YHWH's violence is directed at Egyptians, people like us. How are people of privilege to understand this violence in our Egyptian reading? We must find our own answers to Croatto's questions. "Why does the god of Exodus act violently? Why does God not respect the lives of the Egyptians whose King and whose firstborn he sacrificed?"[40]

Earlier in the chapter we looked at some of the historical roots of the violent images of God. In the remainder of the chapter I offer some ways that first-world Christians can look at the violence of God in Exodus. These are difficult texts that do not offer easy outs, they challenge our images of ourselves and of God. The following is not an attempt to reconcile the irreconcilable; a loving God does not kill children, and the killing of children should be protested in scripture and in the world. Nevertheless, we can grapple with these images in a serious and meaningful way without betraying our conviction that God is not a violent actor.

UNDERSTANDING THE VIOLENCE IN EXODUS

Violence against Oppressors

At the sea YHWH exhibits qualities of the divine warrior, a tribal war-god fighting on the side of Israel, but there is also a moral quality to Pharaoh's defeat. The drowning of the Egyptian army is not a case of one country over another, or even the God of Israel besting the Pharaoh of Egypt; it is the victory of liberated slaves over the shock troops of empire. The Egyptian army was the ultimate tool of imperial violence, and Egypt's chariots, the great symbol of this military violence and imperial power, are specifically targeted in the text. The word chariot appears ten times in Exodus 14, the prose description of the events at the sea,[41] and it is chariots specifically that bring about the army's downfall, "He clogged their chariot wheels so that they turned with difficulty" (Exod. 14:25). Despite the fact that it relies on divine violence, one way for first-world readers to understand the destruction of Pharaoh's army is as Israel's wholesale condemnation of the military violence of empire.

The incident at the sea is somewhat comprehensible for first-world readers. After all, soldiers at war do risk death. The killing of the firstborn, however, is violence of a different order. While the plague against the firstborn strikes at all levels of Egyptian society and targets children, this is not random violence. It is directed specifically at every household that could be seen to uphold the Egyptian empire. But why are children killed?

In Western and European literature and art children are often symbols of innocence. This is not so in the Bible. A clue to understanding the significance of the plague against the firstborn is found in the final phrase of Exodus 12:29, "from the firstborn of Pharaoh who sat on the throne, to the firstborn of the captive who was in the dungeon, and all the firstborn of the livestock." One of the fundamental ways that children are portrayed in the Bible is as possessions, like slaves and livestock. Whether they were prized, abused, or both, children were seen as belonging to their fathers.

Thus, whatever happened to children was not a reflection on them as individuals but on their fathers. In this case, it was a reflection on their Egyptian fathers who participated in empire.

Whether the target is the military enforcers of empire or the prized possessions of the supporters of empire, violence in the first half of Exodus is directed at Egyptians as oppressors and as beneficiaries of empire. As we have documented in previous chapters, these are the ways in which first-world readers most resemble biblical Egyptians. For people of privilege, the essential message is that this violence is directed at us; it is a condemnation of us and our way of life. A chilling truth of this story is that the killing of the firstborn deters Egypt's assaults on Israel only temporarily. We first-world Christians do not stop our voracious consumption even though it is killing our children and children all over the world.

Structural Violence

The existence of injustice in society is the existence of violence.
—Martin Luther King Jr.[42]

Delores Williams calls the black community and black theologians to "explore the moral status of violence in scripture."[43] It is crucial for everyone to interrogate violent models of God, but people of privilege, white people, and North Americans, have a legacy of interpretive power and a history of interpretive abuse. We have been content for a long time to ignore the violence that benefits us, violence in scripture and violence in the world. Therefore we must not be too quick to decry the violence in Exodus, especially when it is directed at us. An exploration of violence in scripture is meaningless without a rigorous examination of the violence in our own lives.

Yes, Exodus is a violent story, but so too is the story of life in the first world. Those of us who enjoy some measure of comfort in so-called developed nations benefit unavoidably from the suffering of others. The history of North America reads like a litany of human misery: conquest, genocide, land theft, and slavery. As we established in previous chapters, we who can afford the necessities that sustain us and the luxuries that entertain us, can do so because their prices are subsidized by laborers in sweatshops, factories, and plantations around the world, working as slaves or earning wages that will not feed their children. At home the rich get richer while infant mortality rates in inner-city neighborhoods exceed those of third-world nations, homeless people die on downtown streets, and prisons have become the new sweatshops. Perhaps the ultimate expression of this violence is the insidious ranking of arms over children's lives and wealthy corporations over poor people. Indeed wealthy nations are like Egypt, "where state and culture [collude] in the perpetuation of slavery and degradation."[44] What can we call this deliberate withholding of even the most basic decency from neighbors in our own cities and towns and around the world? Following the example of Martin Luther King Jr., we can only call it by its name: violence.

One of the great deceptions of North American imperial culture is that it equates success, wealth, status, and power with virtue and hard work, all the while ignoring the structural barriers that keep those who succeed and those who wield power predominantly white, male, and straight. The token presence of a few rich immigrants, white gays, and women renders invisible the vast numbers of ordinary people working incredibly hard simply to survive. Our ideology and identity in North America (in the United States more than in Canada) are focused on the idea of freedom and opportunity. Our collective mythology includes the idea that every person is equally likely to achieve success and to live the good life. Consequently, we regard those who fail to do so as losers rather than victims of a system set against them. A child who has to contend with poor nutrition, poverty, frequent school changes, high teacher turnover, inadequate childcare, racism, death of peers, and a dangerous neighborhood is more likely to go to prison than to complete college. Yet the fact that this child's "failure" is engineered by his country's priorities is all but invisible.

Another aspect of privilege is that when the powerful commit or are a party to violence, it is often performed by others on our behalf; agency is disguised. Those of us who are heirs to Pharaoh's Egypt are insulated by our palace walls. We drive on freeways and walk through tunnels above the city; we do not dwell in it and are untouched by the violence of human misery: latent and overt.

First-world Christians collude with violence; we participate in violence, and we are sustained by violence. To those against whom our violence is directed, who feel its effects in their homes, on their lives, and in their bodies through malnutrition, incarceration, street violence, and poverty, our protestations of innocence testify against us. "We didn't know." "Nobody we know lives like that!" "I can't believe it!" The women and men and children who cling to the lowest rungs of our social ladder face violence every day. For those who live on the front lines, "who live at the shoreline standing upon the constant edges of decision,"[45] there is no question of violence or nonviolence. Instead it is a question of *what kind* of violence: the violence of a respectable-seeming social structure that deliberately strips people of rights, opportunity, and the very stuff of survival, or the violence of resisting such structures.

An Angry God

For most of my adult life I have been moving away from my middle-income, working-class upbringing in an attempt to follow what I believe is the biblical call to come closer to those on the margins. For me this means living in community, struggling together with the urban poor, and working for social change. As this way of living brings me face to face with the latent and not so latent violence of our culture, my own stories parallel the stories of Pharaoh's regime. When I reflect on the violence that my chosen life brings me close to, I understand that God must be angry.

"The Egyptians became ruthless . . . and made their lives bitter. . . . They were ruthless." (Exod. 1:13-14)

When my gentle friend Paddy told me about his job in an Oregon prison, salvaging the still edible loaves from moldy bread that the prison was buying on the cheap and charging the state full price for, I wanted God to share my anger.

When doctors and social workers at a Vancouver hospital discharged Bob, who at age fifty looked eighty and weighed less than one hundred pounds, I expected God to share my outrage. Bob's tiny room would not accommodate his wheelchair, the room was filled with flies and rotted food. The bed was full of his own feces.

When, three days out of prison and full of hope for a new life, Maria died outside at night from hypothermia and too much of her prescription medication, I wanted God to share my fury that there were no shelter beds for women in Tacoma. Maria's friend ran from the homeless camp to flag down a car for help. Saturday morning shoppers would not let their eyes rest on another crazy homeless woman. They kept driving. Maria died.

Then Pharaoh commanded all his people, "Every boy that is born to the Hebrews you shall throw into the Nile." (Exod. 1:22a)

Recently I saw a photograph of a young African American boy, no older than eight, crouched on the stone steps of some vast government building clutching a sign that read, "Do you share my outrage?" The child is dwarfed by the building and by the structures that it represents. He is taking part in a protest against execution, a fate that threatens him as an African American male more than anyone else in his country. In the United States, African Americans make up 12 percent of the population but 40 percent of inmates on death row.[46] African Americans are jailed at a rate eight times higher than that of whites, and the incarceration rate for African American men in the United States is four times what it was in South Africa under apartheid.[47] An African American youth with no prior criminal record is six times as likely to be incarcerated as a white youth charged with the same offense. Black youth make up 46 percent of juveniles tried in adult court and 58 percent of juveniles in adult jails and prisons.[48] How can I fail to share this child's outrage at this blatantly racist system? How can God fail to share his outrage?

Violence and injustice are so pervasive in our culture, in the face of blatant disregard for human life I find myself in need of a God who is outraged and prepared to act: a God who rages. I do not experience the daily violence of the sex-trade workers in my neighborhood, nor racism, nor grinding poverty. I do not live in fear, and I am not in prison. I need to know that God is outraged at injustice, and I live a relatively protected existence. How much more must those who suffer these assaults need the angry face of God?

Rage

Structural violence makes wrath and revenge central to popular resistance culture.

—Willa Boesak[49]

First-world readers must keep in mind that what we are told about the Egyptians in the book of Exodus is told not from the perspective of the Egyptians but from the perspective of the Israelites. Egypt records no plagues, no military defeat, and certainly no loss of six hundred thousand members of its workforce. Egypt's record of Israel is one of utter disregard for an inferior. Pharaoh Mernaptha's boast, "Israel is made that which is not,"[50] is hardly the recounting of Egypt's humiliation. Perhaps, then, the imagery of violent judgment, so strong in Exodus—the plagues, the killing of the firstborn, and the drowning of the army—is not about the nature of God, but rather is an expression of Israel's hatred for Egypt. Perhaps the very violent fate of Egypt is not what *did* happen but what Israel *said* happened, what Israel *wanted* to happen. What does Israel's hatred for Egypt mean for our egyptian reading? What are the modern parallels?

Certainly in the empire that we know, there are members of the disenfranchised who are rightfully enraged. In North America, people of color, indigenous people, the poor, lesbians, gays, bisexuals, transgender people, immigrants, working-class people, and women endure varying levels of systemic violence daily. What is this violence if not an expression of our culture's hatred toward them? And is it any surprise that those who are hated respond with hatred?

> In the process of criminalizing such a large portion of nonviolent people we have set in place the conditions for more long-term violence. You do not willy-nilly arrest a father in front of a son, or break into someone's house looking for some kind of minor drug dealer and throw everyone onto the floor in front of screaming children and upset mothers, and drag people off the way we do routinely in our inner cities, without having it come back at you. You create anger. You nurture alienation.[51]

Although there are African Americans, poor people, gays, and immigrants who, for reasons of survival or self interest, condemn, apologize for, or distance themselves from their own rage and the rage of their sisters and brothers; there are others who claim their rage as justified, healthy, and a tool for change. Willa Boesak, speaking from his context of South Africa under apartheid, says that structural violence, the violence that pervades our daily living, makes wrath and revenge necessary to resistance.[52] He claims that such anger is a mode of connectedness, a vivid way of caring.[53] Z. K. Matthews, also of South Africa, says, "the white man is creating an unfathomable well of hatred against himself."[54] Argentinean Severino Croatto lays full responsibility for the hatred of the disenfranchised squarely at the feet of these who benefit from systemic injustice.

Many of us who fit, however uncomfortably, the model of white liberal or liberal Christian—Egyptians who would ally ourselves with Israel—do not feel ill-will or malice toward those we oppress; we may even feel benevolence or genuine concern. An invisible aspect of our privilege is that we seldom have to question our value or goodness. When we encounter the anger or hatred of marginalized groups or individuals, we are baffled, hurt, and indignant—or, worse, we are discouraged from the work for change. The message that we share responsibility for the hatred directed at us and for the lateral hatred between oppressed groups can compound our despair.

If we persist with hardened hearts in reacting to rage and hatred at a personal and emotional level, then we are doomed like Pharaoh. Violence is about how you act and how your society acts, not about how you feel. Racism is not a sentiment. Classism is not an emotion. Although they have personal aspects, these are social not individual sins; they are systemic in nature. Gustavo Gutiérrez says that from a third-world perspective sin is never fleshless[55] and the flesh that we sin against is not mute; it makes meaning, it cries out to God!

In Egypt the Israelites cry out; the oppressed speak their outrage. But closer to us in time and place, others are crying out. Prisoners, queers, and people of color are transforming *their* anger into holy action. bell hooks says:

> Renewed, organized black liberation struggle cannot happen if we remain unable to tap collective black rage. Progressive black activists must show how we take that rage and move it beyond fruitless scapegoating of any group, linking it instead to a passion for freedom and justice that illuminates, heals and makes redemptive struggle possible.[56]

Robert Goss tells us:

> Anger is not the opposite of love. Rather, anger is a form of love-making that fuels queer justice doing. Gay/lesbian Christians must not avoid the power of their anger.[57]

Arthur Solomon proclaims:

> Almost without exception I have found by going into prisons
> over the past twelve years

that the victims of the prison system
have been ripped off from their families
by the Children's Aid Society
and put into one white foster home after another
and end up in one correctional facility after another.
And their anger and their frustration grows
because they have been ripped off
from their rightful inheritance.
Their inheritance comes from God,
not from Governments or institutions.
The anger that our young people have against a totally
unjust system *is the anger of God*
and it will have to be accounted for.[58]

We, who by reason of race, gender, class, or whatever constellation of privileges we were born under, are the beneficiaries of the system we live in, must listen to the outraged. African American authors Toni Morrison and bell hooks ask whether black folks and white folks can ever *be subject together,* ever truly meet as human and work together, "if white people remain unable to hear black rage, if it is the sound of that rage which must always remain repressed, contained, trapped in the realm of the unspeakable."[59] I contend that unless the privileged can hear the rage of the oppressed we will remain entrenched in our privilege, in the illusions and comforts of Egypt, and whatever stirrings toward justice are alive in the world will leave us behind. Matthews's "unfathomable well of hatred" is sobering; but unless we stand sobered, unless we acknowledge the enormity of the task we face, there is no hope for change.

Judgment and the Knowledge of God

This is the good news! Judgment is daily passed on the oppressors.
—Josiah Young[60]

When Pharaoh does not listen to you, I will lay my hand upon Egypt and bring my people the Israelites, company by company, out of the land of Egypt by great acts of judgment. The Egyptians shall know that I am the LORD, when I stretch out my hand against Egypt. (Exod. 7:4-5)

The rising action of the plague narratives intimates both the depth of Pharaoh's refusal to know YHWH and the certainty that YHWH will be known by Pharaoh and by Egypt. "Yahweh is increasingly known by Pharaoh, as Pharaoh cedes more and more 'territory' to Yahweh and Pharaoh is increasingly humiliated and driven from the field of power."[61] Because of the nature of YHWH, *how* Egypt comes to knowledge of God is directly related to *what* that knowledge entails. "Israel like Pharaoh, does not come to information about Yahweh, but to the liberating reality of Yahweh's sovereign gift of freedom."[62] Thus, both Israel, and Pharaoh come to know YHWH through political praxis: or, as James Cone has it, "there is no knowledge of Yahweh except through his political activity on behalf of the weak and helpless of the land."[63] And God's political action for Israel is a political action *against* Egypt.

For privileged North Americans who read Exodus as Egypt, this is a powerful and frightening assertion. If we cannot or will not know God in the signs around us, we *will* come to know God through destruction and judgment. I am certain that God is a creator and not a deliberate destroyer, but in the world where I live, I see destruction all around me: destruction of oppressed and destruction of oppressors, destruction of lives, of souls, of ecosystems, of communities, and of peoples. I have not dwelt a great deal on the image of God as judge, but I have no doubt that nations, races, classes, and indeed all of creation, judge those of us who have a disproportionate share in causing the destruction all around us.

In the passage quoted above (Exod. 7:4-5) judgment and the knowledge of God are connected. Egypt comes to know YHWH through great acts of judgment. This may be true for us as well. If people of privilege with an earnest desire for solidarity can hear the judgment of those who suffer because of how we live, if we can listen to the cries of creation, hear the rage and not turn from it, then I believe we will come to know a face of God that has until now been hidden from us, a face that is vulnerable, abused, and angry.

CONCLUSION: READING VIOLENT STORIES

Stories are powerful; through telling and retelling they seep into minds and hearts and become part of a people's unconscious. The meaning of stories is not static. Violent stories can be a safe way to express anger and frustration, or they can be used to incite violence in others. Violent stories can be used to excuse, pardon, or explain away ongoing violence, or they may simply reflect a violent world.

Who tells a story and who listens to it can alter a story profoundly. The story of the exodus may have begun with the campfire bravado of escaped slaves and "morphed" into resistance literature, but on its way to the present, the story has been used to mystify domination, encourage group loyalty, foment revolution, and justify slaughter. If a small, oppressed group tells a story about their mighty deeds and God's punishment of their oppressors, the meaning of the story is changed when powerful people appropriate that story and use it to justify their aggression. First-world Christians must keep this in mind as we read the violence in Exodus.

Exodus is our heritage, but it is a troubling heritage: we cannot separate the stories of liberation and resistance from the stories of violence and conquest; the God of Israel's liberation is a violent actor. For those of us with an agenda of justice, social change, and nonviolence, who look to our tradition for support, the temptation is to ignore those texts which justify conquest and condone violence and focus on texts that promote justice. This "reading for the liberative strands of the text" is important because it shows that significant portions of our sacred scripture are focused, however humanly and imperfectly, on justice, resistance to empire, God siding with the oppressed, respectful relationships, and the integrity of creation. In a world that does not share these values and in churches that have lost contact with this radical root, it is important to assert that these are central themes of scripture. But to focus on the aspects of tradition that confirm our beliefs to the exclusion of those texts that say the very opposite of what we believe, abandons those texts to those who would use them for harm. As Robert Warrior cautions us, "these stories of deliverance and conquest are ready to be picked up and believed by anyone wondering what to do about the people who already live in their promised land."[64] What then do we do with our violent heritage?

As we have done in this chapter and will continue to do in this book, first-world Christians can claim our entire heritage. We can look at the violence in our tradition; and we can look at the violence in our lives. We can examine the roots, the history, and the manipulation of violence in stories and in our world. We can speak about violence and against it. We can repent. We can deny that God is capricious, petulant, and violent, without reducing the divine to the status of pet. We can embrace the ambiguity of our heritage, and we can act nonviolently for justice.

8

PHARAOH'S DAUGHTER,
DAUGHTER OF GOD

My sense of the interdependence of all life is, if I may say, born of the teeming Nile. I don't vaunt my own actions, mind you, but look what I did. I made no speeches, declared no contest. I sent no minions to act for me. I reached into the water and drew out one Hebrew child. One. One saved one. An act from which meaning never ceases to flow, through ages and worlds.
                      —The voice of Pharaoh's daughter in "Bitiah"[1]

A compassionate princess saves an infant hero; the daughter of a genocidal tyrant acts in open defiance of her father; a conspiracy of women thwarts the plans of an evil ruler; a haughty princess is the unwitting instrument of God and a clever young girl. Although she merits a spare five verses at the end of the prologue to Exodus, Pharaoh's daughter has captured the minds of centuries of biblical readers. Hers is a story whose gaps call upon the biblical imagination.

Pharaoh's daughter is the clearest example of an Egyptian who acts intentionally for Israel, or at least for one individual Israelite. As people of privilege who would be allies of the oppressed, this passage presents an exciting possibility; a woman of incredible privilege successfully acts in solidarity with the oppressed. Perhaps such action is possible for us. In this chapter we will approach the story of Pharaoh's daughter at three different levels. Let us begin by looking closely at the biblical text.

THE TEXT

A Close Reading

Pharaoh's daughter is inseparable from the other women in this story. The Hebrew name for the book we call Exodus is "These are the names," which are the first words of the book.

These are the names of the sons of Israel who came to Egypt with Jacob, each with his household: Reuben, Simeon, Levi, and Judah, Issachar,

146

Zebulun, and Benjamin, Dan and Naphtali, Gad and Asher. The total number of people born to Jacob was seventy. Joseph was already in Egypt. (Exod. 1:1-5)

These twelve sons precede the whole of Exodus. In the Bible, the number twelve is important: there are twelve tribes of Israel, twelve months of the year, twelve signs of the zodiac, and—in the Christian tradition—twelve apostles. Sons are even more important. They are heirs and the fulfillment of God's promise to Abraham and Sarah; the birth of sons is eagerly anticipated by mothers and fathers. Feminist scholar Jopie Siebert-Hommes points out that in the prologue to Exodus the role of daughter is uniquely emphasized and that there are twelve women mentioned: Shiphrah and Puah, the midwives; a daughter of Levi, Moses' mother; the infant's sister; Pharaoh's daughter; and the seven daughters of the priest of Midian. The twelve tribes of Israel owe their deliverance to twelve daughters through their actions on behalf of life.

Pharaoh's daughter does not appear until Exodus 2:5, but her story is part of the complex structural unit that makes up the first verses of the chapter.

Now a man from the house of Levi went and married a Levite woman. The woman conceived and bore a son; and when she saw that he was a fine baby, she hid him three months. When she could hide him no longer she got a papyrus basket for him, and plastered it with bitumen and pitch; she put the child in it and placed it among the reeds on the bank of the river. His sister stood at a distance, to see what would happen to him.

The daughter of Pharaoh came down to bathe at the river, while her attendants walked beside the river. She saw the basket among the reeds and sent her maid to bring it. When she opened it, she saw the child. He was crying, and she took pity on him, "This must be one of the Hebrews' children," she said. Then his sister said to Pharaoh's daughter, "Shall I go and get you a nurse from the Hebrew women to nurse the child for you?" Pharaoh's daughter said to her, "Yes." So the girl went and called the child's mother. Pharaoh's daughter said to her, "Take this child and nurse it for me, and I will give you your wages." So the woman took the child and nursed it. When the child grew up, she brought him to Pharaoh's daughter, and she took him as her son. She named him Moses, "because," she said, "I drew him out of the water." (Exod. 2:1-10)

As we observed in chapter 2 of this book, Exodus 2:2-10 has a chiastic (sandwich-type) structure in which the position of words conveys meaning. Unlike lists in English, where the most important item is either first or last, the most essential information here appears in the center—in this case, the child.

A   Birth of the *son* (no name)(2:2)

  B   *Mother* lets child go (2:3)

    C   *Sister* (passive) (2:4)

      D   Pharaoh's *daughter*—seeing (2:5)

        E   *The child* (2:6a)

      D'   Pharaoh's *daughter*—compassion (2:6b)

    C'   *Sister* (active) (2:7-8)

  B'   *Mother* gets child back (2:9)

A'   Adoption of the *son* (name) (2:10)

The infant Moses is surrounded and protected by three women. Pharaoh's daughter surrounds him most closely. "At the great crisis point in the story, when the child is given up to the water and he has become unattainable for his mother, even for his sister, it is Pharaoh's daughter who descends into the depths and shows pity."[2]

Pharaoh's daughter is a decisive actor. Her short story is told using a series of powerful verbs. She *goes down* to bathe, *sees* the ark, *sends* her maid, *opens* the ark, *sees* the child, and *has compassion*. She *says*, "This must be one of the Hebrews' children." This deliberate detailing of Pharaoh's daughter's actions parallels the focus on the mother's actions at the beginning of the story. It slows the pace and makes clear that every action represents a choice and a progression toward her saving act.

These early chapters of Exodus tell of a contest between gods: Pharaoh and YHWH. In this cosmic struggle Pharaoh's daughter takes sides. She acts for Israel and on behalf of life. Pharaoh's daughter is clearly on the side of the good; she is compared to God and contrasted sharply with both her father and the pharaoh who succeeds him. When her father orders all Hebrew infant males thrown *into the Nile,* Pharaoh's daughter takes an Israelite infant *out of the Nile.* Pharaoh's daughter recognizes the Israelite child who will become God's messenger, yet Pharaoh refuses to recognize God in the signs or plagues. Pharaoh's daughter conspires and collaborates; her father commands. The pharaohs deal death, while Pharaoh's daughter guards life. Pharaoh hardens his heart, but Pharaoh's daughter has compassion. Because of her compassion she acts in knowing defiance of Pharaoh, her father, her king, and her god.

Compassion is the critical motivator in this short story. In her compassion, which is considered a divine quality, Pharaoh's daughter is likened to God, although God is not mentioned in the story. She delivers Moses from the reedy waters just as YHWH delivered Israel from destruction in the Reed Sea. In Exodus 2, Pharaoh's daughter sees the endangered child, just as God will see the suffering of the Israelites in chapter 3.[3] As God adopts

Israel, she takes Moses as her own, and like God she names: "When the child grew up, she brought him to Pharaoh's daughter, and she took him as her son. She named him Moses, 'because,' she said, 'I drew him out of the water'" (Exod. 2:10).

Moses is an Egyptian name derived from the word for birth. There are numerous examples of names that use Moses as a base and a god's name as prefix: Atmoses, Tutmoses, Ramses. These are translated either "son of the god X" or "the god X is born."[4] Although there are historical references to the name Moses standing alone without the god element, it is fitting that Moses, whose father is "a man of the house of Levi" and who speaks for a God who will not be named, bears this ambiguous appellation, "son of *whom*?" The text offers a Hebrew etymology for the Egyptian word *moshe* (Moses), but it is in reality more of a wordplay. In Hebrew *moshe* is a rarely used verb form meaning "the one who draws out" and not as the text claims "the one who was drawn out."[5] The name points to Moses' future role. So Pharaoh's daughter contributes to the Exodus of the Hebrews not only by saving the savior but by designating him the "drawer out."[6]

Pharaoh's daughter is a forceful actor who commissions the leader of the people; she is compared to God, and she performs a salvific act at a critical time. Clearly she is portrayed positively in the text, yet some commentators persist in projecting their stereotypes onto the biblical text. "As we shall see, there is all the world between the clever Hebrew midwives and the dumb Egyptian princes."[7]

Because she is a woman of status associated with a powerful man, it is assumed that she must be stupid. Ironically one of her greatest acts, the naming of Moses, is counted as evidence of her stupidity on account of her imperfect knowledge of Hebrew. This is especially unreasonable, as etymologies, or stories of the origin of names, often feature grammatical stretches and deliberate misreadings, even by native speakers.[8] The linguistic bending in Exodus 2:10 is well within the norm of biblical name stories. To say that Pharaoh's daughter is foolish or that she was duped is to read not the text but cultural codes that do not admit that women have intelligence or that an enemy might have humanity.

Historical Questions

What sort of life or role did a pharaoh's daughter have? How did adoption work in that time and culture? How could a pharaoh's daughter have brought an Israelite infant into her father's court?

Certainly much more will remain unknown about Pharaoh's daughter than it is possible to know. The text refers to her as "the" daughter of Pharaoh, not "a" daughter,[9] but we do not know if this was intended to imply that she was the only daughter or simply the only daughter present. Was her mother the queen or a slave?[10] If the pharaoh in question were

Ramses II, she would have been one of forty-nine daughters! As a member of the royal family, a pharaoh's daughter would have had some role in the affluent life of the court, but as a woman her power would have been circumscribed. By the time of the New Kingdom (sixteenth to eleventh centuries B.C.E.), ruling-class women could buy and sell property and give legal testimony. Compared to the cultures around them, Egypt accorded women a relatively high status. All land was passed down through the female line from mother to daughter.[11] Egyptian women were equal to men under the law and could conduct business independently. Marriage did not diminish or increase a woman's legal rights or standing.[12] In Egyptian art depictions of women are less common than those of men, and upper-class women are confined largely to the domestic sphere. But women also appear as servants, court musicians and dancers, field workers, and priests. Women's roles were not as controlled and tidy as upper-class family representations show; in sharp contrast to these limited portrayals, Egypt was ruled by a woman several times during the pharaonic era. Probably a daughter of Pharaoh would have had wealth, status, and some power, particularly compared to a laboring slave population.

Pharaoh's daughter's trip to the water accompanied only by her maids indicates a degree of autonomy that may not always have existed for ruling-class women. Ramses III (1194-1163 B.C.E.) is supposed to have boasted, "I enabled the women of Egypt to go her way, her journey being extended where she wanted without any other person assaulting her on the road."[13] Although the Greek historian Herodotus (b. 484 B.C.E.) regarded the Egyptians as fanatical bathers, bathing in the river itself was unusual,[14] but as a literary device it provides a convenient means to get the infant Moses from the Nile to Pharaoh's courts.

The adoption of Moses is historically plausible and an indication of Pharaoh's daughter's autonomy and status. An Egyptian woman could legally adopt children in her own name.[15] There are no laws concerning adoption in the Torah,[16] nor do we know much about the legal aspects of adoption in ancient Egypt,[17] but adoption in various forms was common in Africa and the ancient Near East, and we have examples from both cultures. Esther was adopted and supported by her uncle Mordecai after the death of her parents. "Mordecai had brought up Hadassah, that is Esther, his cousin, for she had neither father nor mother: the girl was fair and beautiful, and when her father and her mother died, Mordecai adopted her as his own daughter" (Esth. 2:7). Hatshepsut (1473-1458), the great woman pharaoh, used a form of adoption to her political advantage. She came to power after the death of her husband and half-brother Thutmose II by acting as regent and parent for Thutmose III, his son by a subordinate wife.[18]

The phrase, "she took him as her son" and the fact that Moses lived as an Egyptian into adulthood support the argument that Moses was legally adopted and Pharaoh's daughter was not a foster parent. The sequence in the story where the child is found, recognized as a foundling, delivered to a wet nurse for set wages, weaned, returned to the finder, and adopted, strongly parallels the pattern and the content of certain Mesopotamian legal contracts regarding the adoption of a foundling.[19] The daughter of Pharaoh became the mother of Moses. This is particularly significant when we consider the importance in Egypt of the mother of the leader. On a pharaoh's tomb, his most important monument, the most important portrait of the pharaoh often showed him enthroned next to his mother.[20]

As for Moses' upbringing in Pharaoh's court, this too is historically possible. A brilliant but risky aspect of the Egyptian court was that the offspring of subject kings and rulers were kept as something between honored guests and hostages. Their presence in court accustomed them to the pharaoh's absolute authority, promoted their fathers' compliance, and assured their own future loyalty.[21] Although there is no textual evidence to suggest that Moses was the son of a client ruler, the possibility is intriguing.

CONTEXT—STEPPING OUT OF THE TEXT

Biblical Context

How does the passage we have been examining fit into the rest of Exodus? The story of Pharaoh's daughter (Exod. 2:5-10) appears at the end of the prologue to Exodus (1:1-2:10). The story preceding it, the tale of the midwives, which we will explore in the next chapter, is either a sequel to the story of Pharaoh's daughter or an alternative version of Moses' endangered infancy and miraculous escape.[22] Together they form a prologue, which is exciting, danger-filled, and sets the stage for the epic to follow. Virtually everything that happens in these early verses has a parallel in the rest of Exodus. Moses is placed among the reeds (*suph*); the Hebrews walk through the Sea of Reeds (*yam suph*). Pharaoh's daughter comes to the river where Moses' sister stands, and Pharaoh comes to the river where Moses stands.[23] This unnamed sister of Moses takes action by the water and later the priest Miriam, sister of Moses, is repeatedly associated with water.[24] Moses, like Israel, is saved from a monarch's threat and watery death.

The verb "to see" (*ra'ah*) conveys a theme through repetition: seeing injustice leads to action for justice. Pharaoh's daughter sees the basket and the infant (Exod. 2:5-6) and rescues him. Moses' mother saw his goodness (Exod. 2:2) and hid him. Moses will see the oppression of his brothers and sisters, and on the mountain he will see God. Finally, seeing is the catalyst for the entire Exodus, when God sees the suffering of the Hebrews in Egypt (Exod. 3:7, 9) and acts for their liberation.

The prologue (Exod. 1:1-2:10) is a platform from which the hero is launched and his dual identity, Egyptian and Israelite, established. The host of strong women actors who conspire to save him are virtually dropped after Exodus 2:19.[25] Yet the story is striking not for the presence of strong women, of whom the Bible boasts many, but for their appearance together and the almost complete absence of men. Although there are numerous parallels between the prologue and the rest of Exodus in theme and literary detail, there is a striking contrast at the level of narrative. In the prologue Israelite and Egyptian women cooperate, communicate, and work together across differences and power differentials to save a child's life. In the rest of the book, Israelite and Egyptian men and gods clash, posture, and engage in violent struggle bringing death and destruction to thousands. What women do is very different from what men do.

Extra-Biblical Context

Beyond Exodus, how does this passage compare with the rest of the Bible? The story of Pharaoh's daughter remains unique for its lack of male characters. In the genealogies of First Chronicles (4:18), there is an ambiguous reference to a Bithiah, daughter of Pharaoh whom Mered married. She may or may not have had anything to do with Moses' adoptive mother.[26] The strongest linguistic connection with another text is the word *teva*. Pharaoh's daughter finds the infant floating in a *teva*. The word has only two uses in the Bible; it describes Moses' basket and Noah's boat. So each story of hope, afloat and imperiled, recalls the other. In terms of form, the Bible has other etymologies and other adoptions. In terms of content, the story of Pharaoh's daughter tells of a righteous Gentile woman who acts on behalf of Israel. Other examples include Jael, who executes Sisera, an enemy general (Judg. 4-5); Rahab, the prostitute of Jericho whose story we heard in chapter 3 of this book, and perhaps the midwives, Shiphrah and Puah, who we will discuss in the next chapter. For first-world readers seeking to be a part of the project of liberation, these women—a seductive murderess, a prostitute, and two lawbreakers—are reminders to us that we might not know what salvation looks like.

Accounts of a national hero's childhood escape are common in various times and cultures. Oedipus, Hercules, Romulus, King Arthur, Snow White, and Superman all began their careers, like Moses, as endangered children rescued by some good fortune. The story of baby Moses and Pharaoh's daughter shares certain characteristics with these notables. The child's father and mother are relatives. Early on there is an attempt on the child's life. The child escapes through the actions of others and is raised by substitute parents. Details of the hero's childhood are sketchy.[27] Two of the many such stories bear further examination, as both come from the ancient Near East and concern infants afloat.

The first, from Ptolemaic Egypt (332-30 B.C.E.), relates how the goddess

Isis saved her son Horus from the god Seth, his uncle, by hiding him in the reeds.

> Seth was ranging about looking for Horus when he was a child in his nest at Khemmis. His mother hid him in a papyrus-(thicket), and Nephthys' mat (?) was over him. She hid [him] as 'Child-who-is-in-the-papyrus-(thicket).

Another version:

> He was sailing about in a boat of papyrus, and Isis said to Thoth, "Let me see my son who is hidden in the marshes."[28]

The second comes from the Legend of Sargon, the "autobiography" of the ruler Sargon (ca. 2300 B.C.E.) composed in the seventh century B.C.E., some sixteen centuries after his death.

> Sargon, mighty king, king of Agade, I-
> My mother is an *enetu*,
> My father I do not know. . . .
> The *enetu*, a mother conceived me,
> In secret she bore me.
> She put me in a vessel of reeds,
> She caulked my opening(s?) with bitumen.
> She cast me into the [ri]ver
> From which I could not rise
> The river bore me be[fore] Aqqi,
> It carried [me] to the water drawer.
> Aqqi the water drawer (dalu), in dip[ping his] b[ucke]t,
> Lo, he raised [me] up.
> Aqqi the waterdrawer, to [his] (adopted) sonship
> [L]o, he raised [me].
> Aqqi the water drawer, to his gardening
> [L]o, [he] set [me].
> [During] my gardening
> Lo, Ishtar fell in love with [me]-
> For [fifty]-five years
> Lo, I wield[ed] the kingship.[29]

The birth narrative of Sargon has numerous parallels with the Moses story, but the details of the basket, "a vessel of reeds caulked with bitumen," are particularly striking and may indicate a direct relationship between the two texts.

Although it has parallels with other birth narratives, the story of Moses and Pharaoh's daughter features some uniquely Israelite qualities. First, the story foreshadows all of the major themes and events of the Exodus. In contrast to many found-hero stories where the finder is a poor, humble person or even an animal, Moses is found by a person of status and some power. Moses' identity is known throughout the story, and he is not completely separated from his family but raised by his mother until he is weaned. The sharpest contrast to and perhaps even a rejection of the lost-hero tradition is that as an adult Moses does not rise from his humble station to glory but rather the reverse: he must leave Pharaoh's palace in order to lead his people.

Pharaoh's daughter merits a mere five verses in the whole of the Pentateuch. Much is communicated in two brief episodes but more is left out. How did she explain Moses' presence? What was her role in Moses' early life? Did she have a child who was killed in the final plague? Did she take part in the Exodus?

The open spaces in her life were seized upon by Jewish sages and biblical commentators. In midrashic texts, the nameless daughter of Pharaoh becomes Thermutis, daughter of Pharaoh's wife Alfar 'anit. She descends to the Nile to bathe because, like all Egyptians, she was stricken with leprosy at the precise moment when an unnamed infant was placed on the water. When she retrieves his ark she is cured. Thermutis contracts the infant's mother as a nurse because he refuses the breast of any Egyptian woman. She then feigns pregnancy, anticipating the weaned child's arrival. Thermutis names the child Moses, and The Holy One, blessed be He, says to her, "Moses was not thy child, yet thou didst treat him as such. For this I will call thee My daughter, though thou art not My daughter."[30] Thus she is given the Hebrew name Bithiah, "daughter of God," which corresponds to the name in 1 Chronicles 4:17. Further, she is rewarded by being permitted, like Enoch, to enter paradise alive.[31]

Feminist biblical scholars in our time have studied the story of Pharaoh's daughter. Cheryl Exum, who has spent considerable time on this story, reminds us that the text is a construction by and for a community centered on male power, and she invites us to "step outside the ideology of the text" for a different look at what it might mean.[32] Yes, Pharaoh's daughter and the other women in the prologue are positively portrayed; but what function does a positive portrayal serve in a scripture where women are largely absent and in a culture where women's power is denigrated? Looking at the story in terms of gender politics reveals more than a tale of heroic women.

A recurring theme in Exodus is that God uses the weak to overcome the powerful. Viewed from this perspective we see a "great" Pharaoh who is so foolish that even women can outwit him (although it takes several of them to do it). The prologue concerns the birth and survival of infants so "naturally" this is a sphere for women. The women of the prologue are heroic and significant contributors to the life of the people, but the arena for their saving deeds is that of childcare and mothering. Exum sees this passage as rewarding women's complicity in patriarchal structure and as small compensation for women's virtual absence from the rest of Exodus.

STEPPING BACK INTO THE TEXT

Three Feminist Portraits

The third way we will examine the text is sort of a self-conscious combination of the previous two. Combining the insights from close reading of the text and from the passages' various contexts—especially the reader's own first-world context—we can step back into the text and engage it in a powerful new way.

In the past years feminist scholars have brought new insights and tools to the task of biblical hermeneutics (understanding the Bible). Elisabeth Schüssler Fiorenza, an important early proponent of feminist biblical interpretation, describes a fourfold feminist hermeneutical process involving hermeneutics of suspicion, remembrance, proclamation, and creative actualization.[33] Other feminist biblical scholars have used a combined hermeneutic of invention to interrogate texts in a manner that is accessible and creative.[34]

> You say there are no words to describe this time, you say it does not exist. But remember. Make an effort to remember. Or, failing that invent.[35]

Three recent examples show the range and possibility of such a hermeneutic. Patricia Williams is a black law professor and journalist; Norma Rosen is a Jewish novelist and essayist; and Nancy Lee is a biblical scholar who has studied in Croatia. These three U.S. academics are grounded in different traditions of inquiry and seek to address different issues, but each uses the passage on Pharaoh's daughter as her starting point for making meaning through story.

Norma Rosen, a fiction writer, develops the character of Pharaoh's daughter as she has Bitiah give a hilarious interview to a reporter from the Jewish press. Although she grounds her work in the rabbinic midrash, Rosen is concerned with questions of gender and modern Judaism. She uses insights from feminism to interrogate scripture. Bitiah speaks to the reporter about personal relationships and personal theology.

> "Yes, Pharaoh let his people suffer through these plagues of blood, boils, lice, rats, darkness and wouldn't give in. But what about the hard heart of the Hebrew God? Who made *that* happen? Couldn't God, through his mighty power, have shortened the contest so that the side he was going to help, the Hebrews, would be released at once? Weren't they still

suffering, dying of starvation and exhaustion at their day-and-night brick making during the weeks of this contest of might! Did God forget that the purpose of the whole thing was to relieve the suffering of the Hebrews? Did Pharaoh forget he was the father of his own people? The mighty monarchs shut their ears to the groans around them, the sights and smells of rotting flesh that fell on Jew and Egyptian alike. . . ."

"In Exodus 6:5, God heard the outcry of the Hebrew slaves. And awarded them as spoils to the victor [Moses]."[36]

"[My father the Pharaoh] was not the tyrant you media people like to portray. You have no idea how loving he was to me."[37]

Rosen vividly portrays a very privileged Pharaoh's daughter who scathingly exposes the ironies of the plague narratives. In keeping with Bitiah's character, class is everywhere evident but never questioned.

Patricia Williams identifies with Pharaoh's daughter as a woman of privilege who has just adopted a son; and she uses both her own story and that of Pharaoh's daughter to explore the American motherhood mythos. In her essay "In Search of Pharaoh's Daughter," a call-and-response patchwork of tales, Williams juxtaposes her experiences as a black adoptive single mother with the prologue to Exodus.[38] She places social analysis beside brief biblical passages quoted from the King James Version. Pharaoh's persecutions are juxtaposed with the crisis in childcare experienced by impoverished mothers. The Israelites' bitter service is loosely linked to the racialization of the politics of single motherhood.

Until the day-care crisis for all women is addressed in material terms, the cost of having children remains prohibitive yet strangely unacknowledged, for poor working women and for middle-class women alike—and God help women on welfare. This is so regardless of whether one is married, although the burden obviously falls disproportionately on poor single women.

Therefore they did set over them taskmasters to afflict them with their burdens. And they built for Pharaoh treasure cities, Pithom and Raamses. But the more they afflicted them, the more they multiplied and grew. (Exod. 1:11-12 KJV)[39]

Using the story of Pharaoh's daughter, Williams repudiates a culture that punishes and blames the poor, women, people of color, and children for their impoverishment. Her sharp social commentary shows up our cultural contradictions and hypocrisy regarding reproductive choice, the value of children, race, motherhood, and reproductive technology.

Nancy Lee uses the story of Pharaoh's daughter to illuminate her experience as an, "outsider-in-residence" in the former Yugoslavia. In what she describes as a sociological read, Lee places her analysis of the text next to voices of lament from Bosnia and Croatia. Kata Solji, a Croatian mother whose four sons were killed in the war, could be speaking to an Israelite mother at the Nile or an Egyptian mother by the Reed Sea:

> Into the Danube, Mother, throw the white flower,
> Let the whole world know, down the length of the river
> Of your grief and of your pain . . .
> Decorate the unknown grave of your children![40]

Lee claims that Pharaoh's daughter's response to the crying infant follows the biblical tradition of lament and redemption and models the appropriate human response to genocide. "She must cross dangerous social and ethnic boundaries to help, regardless of her father's pervasive policy."[41] Pharaoh's daughter's acts of compassion stand in stark contrast to the violent acts of YHWH. In this passage, the divine response to the genocide of Israel is the killing of Egyptian firstborn children. Lee says this is "highly problematic ethically, limited by ancient social practices, open to dangerous application and should finally be critiqued rather than glossed over in this paradigmatic story."[42]

Bringing their own concerns and contexts, Rosen, Williams, and Lee step into the text in a new way. Through their readings, the spare tale of an infant and a king's daughter expands and unfolds. These feminist scholars find in the story critical issues: gender, religion, race, class, and genocide, and profound human experiences: pride, lament, grief, hope, mystery, and outrage. What can we privileged first-world readers learn about ourselves in this story?

What I find unsatisfying in the story of Pharaoh's daughter is the same absence, which has engaged centuries of readers: Pharaoh's daughter comes on stage for five verses, returns to the palace, and we never hear from her again. Somewhere in the space between v. 10 and v. 11 Moses grows from infant to adult and Pharaoh's daughter disappears. Everything we "know" about the palace life of Moses is by implication and conjecture. What happened to Pharaoh's daughter? What happened to the defiant actor who took a condemned stranger into her home? The narrative framework is so spare we have no choice but to hang our own assumptions and aspirations on it. As for Pharaoh's daughter, I imagine her life after v. 10 would have followed one of two paths.

Pharaoh's Daughter: Princess

The first possibility seems the most likely. I imagine a princess who stays a princess, who extends her privilege temporarily to an endangered infant but does not really change very much. This woman is complicit in the structures she defies; her privilege so insulates her that she never questions it.

Norma Rosen captures the self-absorbed attitude of such a princess, "I don't mind if other people's plans work out for them if they suit my purpose as well."[43] Pharaoh's daughter sees difference: "this must be one of the Hebrews' children." But if she questions it at all, it is at the level of personal morality and prejudice. Like people who claim to be "color-blind," saying "I don't even notice what color a person is, I treat everyone the same," she refuses to acknowledge the systemic difference in treatment experienced daily by those who do not fit the dominant norm in terms of race, class, and so on.

Pharaoh's daughter's story has parallels in a modern phenomenon. Over the past forty years, increasing numbers of mostly white, middle-class North Americans and Europeans have adopted children across lines of race, nation, color, class, and culture. Although few situations are as stark as the adoption of a condemned slave by a princess, the parallels are disturbing. Obviously any adoption has some economic implications and messages about who is fit, capable, and worthy of raising children, but in the United States, adoption regulations and practices, along with media characterizations of minority mothers conspire to tell us that only the elite are worthy parents.

> One is left with the impression that the rights to children, intimacy, and privacy are the rewards of wealth; one is left with an image in which mainstream society's punitive and oppressive desire to make poor blacks literally disappear wins acceptance when reexpressed as *their* uncontrolled desire for babies *they* can't afford.[44]

I was raised on evening television sit-coms featuring cute black children with white parents. I grew up and attended school with a number of black and Native children who had been adopted into white families. The prevailing wisdom of the day was to ignore difference because love could make up for any social inequity. But as children we knew that the pain and the power of unacknowledged racism was always present, as angry and as palpable as the alcoholism, mental illness, and child abuse we were compelled to ignore. In recent years adults have attested to what we children knew.

The United Nations defines "forcibly transferring the children of the group to another group" as an aspect of genocide.[45] First Nations people in Canada, the United States, and Australia have attested to the suffering that such adoptions have caused in terms of isolation, alienation, and loss of culture. In 1971, the National Association of Black Social Workers in the United States issued a statement on the harm done to black children adopted into white families. Their concluding statement was that "love is not enough." In 1991, Morris Jeff Jr. reiterated this theme, saying: "Placing African-American children in white European American homes is an overt hostility, the ultimate insult to black heritage . . . it is a simple answer to a complex situation. It causes more problems than it solves."[46]

Internationally, the inequity between North and South is the reason many southern children are available for adoption. Significant numbers of children adopted from the Southern Hemisphere are not orphans. In some cases the adoption of southern children into the North is a virtual industry. This is part of a global trend where southern women and women of color are increasingly servicing the reproductive "needs" of the white North. These services include domestic labor and home support, providing babies for adoption and outright trafficking, and surrogate motherhood.[47]

The adoptive parents I knew as a child and those who are adopting today are for the most part good people desiring to do a good thing while at the same time meeting their own needs. Despite their individual virtue, they are part of a social pattern that has caused enormous harm to people and communities of color, a pattern of institutionalized racism. Like Pharaoh's daughter, they raised an endangered child to their own level of privilege; they did not seek to change the situation of the child's parents.

The Pharaoh's daughter who follows this path manages to keep her fragile world of privilege intact. She draws the child from the water, but she does not draw a connection between her own life of luxury and the Israelite families who are forced to throw their children into the Nile.

Despite the troubling issues raised by this version of Pharaoh's daughter, there is a strong tradition that insists on the sufficiency of her single virtuous act. "The Holy One, blessed be He, said, 'Moses was not your son, yet you called him son. You are not my daughter, yet I will call you my daughter.'"[48] The stories that laud Pharaoh's daughter express our desire that a single beautiful act should be sufficient to wed us to the plan of the liberating God. They promote the patriarchal idea that being a great man's mother is a glory in itself. These interpretations try to tame and control a text that refuses easy answers. They counter the evidence of the exodus and the desert wanderings, the long hard struggle that among other things shows that to be a part of God's project involves painful change.

Pharaoh's Daughter: Class Traitor

The second scenario for Pharaoh's daughter is more hopeful although it seems much less likely. It is possible that Pharaoh's daughter's act by the river was the beginning of her defection from the courts of Pharaoh and the empire of Egypt. To explore this possibility I imagine a conversation between Pharaoh's daughter and my friend Rosie, who never fails to ask me difficult questions about my own life choices.

When Pharaoh declared that all Hebrew boys born were to be thrown into the Nile, Pharaoh's daughter brought an Israelite boy to live in the palace. In 1995, when Mike Harris's Conservative Party government brutally cut social programs to the very poor in Ontario, Rosie and her husband invited two homeless teenagers to come and live in their house. If Pharaoh's daughter's life was unchanged, Rosie's was not. There were fights, pets, screaming, thefts, disappearances, negotiations, reconciliations, and a hole punched in the kitchen wall.

Rosie and Pharaoh's daughter are sitting in Rosie's kitchen in Toronto, drinking tea and eating fresh bread.

R: What were you thinking!? Is compassion some kind of temporary insanity that just comes over you?

PD: Honestly, at the outset I wasn't thinking much. I saw something I wanted and I took it, but it wasn't greed, more like an incredibly pure desire and a sense of connection with this live helpless thing.

R: So what happened when you brought him home? Didn't a baby interfere with your . . . uh. . . lifestyle?

PD: What he interfered with was my vision. I started to see things that were invisible.

R: What are you talking about?

PD: Because my son was a Hebrew, because I loved a Hebrew, the Egypt I loved looked different. In the palace I was nourished and cherished. I mean, I knew my place as a woman and a daughter, but I was beautiful, a potential bride for my brother, the next pharaoh. I was valued. I had what I wanted and I knew where I belonged. But then with the baby I had to think about things I'd always taken for granted. The hands that made the food I ate and the clothes I wore were slave hands, Hebrew hands. And they were by no means soulless and stupid.

I tried to pretend that Moses was exceptional, and he was, every baby is, but . . . he wasn't any different from the rest of the Hebrews.

Well, I know myself from being ignored and having to use a more subtle influence that some of the greatest minds in court belong to those carrying fans, sweeping corridors, and bearing platters.

R: Babies change your life alright. But when the kids stayed with us I questioned myself a lot.

PD: It made me feel terrible about myself. Everything I'd loved was tainted. Everything I believed was mine because I deserved it, earned by the status of my father. . . . I knew he wasn't a god, I'd seen my mother and the other wives manipulate him, I'd heard advisors mock him in the halls, but he worked hard and had big plans for Egypt. The good things we had I believed were a sign of the gods' favor and a reward for our hard work. It's *hard work* to manage an empire!

But this baby made me feel like I had something I didn't deserve. It made me sick.

R: So?

PD: So I stayed sick for a while, stopped seeing my friends, stopped taking part in much of anything, but I can't keep on like this forever, I feel like I have to do something, I'm afraid my son will grow to hate me. I love my son but I keep looking back to that day by the river and I know from the moment my hand was on that basket something was working in me, I couldn't go back to not knowing.

What did Pharaoh's daughter do with her knowledge? From midrash to Hollywood, exegetes have been profoundly unwilling to leave her in Egypt unrewarded. But the wilderness sojourn that was so fraught with doubt and failure for Israel would have been harder still for an Egyptian princess. Alone, nationless, and accustomed to luxury, what would her exodus have been? Was she distrusted by the Israelites or overpraised? Either way, her journey out of Egypt must have been arduous and lonely.

CONCLUSION

For those of us who live lives of privilege, like Pharaoh's daughter we face two paths. We can congratulate ourselves and be praised for acts of charity, or we can open ourselves to the life-changing consequences of compassion. If Pharaoh's daughter stays in the palace, the consequence is not death. Like privileged modern readers, she is faced with the choice between a comfortable existence that stifles and a new life with God's people, a life that is hard, unfamiliar, and sometimes lonely but deeply joyful.

The story of Pharaoh's daughter is in some ways woefully inadequate. It does not give us instructions for opening ourselves to compassion, but the wording does leave us a few clues. Pharaoh's daughter is a decisive actor. She works together with other women despite differences in class, nation, and age; she forms alliances. Action, compassion, and relationship are the critical factors in this short story of salvation. I think the greatest gift of this passage is found in the interaction between Pharaoh's daughter and Moses' sister, two women who we know only through their relationship to men.

His sister stood at a distance, to see what would happen to him.

The daughter of Pharaoh came down to bathe at the river, while her attendants walked beside the river. She saw the basket among the reeds and sent her maid to bring it. When she opened it, she saw the child. He was crying, and she took pity on him, "This must be one of the Hebrews' children," she said. Then his sister said to Pharaoh's daughter. "Shall I go and get you a nurse from the Hebrew women to nurse the child for you?" Pharaoh's daughter said to her, "Yes." So the girl went and called the child's mother. (Exod. 2:4-8)

What happens here is subtle and yet incredibly profound. A woman of rank, privilege, and power, in a crisis situation, listens to perhaps the least powerful person she is likely to encounter: the female child of a slave. And she allows the child to offer the plan, to tell her what to do. To listen and to be directed by the least may be the beginning of our journey out of Egypt.

How did Moses' mother + sister conspire beforehand? What about Moses' father. Did he buy into the plan? What might the conversations between mother + daughter have been? What if the princess had not chosen to rescue the child but instead throw him back into the water - what response then?

What led them to think that this princess would perhaps respond in the way she did? Was there a rel. there between them? Something about her?

Was there prayer b/4, during, after? What was the response of other Hebrew mothers? No jealousy? any revealing of the plan to the powers that be?

9

SHIPHRAH AND PUAH

The Power of Refusal

They don't lie . . . they simply do not tell the whole truth. It is the conventional weapon of the powerless, especially women in the Old Testament, against those in power: the weapon of deception where the "truth" is not defined by the powerful, but becomes the priority of the underclass to interpret and shape according to their own reality. The refusal to tell the "truth" becomes tantamount to the refusal to obey.
—Renita Weems[1]

Exodus 1:15-21, the story of the midwives, is incredibly rich, politically and theologically. The text addresses gender, class, genocide, group identity, wisdom, birth, civil disobedience, and God. Despite its richness and depth, the story of the midwives is not well known, perhaps because it is a story of women that precedes the story of a male hero.

MIDWIVES OF THE HEBREWS

For readers identifying with Egypt, the most important question about this passage is the nationality of the midwives. The Masoretes, who added vowel points to the text, understood the word "Hebrew" to be an adjective in this passage, but the unpointed text is ambiguous. "The midwives to the Hebrews" could indicate Hebrews themselves or non-Israelites who perform this function for the Hebrews. The evidence and arguments for the midwives' Hebrew identity are as follows. Shiphrah and Puah are Semitic names. Midwives are usually of the same or lower social station as the women they serve. The women refuse to kill Hebrew infants. Finally in the middle of the description of the midwives' reward of "families," houses, or lineages is the phrase, "the people multiplied and became very strong" (Exod. 1:20). The midwives' reward parallels the increase of the Israelites.

163

Equally compelling evidence supports the idea that the midwives were Egyptian. The women have easy access to Pharaoh. They are expected to kill Hebrew children. They have some knowledge of Egyptian women in childbirth.[2] The most convincing argument for their Egyptian identity is that in the narrative, the midwives' "fear of God" is presented as a surprise.[3] Why should Egyptian women fear God and not Pharaoh? Ellen Frankel, in her commentary on the Torah, has Hagar the Egyptian, a character from Genesis, suggest that these women may not be Israelites without insisting that they are Egyptians.[4] Historically this is perfectly possible, but there is no narrative reason to have midwives of a national identity other than Israelite or Egyptian.

Are the midwives Israelite or are they Egyptian? For centuries this question has been argued; the earliest recipients of this story may have known the answer, but readers since have not. For us, ambiguity enriches the text. The uncertainty offers us the possibility of the following reading. From midrash to modern day, most readers have assumed that the midwives are Israelite characters; few focus on Egyptian possibilities. Ours is not such a reading. Confident that people of privilege can be part of God's liberation project, we will assume that the midwives are Egyptian allies of Israel.

THE TEXT

The king of Egypt said to the Hebrew midwives, one of whom was named Shiphrah and the other Puah, "When you act as midwives to the Hebrew women, and see them on the birthstool, if it is a boy, kill him; but if it is a girl she shall live." But the midwives feared God; they did not do as the king of Egypt commanded them, but they let the boys live. So the king of Egypt summoned the midwives and said to them, "Why have you done this, and allowed the boys to live?" The midwives said to Pharaoh, "Because the Hebrew women are not like the Egyptian women; for they are vigorous and give birth before the midwife comes to them." So God dealt well with the midwives; and the people multiplied and became very strong. And because the midwives feared God, he gave them families. Then Pharaoh commanded all his people, "Every boy that is born to the Hebrews you shall throw into the Nile, but you shall let every girl live." (Exod. 1:15-22)

Literary Issues

The NRSV translation above is flowing and comprehensible, but it smoothes over some rough spots in the text, like the midwives' nationality, which scholars have debated for centuries. Compare the NRSV translation to this version by Everett Fox, which follows the Hebrew very closely.

Now the king of Egypt said to the midwives of the Hebrews—the name
of the first one was Shifra, the name of the second was Pu'a—
He said:
When you help the Hebrew women give birth, see the supporting-stones:
If he be a son, put him to death,
But if she be a daughter, she may live.
But the midwives feared God,
And they did not do as the king of Egypt had spoken to them,
They let the (male) children live.
The king of Egypt called for the midwives and said to them:
Why have you done this thing, you have let the children live!
The midwives said to Pharaoh:
Indeed, not like the Egyptian (women) are the Hebrew (women),
Indeed, they are lively:
Before the midwife comes to them, they have given birth!
God dealt well with the midwives.
And the people became many and grew exceedingly powerful.
It was, since the midwives feared God, that he made them households.
Now Pharaoh commanded all his people, saying:
Every son that is born, throw him into the Nile,
But let every daughter live.[5]

Notice where the translations differ. What do the midwives see? Who is
allowed to live? What is the midwives' reward? Does the story concern
boys and girls or sons and daughters?

As with the story of Pharaoh's daughter, the midwives' story is expressed
in a chaiastic structure with critical word patterns repeating at each level:

A   1:15, 16   King of Egypt says to midwives, kill *sons,* let
                daughters live"

  B   1:17a   *Midwives fear God*

    C   1:17b   Midwives do not *do* as told, *let children live*

      D   1:18a   King calls midwives and says

    C'   1:18b   "why did you *do* this, and *let children live?*"
                (accusation)

  B'   1:21   Because *midwives feared God,* rewarded with houses

A'   1:22   Pharaoh commands all people throw *sons* in Nile, let
            every *daughter live* (emphatic)[6]

At the outside of the structure stands the king of Egypt, agent of death.
Toward the center are the midwives, actors on behalf of life. Separating the

two is the fear of God.[7] As in any chiastic structure, the central point is all-important. The crisis moment of the story occurs when the midwives are called before Pharaoh: the agent of death and the actors for life meet face to face. Indeed, as we will explore later, the midwives are called to stand trial for their actions.

Although the central unit, Pharaoh's accusation, is critical, in this passage events escalate in importance from start to finish, culminating in a campaign of genocide that involves the whole nation. After the midpoint of the story (Exod. 1:18), the passage is increasingly elaborate, with the second half of the structure conveying much more detail regarding the designs of Pharaoh, the resistance of the midwives, and the action of God. As Pharaoh's plan escalates in malevolence against its intended victims, the plan diminishes in accuracy. At the outset the king of Egypt's plan is calm, focused, and deadly although relatively small in scale. Two midwives are to kill sons and spare daughters. But once he has been defied, in his rage and fervor Pharaoh sows the seeds of his own defeat. He commands all his people to throw sons into the Nile but let every daughter live![8] This new order obligates many more to take part in the killing, but it offers two significant outs, both of which are exploited by the narrators. A child thrown into the river can be pulled from it alive, and a living daughter can do much to overthrow the plans of a king.

This is a story of resistance to genocide. Jopie Siebert-Hommes has looked at the text in detail and observed that the midwives' success in thwarting Pharaoh is due in some part to their refusal to recognize the sex distinction that Pharaoh makes, a subtlety not apparent in English translation. The king of Egypt orders *sons* put to death and concedes that *daughters* may live (Exod. 1.16) but the midwives let *"the children" (yeladim)* live.[9] The word *yeladim* can mean either male children or simply children, because in Hebrew the masculine plural form can refer to boys alone or boys and girls both.

Later in the text the role and importance of daughters are emphasized through repetition and wordplay. The midwives are among the twelve daughters of the prologue, and they are instructed, "if she is a daughter (*bat*) she may live," and they are rewarded with houses (*batim*). The word "house" also features in an inter-language wordplay. "Pharaoh" means "great house" in Egyptian while Pharaoh's opponents, the midwives, are given *houses* as their reward by God. Another wordplay in this passage has to do with seeing and fearing. The king of Egypt tells the midwives to "see the birthstones" but the midwives instead "fear God." These two verbs, to see (*ra'ah*) and to fear (*yare'*) contain the same letters in Hebrew but in different order. This visual and phonetic pun reinforces the whole point of the story, which is that the midwives by their deliberate refusal to cooperate turn Pharaoh's plan for destruction "inside out and upside down."[10]

Historical Issues

While the words and passages above make thematic points or raise narrative questions, other parts of the text invite us to address historical issues or lend insight into the world of the ancient Near East. What do we know about midwives and birth in ancient Egypt? What about infanticide?

Midwifery, that is, female assistance at birth, is common in many cultures and is referred to elsewhere in the Bible. According to Nahum Sarna, midwives in Egypt were held in some esteem and would therefore have had a certain degree of autonomy.[11] Additionally, unlike in modern delivery rooms, birth in ancient Egypt was a fairly private event providing opportunity for "discreet" infanticide.

The names of the midwives have some historical significance. Shiphrah and Puah are Semitic names. Shiphrah means "beauty" in Hebrew, and the name appears in an eighteenth-century B.C.E. list of slaves belonging to an Egyptian household.[12] Puah is the name of a heroine in Ugaritic literature. The name probably means "girl," although other commentators render it "splendor/splendid."[13] More significant than the meaning of their names is the fact that these women are named at all, particularly when the king of Egypt is not named. The effect on the reader attests to the skill of the narrators: we remember the insignificant and forget the mighty; we feel close to the midwives and alienated from the powerful pharaoh. The importance of the midwives is further emphasized by the fact that the word "midwives" is used seven times in the seven-verse passage.

In Exodus 1:16 above, there is a phrase translated in the NRSV as, "see them on the birthstool" and by Fox as, "see the supporting-stones." Other translations include "look at the birthstool" (Tanakh); "see them upon the stools" (KJV); "look at the birthstool";[14] and "see them upon the birthstool."[15] The contested word in the passage is *obnayim*, which is very close to the dual form of stone, that is "the two stones." The only other place in the Bible where the word appears is Jeremiah 18:3, where it refers to a potter's wheel, obviously not an appropriate translation in this context. All commentators assume that the word means "the two stones," but what that might signify has been the subject of much research and speculation. If the midwives are directed to look at each infant, the stones might be the genital area or might refer to testicles specifically, although there is no other use of this euphemism in the Bible. If the midwives are to look at the whole birthing area, the stones could refer either to the stone pedestals upon which women rested their legs during labor, or the bricks upon which Egyptian midwives placed newborn infants.[16] Each of these possibilities has been researched, argued, and championed by different scholars.

The conclusion of the story points to another historical issue, which is obscured from modern readers because we share a common assumption with its creators, or perhaps its transmitters. The story of the midwives ends with Pharaoh's command that all his people kill Hebrew boys, thus setting the stage for the story of Pharaoh's daughter and the abandoned baby. Although the endangered infant-hero is a common literary genre, the Israelites did not practice population control by infant exposure. Therefore, in order to have a story about an abandoned infant, extraordinary circumstances are demanded.[17] The assumption we share with the biblical authors is that an Israelite family would only abandon a son under terrible circumstances. Pharaoh's genocidal command is the terrible circumstance that links these two stories; it seems to be a late addition to the text. This is further supported by the fact that Pharaoh's campaign against infants is not referred to again in Exodus, and outside Exodus only briefly.

More Bitter Than Death the Woman Who Is a Trap, Whose Heart Is Snares and Nets (Ecclesiastes 7:26)

Beyond the book of Exodus, Shiphrah and Puah fit into a common biblical pattern; they are women who lie for their people. Deception in word or deed is a characteristic of many biblical women. Whether they are commended or condemned, Rebekah, Potiphar's wife, Rachel, Achsah, Lot's daughters, Delilah, Jezebel, Michal, Rahab, Jael, Ruth, and Tamar are all depicted as liars. How do the midwives fit this pattern?

> So the king of Egypt summoned the midwives and said to them, "Why have you done this, and allowed the boys to live?" The midwives said to Pharaoh, "Because the Hebrew women are not like the Egyptian women; for they are vigorous and give birth before the midwife comes to them." (Exod. 1:18-19)

Commentators tell us that Pharaoh's stated desire to "deal shrewdly" with the Hebrews is contrasted with the midwives' unassuming but clever reply. Let us examine this reply more closely. When accused by the pharaoh, the midwives do not respond in outright defiance, they do not say, "We delivered Israelite boys and did not kill them because we fear God and yours is an unjust law." Neither do they respond with an utter falsehood, "We have killed X number of babies," or "We have not been able to attend a single birth." Yet what the midwives say cannot be true. If the women of Israel did not need midwives there would be no midwives to the Hebrews. Their answer is deceptive and oblique, but it enables them to continue their work.

"The Hebrew women are not like the Egyptian women" (Exod. 1:19). In a situation of power differentials, the midwives exploit Pharaoh's assumptions about difference.[18] Pharaoh fears the Hebrews, and fundamental to his dread, which spawns repression, is the assumption that Egyptians and Hebrews are different;[19] the increase of Israel somehow threatens Egyptian security. As Pharaoh accelerates his campaign against the

Israelites, he tells the midwives to kill Hebrew boys. He assumes that the birth of a Hebrew boy threatens Egypt in a way that the birth of a Hebrew girl does not. Pharaoh assumes that to be born male is politically and socially different from being born female. With these assumptions of difference are encoded assumptions about worth and value, assumptions that Pharaoh makes and assumptions that the narrators make.

At the level of the text, Pharaoh assumes that men are more valuable than women and that Egyptians are more valuable than Hebrews. The narrators, through the midwives, exploit Pharaoh's ignorance of childbirth and his assumption that Egyptians and Hebrews are different. As it continues, the story promotes the narrators' counter-assumption that it is Israelites, not Egyptians, who are more valuable. The assumption that men are more valuable than women is not questioned.

In a text that seems to laud them, the midwives are at the same time diminished. Pharaoh, the greatest and wisest Egyptian, is outwitted by mere women. Unlike other stories where God uses a lowly man to defeat the mighty, here it takes two midwives to defeat Pharaoh. While this is a far more realistic portrayal of how active resistance works through collaboration and how God works through human agents, in contrast to the stories of lone male heroes like Moses and David, the women are diminished by the fact that they work together. Pharaoh is so foolish that he is defeated by women, but it takes several of them—midwives, Moses' mother and sister, Pharaoh's daughter—to do it.

The midwives contrast Egyptian and Israelite women across the lines of class, race, and power which separate them, to the effect in the narrative of trapping Pharaoh in his own ignorance and prejudice. The meaning of the word (chayeh) used by the midwives to describe the women of Israel to Pharaoh is uncertain. It comes from the root for the word "life" and could mean vigorous, lively, and full of life, or it could mean animal-like.[20] If we read the word as "lively," the midwives could have been insulting Pharaoh as they deceived him, contrasting the death-dealing king and his people with Israelites so full of life and strength and vitality that they found midwives unnecessary.

If we read the word as "animal-like," then the midwives capitalize on a derogatory stereotype: "The Hebrew women are not like the Egyptian women; they are *like animals*, they give birth before the midwives come to them" (Exod. 1:19). This "clever reply" has disturbing modern parallels. In the present and recent past there are numerous examples of (usually) white people using just this argument to illustrate the supposed inhumanity of those whom they oppress, and to justify their own inhumanity toward them. "They are just like animals, look at how they have babies!" Dehumanization of the oppressed, especially in relation to reproduction, is one of the hallmarks of racism in the Americas; but the derisive "they breed like animals" has been used most often against the poor. The modern manifestations of this prejudice are sad and ironic. The overmedicalization of childbirth causes women of privilege serious spiritual, emotional, and even physical harm, while lack of medical care to poor women and women of color has made childbirth and complications from pregnancy a scandalous health threat for some populations. Even if *chayeh* is not translated as "animal-like," the implication remains. Clearly the text is written from a perspective that is pro-Israel: Israelite receivers of the text would have known the midwives' answer for a ruse and may even have enjoyed affirming their difference from the Egyptians, but capitalizing on a derogatory stereotype is problematic for modern readers.

Renita Weems believes that the narrator has the midwives exploit Pharaoh's assumptions about difference but does not question them.[21] A careful reading of the passage suggests another possibility. In allowing "the children" to live, the midwives oppose Pharaoh's assumption that boys and girls are of different value. In deceiving Pharaoh they indeed exploit his assumptions about the differences between Egyptians and Hebrews, but we do not know if they accept them or not. The midwives, who would have known precisely what level of care in delivery the women of Israel required, may have chosen to use Pharaoh's prejudice against him while clearly recognizing it as such, in which case the passage satirizes his prejudice rather than reinforcing it.

Over time understandings and responses to the midwives deception have varied. Rabbinic commentators focused on the increase of the Israelites. For early and medieval Christian interpreters, Shiphrah and Puah's story is a central event in the first chapter of Exodus. Church fathers Augustine and Gregory were deeply concerned that the midwives were rewarded for lying. Both conclude that lying is never justified and always unacceptable; thus whatever reward the midwives received was not what it might have been had they not lied. During the Reformation, Calvin agreed that lying is reprehensible and displeasing to God, but Luther regarded the story as a model for Christian living in time of persecution. Since then, Protestant commentators have tended to defend the midwives, some to the extent of declaring that they did not lie.[22]

The text and most commentators concur that the midwives do lie, a conclusion that has a compounded meaning in light of the fact that so many biblical women are depicted as liars. While any person may choose deception at any time, and survival is the imperative of the oppressed, there is an overwhelming message in the Bible: women lie. In this context we must interrogate the scriptures further. Why are biblical women such liars? What these tales of lying women consistently omit or underplay is that these women are of inferior status to the men they lie to. Deception is consistently linked to lack of power.[23] In the case of the midwives, to defy Pharaoh openly would be to risk not only their own lives but the lives of the Hebrew infants as well. Looking at the text with this information, we can conclude that the midwives boldly take the prerogative of the powerless and define for themselves what truth is. Further, we can say that when women are continually depicted as liars and judged more harshly than men for lying, and when power differentials are ignored, then it is the texts, not the women, that lie.

[handwritten margin notes: more harshly; women judged, complaining or reading; when dying, too!]

Fear of the LORD Is Instruction in Wisdom (Proverbs 15:33)

Two ordinary women find the courage to defy and deceive a king. How could such a thing have happened? In the text, the repeated reason for the women's action is that the midwives feared God. This is the first mention of God in Exodus; who is this God whose first mention inspires such fear? Fear is emphasized by repetition in the passage. What does it mean to fear God?

Fear of God is a tradition from wisdom literature that means much more than to be afraid of God or of God's punishment.[24] To fear God, in wisdom literature, is to act according to basic ethical principles. How would the Egyptian midwives have come to such wisdom? First of all, Egyptian wisdom literature is very similar to the wisdom tradition of the Hebrew Bible.[25] Second, there are numerous incidents where foreigners are described as capable of fearing God; fear of God is not the exclusive prerogative of the Israelites. But how could a non-Israelite come to know and fear the God of Israel? In the wisdom tradition a person attains wisdom by observing particular patterns in creation and in human interactions and discerning an underlying order. To act in accordance with this order is to do the will of God.[26]

Although they were in Israelite homes at Pharaoh's order, being a midwife is an occupation with an abundance of entry points for grace. When I have examined this text with study groups using simple dramatization and first-person storytelling, ordinary readers are quick to grasp how Shiphrah and Puah learned their fear of God through their work as midwives.

"I'm a midwife, my job is helping babies get born."

"There is no way after coaching a woman through hours of labor I could take her child and kill it."

"I'm a mother and I help women become mothers—I guess I just can't help being on the side of life. It doesn't matter to me what Pharaoh says."

"How can a little child be a threat to anything?"

By observing in their daily work a pattern of life and creation, Shiphrah and Puah discerned an order to which they were committed. When Pharaoh's command contradicted that order, they could not obey. Fear of God in the midwives' case meant exercising compassion, observing their own feelings toward women and infants, and having faith in the force of life itself.

In the Bible, one means of attaining wisdom is through the observation of human interactions and power dynamics. Egyptian "midwives to the Hebrews" had an opportunity for wisdom unavailable to most Egyptians. As midwives Shiphrah and Puah would have had intimate access to the lives of Israelites in an intense setting. They would have had the opportunity to observe and analyze patterns of power that might have been invisible to ordinary Egyptians. Everyday contact would have shattered some assumptions about difference and led to new understandings. Poor Egyptians and Israelite slaves had common interests; there is an inherent dignity in other ways of life; goodness and life are not dependent on Pharaoh.

Admittedly such wisdom would have been difficult to attain. As instruments of Pharaoh's rule in the homes of a subject people, Shiphrah and Puah would have been neither liked nor trusted. Across such a divide of power and distrust, how would they have had the tools to understand or correctly interpret what they saw? How could they have had the courage to act on their understanding? One answer to these questions addresses another inconsistency in the text. Numerous commentators have pointed out that such an increasing nation as Israel would have required more than two midwives. Perhaps then the story of Shiphrah and Puah is the story of the exception. Out of all the midwives to the Hebrews, no doubt some had compassion for the women they attended, but only these two dared to defy Pharaoh. Midrash tells us that other Egyptian women acted as guards within Hebrew homes and would bring their own weeping infants with them to evoke the sympathetic cries of hidden children.[27]

However it happened, the midwives feared God, and their fear of God led them to take radical action for life. In Shiphrah and Puah, first-world readers of privilege have a story of ordinary women who act courageously, defying authority and breaking the law to do what they believed right, a story of civil disobedience.

CIVIL DISOBEDIENCE

The way I see the world is strictly illegal
to wit, through my eyes

is illegal, yes;
to wit, I live
like a pickpocket, like the sun
like the hand that writes this, by my wits

This is not permitted
that I look on the world
and worse, insist that I see
what I see
—a conundrum, a fury, a burning bush.

—Daniel Berrigan[28]

Civil Disobedience in the Bible

In the center of the story of Shiphrah and Puah, at the midpoint of the chiasm, the king of Egypt summons the midwives and speaks to them. "Why have you done this (thing), and allowed the boys to live?" (Exod. 1:18, Fox). His language points out that their simple noncooperation, "they did not do as the king of Egypt commanded them," is an overt act of defiance, "Why have you done this (thing)?" In fact, he makes a formal legal accusation. In the courts of Pharaoh, two midwives who defied him are charged with a felony.[29] As Weems has it, "the women stand in the royal chambers and defy the Pharaoh long before Moses and Aaron would."[30] In his book *Civil Disobedience in Antiquity*, David Daube calls the story of Shiphrah and Puah *"the oldest record of civil disobedience in world literature."*[31] This first civil disobedience action is the prototype, which spawns a mass resistance movement—the exodus itself.

Civil disobedience is nothing more than choosing to disobey a law for reasons of conscience; it is a modern concept, but the story of Shiphrah and Puah is one of numerous accounts in the Hebrew Bible of people who act according to the laws of God rather than the laws of some king or ruler. The frequency with which the Bible portrays salvation as contingent on acts of noncooperation with authority is not a coincidence but something of an imperative.[32]

Tobit is persecuted for burying the bodies of Jews executed by Sennacherib of Assyria. The prophet Micah is jailed for defying King Ahab. In the book of Daniel, which Daube describes as "a veritable charter of civil disobedience by a religious minority,"[33] Daniel and his companions, exiles in Babylonian court, refuse ritually unclean food and are cast into the fiery furnace. Surviving unharmed, Daniel breaks the law again by praying to the God of Israel and not Nebuchadnezzar, the king of Babylon. He receives a second death sentence and is thrown into a den of lions. Again he escapes unharmed. The second book of Maccabees includes the story of a mother and her seven sons who defy imperial law. For their refusal to break Jewish dietary law and eat pork, the seven young men are tortured, mutilated, and killed one by one before their mother. Then she too is killed.

This mother's story is one of many in which biblical women break the law in acts of resistance. In the story we examined in our last chapter, Pharaoh's daughter does precisely the opposite of what her father commanded and draws Moses *out of the Nile*. In Canaan, Rahab of Jericho protects and saves Joshua's men, thereby saving her own family. Michal defies the order of her father, King Saul, and saves the life of David. Rizpah stages a solitary public vigil against King David's command forbidding the burial of her sons. Vashti refuses to be displayed before the king's guests, and Esther, in an attempt to save her people, risks her life by approaching the king unsummoned. These women commit acts that are political and at the same time deeply spiritual and relational. When we consider how few women are mentioned in the Bible, the incidence of women who commit what would now be defined as civil disobedience is astonishing. As people who claim the Bible as our heritage, we must reclaim these foremothers of civil disobedience and come to know their stories.

Because the main focus of this section is Christian involvement in civil disobedience, this is one of the very few places in the book where we will deal specifically with Christian scriptures. Gandhi, the great prophet and practitioner of nonviolence, wrote that Jesus was "the most active resister known perhaps to history. This was nonviolence par excellence."[34] Because of writing and actions of Gandhi, Martin Luther King Jr., Leo Tolstoy, John Woolman, and others, the nonviolent campaign of Jesus is well documented, if not well known to most Christians. Jesus was involved in acts of civil disobedience which the Gospel writers understood in terms of Daniel, Exodus, and the Prophets. He healed on the Sabbath; he touched lepers; he challenged the authority of Rome. Jesus' symbolic destruction of the temple, overthrowing the tables of the money-changers, was a decisive act of civil disobedience, which according to the Synoptic Gospels led to his arrest and subsequent execution.

Because civil disobedience in the Gospels is of interest mainly to Christians and because the theology of most Christians involved in civil disobedience is very Jesus-centered, the civil disobedience of those who surrounded Jesus is seldom considered. Yet Jesus was consistently involved and associated with people doing active resistance; he was part of a resistance movement. Jesus was probably a disciple of John the Baptist, a fiery radical and unauthorized leader whose arrest and execution started Jesus' own work. Jesus' companions broke laws regarding diet, ritual cleansing, and work on the Sabbath—all purity laws, but with political content. A woman who was legally unclean, and as such prohibited from being in a crowd where she might contaminate others, deliberately reached out and grabbed hold of a holy man's garment. In the city of Jerusalem ordinary people enacted a massive street theater and civil disobedience demonstration: crowds marched in the streets bearing palm branches and declared Jesus king. When Jesus was executed, he was in the company of "bandits," a term referring to peasant outlaws, regarded by the powers that be as criminals and by the peasantry as heroes[35]—certainly not nonviolent, but direct action protesters nonetheless.

It is a serious oversight to separate Jesus' actions from the actions of his friends and contemporaries. It makes him into someone of unattainable status, reduces his actions to symbols, and takes a flesh-and-blood man out of the real world. It diminishes his companions to suggest that they had no influence on him, and it reduces us to powerlessness as well.

Jesus is like the whitecap on a wave. The whitecap is momentarily set off from the swell that is pushing it up, making us notice it. But the visibility of the whitecap, which draws our attention, rests on the enormous pushing power of the sea.[36]

It is deceptive and diminishes the power of Jesus' civil disobedience to suggest, in the face of evidence to the contrary, that he was a lone actor. Although there are incidents of solitary individuals like American antiwar protester Ammon Hennacy, German conscientious objector and martyr Franz Jägerstätter, and Israeli nuclear whistle-blower Mordechai Vanunu doing civil disobedience, civil disobedience is most effective when others take part. Most civil disobedience actions involve a group of people filling various roles, most of which do not involve risk of arrest. The fact that the campaign of the Jesus movement was not limited to the acts of Jesus is illustrated by the fact that after the execution of Jesus, his friends and followers continued their campaign of active resistance to Rome in a time when "by the laws of the empire, to be a Christian at all was to be in a state of civil disobedience."[37]

Modern Civil Disobedience

Biblical accounts of civil disobedience are myriad, and doubtless groups and individuals engaged in acts of civil disobedience in the centuries before pharaonic Egypt. In subsequent centuries, nonviolent actors have risked consequences that range from ridicule to death, by asserting religious freedom, resisting genocide, protecting ancient forests, defending tribal land, and escaping slavery. For most North Americans, however, civil disobedience seems to be viewed as the province of saints and heroes, naive idealists, or dangerous radicals. Despite being seen as marginal, many benefits that we take for granted, such as the weekend, free speech, or eight-hour work days, were won through direct action and campaigns of civil disobedience. In truth, ordinary people are choosing to take part in civil disobedience in ever-increasing numbers.[38]

There are numerous strategies and philosophies of nonviolent civil disobedience. I have some experience with Buddhist, Wiccan, feminist, labor, and anarchist traditions (which are not, by the way, mutually exclusive), but I am grounded in the radical Christian activist tradition of Dr. Martin Luther King, Dorothy Day, Cesar Chavez, the Berrigans, and others. These thinkers and actors have reflected to some degree on the biblical roots and the ethical mandates for civil disobedience: "We Christians are called to rediscover ourselves as people who hold allegiance only to God, as a people who practice, proclaim and promote God's way of nonviolent love and justice for all."[39]

But it is the observations of actors reflecting on their *experience* of engaged resistance that resonate most with the story of Shiphrah and Puah. This six-verse story of two thirteenth-century B.C.E. Egyptian characters, whose historical credentials are extremely doubtful, cannot be a biblical blueprint for Christian nonviolence; but the story's parallels with modern activism provide an opportunity to explore certain aspects of civil disobedience in the Christian activist tradition.

The text, for all its brevity, tells a surprising amount about the two women. Shiphrah and Puah are in a position of moderate power: they have access to Pharaoh; they are somewhat autonomous, can move about freely, and are of higher social status than the Israelite women they attend. At the same time, they are working women, not part of the court or the leisure class; and like all Egyptians, they are subjects of Pharaoh.

Throughout history many nonviolent thinkers have pointed out that civil disobedience and nonviolent resistance are frequently tools of the relatively powerless. There are a number of reasons that this is so: the powerful few rely on the consent of the powerless many; civil disobedience is most effective when used in large numbers. The powerless do not make the laws and do not have means to change them, and although nonviolence is universally available, the powerful have more expedient tools of coercion at their disposal. Shiphrah and Puah do not fit this pattern; they are not among the least powerful, but neither are a significant group of nonviolent practitioners today.

Shiphrah and Puah's situation has parallels to the situations of many first-world Christians involved in the work of civil disobedience and nonviolent resistance. For the most part, persons currently involved in Christian-based civil disobedience campaigns like Plowshares, School of the Americas Watch, and Nevada Desert Experience are white, educated, and have access to middle-class resources. We are not the elite, but neither are we the very poor. Like Shiphrah and Puah, we are persons of moderate privilege and power who oppose some aspect of the reign we live under. Many Christian activists come to civil disobedience from a context of struggle with our own inherited race and class privilege. But like Shiphrah and Puah, we join with one another in resisting death and empire in the situations where we find ourselves.

The midwives' noncooperation with Pharaoh is directly related to their understanding of the divine. "But the midwives feared God; they did not do as the king of Egypt commanded them, but they let the boys live" (Exod. 1:17). Activists from different traditions also understand their civil disobedience in religious and spiritual terms. Rabbi Abraham Joshua Heschel said that when he marched with Dr. Martin Luther King into Selma, he felt as if his legs were praying.[40] Buddhist monk Thich Nhat Hanh speaks of engaged Buddhism. Starhawk has numerous books describing how her activism is an expression of her Wiccan practice. Many people I know describe a sense of inner peace, a call, or a kind of deep rightness associated with civil disobedience actions in which they have taken part. I too have had this experience. The first time I risked arrest in a civil disobedience action, I was filled with joy and the absolute surety that there was no other place I could be at that moment and no other thing I could be doing. In Christian terms this is a sacramental experience—a moment when the divine is intensely present in human experience. John Dear, nonviolent activist and Jesuit priest, is the best articulator of this understanding: "If civil disobedience is enacted in a prayerful spirit of nonviolent love, it takes on the nature of a sacrament. When civil disobedience is engaged in a prayerful spirit of nonviolent love as a sacrament, *God is present.*"[41]

So what did Shiphrah and Puah do? They invited God to be present. And God responded. The first mention of God in Exodus is in 1:17, "but the midwives feared God," and the first action of God in Exodus is in 1:20, "God dealt well with the midwives." Shiphrah and Puah celebrated the sacrament of civil disobedience.

According to Hebrew Bible scholar Brevard Childs, the midwives were charged with a felony,[42] but what happened next is unclear. The midwives put forward their defense: "Because the Hebrew women are not like the Egyptian women; for they give birth before the midwife comes to them" (Exod. 1:19). This defense has a number of holes in it, but there is no cross-examination. The text moves immediately to the action of God, "God dealt well with the midwives" (Exod.1:20). We do not know what happened in the court of Pharaoh. Were the midwives acquitted? Were the charges dropped? Felony charges are no small thing. In the United States if you are convicted of a felony you lose the right to vote. (There are some communities where 25 percent of adult men cannot vote because of this law.[43])

Although the text seems to imply that the midwives were able to enjoy God's reward, Shiphrah and Puah do not speak or act again after Exodus 1:19. We know for certain that God rewarded them, but we do not know whether Pharaoh punished them. The women may have served prison sentences. Indeed if, the "*houses*" of v. 1:21 refer to their many descendants and not to actual buildings, they may even have been executed. We do not know. This aspect of the story is similar to modern civil disobedience campaigns in that before, during, and even after a specific action or campaign we are seldom able to assess its full impact. Civil disobedience is frequently met with some form of the question Why? What good does it do? What good does it do to hammer on the nose cone of a missile? What good are you doing in jail? What good is an action few will hear about and fewer still understand? What's the point? Why are you doing this? These are important questions, and the answers range from personal to systemic. But the true impact of a particular action may only be revealed in time, as is true in the case of the midwives' action.

Although the midwives themselves are "dealt well with," the consequence of their action for Israel is an escalation in Pharaoh's campaign. Instead of two henchwomen, who are bound to miss some births, all the people of Egypt are commanded to take part in the campaign of genocide. Resistance seems to have made the situation worse.

But a longer view shows exactly what civil disobedience can achieve. By refusing as individuals to cooperate with Pharaoh's campaign, the midwives do far more than keep themselves "pure." They force Pharaoh to seek other accomplices. They blow open his covert campaign causing him to reveal clearly that he is on the side of death. Shiphrah and Puah publicly

communicate both that they are unwilling to kill for Pharaoh and that
resistance is possible. They effectively do what Martin Luther King Jr.
called "arousing the consciences of the community over its injustice."[44]
The story of the midwives' refusal is followed immediately by the civil disobedience of Moses' mother, who does not throw her baby into the Nile
but places him safely in a tiny boat. Moses' sister then boldly confronts the
daughter of Pharaoh, conspiring with her to save the infant Moses. Each
act of civil disobedience inspires the next. Is it any wonder that Moses
becomes a resistance leader with such women influencing his early life? The
baby in the basket becomes the man who demands that his people be free
to worship God and then marches with a band of slaves out of the house
of bondage. The midwives' civil disobedience is the beginning of the end of
Pharaoh's tyranny.

CONCLUSION

For readers who identify with Egypt, reading Shiphrah and Puah as
Egyptian allies of Israel offers much insight. Their story tells of the transition from ordinary to extraordinary. From a wisdom perspective Shiphrah
and Puah are women who by simple observation in their daily lives—
watching babies get born, seeing how other families live, observing power
relationships—come to the fear of God, or to *wisdom*. In terms of action,
theirs is a story of how simple refusal to cooperate with evil—not killing
babies—becomes a pivotal act: the first recorded civil disobedience action
and the starting point for the exodus. Without making them into fixed and
flawless role models, first-world Christians can reclaim Shiphrah and Puah
as courageous foremothers who acted together and were not paralyzed by
their privilege. Let us celebrate the story of courageous women who acted
against the grain, as we live our own stories of resistance to empire.

10

OTHER EGYPTIANS

Despite the fact that scholars from various other disciplines have argued that Moses must be Egyptian, nearly all biblical scholars have refused even to entertain this possibility. Several factors have conspired to make this so. The first is anti-African sentiment, both on the part of Priestly editors of the biblical text[1] and centuries later from biblical scholars themselves. The second factor is that scholars have tended to treat race, religion, and nation as identical. The third reason that scholars refuse to address the possibility that Moses was Egyptian is that biblical scholarship is, for the most part, practiced by Jews and Christians, and this refusal is an act of loyalty to faith. All three factors share the assumption that, were Moses Egyptian, this would somehow dilute or diminish his Jewishness.

African American biblical scholar Randall Bailey has marshaled the following textual and historical evidence in support of Moses' Egyptian identity.[2] Moses' lineage is unclear; there are two conflicting Israelite genealogies for Moses. Moses is a known Egyptian name, and the story for the Hebrew homonym (Moshe, "I drew him out of the water" [Exod. 2:10]) is probably not intended to be taken literally. When the daughters of the priest of Midian encounter Moses at the well (Exod. 2:19), they identify him as Egyptian. Finally, prior to the exile, Egyptians were highly regarded in Israel, so an Egyptian leader would have been a sign of prestige.

As we noted in earlier chapters, the stories of the midwives, Pharaoh's daughter, and the infant Moses (Exod. 1:15-2:10) were composed after the accounts of Moses' call, rise to leadership, and encounters with Pharaoh. Bailey claims that the stories of the prologue are Priestly attempts to explain why an Egyptian led Israel out of Egypt.[3] "As one looks at material in later units the clear message is that Moses is Egyptian."[4] Bailey contends that Exodus 3:1 is actually the first introduction of Moses: "Moses was keeping the flock of his father-in-law Jethro, the priest of Midian; he led his flock beyond the wilderness, and came to Horeb, the mountain of

God" (Exod. 3:1). Here the reader learns Moses' Egyptian name, his occupation, and his relation to his employer.

Bailey's reading puts a fascinating spin on Moses' encounter with the God of Israel in the bush that burns but is not consumed.

> "So come, I will send you to Pharaoh to bring my people, the Israelites, out of Egypt." But Moses said to God, "Who am I that I should go to Pharaoh, and bring the Israelites out of Egypt?" He said, "I will be with you; and this shall be the sign for you that it is I who sent you: when you have brought the people out of Egypt, you shall worship God on this mountain."
>
> But Moses said to God, "If I come to the Israelites and say to them, 'The God of your ancestors has sent me to you,' and they ask me, 'What is his name?' what shall I say to them?" God said to Moses, "I AM WHO I AM." He said further, "Thus you shall say to the Israelites, 'I AM has sent me to you.'" God also said to Moses, "Thus you shall say to the Israelites, 'The LORD the God of your ancestors, the God of Abraham, the God of Isaac, and the God of Jacob, has sent me to you':
>> This is my name forever.
>> and this is my title for all generations." (Exod. 3:10-15)

Notice the use of pronouns, God does not call the Israelites Moses' people, nor does Moses claim Abraham, Isaac, and Jacob as his ancestors. Moses identifies and is identified as an outsider. Read in this light, the sense behind Moses' questions and protestations becomes strikingly clear.

> "Who am I [*an Egyptian*] that I should go to Pharaoh, and bring the Israelites out of Egypt?" (Exod. 3:11)

> "If I come to the Israelites and say to them, 'The God of your ancestors has sent me to you,' and they ask me [*as a test*], 'What is his name?' what shall I say to them? [*since I don't know your name*]" (Exod. 3:13)

Moses the Egyptian knows nothing about this God of the Israelites.

For those of us reading Exodus and identifying with Egypt, is there anything to be gained from reading Moses as Egyptian?

There are certain parallels between the biblical accounts of Moses' life and the lives of privileged people who want to work for justice. "Who am I that I should go?" "What if they ask me your name?" "What if they don't believe me?" "What if they don't listen to me?" "I'm not a good speaker, please send someone else." These repeated attempts of Moses to avoid God's call are part of the prophetic call formula.[5] But like Moses, those of us who would oppose injustice, and especially injustice that benefits us, must also do battle with our own internal resistance. We must answer the voices from our families, our friends, our culture, and our heads that tell us that the forces we are fighting are too strong, that we cannot make a difference, and that the best we can do is to take care of our loved ones—the voices that say that our efforts help no one and harm us.

Moses left the city and the trappings of his privileged youth; afraid for his life he fled Egypt and tended sheep in the wilderness. Some of us who leave empire also make dramatic breaks from our past. By giving away money, quitting a job, joining a community, or coming out as lesbian, gay, bisexual, or transgender, we act out our defection from the order we once supported, if only by our silence. Others of us are more methodical, disentangling ourselves from empire's thorns slowly and deliberately. For some, Moses' flight from city to wilderness is critical. To resist empire we must move, if only temporarily, from its centers where the constant messages of consumption, competition, comfort, and control drown out the voice of God. In gardens, farms, deserts, and forests modern fugitives from the city are reconnecting to an order that is older and deeper than empire. Fast or slow, in the city or outside of it, those of us who would be part of God's project must declare that we no longer belong to Egypt: and when we do, no matter how pervasive and rooted in us empire is, we, like Moses, have the divine assurance, "I will be with you" (Exod. 3:12a).

Moses saw the burning bush but it was not until he *turned aside* and *looked* that God spoke to him. God will not be coerced or manipulated, but people of privilege who wish to find God can cultivate that possibility. We can place ourselves in the way of change's possibility and open ourselves to difference.[6] An important way for first-world Christians to open ourselves to difference, *to turn and look*, is by working together with people of race, class, orientation, and nationality different from our own. Moses worked with Aaron, Zipporah, Miriam, and Joshua; he did not act alone. As Randall Bailey says, reading Moses as an Egyptian leader of Israel, "suggests that the liberation narratives of Exodus originally spoke to class struggle along with national struggles. It also suggests that coalitions among people across class and national lines within such struggles are a model for consideration for our current liberation efforts."[7]

The Israelites did not follow Moses unhesitatingly; they were mistrustful and questioning.

> They said to Moshe:
> Is it because there are no graves in Egypt
> that you have taken us out to die in the wilderness?
> What is this that you have done to us, bringing us out of Egypt?
> Is this not the very word that we spoke to you in Egypt,
> saying: Let us alone, that we may serve Egypt!
> Indeed better for us serving Egypt
> than our dying in the wilderness! (Exod. 14:11-12, Fox)[8]

Modern activists who come from privilege face a similar situation. Even after we believe we have proven ourselves allies of the oppressed, those of us who have the incredible privilege of choosing whether or not we deal with racism, homophobia, or any other manifestation of dominance, will continue to lack credibility with those who have no choice. Race and class traitors must always be about the work of proving ourselves trustworthy.

Although reading Moses as an Egyptian offers first-world readers some insights, it is a reading that must be exercised with caution and attention to the power dynamics and differentials involved. Randall Bailey's primary concern in reading Moses as an Egyptian is to reclaim his African identity; our primary concern is to understand Moses as a person of privilege who acted against empire. While these readings overlap, Bailey is consciously reading from below, and we are consciously reading from above. So while Bailey says, Moses was *African*, we say Moses was of the elite. Prior to the Babylonian Exile of the sixth century B.C.E., these two assertions might have had almost identical meanings for readers in Israel, but in the centuries of intervening history and among a vast audience of modern readers, African and elite have come to be almost opposites.

In the story of the exodus it is very unlikely that race, as we understand it today, was an issue. Indeed race as we understand it is a fairly recent invention. Consider that the final editor of the text would have us believe that Moses, an Israelite, was raised in Pharaoh's court without question as to his identity. When he encounters Zipporah and her sisters at Midian, they recognize him as an Egyptian.

> When Pharaoh heard of it, he sought to kill Moses. But Moses fled from Pharaoh. He settled in the land of Midian, and sat down by a well. The priest of Midian had seven daughters. They came to draw water, and filled the troughs to water their father's flock. But some shepherds came and drove them away. Moses got up and came to their defense and watered their flock. When they returned to their father Reuel, he said, "How is it that you have come back so soon today?" They said, "An Egyptian helped us against the shepherds; he even drew water for us and watered the flock." (Exod. 2:15-19)

Whatever distinguishes Israelites from Egyptians it is not skin color, hair texture, facial features, or physical stature. In Exodus the Egyptians, and particularly Pharaoh, lie about the Israelites, denigrate the Israelites' religion; they fear the Israelites and project their own violence onto them. The way that they manipulate difference is strikingly like the way that racism operates in North America.

For white readers and people of privilege it is important that, in reading Moses as Egyptian, we do not promote racism and classism, implying that only privileged groups produce leaders. It is a historical fact that as popular figures gain ascendancy, the attributes and actions of others are accredited to them, just as Miriam's Song at the Sea was attributed to Moses. For this reason we know very little about the peers and companions of heroes and superstars like Moses. Nevertheless, in our egyptian reading of Moses, people of privilege must emphasize what we know, that he worked with others across boundaries of nation and class.

OTHER EGYPTIANS

In previous chapters we have looked at several major Egyptian characters in Exodus. The pharaohs were living embodiments of empire who opposed and confounded liberation at every turn. Pharaoh's daughter was the savior of the savior. At the very least she engaged in one beautiful and saving act, and she may even have begun a true defection from the courts of Pharaoh that one day by the river. Shiphrah and Puah were the foremothers of civil disobedience. In this chapter we see that Moses himself may have been an Egyptian acting on behalf of God's justice. For modern readers who identify with Egypt, each of these characters and stories offers parallels and possibilities for our own lives, but heroes and royalty are not always easy to identify with. Are there any ordinary Egyptians in Exodus? And are these Egyptians part of the project of liberation? In chapters 4 and 5 of this book we looked at Egypt from a broad perspective. Now we will look at some of the specifics and complexities of the text, examining minor characters who are only briefly mentioned.

Those Officials of Pharaoh
Who Feared the Word of YHWH

Those officials of Pharaoh who feared the word of the LORD hurried their slaves and livestock off to a secure place. (Exod. 9:20)

With each successive episode of the plague narratives, the obstinate pharaoh had to face his diminishing ability to control the situation and even to control his own subjects. Although the narrators' chief concern seems to have been to discredit Pharaoh, Exodus 9:20 above also conveys the fact that not all Egyptians agreed or fully cooperated with Pharaoh. The fact is that individual Egyptians had agency, and this is very good news for those of us identifying with Egypt.

George Pixley suggests that the historical kernel behind the mention of these free-thinking officials are those state bureaucrats who allied themselves with the peasant uprising against the Canaanite city-states sparked by Israel's arrival in Canaan.[9] In the text, the officials who fear the word of the LORD are neither praised nor condemned; their actions are simply recorded. Having endured blood, frogs, insects, cattle disease, and boils with no opportunity for respite, when a warning comes they take the opportunity to save their property, hurrying their slaves and livestock off to a secure place. Clearly they are acting out of self-interest, but even this is more than Pharaoh will do.

Exodus 9:20 explains the official's actions in terms of fearing the word of the LORD. If we recall from the previous chapter the definition of fear of the LORD as wisdom, it is clear that acting out of self-interest is not necessarily at odds with wisdom. Individuals come to wisdom, or fear of YHWH, through observing the world around them, particularly the natural world. The officials of Pharaoh observe Pharaoh's diminishing control and the increasing devastation of their country, their homes, and their wealth. Obviously for these officials, Pharaoh's rule no longer protects them or their interests. "Pharaoh's courtiers . . . do not actually join Moses and the undertaking pursued by him and his class. They do however respect it, and place their personal interest, threatened by the violence predicated in Yahweh's message, ahead of their class solidarity with Pharaoh."[10]

Although there is only one verse referring to the officials of Pharaoh who feared the word of YHWH, their presence at all is a gift to first-world readers. For those of us awakening to the knowledge that empire is a construction of pride, coercion, and domination that can only consume and does not ultimately serve us, servants of Pharaoh who fear the word of YHWH is what we seek to be. If we, like the servants of Pharaoh, can break class solidarity, whether for self-interest or altruism, we will have shattered one of the most powerful holds that empire has over us. Class identification is deeply ingrained in us even as we deny the classed nature of our society.

> The closest most folks can come to talking about class in this nation is to talk about money. For so long everyone has wanted to hold on to the belief that the United States is a class-free society—that anyone who works hard enough can make it to the top. Few people stop to think that in a class-free society there would be no top. While it has always been obvious that some folks have more money than other folks, class difference and classism are rarely overtly apparent, or they are not acknowledged when present.[11]

The passage about the God-fearing officials offers us very little, but if we bring our own stories to it, we can imagine new endings that remain true to the roots of the story itself. What if, as it did for Pharaoh's daughter, a single act motivated by self-interest became a catalyst for change in the lives of these Egyptians? Might not some of these Egyptians have given gifts to their departing neighbors to start them out on their new lives? Might not a few of those who gave gifts have chosen to throw their lot in with their allies and march out of Egypt with the mixed multitude?

Egyptians Who Gave Them
Jewelry and Clothes

Three times in Exodus an event just prior to the Israelites' departure is described. The Israelites ask their neighbors for valuable goods—jewelry and clothing—and because YHWH has put them in good favor with Egypt, the Egyptians give these willingly. Israel then departs suddenly, thus plundering Egypt. The incident is first mentioned in the call of Moses.

> "I will bring this people into such favor with the Egyptians that, when you go, you will not go empty-handed; each woman shall ask her neighbor and any woman living in the neighbor's house for jewelry of silver and gold, and clothing, and you shall put them on your sons and on your daughters; and so you shall plunder the Egyptians." (Exod. 3:21-22)

Later (Exod. 11:2) YHWH tells Moses to instruct the people to carry out this plan; and in Exodus 12, the event is recorded as accomplished. In Psalm 105, which includes one of the independent versions of the plagues, there is a fleeting reference to perhaps the same event, "He brought them out with silver and gold" (Ps. 105:37).

Although the story uses the Hebrew verb *natsal*, "to strip or plunder,"[12] a word meaning theft by a conquering military force, what is described is asking for goods, receiving them, and departure. Most exegetes assume that this is a story of wit and deception. The Israelites borrowed expensive goods and then left without telling the owners.[13] The reference to plunder is humor; how else but through deception could a small, unarmed group plunder a wealthy empire with a standing army? And who but such a band would consider some clothing and jewelry plunder?

From the rabbinic age to the present, readers have felt compelled to defend or justify the Israelite deception. One argument is that by taking clothing and valuables the Israelites were acquiring just wages for their years of uncompensated labor in Egypt. Other scholars make a similar argument, connecting the Exodus passages with Deuteronomy 15:13-14:

> And when you send a male slave out from you a free person, you shall not send him out empty-handed. Provide liberally out of your flock, your threshing floor, and your winepress, thus giving to him some of the bounty with which the LORD your God has blessed you.

These scholars say that according to the law, the Israelites, as freed slaves, were entitled to a portion of the slaveholders' assets and goods. The effectiveness of these arguments is diminished by the fact that the ordinary Egyptians who were neighbors of Israelite slaves were probably not slave holders and did not benefit from Pharaoh's building projects any more than ordinary Americans benefit from U.S. military spending.

In the second chapter of this book, we observed that Exodus is not a seamless composition but a patchwork of stories representing different times and perspectives. If we look at the despoiling of the Egyptians apart from the rest of the Exodus narrative, less is required in the way of mental gymnastics to explain Israel's actions.

The three renditions of the plundering of Egypt are related to one another, but they do not have any clear connection with the other literary units in Exodus: plagues, Passover, sea. Rather, they represent a very stark version of the exodus consisting only of escape and clandestine flight. In this minimalist exodus it is easy to imagine a situation that might have given birth to a story of plunder: a boastful campfire scene where each person bests the last by revealing what great spoils they have taken from Egypt.

> Well I went down to the rich man's house
> And I took back what he stole from me
> Took back my dignity
> Took back my humanity.[14]

This is a tale of slave escape; and in the tradition of Brer Rabbit and other tricksters it requires no apology for taking from the oppressors. This is a story that delights in "getting over." Indeed the so-called plunder of the Egyptians is the climax of this version of the exodus.

For first-world readers, I propose yet another reading of this story, or at least a reading to accompany the aforementioned popular understandings. Based on the second rendition of the story (Exod. 11:2-3), I argue that Egyptian women gave valuables to the departing Israelite women as a conscious act of solidarity.

Let us look at all three versions of the story together.

"I will bring this people into such favor with the Egyptians that, when you go, you will not go empty-handed; each woman shall ask her neighbor and any woman living in the neighbor's house for jewelry of silver and gold, and clothing, and you shall put them on your sons and on your daughters; and so you shall plunder the Egyptians." (Exod. 3:21-22)

Tell the people that every man is to ask his neighbor and every woman is to ask her neighbor for objects of silver and gold. The LORD gave the people favor in the sight of the Egyptians. (Exod. 11:2-3a)

The Israelites had done as Moses told them; they had asked the Egyptians for jewelry of silver and gold, and for clothing, and the LORD had given the people favor in the sight of the Egyptians, so that they let them have what they asked. And so they plundered the Egyptians. (Exod. 12:35-36)

All three versions of the story include the same basic facts: Egyptians and Israelites are neighbors; Israelites are to ask for silver and gold; Egyptians favor Israelites. In both Exodus 3:22 and Exodus 11:2, women are told specifically to request goods from their female neighbors. What Exodus 11:2 lacks is the narrators' *interpretation* of the events, "thus they plundered the Egyptians."

Unlike parts of the plague narratives where the Israelites are ghettoized in Goshen, this passage (Exod. 11:2) assumes that Egyptians and Israelites lived side by side as neighbors. Although proximity can breed or exacerbate animosity, those who share a location also share certain experiences. If the neighborhood floods, everybody gets wet; in a fire, anyone's house can burn; downwind from the medical incinerator, everybody's kids get sick; and when the water is cut off, someone in every house must carry buckets. For the most part, in ancient times and in our own, neighborhoods house people of similar economic levels. Egyptians who lived next to Israelite laborers would have been peasants, not courtiers. Whatever ethnic, religious, racial, or cultural differences might have divided them, poor Egyptians had a great deal in common with their Israelite neighbors. As Michael Walzer says, the Israelites were not the only oppressed in Egypt, "many Egyptians were similarly subject."[15]

Exodus 11:2 states that Israelite men were to ask their male neighbors for valuables and that Israelite women were to ask their female neighbors. In Exodus 3:22, the instructions are only for women. For most of Exodus, women's presence and activity are not mentioned, so why do women appear in these passages? Perhaps the implication is that men and women had jurisdiction over different kinds of property, say cordless drills and hand mixers, but the goods mentioned are not sex specific, in Egypt men were as likely as women to have ornaments of silver and gold. Something else is going on here, something to do with women.

Julian Morgenstern argues that "clothing and jewelry" is a formula that refers specifically to brides and therefore women. According to Morgenstern the original parts of the tradition refer only to women and the men were added to the text later.[16] The other Egyptian women in Exodus are Pharaoh's daughter, who defies Pharaoh by saving a Hebrew infant, and Shiphrah and Puah, who break Egyptian law by refusing to kill Hebrew babies. Outside of the "plunder" passages, the only time Egyptian and Israelite women are mentioned together Pharaoh's daughter, her servants, Moses' mother and her daughter collaborate to save the infant Moses (Exod. 2:1-10). Perhaps the presence of Israelite and Egyptian women together indicates that this too is a story of collaboration across lines of difference.

In ancient Egypt, women, more than men, moved in the domestic sphere, thus neighbors impacted women's lives more than men's. Egyptian and Israelite women may have shared childcare or food.[17] I think this is not a story of great spoils from the rich man's house but rather one of simple gifts from one poor woman to another. After all, what good would fine clothes be in the wilderness, or gold and silver in a land of milk and honey? This giving is not an act of charity or *noblesse oblige* imposed by the wealthy. Like Pharaoh's daughter, the Egyptian women respond to the prompting of their Israelite neighbors with humanity.

Despite what readers, commentators, and translators[18] have assumed, the text does not say that the Israelites asked to *borrow* objects of silver and gold. It says that they asked for and received them. According to the text, the Egyptians gave the Israelites these goods because YHWH gave the Israelites favor in the sight of the Egyptians. The Egyptians *liked* the Israelites; they thought well of them. This manifestation of YHWH's power stands in stark contrast to the destruction of the plagues and at the sea.

> Yahweh's victory is not only through force. In part, it comes about through a change of heart within some of the Egyptians. Just as Pharaoh's daughter had pity on the infant who she *saw* in the basket, so God will give the Israelites favor "in the *sight* of the Egyptians" (RSV following the Hebrew). So when each departing Israelite woman asks her neighbor for a parting gift, it will be freely given.[19]

Perhaps in this version of the exodus the power of YHWH is something so different from anything Egypt or Israel has ever known that it can change the meaning of the word plunder. The power of YHWH and the solidarity of women changed the relationship between Egyptian and Israelite: "The LORD had given the people favor in the sight of the Egyptians, so that they let them have what they asked" (Exod. 12:36). And if the power of YHWH and the experience of being neighbors could soften the hearts of ordinary Egyptian women, then there is hope for those of us who live under empire today.

Modern Solidarity and Sabbath Economics

Some Egyptians experienced a change of heart and acted in conscious solidarity with their oppressed Israelite neighbors. Privileged readers of Exodus today have an example of first-world Christians doing the same. Through the Jubilee movement, people of debt-impoverished nations and people of wealthy nations are working together in solidarity using a very old idea. The Deuteronomy passage regarding compensation for released slaves (15:13-14), which we looked at earlier, is an example of the biblical tradition of Sabbath economics. The theme of Sabbath economics pervades both Christian and Jewish scriptures and is focused on abundance, dependence on the earth, just distribution of resources, and the idea that there is enough for everyone. The manna of Exodus 16 exemplifies this understanding of God's and earth's abundance: everyone has enough but it is impossible to hoard. The Jubilee year, best described in Leviticus 25, was a legal codification of Sabbath economics. Every fifty years the inevitable distortions, inequalities, and accumulations of daily commerce were leveled: land was restored to its original owners, captives were released, fields were to lie fallow, and debts were canceled. The responsibility for keeping these laws fell largely to those who had accumulated wealth.

In the late 1990s, with the approaching turn of the millennium, liberal church groups became interested in the idea of Jubilee and began to explore the idea through economic research, biblical study, educational campaigns, and North–South dialogue. The most notable result of this commitment of time and energy has been a strong ecumenical movement calling for the cancellation of international debt of the world's most impoverished nations. Despite its flaws and limitations[20] the Jubilee 2000 movement has brought the subject of international debt to the pulpits and pew bulletins of mainline churches in the Northern Hemisphere. Jubilee has been an entry point for more traditionally conservative church people into the growing anti-globalization movement. Jubilee activists played a significant role in the enormously successful demonstrations against the World Trade Organization in Seattle in 1999. Jubilee marches and demonstrations, international signature campaigns, and lobbying have gained the attention of the world media. Recently the various Jubilee campaigns have held demonstrations at meetings of the International Monetary Fund, the World Bank, and the G-8; have monitored corruption in the administration of debt relief; and have continued to demand cancellation of the debts of the world's most impoverished nations.[21] So it is possible for ordinary Egyptians and North Americans to act in solidarity with their neighbors.

The Mixed Multitude

The Israelites journeyed from Rameses to Succoth, about six hundred thousand men on foot, besides children. A erev rav also went up with them, and livestock in great numbers, both flocks and herds. (Exod. 12:37-38)

Exodus 12:38 is the only place in the Bible where the expression *erev rav* appears. *Rav* is a common word, appearing more than four hundred times in the Hebrew Bible; it is translated as "numerous, much, many, great, plentiful, enough, and abundant."[22] The only other occurrence of the word *erev* is Leviticus 13:48-59, where it is a technical term in weaving, but the meaning of the word is mixture or combination. Translations of the phrase *erev rav* do not vary a great deal: mixed crowd (NRSV), numerous strangers,[23] many strangers,[24] mixed multitude (following the Septuagint), people of various sorts.[25] It would seem that the sense of the phrase is reasonably clear: a great mixture or a large group of people who are not Israelites. The composition of the group, however, is unclear; the text offers no explicit social or ethnic indicators as to who might have shared the exodus with Israel and why.

Because for some people the question, Who made the exodus? raises other questions: Who is included in the covenant? Who is a Jew? Who is in and who is out? Various interpreters' answers to these questions influence how they read Exodus 12:38. In the midrashic writings the rabbis said that the reference to the mixed multitude indicates that not only Israel, but the whole of humanity, was brought out of Egypt.[26] Jewish biblical scholar Jon Levenson is adamant that Exodus is too specifically about Jewish liberation and religious identity to be used credibly by non-Jews as a liberation text.[27] He argues based on the parallel passage in Nehemiah 13:3, that the phrase should be translated, "a large number of people of mixed blood."[28] That is to say the mixed multitude consisted of people with one Israelite parent. George Pixley, a Latin American liberation theologian, says Exodus 12:38 shows that people of every class took part in the exodus.[29] Rita Burns, an American feminist employed at a Catholic university, gives a very open definition of those who left Egypt: "it is not unlikely that the one common element which was shared by members of the exodus group was not blood kinship or faith but a marginalized social status."[30] It certainly makes sense that during this early formative period, Israel would have been a flexible and open community.

Although the mixed multitude is not described, there are clues to their identity in surrounding and similar material. Immediately following the reference to the mixed crowd are instructions for the Passover, including what to do if, "an alien who resides with you wants to celebrate the passover to the LORD" (Exod. 12:48). The passage about the mixed multitude (Exod. 12:38), is often paired with Numbers 11:4, where the Israelites and others with them in the wilderness, cry out for the good things of Egypt.

> The rabble among them had a strong craving; and the Israelites also wept again, and said, "If only we had meat to eat! We remember the fish we used to eat in Egypt for nothing, the cucumbers, the melons, the leeks, the onions, and the garlic, but now our strength is dried up, and there is nothing at all but this manna to look at." (Num. 11:4-6)

These passages are linked because in the Septuagint, a Greek translation of the Hebrew Bible begun in Egypt in the third century B.C.E., mixed crowd (*erev rav*) and rabble (*asaph suph*) are both translated as "mixed multitude."[31]

Most commentators conclude from the textual and historical evidence that there were people who neither identified as Israelite nor were identified by others as Israelite, who took part in the exodus and dwelt in the wilderness. They do not, however, go so far as to suggest what seems obvious to me: that Egyptians took part in the exodus.

Exodus 11:5, "from the firstborn of Pharaoh who sits on his throne to the firstborn of the female slave who is behind the handmill," suggests that Egyptians were also slaves in this house of bondage. Leviticus 24:10 tells that "a man whose mother was an Israelite and whose father was an Egyptian, came out among the people of Israel," that is, he made the exodus. In Deuteronomy 23:7, the Hebrews are commanded, "you shall not abhor any of the Egyptians, because you were an alien residing in their land."

According to the midrash, Pharaoh's daughter was an Egyptian who made the exodus.[32] These traditions indicate that there were Egyptian slaves in Egypt, that some Egyptians may have made the exodus and that Egyptians lived among the Israelites post-exodus. The fact that the final description of those Egyptians who aided their neighbors with gifts of jewelry and clothing directly precedes the passage about the mixed multitude strongly suggests a connection between these two groups. However, the most obvious reason to assume that there were Egyptians in the mixed multitude is the simple fact that in Exodus, Egyptians and Israelites are the only peoples mentioned in Egypt. It stands to reason then, if some non-Israelite group were leaving Egypt, at least some Egyptians would be included.

CONCLUSION

What lessons do the stories of these "other" Egyptians offer first-world Christians who "want to be in that number?" Like the officials of Pharaoh, we need to observe the world around us and to seek wisdom, not glibly identifying with the class above us.

> Ideologically, through mass media seduction, many of the world's have-nots take on the thoughts and values of ruling classes. In everyday life they ideologically join with the rich to protect the class interests of the wealthy.[33]

We need to know our neighbors and, like the Egyptian women, offer them concrete support and act in solidarity with them. The final and most difficult lesson from these Egyptian characters is that we first-world Christians must be willing to risk leaving the security of all we have known and walk out of empire.

In truth, the story of Moses the Egyptian and the stories of these other Egyptians are not a lot to go on. Exodus paints a scathing portrait of empire in which first-world Christians can recognize ourselves, but Exodus is very much Israel's story. Although occasionally generous in the depiction of class and race traitors, like Pharaoh's daughter and the midwives, Exodus does not offer privileged readers much in terms of *how* such change comes about, nor should it. It is not the oppressed's job to teach us to stop oppressing. It is their job to tell us to stop. When they have—and they *have*, clearly and repeatedly—it is our job to learn how. Further, Exodus is a story about leaving Egypt physically and therefore offers little by way of example for resisting empire while still in it. The state of global capitalism is such that not even the most remote-dwelling, traditionally living indigenous person is unimpacted by empire. Thus none of us has the option of leaving. For these reasons my hope for change is located in a large part outside of the text. In the final chapter we will look beyond Exodus.

PART THREE
BEYOND EXODUS

11

SETTING THE PEOPLE FREE

A Commissioning

This book was written out of loyalty to white middle-income church people, the people who, mostly unintentionally, taught me to love the Bible. I am angry that these who are my people—at least as much as the street folks and addicts, prostitutes, and mentally ill who now occupy my days— hear biblical readings that are almost exclusively personal. These personal readings "turn the Bible's religious passion for social justice into a teaching about individual salvation which has the net effect of rationalizing and perpetuating social inequity."[1] In the case of Exodus, such personalized readings ask middle-class people, "What keeps you from being liberated?" Readings of Exodus that focus on how the affluent are oppressed fail. They fail the poor by making their suffering invisible, they fail the text by making its political, community message psychological and personal, and they fail the rich by fearing to challenge them to the hard change and repentance that is liberation. My goal in writing is that people of privilege who identify as Christian will come to take the Bible's passion for justice seriously in their own lives and become involved in the work of justice. My hope is that my people will come out of empire.

A fundamental premise of this book is that first-world Christians, reading together, can use the sacred gift of our tradition to grapple with and live out our own stories in the empire of global capitalism. The Bible is a gift of our ancestors born of the love of God and struggle to do right in the world. In our modern self-absorption and shortsightedness, we have lost all reverence for the wisdom of our ancestors. It is difficult for modern people, and especially middle-class white people, to admit that anybody knows better than us, let alone people who lived thousands of years ago. But Exodus asks questions that are relevant beyond the book's ancient African and Near Eastern contexts.

- Who controls the land?
- Does the earth have its own integrity?

- Do poor people matter?
- Does power automatically deserve allegiance?
- How do you know if the law is right?
- Where do good things/good life come from?
- What is God like?
- Is empire the only way to live?
- What determines membership in a group?
- What are the characteristics of empire?

These questions are as relevant to those of us living under global capitalism today as they were thousands of years ago. In the previous chapters we explored some of these questions. Before we look at the task of leaving empire, let us briefly revisit some of the answers we have gleaned from Exodus.

A REVIEW

The core argument of this book is that first-world Christians have more in common with Egypt than with Israel in Exodus, and that this is a hermeneutical key that can unlock both Exodus and our own lives. Through the characters of the two pharaohs and the functioning of Egypt, Exodus presents us with a centuries-old portrait of empire from the perspective of the oppressed. From our context of today's global economy we can see how empire has changed over time. We can look at the qualities of empire: exploitation, slavery, genocide, deceit, and the various ways that people of privilege participate and collude in them. Looking specifically at the land of Egypt in Exodus allows us to focus on environmental/ecological issues in our own time, particularly issues of women and the environment and the connections between modern corporate exploitation of the natural world and of other humans.

Exodus is pervasively and disturbingly violent, with the pharaohs and YHWH being the most violent actors. Honestly addressing this violence in scripture can help us to address the structural violence in our own culture and to ask who carries it out and against whom. Exploring the violence in Exodus causes us to look at the connections and differences between violent stories and violent actions. First-world Christians can use the stories of Egypt in Exodus as a means of exploring our own participation in the modern empire of global capitalism. Knowing and recognizing our patterns of addiction to empire is the first step to breaking them.

In Exodus, Shiphrah and Puah and Pharaoh's daughter are Egyptian women from different levels of privilege who defy the law and act courageously with and on behalf of the oppressed. There are hints and indicators that other Egyptians too were part of the exodus project. The great gift of these stories is that the Israelite narrators of Exodus considered Egyptians to be capable of such acts of solidarity. This is an enormous vote of confidence for those of us who seek to live counter to empire today. However, the stories also show some of the complexities and ambiguities of trying to live and act in solidarity, the pitfalls of trying to cross, not from Egypt to Canaan, but simply from power to less power. According to Gregory Baum, a Canadian theologian, Israel's dissent and mutiny in the wilderness attest to the ambiguity of the people's commitment to liberation.[2] How much more ambiguous is the commitment of the privileged to liberation when in material terms we stand to lose?

Reading the Bible as we have in this book, as sacred story, can be tremendously valuable for people of privilege. Exodus is neither a history text nor a personal instruction book for life. Using the tools of critical scholarship, we can bring our minds to scripture and understand how a passage's very specific context might be compared to our own. Grappling with the parts of the text that disturb us or are at complete odds with our own values inoculates us against using the dangerous phrase "the Bible says" as a hammer or a weapon. By placing our egyptian reading of Exodus beside other liberation readings we open ourselves to critical evaluation from others seeking justice, and we are prevented from imagining that we have the one true interpretation. At the same time, being grounded in our own social and political context and being clear about our own assumptions and values provides a basis from which to evaluate our own and others' interpretations. Thus we can stand firm in our commitment to justice and need not fall into the fallacy of asserting that all interpretations are equally valid.

WHERE DO WE GO FROM HERE?

The Exodus authors had confidence that people of privilege could actively resist empire and be allies of the oppressed, but in the modern world of global capitalism this is a tremendous task. We are seeking in some real sense to leave behind everything we have known, for we have been raised and nurtured on empire. The challenge we face is compounded by the fact that we do not have the option of simple departure. We cannot, like Israel, go feral. There is no Promised Land lying empty and waiting for us; indeed there was not for Israel. Corporate globalization is such that the most remote enclaves and peoples are still touched by it. We must then resist empire while remaining somehow within it.

Empire surrounds us so completely that it is essentially invisible. Pop machines, skyscrapers, automobiles, television—the most ordinary stuff of our lives—is the effluvium of empire. We are continually plied with comfort and convenience that muffle any question or protest. But the fact that affluent lives may still be filled with suffering and struggle can render privilege invisible to those who have it. Those of us who would resist empire are faced with a difficult task. To see the luxury that surrounds us as anything but right and normal puts us profoundly out of step with our peers. Questioning empire, let alone saying no to it, seems impossible, absurd. What empire offers us is fun, fast, and glitzy, but more than anything else, it is normal.

By contrast, resistance and the work of solidarity are sometimes slow, boring, and inconvenient. Friends, family, and the people we love may not understand what we are trying to do. This can be lonely and alienating. It can be even more lonely when those whom we seek to join and support do not welcome us with open arms. When our intentions are good it can be hard to realize that the oppressed have every reason to mistrust us. Religion too can impede our task, for since the time of Constantine, the church has supported and modeled itself after empire. By all that empire has taught us to value, becoming allies of the oppressed is an exchange in which we stand to lose.

Corporate capitalism so pervades our lives and our planet that any resistance we offer seems terribly small. Success is one of the key elements of empire's mythology. For those of us raised on this myth it can be incredibly frustrating to feel that our efforts are futile or that we are constantly failing. When we cannot hope to win it is difficult for us to resist. Global capitalism is profoundly opposed to love of humanity, love of the earth, and love of God. A system based on domination cannot be fixed, but we can offer alternatives. Winning is not the overthrow of empire; it is any action that suggests that empire is not the only way.

We are faced with an enormous task, but this is the stuff that great stories are made of: leaving behind what has always represented security, starting out on a journey of discovery that will show us what lies behind the world we know. In order to survive in this new world we will need new ways of thinking and acting. In the introduction to this book, I laid out certain criteria for the evaluation of this reading of Exodus: dangerousness, subversiveness, insightfulness, usefulness, creativity, ferocity, rigor, honesty, joy, and faithfulness. In these last pages of this book I want to focus specifically on the criterion of usefulness. It is not enough that people read this book; it is my hope that through this reading people will come together to act for change. To do this we will need to change the ways we think, and speak, and act.

Old/New Ways of Thinking

As feminists have been saying for decades now, language is important. If we are to live a new way, then we require a new vocabulary. In the Christian tradition, on the political left, and in personal recovery and labor movements, there is a wealth of concepts and ideas that speak to our task of liberation, if we truly examine them. Hidden in the seemingly banal language of staid institutions are some radical roots. The following is an exploration of some ideas that first-world Christians can use to begin and to continue our resisting empire. This is not a complete project but a start: there are gaps and overlap; some ideas are connected and others are not.

Salvation

For most of us salvation seems to be concerned with our souls' destination after death. Christians of most varieties recognize Jesus as a savior, who through his living, suffering, dying, and rising, saved the world from sin. Individual Christians have a part in salvation—that is, we secure our place in heaven—either through baptism, absolution, good works, the grace of God, or some combination of these. For centuries this has been Christianity's interpretation of what happened to Jesus, how the Messiah could have died, and what that has to do with us.

For a long time the poor and people who are hungry have critiqued this "pie in the sky when you die" theology. Liberation theologians from different locations have challenged the notion of Jesus as savior and offer in its place a different interpretation. They say that from Genesis to Revelation, one of the most important biblical themes is liberation: freedom, justice, and dignity for the oppressed in this world. This is more in keeping with the Jewish tradition of the Messiah, a political deliverer on earth. Jesus died, according to this interpretation, not because God willed it, or stood aside and let it happen, but because Jesus defied empire. His death was the consequence of the way he lived, and the resurrection was God's vindication of Jesus' call for justice in the world.

According to this interpretation, God is more concerned with corporate sin, the sins of groups and classes, than with individual sin; and sin is most accurately defined as passivity in the face of injustice. Salvation, then, is not something that happens to individuals while we quietly assent. Salvation is participatory, and the means of participation is action for justice in this world. Salvation is not a destination but the journey, and salvation means acting in solidarity with one another.[3] For those of us who seek to live an alternative to empire, a notion of salvation which requires us to act for justice in the world is tremendously relevant.

Solidarity

Solidarity is a word heard often on the lips of white liberals and gender-based feminists who, like Pharaoh's daughter, want the poor painlessly raised to their own level of privilege and consumption. But solidarity is more than that.

Focus on solidarity calls for an end to facile adoption of the rhetoric of solidarity by Celtic-, Anglo-, European-American feminists, while they ignore and, sometimes consume the experiences and voices of the marginalized and oppressed, while ever adroitly, dodging the penitential call to conversion—to authenticity in word and deed.[4]

Too often those who speak of solidarity confuse it with surrogates: charity, paternalism, control, and the exercise of authority.[5]

The true meaning of solidarity is under serious attack and runs the risk of being drastically changed. The proof of this is how fashionable its usage has become, how easily it rolls off the tongues of all sorts of speakers, how unthreatening it is. If the true meaning of solidarity were understood and intended, visible radical change would be happening in the lives of those who endorse it with their applause.[6]

Solidarity is the recognition of our own complacency in the interconnected structures of oppression, our shared interest and responsibility across lines of difference, our accountability to those with less power, and our commitment to take action, persistently and with others, to challenge and change all forms of domination and injustice—from which we benefit and by which we are harmed. Solidarity involves both personal transformation and concrete work for social change; it requires first-world Christians and people of privilege to place ourselves in the way of conversion.[7]

Conversion

Conversion is a church word, popular in churches that claim to be apolitical but in fact support the status quo. But conversion is transformation: a change of heart in both the Hebrew and the English sense of the word heart. As with Pharaoh's heart, conversion involves an increase in courage, resolve, and determination, but it also requires an increase in love, compassion, and openness. Conversion is a change of heart that compels us to take new action, or the same action differently.

Christians tend to understand conversion on the "road to Damascus" model. We get knocked off our horse and then—bam—effortless, instantaneous, and once and for all, we are made new. While it is true that events like this happen, these experiences are more accurately moments of profound awareness of the loss and joy of our conversion, not conversion itself. Conversion is not an event but a process, and if it is not ongoing, all we have is the memory of moments of clarity.

Yet, conversion cannot be willed, neither can it be manipulated. It is possible when we place ourselves in the way of change's possibility, when we open ourselves to difference. Still, conversion is always tenuous, always precarious; while difficult to achieve, it is even more difficult to sustain.[8]

While we cannot will or manipulate conversion, there are ways that persons of privilege can either shield ourselves from the opportunity for conversion or "place ourselves in the way of change's possibility." We can do this through our attitudes but more concretely by where we physically locate ourselves. You can be as open to difference as you want in suburbia, but you'll be hard pressed to find much. People of privilege must talk and work together as equal partners with people who do not resemble us, people who may make us uncomfortable: poor people, people of color, queer people, people with disabilities, young people. If first-world Christians understand conversion as a process that requires us to work across lines of difference we will continue to be converted to the sometimes uncomfortable work of liberation.

Humility

Now the man Moses was very humble. (Num. 12:3a)

African American feminist theologian Shawn Copeland calls for "a new and bold expression of the virtue of humility."[9] People of privilege must practice humility in order to listen to and work with people who experience oppression. First-world Christians need to reclaim the virtue of humility. According to Webster's dictionary, to be humble is "having or showing a consciousness of one's defects or shortcomings; not proud; not self-assertive; modest." Humility as it is understood in Western culture, refers almost exclusively to individuals and, while we may praise someone's modesty (usually at their funeral) humility is not a virtue that is sought after. In the United States especially, it is not a good thing to be "not self-assertive." We firmly believe that each person, especially each man, should be recognized and compensated for his accomplishments. Because of our great cultural arrogance, humility is even less valued at the group or national level.[10] We are entirely unconscious of our defects and shortcomings.

Until recently it has been almost impossible for first-world people, particularly those of northern European heritage, to imagine that our qualities, values, possessions, activities, and way of life were not simply the best. Yet the kind of humility required for true solidarity and working with others demands that first-world Christians recognize that our way is only one of many. The practice of this kind of humility is difficult for those who have always lived with a sense of entitlement. It involves not speaking first, sometimes not speaking at all, waiting to be asked, questioning our assumptions, not setting the pace, not having or getting to be right.

Passion

In the Christian tradition, "passion" has held two meanings that seem very different. The first is sexual lust and the second is Jesus' experience from the time of the Last Supper until his death: mostly suffering. These apparent opposites each represent an aspect of passion. Passion is about intimacy, intensity, deep connection, love, and physical bodies. Passion is also about being in touch with a suffering world, knowing that we are harmed by the suffering of others; and passion is about living wholly for justice in a way that puts us in conflict with the powers of domination. The church, in its desire for control, has distorted these aspects of passion by venerating one and denigrating the other such that they are reduced to bad sex and good suffering. Churches, especially mainline Protestant denominations, out of a fear of God's spirit and our own creatureliness, have projected all our passion onto others: to women, to people of color, to queers, and even to other, poorer churches. Where we cannot project our passions we have buried them. When we deny our desires and refuse to feel our feelings, the result is first-world despair and our inability to act for justice despite a wealth of resources. As queer theologian Carter Heyward says, "the church has become a passionless institution."[11]

But passion is a gift from God, a way of life that embraces abundance. The great figures of our tradition—Eve, Moses, the Prophets, Mary, Jesus—all lived lives of passion. If first-world Christians can connect with the knowledge that every human and all of creation are beloved of God and profoundly deserving of justice and dignity, then we will be set on fire for the work of justice. We must find the courage to connect with this deep well of passion within us, for the time will come when it is not enough to be good or to act out of duty, and only passion will sustain us. In the words of Coleen Fulmer's song:

> God is passionate life
> Strong and vibrant in us
> As we seek justice
> For all people.[12]

Vigilance[13]

By ecclesial definition, a vigil is a devotional watch on the eve of some fast or holy day. This tradition of preparing our hearts and spirits for some especially sacred event runs counter to the logic of empire. Vigil does not ask that we accomplish something; instead it affirms that our presence itself has meaning, that our attention is a valuable currency. Both deliberately and unintentionally modern vigils attest to the power and possibility of the tradition of vigilance.

In the alley in my neighborhood where a young man was shot and killed, family, neighbors, and church people come to pray and remember and together take back the street too dangerous for one person to walk alone.

In Seattle, through a bitter rainy week in winter, a few hundred individuals refused to leave the front doors of the county jail. They sang and danced and chanted and drummed, built tents, made speeches, set up a kitchen and held meetings until their companions were released.

After gay city council member Harvey Milk and San Francisco mayor George Moscone were murdered by homophobic council member Dan White, thousands of people spontaneously filled the streets and marched to city hall in silence.

In secular terms a vigil is "a purposeful or watchful staying awake during the usual hours of sleep." Throughout scripture we are urged repeatedly to see, to hear, to listen, to wake up, and to pay attention to that which surrounds us; in short, we are called to be vigilant. "Are you asleep? Could you not keep awake one hour? Keep awake and pray that you may not come into the time of trial" (Mark 14:37b-38a).

One of the deceptions of empire is that it can make us believe that there is nothing else. It keeps us asleep to the real workings of the world, to environmental destruction, and to the increase in global poverty. We need this call to vigilance; we must wake up.

As individuals, first-world Christians can practice vigilance by asking ourselves difficult questions and by practicing a kind of political mindfulness as we walk through the world. Concretely we can know where what we purchase comes from, and we can research and monitor the covert machinations of institutions and corporations. But perhaps more importantly we can be vigilant together. We can agree with companions to examine our lives together, not to soothe each other's egos or talk each other out of guilt but to question one another in love so that we stay awake and vigilant in the face of a system that would make commodities of us all.

Recovery

First-world participation in empire, through the consumption of products and ideology, involves deliberately choosing actions that we know will harm ourselves and others. Although we are aware that our way of life is predicated on structural and military violence, the widening gap between rich and poor, and environmental destruction that threatens much of life on the planet, we are either unable or unwilling to stop. We are, in effect, addicted to our way of life. Obviously simply being aware of the problem has not led to change. We are in need of some model that can help us change our behavior.

The recovery movement, particularly twelve-step programs, has an understanding of addiction that parallels the ways in which first-world people participate in empire. Like other addictions, empire makes us comfortable and numb, assuring us that we don't have to deal with troubling issues. Participation in empire is socially reinforced, and it keeps us from being alone. Empire makes us feel good, while masking our deeper needs. We cannot imagine living without it. Empire has all the hallmarks of a drug.

The precepts of the recovery movement include repentance, reparation, and responsibility, practices that can be applied to and adopted by first-world Christian's seeking to resist global capitalism.[14] In order to leave empire, each of us must acknowledge that we are addicted to a destructive system and cycle of behavior. Recovery is rooted in our own experience, but it is not possible without God and without the support of others. To recover we need to tell our stories and listen to the stories of others. We must rigorously examine ourselves and our lives. Addiction is almost never one person's problem. To change our behaviors and learn new ones, we may have to stop seeing old friends and learn to trust new ones. Recovery takes a long time and relapse is not failure but part of the process. Finally, recovery is the promise of a new life of freedom and the call to bring others out with us.

Apocalypse

> Nobody would let the others know that he saw nothing, for then he would have been shown to be unfit for his office or too stupid. None of the Emperor's clothes had ever been such a success.
> "But he has nothing on at all," said a little child.
> "Good heavens! Hear what the innocent child says!" said the father, and then each whispered to the other what the child said: "He has nothing on—a little child says he has nothing on at all!" "He has nothing on at all," cried all the people at last.[15]

Like the townspeople in the children's story of the naked emperor, we have all consented to empire's illusion. Despite the evidence of centuries of history and thousands of peoples and cultures to the contrary, we all agree that global capitalism is not simply the best but the only way. We agree to the lie because our neighbors do, and none of us wants to be thought a fool.

First-world Christians have the experience of living simultaneously in two worlds. We live under the empire of global capitalism, the elaborate dream world to which the culture around us consents. We also live in the kingdom, the beloved community, or the new society in the shell of the old, a world beyond empire, which we believe in, catch glimpses of, and seek to make real. In biblical literature and Christian thought, the root of the apocalyptic tradition addresses our situation of living simultaneously in two worlds. Apocalyptic literature is not about the end of the world but about unmasking the dominant illusion. The Greek word *apokalypsis,* the name of the last book in the Christian Bible, literally means unveiling or revelation.

Apocalyptic literature is specifically about empire. In dreams and symbolic language, the books of Daniel and Revelation depict the Seleucid and Roman empires as monstrous distortions that have already fallen. According to New Testament scholars Wes Howard-Brook and Andrew Gwyther, "biblical apocalypse is adamant that both the various empires of history, and more fundamentally empire itself, will not stand forever."[16] In apocalyptic time, God's overthrow of empire is both ongoing and already accomplished. Humans are called to celebrate the defeat of empire while at the same time participating in its ongoing overthrow through active nonviolent resistance.

First-world Christians can use the language of apocalypse to talk about the two worlds in which we live and address the seeming contradictions that we face. Rooted in a tradition of resistance to empire that is centuries old we can come to live more and more in the new society. We can assert with our voices and our lives that those who are most rejected are truly valuable, that there is power in what is fragile and vulnerable, that the poor have riches beyond measure, and that tyranny does not have the last word.

> Babylon is fallen, is fallen, is fallen
> Babylon is fallen to rise no more![17]

New Ways of Acting

New ways of thinking, perceiving, understanding, and describing the world, injustice, and our struggle to make change are only useful insofar as they impact our behavior. To make change in the world we must also have new ways of acting.

I don't like to be told what to do and I don't like telling others what to do, but I have been inspired recently by one of my community members to show people what is possible. Michael runs a very simple project. He drives around town in the morning and in the evening distributing food and blankets to people on the street who are cold and hungry. When visitors come to our community they sometimes ride along with him. In Spokane and San Francisco young people who went out with Michael have begun their own blanket projects. In this spirit I offer the following list. Like the list of vocabulary, this a partial exploration of a few possibilities. It is not meant to be exhaustive but to offer encouragement on the journey out of empire.

Community

We have all known the long loneliness and we have learned that the only solution is love and that love comes with community.

—Dorothy Day[18]

For most of our existence on earth, human beings have lived in tribal, communal, or extended-family settings. From the early church to base ecclesial communities, the history of Christianity has been a story of communities. Franciscan sisters, Anabaptist farmers, and Latin American base communities have all, in their living, working, and sharing together, attempted to show the world and one another that salvation is not only an individual journey. Today there are intentional Christian communities of all kinds all over the world: Catholic Workers, L'Arche homes, urban squatters, house churches, and farming communities just to name a very few. Although they vary greatly in size, focus, composition, perspective, and work, all have the desire for daily life to reflect gospel values, and all affirm that practical and simple acts are sacred: eating together, sharing stories, playing, working, disagreeing, and laughing.

In contrast, for most first-world Christians today, especially in urban settings, our "worshiping community" is a group of people that we see for a few hours a week in a structured and impersonal setting. In our home lives we are equally isolated. Despite its being less and less the reality, the fundamental unit of our society is supposedly the two-parent nuclear family. Ideally and potentially a haven of strength and nurture, it is more often a tiny totalitarian state of abuse and dysfunction. Many of us experience little in the way of support from our church community or extended family. Much of our first-world hardness of heart is born of this isolation and focus on the individual. Our sense of self becomes distorted by hubris or surplus powerlessness because we do not have companions to reflect back to us our true state. Like Pharaoh, privileged Westerners are closed up behind palace walls.

In our isolation many of us have a deep desire for community, home, and a sense of belonging, but we are afraid as well. "Oh, no. I couldn't live like that; it's too strange, too difficult, too saintly, too chaotic, too messy, too risky." Community can be all these things, for we continually rub against one another in all our pride and humanity and brokenness. To live together we must examine our values, our roots, and our histories. This is hard work but it can be deeply joyful. For people who are drawn to community but are fearful, it is possible to start slowly. Become part of the extended circle of an existing community. Have a monthly meal with friends and neighbors; talk about community, or empire, or resistance. Trade childcare, or goods, or services. For those already living community in some way, it is always possible to go deeper. In community, first-world Christians can manage the daunting task of living differently from those around us because we do so together; we have companions. As Exodus tells us, for Egyptians as well as Israelites, "the desert can be crossed only in community."[19]

Connection with the Earth

An incredibly important gift that first-world Christians can give ourselves is to nurture our connections with the earth. This need not be an expensive consumer experience: buying hundreds of dollars worth of equipment and driving many miles to an overused national park. You do not have to spend the next six months on a platform fifty feet up a red-wood tree. Nor do white people need to go looting other cultures for *authentic* ways of relating to the earth. As part of creation we are already connected to the earth. There are lots of simple ways to cultivate that connection. Get a houseplant; look at clouds; walk your neighborhood; read food labels; go to an unpaved place; take the back roads. Open your senses to what is around you, to what you see, hear, and smell. Ride a bike; plant a tree; stand in the rain; walk with a child. Even if you live in the middle of the city, the earth, like God, is not as far away as you imagine. Nurturing these connections is integral, not alien, to our faith; the Bible is full of stories of deep connection to the earth. Coming to know creation with bodies and hearts can give us tremendous spiritual grounding and a passion to protect the earth.

We can also come to know the nonhuman world with our minds. Many of us in the first world are woefully ignorant about our immediate environments. Where does the water come from before it gushes from the tap? Where does it go after it swirls down the drain? What generates the power behind the wall switch? Where does our gas come from? Where does the garbage go after the can? What plants are native to this place? Which ones are introduced? What grows in the fields outside town? Who owns them? Who works there? Where do the crops go? What animals live here? What is that smell in the air? What is in the soil? Is the water safe to swim in? Who are the big polluters where we live? The more we know about where we live and how we fit into our local ecosystem, the better we can judge what issues are critical, and what must be dealt with immediately. Following even one thread in this complicated web can increase our sense of ownership, belonging, and commitment and decrease our feelings of alienation and helplessness.

Middle-income people have homes, property, vehicles, and tremendous consumer influence. We can choose to use these privileges to increase our isolation and alienation from other humans and the rest of creation. We can pollute and consume and treat nature as a product that is only available to the elite. Or we can use these advantages to nurture our connection with the earth. If we open ourselves to the earth, we open ourselves to change; and small change can lead to bigger change. A plant can become a community garden; a walk in the park can lead to cleaning up a stream; reading labels can spark a consumer boycott.

Public Liturgy

Although prayer has many manifestations in many traditions —fasting, drumming, silent meditation, petition, recitation of texts, dance—for the most part prayer is regarded in the first world as a passive, non-threatening, personal activity. Prayer as active public participation in the world is barely considered. Those of us who take part in Sunday worship in main-line (read middle-class) churches find it unfailingly polite. Any conflict or painful content in scripture or in sermon is glossed over or used to heighten the interest of a passive audience, but it never interferes with the take-home, feel-good message. This bland fiction represents neither the biblical stories from which our tradition is grown nor the lives of anyone who attends the service. It leads to the bizarre situation where the screaming tirades of prophets and the bloody execution of a peasant leader are presented in passionless monotone to rote responses from people in the midst of modern tragedies and anguish at least as compelling as the texts. Those whose church attendance consists of weddings, funerals, baptisms, and perhaps Christmas or Easter services are even more likely to experience the idolization of sentimentality and comfort than an encounter with the living God. What would happen to our worship if Christians took seriously our tradition's call to resist empire and work for justice?

As we discussed in the sections on civil disobedience and vigilance, some worshiping communities and resistance groups do just that. Powerful political interpretations of fasting, pilgrimage, exorcism, repentance, and lament are being carried out at sites of corporate, government, and military violence: court houses, consumer outlets, military bases, prisons. Individuals and groups are taking on consumer boycotts and letter-writing campaigns as spiritual disciplines.

Not all public worship is focused on the negative or on the large scale; we can also celebrate what we truly value: friendship, change of season, political victories, coming of age. I heard recently of two very beautiful nontraditional liturgies. In the first, two young parents made a public declaration of their commitment to their children. As a symbol of this covenant, they took and wore thin, fragile rings, each one representing one of their children. In the second service, a straight woman and a gay man who had been married for many years, marked the occasion of their divorce, each lighting individual candles from a single flame and promising that as they went on to new lives they would continue to love and support each other.

For those of us who consider an outdoor sunrise service at Easter the height of liturgical daring, singing loudly on a street corner, praying in the mall, or kneeling down at an arms trade show represent exquisite humiliation. These experiences are nothing like the serenity and familiarity that we have come to imagine are the only voices of God. If what we say in church is not empty platitude, why are we ashamed to make our faith public? Our reluctance to bring our worship out into the marketplace, the site of imperial religion, is influenced by the fear of any public prayer being mistaken for a sign of allegiance to a right-wing ideology, but it is also a measure of empire's hold over us. To pray only in private is to cede public space to the forces of global capitalism. First-world Christians can and must take our worship to the streets; they belong to us. The socially transformative power of our tradition is limited only by our creativity and courage.

Cultural Work

No matter our capacity to inform, it is our ability to inspire that will turn the tides.
—Syracuse Cultural Workers' Mission Statement[20]

While visiting the Open Door Community in Atlanta, Georgia, I heard the following story. A dedicated young American woman was doing some sort of human rights work in El Salvador. She was invited to a party but declined because she had too much work to do. Later the people who had invited her told her, "You're not going to last here, you're going to go back North." She was hurt and indignant: "What do you mean?" "The ones who don't come to parties always leave." They knew that unless we make a place for play and for beauty in our work we will begin to do harm to ourselves and others. Any change movement without joy or beauty is not sustainable.

It used to be that art was a part of everyday life. Everyone knew who was the best local storyteller, poet, carver, painter, dancer, weaver, or musician. Many people had some proficiency in one or two of these skills and were not ashamed to enjoy or share them. Now few of us produce any kind of creative work beyond childhood, and those of us who do wear the elevated and suspect title of artist.

Several factors have conspired to make "art" a commodity produced and consumed by a very few. With the advent of mass communication, the best has (as Daniel Berrigan put it) become the enemy of the good. Why, when at the flip of a switch, we can hear the greatest saxophone player who ever lived, would we bother to listen to the so-so squawking of the guy down the street? The next culprit is industrialization. For almost all of us in the first world, every aspect of our lives has been industrialized. The clothes we wear, the food we eat, the utensils we eat from were all produced in factories. We don't have to make soap, or jewelry, or lullabies. Factories produce everything we need—and many things we don't need— much more efficiently and effectively than we ever could. As a result we are profoundly alienated from the physical stuff of our everyday lives. Finally, art has become the province of the elite. One of the lies of imperial culture is that beauty is a signifier of value; thus poor people, who are not valued, cannot produce, afford, or appreciate art. The "WHY CHEAP ART? Manifesto" from Bread and Puppet theater in Vermont expresses a joyful alternative to the commodification of art.

PEOPLE have been THINKING too long that
ART is a PRIVILEGE of the MUSEUMS &
the RICH. ART IS NOT BUSINESS!
It does not belong to banks & fancy investors
ART IS FOOD. You can't EAT it BUT it FEEDS
you. ART has to be CHEAP & available to
EVERYBODY. It needs to be EVERYWHERE
because it is the INSIDE of the WORLD.
ART SOOTHES PAIN!
Art wakes up sleepers!
ART FIGHTS AGAINST WAR & STUPIDITY!
ART SINGS HALLELUJAH!
ART IS FOR KITCHENS!
ART IS LIKE GOOD BREAD!
Art is like green trees!
Art is like white clouds in blue sky!
ART IS CHEAP!
HURRAH![21]

The human potential to create is a gift from God and a gift that each one
of us possesses. If we tap into the well of our creativity, it will nourish our
spirits for the work we have to do. Some of us have been deeply shamed
about our ability to create, but if we can begin to make art again, to deny
that there is high and low art, we will make a breach in the fabric of imperial culture. Individuals and communities that make beautiful and func-
tional soap, pottery, bread, candles, or coffins are not bringing global
capitalism to its knees, but we are showing determinedly that it is not the
only way to live—and that itself is a victory. Christians who seek to live in
resistance must remember Dorothy Day's favorite quotation, "the world
will be saved by beauty," and act as if this is so.

Building Alliances

The Christian left has been criticized by other activists for being insular
and ineffective. To some extent this criticism is deserved. Our membership
is predominantly white and middle-class, and our interaction with poor
people, people of color, and people with disabilities is often limited to
lamenting their absence from *our* groups or including them at the level of
tokenism. When we engage in actions, they tend to be safe, symbolic, and
choreographed, relying heavily on the privilege of "good relationships with
the authorities" and doing little to bring about real change. To be truly
effective and to be true to our tradition requires much more from us than
this. We are called to act in solidarity, and this means building alliances.

There are lots of models for building alliances. Some are short-term and
fleeting, for example, two or three affinity groups joining together in a
street blockade for a period of hours. Others involve a long-term commit-

ment, for example, a sister-parish relationship where two congregations, usually of different economic levels, sometimes in different countries, sometimes in different parts of the same city, support each other through donations, visits, and shared projects. Each kind of alliance has its own strengths and pitfalls, but in almost every case working together across difference is hard work. Even somewhat similar groups can have different needs, tactics, perspectives, ways of communicating, models of leadership, and means of decision making. These differences increase as the distance between the groups increases. Building alliances presents specific challenges for people of privilege who are not used to negotiating two or more sets of norms and standards for behavior. Poor people, queers, and people of color have to do this all the time. In order for first-world Christians to work together with others we need to identify to ourselves what it is we fear we will lose: identity, control, smooth-running meetings, comfort and security, clear focus. Then we need to be clear whether these are essentials we need to defend or comforts we are willing to risk for the possibility of true solidarity.[22]

Educating Ourselves

In chapter 6 of this book we looked at some alternative translations or paraphrases for the passages about Pharaoh's hard heart. We spoke about his dull mind or rigid understanding. Like Pharaoh, first-world Christians limit our attention and understanding to that which is familiar and untroubling, despite our easy access to a wealth of information. In so doing we create a climate where the most persistent and brazen of empire's falsehoods—human progress is measured by economic growth; globalization of capital benefits poor and rich alike; what is good for business is good for people; the global economy is self-regulating—are simply accepted.

It is easy to be mystified and intimidated by "experts" and comfortable to be lulled by the trivial or dazzled by the spectacular, but each of us is capable of engaging with the complexities of global capitalism, and each of us is called to do so. We can begin to critique the messages that bombard us by asking questions. Is that really so? Who benefits and who is harmed? Could things be different? Has it always been this way? What is true for women? What is true for people of color? What is true for poor people? We can seek the answers to these questions by reading or watching against the sanctioned story on the news, looking for what is absent. Better still, we can turn off the dominant narrative and seek alternatives beyond the mainstream media. The independent media centers, which grew out of the anti-globalization movement, are a brilliant and creative tool for people with access to computers and the Internet to share their versions of the news.[23] Communities of resistance can support one another in our search for different answers. We can study together, invite speakers to our church or study group, discuss books, or hold roundtable discussions.

We need to educate ourselves about economic issues at various levels.

This is a difficult task not only because the global economy is complex, but also because "experts" who know the most about global economics are generally supporters of the current system and unlikely to critique it. Recently, however, there have been growing numbers of people who question the message that social and environmental justice are too expensive and that the role of governments is to protect property rights and promote trade. The language of economics is a code that neither represents nor measures the well-being of real people. International trade agreements like NAFTA, MAI, GATT, WTO, and FTAA and money-lending institutions like the World Bank and the International Monetary Fund erode national sovereignty and increase the rights and powers of corporations. Growing numbers of people from various walks of life are challenging the ideology of unlimited economic growth and using the meetings of these structures as educational tools to build movements for real change.

The study and challenge of large-scale economics have led some people to develop small-scale alternatives to participating in a system that moves capital from the poor and middle classes to the already rich. Food cooperatives, credit unions, and fair trade products are fairly mainstream examples. Some communities are experimenting with barter systems, local currencies, skill-shares, and tax resistance. Ordinary people can challenge the ideology of globalization through withdrawal of their participation and by deliberate lived alternatives.

History is another area where we need to educate ourselves. Empire tells us that we live in an endless present. The way things are is the way things have always been. To come out of empire, first-world Christians must challenge that lie by coming to know history for ourselves. To be in successful resistance to empire we need to know the history of the empire we oppose. How did it come about? What are its strengths and weaknesses? History is for the most part written by the winners, so we must seek information in sources other than mainstream history books. Fortunately the dominant mythology is so widely accepted that alternatives are not suppressed; they are simply, and much more effectively, ignored. Alternative and "people's" histories are fairly easy to find in public libraries and (endangered) independent bookstores.

Alongside the history of empire we can study and reclaim the history of resistance to empire. Global capitalism did not appear fully formed at the dawn of time; its rise was engineered and was by no means unopposed. There is a rich tradition of resistance to tyranny throughout history; the things that we seek to do now and the ways that we seek to live are neither new nor impossible. Christians who want to live outside of empire have a legacy from our predecessors whose successes and failures can instruct and inspire us.

We can also study the history of our immediate ancestors. Learning our family histories can give us a personal entry point into the history of our country and the fluidity of the dynamics of class. Where did we, personally, come from? Knowing our past can ground us in a sense of cultural identity that white people especially seem to lack.

Economics and history are only two of many areas in which first-world Christians need to educate ourselves. The environment, racism, militarism, labor, indigenous rights, and other issues all require our attention. Obviously we cannot personally research every issue, but neither can we refuse to do anything. A simple strategy is for each person to commit to learn about a single issue and know who to ask about the rest.

IN CLOSING

A list of precepts and prescriptions can seem vague or abstract, and these proposed ways of thinking and acting may be daunting, especially if they are new. Truly the call to live counter to the world around us carries rigorous demands, but the new life we are promised is exciting and joyful. In small ways all around the world there are individuals, organizations, and communities living out their resistance to empire, simply and creatively. Gandhi called these efforts "experiments in truth." As we undertake our own experiments, first-world Christians can be sustained and strengthened by stories: our biblical heritage.

The heritage of Exodus is a great and honest gift for privileged readers. Exodus does not diminish the seduction and appeal of empire, nor does it pretend that salvation can be found there. By reading Exodus and identifying with the Egyptians we have faced hard truths about ourselves and the way we serve the empire of global capitalism. Like Egypt, we are complicit in oppression, slavery, and genocide. Facing these truths is the beginning of true conversion. First-world Christians live daily in the centers of global capitalism, but together with Shiphrah and Puah and Pharaoh's daughter, with one another, and with whoever will have us as allies, we can come out of empire. "Exodus is the journey of the whole of humanity and of creation toward the resurrection of all flesh and the renewal of heaven and earth."[24] Amen.

NOTES

INTRODUCTION

1. Wes Howard-Brook, "Reading for/about Our Lives: Politics, Poetics and Person-hood in the Fourth Gospel" (paper presented to the meeting of the Johannine Literature Section of the Society of Biblical Literature at the annual meeting in New Orleans, Louisiana, November 25, 1996), 5, 12.

2. Mary Ann Tolbert, "Reading for Liberation," in *Reading from This Place*, ed. Fernando F. Segovia and Mary Ann Tolbert (Minneapolis: Fortress Press, 1995).

3. Robert Allen Warrior, "A Native American Perspective: Canaanites, Cowboys and Indians," in *Voices from the Margins: Interpreting the Bible in the Third World*, ed. R. S. Sugirtharajah (Maryknoll, N.Y.: Orbis Books, 1991), 283.

4. I use YHWH rather than Yahweh out of respect for the Jewish prohibition against speaking the name of God and because we do not know how the word was pronounced.

5. Mary Ann Tolbert, "The Politics and Poetics of Location," in *Reading from This Place*, ed. Segovia and Tolbert, 309.

CHAPTER 1
HISTORY, LITERATURE, AND STORY

1. Bruce M. Metzger, "Sortes Biblicae," in *The Oxford Companion to the Bible*, ed. Bruce Metzger and Michael D. Coogan (New York: Oxford University Press, 1993), 714-15.

2. Jon Levenson, *Sinai and Zion: An Entry into the Jewish Bible* (San Francisco: HarperSanFrancisco, 1985), 40.

3. Rita Burns, "The Book of Exodus," in *Exodus, a Lasting Paradigm*, ed. Bas van Iersel and Anton Weiler (Edinburgh: T & T Clark, 1987), 11.

4. Randall C. Bailey, "Africans in Old Testament Poetry and Narratives," in *Stony the Road We Trod: African American Biblical Interpretation*, ed. Cain Hope Felder (Minneapolis: Fortress, 1991), 168.

5. B.C.E. stands for Before the Common Era and refers to the same time period as B.C. It is a Jewish historical term that emphasizes that, for most people, the birth of Jesus is not time's most significant marker.

6. Levenson, *Sinai and Zion*, 10.

7. Pinchas Lapide, "Exodus in the Jewish Tradition," in *Exodus, a Lasting Para-digm*, ed. Bas van Iersel and Anton Weiler (Edinburgh: T & T Clark, 1987), 47.

8. Quoted in Nahum M. Sarna, *Exploring Exodus: The Heritage of Biblical Israel* (New York: Schocken Books, 1986), 11.

9. Ibid., 12.

10. Robert R. Stieglitz, "The Lowdown on the Riffraff," *Bible Review* 15 (August 1999): 54.

11. The text says, "about six hundred thousand men on foot, besides children" (Exod. 12:37). Including women would at least double the number. Although the text uses the word thousands (*eleph*), some commentators suggest that this refers to military

companies or extended families; others suggest that 600,000 is a stereotypical exagger-
ation of the population of Israel at the time of the united monarchy. See Sarna, *Exploring Exodus*, 94-102; William H. C. Propp, *Exodus 1-18: A New Translation with
Introduction and Commentary* (New York: Doubleday, 1999), 414.

12. Anthony R. Ceresko, *Introduction to the Old Testament: A Liberation Perspective* (Maryknoll, N.Y.: Orbis Books, 1992), 18.

13. Unless otherwise indicated, all biblical selections are from the New Revised Standard Version of the Bible, copyright 1989 by the Division of Christian Education of the
National Council of the Churches of Christ in the United States of America.

14. I use YHWH rather than Yahweh out of respect for the Jewish prohibition against
speaking the name of God and because we do not know how the word was pronounced.

15. Carol Meyers, *Discovering Eve: Ancient Israelite Women in Context* (New
York: Oxford University Press, 1988), 122-38.

16. Hebrew translation after William Holladay, *A Concise Hebrew and Aramaic
Lexicon of the Old Testament* (Grand Rapids: Eerdmans, 1988), 17. All English translit-
erations for Hebrew words follow Robert Young, *Young's Analytical Concordance to
the Bible* (Grand Rapids: Eerdmans, 1970).

17. Virginia Ramey Mollenkott, *The Divine Feminine: The Biblical Imagery of God
as Female* (New York: Crossroad, 1983), 57.

18. W. F. Albright, quoted in John Huesman, "Exodus," in *Jerome Biblical Commentary*, ed. Raymond E. Brown, Joseph A. Fitzmyer, and Roland E. Murphy (Englewood Cliffs, N.J.: Prentice Hall, 1968), 54.

19. Quoted from the Christian Community Bible (CCB) version of the Bible, copyright 2000 by Bernardo Hurault, Claretian Publications, Quezon City, Philippines.

20. Carol Meyers, "Miriam the Musician," in *A Feminist Companion to Exodus to
Deuteronomy*, ed. Athalya Brenner (Sheffield: Sheffield Academic Press, 2001), 207-30.

21. Reprinted by permission from Merle Feld, *A Spiritual Life: A Jewish Feminist
Journey* (New York: State University of New York Press, 1999), © 1999, State University of New York. All rights reserved.

22. Everett Fox, *The Five Books of Moses: Genesis, Exodus, Leviticus, Numbers,
Deuteronomy: A New Translation with Introduction, Commentary, and Notes* (New
York: Schocken Books, 1997), xx.

23. Jopie Siebert-Hommes, "But if She Be a Daughter . . . She May Live!," in *A Feminist Companion to Exodus to Deuteronomy*, ed. Athalya Brenner (Sheffield: Sheffield
Academic Press, 1994), 71.

24. Levenson, *Sinai and Zion*, 20-21.

25. Roland Murphy, quoted in Denise Nadeau and Laurel Dykstra, "Jubilaction:
Engaging with a Feminist Jubilee in a Multi-faith and Secular Context," in *Jubilee
Wealth and the Market: Share the Wealth*, ed. John Miheve (Toronto: Canadian Ecu-
menical Jubilee Initiative, 1999), 102.

26. Levenson, *Sinai and Zion*, 39.

27. Ceresko, *Introduction to the Old Testament*, 104.

28. Dorothy Allison, *Two or Three Things I Know for Sure* (New York: Dutton,
1995), 51.

29. Bronislaw Milinowski, quoted in Michael Parenti, *Land of Idols: Political
Mythology in America* (New York: St. Martin's Press, 1994), 98.

30. Leslie Marmon Silko, quoted in Ched Myers, *Who Will Roll Away the Stone?:
Discipleship Queries for First World Christians* (Maryknoll, N.Y.: Orbis Books, 1994),
xix.

31. Bishop Ruíz, quoted in Jim Hodgson, "A Collaboration against Hatred, Churches
Meet to Seek Peace in Chiapas," *Sojourners* 27, no. 1 (January-February 1998): 11.

32. Judith Plaskow, *Standing Again at Sinai: Judaism from a Feminist Perspective*
(San Francisco: HarperSanFrancisco, 1991), 33.

33. David Tracy, "Exodus: Theological Reflection," in *Exodus, a Lasting Paradigm*, ed. Bas van Iersel and Anton Weiler (Edinburgh: T &T Clark, 1987), 121.

34. Mary Ann Tolbert, "Reading for Liberation," in *Reading from This Place*, ed. Fernando F. Segovia and Mary Ann Tolbert (Minneapolis: Fortress Press, 1995), 270.

35. *Passover Haggadah*, quoted in Susan Schneider, *Jewish and Female: Choices and Changes in Our Lives Today* (New York: Simon & Schuster, 1984), 110.

CHAPTER 2

READING EXODUS AS ISRAEL

1. Tanakh is an acronym that stands for the three parts of the Jewish Bible: T = Torah (the Law); N = Nevi'im (the Prophets), and K = Kethuvim (the Writings).

2. Everett Fox, *Now These Are the Names: A New English Rendition of the Book of Exodus* (New York: Schocken Books, 1986).

3. This version is called the Septuagint, from the Latin for "seventy." The legend is that it was translated by seventy-two scholars, six from each of the twelve tribes, each of whom completed identical translations at the same moment.

4. Reprinted by permission from Merle Feld, *A Spiritual Life: A Jewish Feminist Journey* (New York: State University of New York Press, 1999), © 1999, State University of New York. All rights reserved.

5. Randall Bailey, "The Danger of Ignoring One's Own Cultural Bias in Interpreting the Text," in *The Bible and Post-colonialism*, ed. R. S. Sugirtharajah (Sheffield: Sheffield Academic Press, 1998), 76.

6. The Hebrew term for the Red Sea is *yam suph*, "sea of reeds." As lake and sea are not distinct terms, this body of water is not necessarily or even likely to be identified with the modern Red Sea (see Denis Baly, "Red Sea," in *Harper's Bible Dictionary*, ed. Paul Achtemeier [San Francisco: HarperSanFrancisco, 1996], 858).

7. The nongeographic divisions follow Brevard Childs (*The Book of Exodus: A Critical Commentary* [Philadelphia: Westminster Press, 1974], xii-xiii) and Richard J. Clifford ("Exodus," in *The New Jerome Biblical Commentary*, ed. Raymond E. Brown, Joseph A. Fitzmyer, and Roland E. Murphy [Englewood Cliffs, N.J.: Prentice Hall, 1990], 45). The descriptions are my own.

8. Frank Moore Cross, *Canaanite Myth and Hebrew Epic* (Cambridge, Mass.: Harvard University Press, 1973), 104n, 124.

9. Anthony R. Ceresko, *Introduction to the Old Testament: A Liberation Perspective* (Maryknoll, N.Y.: Orbis Books, 1992), 76.

10. Rita Burns, "The Book of Exodus," in *Exodus, a Lasting Paradigm*, ed. Bas van Iersel and Anton Weiler (Edinburgh: T & T Clark, 1987), 16.

11. Marcus J. Borg, *Meeting Jesus Again for the First Time: The Historical Jesus and the Heart of Contemporary Faith* (San Francisco: HarperSanFrancisco, 1994), 121-22.

12. Pinchas Lapide, "Exodus in the Jewish Tradition," in *Exodus, a Lasting Paradigm*, ed. Bas van Iersel and Anton Weiler (Edinburgh: T & T Clark, 1987), 52.

13. Ibid.

14. Judith Plaskow, *Standing Again at Sinai: Judaism from a Feminist Perspective* (San Francisco: HarperSanFrancisco, 1991), 29.

15. *The Union Haggadah Home Service for the Passover* (Cincinnati: Central Conference of American Rabbis, 1923), 20.

16. Martha Shelley, *Haggadah: A Celebration of Freedom* (San Francisco: aunt lute books, 1998), 15-16.

17. Plaskow, *Standing Again at Sinai*, 57-58.

18. Michael Lerner, "Editorial," *Tikkun* (March/April 1999): 6.

tikkun olam

19. José Severino Croatto, "The Socio-Historical and Hermeneutical Relevance of the Exodus," in *Exodus, a Lasting Paradigm,* ed. Bas van Iersel and Anton Weiler (Edinburgh: T & T Clark, 1987), 125.

20. Jay Casey, "The Exodus Theme in the Book of Revelation against the Background of the New Testament," in *Exodus, a Lasting Paradigm,* ed. Bas van Iersel and Anton Weiler (Edinburgh: T & T Clark, 1987), 34.

21. Michael Walzer, "Exodus and the Theory of Holy War," *Harvard Theological Review* 61 (1968): 4.

22. John Newton, "Analysis of Programmatic Texts of Exodus Movements," in *Exodus, a Lasting Paradigm,* ed. Bas van Iersel and Anton Weiler (Edinburgh: T & T Clark, 1987), 59.

23. Christa K. Dixon, *Negro Spirituals from Bible to Folksong* (Philadelphia: Fortress Press, 1976), 23.

24. Judith Plaskow distinguishes between anti-Semitism and anti-Judaism ("Anti-Judaism in Feminist Christian Interpretation," in *A Feminist Introduction,* vol. 1 of *Searching the Scriptures,* ed. Elisabeth Schüssler Fiorenza [New York: Crossroad, 1995], 117-29).

25. Although there is evidence that this is again a conflict among Jews, from very early on the passages have been used by Christians against Jews.

26. Jon Levenson, cited in Walter Brueggemann, "Pharoah as Vassal: A Study of a Political Metaphor," *Catholic Biblical Quarterly* 57 (1995): 27-51.

27. Plaskow, "Anti-Judaism in Feminist Christian Interpretation," 117-29.

28. Newton, "Analysis of Texts," 60.

29. Doris L. Bergen, *Twisted Cross: The German Christian Movement in the Third Reich* (Chapel Hill: University of North Carolina Press, 1996), 147.

30. Robert Goss, *Jesus Acted Up: A Gay and Lesbian Manifesto* (San Francisco: HarperSanFrancisco, 1993), 11.

31. Michael Walzer, *Exodus and Revolution* (New York: Basic Books, 1985), 4.

32. Mary Ann Tolbert, "The Politics and Poetics of Location," in *Reading from This Place,* ed. Fernando F. Segovia and Mary Ann Tolbert (Minneapolis: Fortress Press, 1995), 317.

33. Bishop Ruíz, quoted in Jim Hodgson, "A Collaboration against Hatred: Churches Meet to Seek Peace in Chiapas," *Sojourners* 27, no. 1 (January-February 1998): 11.

34. Leonardo Boff, *When Theology Listens to the Poor* (San Francisco: Harper & Row, 1988), 22.

35. Margaret Eletta Guider, *Daughters of Rahab: Prostitution and the Church of Liberation in Brazil* (Minneapolis: Fortress Press, 1995), 19.

36. Gustavo Gutiérrez, quoted in John O'Brien, *Theology and the Option for the Poor* (Collegeville, Minn.: Liturgical Press, 1992), 24; Croatto, "The Socio-Historical and Hermeneutical Relevance of the Exodus," 126; idem, *Exodus: A Hermeneutics of Freedom* (Maryknoll, N.Y.: Orbis Books, 1981), iv; Leonardo Boff, quoted in Dan Cohn-Sherbok, *Exodus: An Agenda for Jewish-Christian Dialogue* (London: Bellew, 1992), 77.

37. Juan Alfaro, "God Protects and Liberates the Poor—O.T.," in *Option for the Poor: Challenge to the Rich Countries,* ed. Leonardo Elizondo and Virgil Elizondo (Edinburgh: T & T Clark, 1986), 28.

38. Gustavo Gutiérrez, *A Theology of Liberation: History, Politics and Salvation* (Maryknoll, N.Y.: Orbis Books, 1973), 155.

39. Alfaro, "God Protects," 29.

40. Gustavo Gutiérrez, quoted in Dan Cohn-Sherbok, *Exodus: An Agenda for Jewish-Christian Dialogue* (London: Bellew, 1992), 31.

41. Leonardo Boff and Clodovis Boff, *Introducing Liberation Theology* (Maryknoll, N.Y.: Orbis Books, 1987), 11-21.

42. This resistance has come not only from repressive governments but also from churches more inclined to serve the powerful than the powerless.

43. James Cone, *God of the Oppressed* (Maryknoll, N.Y.: Orbis Books, 1997), 59.

44. For a succinct description of this emergence, see Josiah Young, "Exodus as a Paradigm for Black Theology," in *Exodus, a Lasting Paradigm,* ed. Bas van Iersel and Anton Weiler (Edinburgh: T & T Clark, 1987), 94.

45. Cone, *God of the Oppressed,* 10.

46. Paul Laurence Dunbar, "An Antebellum Sermon," lines 29-32, cited in David T. Shannon, "'An Antebellum Sermon': A Resource for an African American Hermeneutic," in *Stony the Road We Trod: African American Biblical Interpretation,* ed. Cain Hope Felder (Minneapolis: Fortress Press, 1991), 110.

47. Cain Hope Felder, "Introduction," in *Stony the Road We Trod: African American Biblical Interpretation,* ed. Cain Hope Felder (Minneapolis: Fortress Press, 1991), 9.

48. These are verses 1 and 18 of the twenty-five sung by the Fisk Jubilee Singers. They were the first black choir to tour Europe, raising money to fund education for black students. See Dixon, *Negro Spirituals from Bible to Folksong,* 22, 29.

49. James Deotis Roberts, *A Black Political Theology* (Philadelphia: Westminster Press, 1974), 105.

50. James Cone, *A Black Theology of Liberation,* 20th anniversary edition (Maryknoll, N.Y.: Orbis Books, 1990), 59.

51. James Cone, quoted in Josiah Young, "Exodus as a Paradigm," 95.

52. James Deotis Roberts, *Liberation and Reconciliation: A Black Theology* (Maryknoll, N.Y.: Orbis Books, 1994), 29.

53. Quoted in Josiah Young, "Exodus as a Paradigm," 93.

54. Ibid., 98.

55. This is due perhaps to the fact that the danger they face is because of their race and not their theology; thus they do not put one another at risk by disagreeing.

56. bell hooks, *Yearning: Race, Gender, and Cultural Politics* (Boston: South End Press, 1990), 6.

57. Delores Williams gives an excellent short version of this twenty-year conversation; see *Sisters in the Wilderness: The Challenge of Womanist God-Talk* (Maryknoll, N.Y.: Orbis Books, 1993), 170-75.

CHAPTER 3

PROSTITUTES, SLAVES, AND CANAANITES

1. Norman K. Gottwald, Margaret Eletta Guider, and Walter Brueggemann each give succinct but different reviews of these critiques. See Norman K. Gottwald, "The Exodus as Event and Process: Test Case in the Biblical Grounding of Liberation Theology," in *The Future of Liberation Theology: Essays in Honor of Gustavo Gutiérrez,* ed. Marc H. Ellis and Otto Maduro (Maryknoll, N.Y.: Orbis Books, 1989), 250-71; Margaret Eletta Guider, *Daughters of Rahab: Prostitution and the Church of Liberation in Brazil* (Minneapolis: Fortress Press, 1995), 20 n. 5; Walter Brueggemann, "Pharoah as Vassal: A Study of a Political Metaphor," *Catholic Bibilical Quarterly* 57 (1995): 27-51.

2. Judith Fetterly is referring specifically to gender identification here, but her point applies to all manner of differences between reader and character (Fetterly, quoted in Cheryl Exum, "The Hand that Rocks the Cradle," in *Plotted, Painted and Shot: Cultural Representations of Biblical Women* [Sheffield: Sheffield Academic Press, 1996], 101).

3. Sor Juana Ines de la Cruz, quoted in Guider, *Daughters of Rahab,* 37. Sor Juana

(1651-1695) was a Mexican nun; she is noted today as the first woman theologian of the Americas.

4. Rita Nakashima Brock and Susan Brooks Thistlethwaite, *Casting Stones: Prostitution and Liberation in Asia and the United States* (Minneapolis: Fortress Press, 1996), 109.

5. Guider, *Daughters of Rahab*, 23-24.

6. Ibid., 21-22.

7. Ibid., 23.

8. Ibid., 22 n. 11.

9. Ibid., 170-71.

10. Susan Tucker, *Telling Memories among Southern Women Domestic Workers and Their Employers in the Segregated South* (New York: Schocken Books, 1988), 207.

11. For the full citation, see Alice Walker, *In Search of Our Mothers' Gardens: Womanist Prose* (San Diego: Harcourt Brace Jovanovich, 1983), xi.

12. Delores S. Williams, *Sisters in the Wilderness: The Challenge of Womanist God-Talk* (Maryknoll, N.Y.: Orbis Books, 1993).

13. Ibid., 4.

14. Renita J. Weems, "A Mistress, a Maid and No Mercy (Hagar and Sarah)," in *Just a Sister Away: A Womanist Vision of Women's Relationships in the Bible* (San Diego: LuraMedia, 1988), 1-21.

15. Williams, *Sisters in the Wilderness*, 144.

16. Ibid., 144, 147.

17. Ibid., 149.

18. Ibid., 150.

19. Ibid., 151.

20. Arthur Solomon, "My Relations: O Canada," in *Eating Bitterness: A Vision Beyond the Prison Walls: Poems and Essays of Arthur Solomon* (Toronto: NC Press, 1994), 60-61.

21. Robert Allen Warrior, "A Native American Perspective: Canaanites, Cowboys and Indians," in *Voices from the Margins: Interpreting the Bible in the Third World*, ed. R. S. Sugirtharajah (Maryknoll, N.Y.: Orbis Books, 1991), 288.

22. Ibid.

23. Kwok Pui-lan, *Discovering the Bible in the Non-Biblical World* (Maryknoll, N.Y.: Orbis Books, 1997), 98.

24. Warrior, "Native American Perspective," 290.

25. Ibid., 292.

26. Ibid., 294.

27. Ibid., 292, 293, 294.

28. John McCutcheon, "You Gotta Know When to Move," *What It's Like*, Rounder Records, 1990 (Appalsongs: ASCAP).

29. Guider, *Daughters of Rahab*, xiii.

30. Williams, *Sisters in the Wilderness*, 149.

31. Warrior, "Native American Perspective," 293. We will take up Warrior's question of how the land is ignored in chapter 5.

32. Norbert Greinacher, "Liberation Theology in the 'First World'?" in *Option for the Poor: Challenge to the Rich Countries*, ed. Leonardo Elizondo and Virgil Elizondo (Edinburgh: T & T Clark, 1986), 81.

33. Jon Sobrino and Juan Hernandez Pico, *Theology of Christian Solidarity* (Maryknoll, N.Y.: Orbis Books, 1985), 26.

34. The term "first-world, North American" expresses the intersection of my economic and geographic realities. Not all North Americans live in the first world, whether they are Canadians, Americans, or Mexicans, and neither is North America an accurate term to describe only the United States and Canada.

35. Mary Ann Tolbert points out that having expended effort to obtain some aspect of privilege obscures it as privilege and can lead to the conclusion that it is earned ("Reading for Liberation," in *Reading from This Place*, ed. Fernando F. Segovia and Mary Ann Tolbert [Minneapolis: Fortress Press, 1995], 264).

36. At the University of Montreal Engineering School on December 6, 1989, fourteen young women were killed and thirteen others injured when Marc Lepine entered a classroom, ordered the men to leave, and began firing on the women, shouting, "You're all a bunch of feminists, and I hate feminists" (Lynn Granke, "Canada after the Massacre," in *Women, Violence and Non-Violent Change*, ed. Aruna Gnanadason, Musimbi Kanyoro, and Lucia Ann McSpadden [Geneva: WCC Publications, 1996], 81). The names of the women who were killed are Genevieve Bergeron, Helene Colgan, Nathalie Croteau, Barbara Daigneault, Anne-Marie Edward, Maud Haviernick, Barbara Maria Klucznik, Maryse Laganiere, Maryse LeClair, Anne-Marie Lemay, Sonia Pelletier, Michele Richard, Annie St. Arneault, and Annie Turcotte (from Jennifer Scanlon, "Educating the Living, Remembering the Dead: The Montreal Massacre as Metaphor," *Feminist Teacher* 8 [1994]: 75).

37. Wright was shot and killed while hiking the Appalachian Trail with her lover, Claudia Brenner (Claudia Brenner, "Survivor's Story: Eight Bullets," in *Hate Crimes: Confronting Violence against Lesbians and Gay Men*, ed. Gregory M. Herek and Kevin T. Berrill [Newbury Park, Calif.: Sage Publications, 1992], 11-15). Brandon Teena, born Teena Brandon, was killed at age nineteen by companions who discovered his transgender identity (*Boys Don't Cry: The Brandon Teena Story*, Twentieth Century Fox, 1999, Beverly Hills, California]). Matthew Shepard was brutally beaten and left tied to a fence to die (Beth Loffreda, *Losing Matt Shepard: Life and Politics in the Aftermath of Anti-Gay Murder* [New York: Columbia University Press, 2000]).

38. Kevin T. Berrill, "Anti-Gay Violence and Victimization in the United States: An Overview," in Herek and Berrill, *Hate Crimes*, 19-24; Carol J. Adams, "Toward a Feminist Theology of Religion and the State," in *Violence against Women and Children: A Theological Sourcebook*, ed. Carol J. Adams and Marie Fortune (New York: Continuum, 1995), 15. Statistics on violence against women, children, and queers are all too quickly out of date, and incidents of violence are notoriously underreported. But even the most conservative reports estimate that two-thirds of all homosexuals have experienced verbal abuse because of their sexuality, and one-third have experienced physical abuse. (Gay men reported a higher rate of physical abuse than women, and transgender people the highest). Between one-third and one-half of all women in the United States will experience physical or sexual assault during their lifetime.

39. Margo Adar and Sharon Howell, "The Subjective Side of Power," in *Healing the Wounds: The Promise of Ecofeminism*, ed. Judith Plant (Toronto: Between the Lines, 1989), 221.

40. Audre Lorde, *Sister Outsider* (Trumansburg, N.Y.: Crossing Press, 1984); Gloria Anzaldua, *Borderlands/La Frontera: The New Mestiza* (San Francisco: Spinsters/aunt lute books, 1987).

41. Mary Ann Tolbert, "The Politics and Poetics of Location," in *Reading from This Place*, ed. Fernando F. Segovia and Mary Ann Tolbert (Minneapolis: Fortress Press, 1995), 309.

42. James Tate, quoted in David Tracy, *The Analogical Imagination: Christian Theology and the Culture of Pluralism* (New York: Crossroad, 1986), 447.

43. Tolbert, "Politics and Poetics of Location," 309.

44. David Tracy, "Exodus: Theological Reflection," in *Exodus, a Lasting Paradigm*, ed. Bas van Iersel and Anton Weiler (Edinburgh: T & T Clark, 1987), 122.

45. Tolbert, "Politics and Poetics of Location," 315.

46. Robert Goss, *Jesus Acted Up: A Gay and Lesbian Manifesto* (San Francisco: HarperSanFrancisco, 1993), 91-92. The story is also about the use of sex for control and the value of male strangers over daughters.

47. Marcus J. Borg, *Meeting Jesus Again for the First Time: The Historical Jesus and the Heart of Contemporary Faith* (San Francisco: HarperSanFrancisco, 1994), 124.

48. Tolbert, "Reading for Liberation," 265.

CHAPTER 4
EGYPT AS EMPIRE

1. Robert McAfee Brown, *Unexpected News: Reading the Bible with Third World Eyes* (Philadelphia: Westminster Press, 1984), 43-44.

2. Rosalie David, *Handbook to Life in Ancient Egypt* (New York: Facts on File, 1998), 89-90.

3. Juan Alfaro, "God Protects and Liberates the Poor—O.T.," in *Option for the Poor: Challenge to the Rich Countries*, ed. Leonardo Elizondo and Virgi Elizondo (Edinburgh: T & T Clark, 1986), 27.

4. Michael Walzer, *Exodus and Revolution* (New York: Basic Books, 1985), 21.

5. Duane L. Christensen and Jo Milgrom, "Encountering the Exodus Story Through Handmade Midrash," in *Experiencing the Exodus from Egypt*, ed. Duane L. Christensen (Berkeley: BIBAL Press, 1988), 7; William Holladay, *A Concise Hebrew and Aramaic Lexicon of the Old Testament* (Grand Rapids: Eerdmans, 1988), 211.

6. Martha Shelley, *Haggadah: A Celebration of Freedom* (San Francisco: aunt lute books, 1997), 5; Christensen and Milgrom, "Encountering the Exodus Story," 7.

7. Richard J. Clifford, *The Wisdom Literature* (Nashville: Abingdon Press, 1998), 47.

8. Randall C. Bailey. "Beyond Identification: The Use of Africans in Old Testament Poetry and Narratives," in *Stony the Road We Trod: African American Biblical Interpretation*, ed. Cain Hope Felder (Minneapolis: Fortress Press, 1991), 172-78.

9. Jon Levenson, *Sinai and Zion: An Entry into the Jewish Bible* (San Francisco: HarperSanFrancisco, 1985), 23.

10. Anthony R. Ceresko, *Introduction to the Old Testament: A Liberation Perspective* (Maryknoll, N.Y.: Orbis Books, 1992), 81.

11. Porter was a student of Agosto Boal, the great Brazilian popular theater educator and creator of "the theatre of the oppressed."

12. I have been fortunate to read Exodus with a number of first-world groups in different stages of engagement with action for social change and at different levels of awareness about their own privilege. Catholic Workers, students, exposure tour participants, and parish groups have joined me for workshops, courses, and shorter classes exploring how Egypt might be a hermeneutical key to our own experiences of empire.

13. Phyllis Trible, *Texts of Terror: Literary-Feminist Readings of Biblical Narratives* (Philadelphia: Fortress Press, 1984), 2.

14. Stanley Rothman, quoted in Joan Chittister, "Heart of Flesh: A Feminist Spirituality for Women and Men" (keynote address at Call to Action National Conference, Detroit, Michigan, November 15, 1997).

15. Wes Howard-Brook and Anthony Gwyther, *Unveiling Empire: Reading Revelation Then and Now* (Maryknoll, N.Y.: Orbis Books, 1999), 236.

16. Winona Stevenson, "Colonialism and First Nations Women in Canada," in *Scratching the Surface: Canadian Anti-Racist Feminist Thought*, ed. Enakshi Dua and Angela Robertson (Toronto: Women's Press, 1999), 50.

17. Although much has been made of globalization as a new phenomenon, labor writer Ellen Meiksins Wood points out that our current situation was described by Marx in 1848 as the logical conclusion of capitalism (Ellen Meiksins Wood, "Labor, Class, and State in Global Capitalism," in *Rising from the Ashes? Labor in the Age of "Global" Capitalism*, ed. Ellen Meiksins Wood, Peter Meiksins, and Michael Yates [New York: Monthly Review Press, 1998], 5).

18. Mary Zepernick, "Man Corporate on Top of the World," in *Defying Corporations, Defining Democracy: A Book of History and Strategy*, ed. Dean Ritz (New York: Apex, 2001), 75.

19. Wood, "Labor, Class, and State," 12.

20. Jane Anne Morris, "Help! I've Been Colonized and I Can't Get Up," in *Defying Corporations, Defining Democracy: A Book of History and Strategy*, ed. Dean Ritz (New York: Apex, 2001), 10.

21. Jeremy Brecher, Tim Costello, and Brendan Smith, *Globalization from Below: The Power of Solidarity* (Cambridge, Mass.: South End Press, 2000), 6-7.

22. Walter Brueggemann, "Pharoah as Vassal: A Study of a Political Metaphor," *Catholic Biblical Quarterly* 57 (1995): 46 n. 53.

23. Marilyn Voran, *Add Justice to Your Shopping List* (Kitchener, Ontario: Herald Press, 1986), 23.

24. David Korten, *When Corporations Rule the World*, 2nd ed. (San Francisco: Berrett-Koehler, 2001), 217.

25. Christopher Scheer, "'Illegals' Made Slaves to Fashion," *The Nation*, September 11, 1995, p. 237.

26. Stephen Oates, *Let the Trumpet Sound: The Life of Martin Luther King Jr.* (New York: New American Library, 1982), 84.

27. James Cone points out that we are much quicker to recognize the racism of the American South than the North, but that both exist (James H. Cone, *Martin & Malcolm & America: A Dream or a Nightmare* [Maryknoll, N.Y.: Orbis Books, 1991], 55).

28. Rita Nakashima Brock and Susan Brooks Thistlethwaite, *Casting Stones: Prostitution and Liberation in Asia and the United States* (Minneapolis: Fortress Press, 1996), 31.

29. Ibid., 161.

30. Michele Durkson Clise, *Stop the Violence Please* (Seattle: University of Washington Press, 1994), 54.

31. *Justification for the Abolition of the Prison Industrial Complex—Forty Acres and a Mule: An Educational Guide for White People of Conscience* (pamphlet from conference entitled "Critical Resistance: Beyond the Prison Industrial Complex," held September 25-27, 1998, at the University of California, Berkeley, California), 8.

32. Quoted in James Cone, *God of the Oppressed* (Maryknoll, N.Y.: Orbis Books, 1997), 200.

33. Nahum M. Sarna, *Exploring Exodus: The Heritage of Biblical Israel* (New York: Schocken Books, 1986), 21.

34. Walzer, *Exodus and Revolution*, 26.

35. Although the fact is not taught in Canadian schools, enslavement of black and Native people was common during the 1700s and 1800s in New France and Upper Canada (Howard Adams, *A Tortured People: The Politics of Colonization* [Penticton, B.C.: Theytus Books Ltd., 1995], 47-57). In U.S. schools slavery is taught as something that was confined to the South (James W. Loewen, *Lies My Teacher Told Me: Everything Your American History Textbook Got Wrong* [New York: New Press, 1995], 159).

36. W. E. B. DuBois, "Of the Black Belt," in *The Souls of Black Folk: Essays and Sketches* (Greenwich, Conn.: Fawcett, 1961), 98.

37. Korten, *When Corporations Rule the World*, 304.

38. *Justification for the Abolition*, 93.

39. According to Mike Davis, the prison industrial complex is characterized by (1) exponential expansion of prisons and jails and rising numbers of female and male prisoners from some communities of color; (2) the symbiotic relationship between private corporations and the prison industry; (3) the reliance of many communities on "corrections" for economic vitality, particularly in the aftermath of economic migration

to the third world; (4) mounting political influence of the "correctional community"; (5) the collaboration of politicians and of corporate media in criminalization of communities of color, especially youth of color, and representing prisons as the catchall solution to social problems (Mike Davis, "Hell Factories in the Field," *The Nation*, February 20, 1995, 229).

40. Scott Christianson, *With Liberty for Some: 500 Years of Imprisonment in America* (Boston: Northeastern University Press, 1998), 303.

41. Eve Goldberg and Linda Evans, *The Prison Industrial Complex and the Global Economy* (San Francisco: Agit Press, 1998), 11.

42. Kevin Bales, *Disposable People: New Slavery in the Global Economy* (Berkeley: University of California Press, 1999), 3, 26.

43. Ibid., 8-9. This is a low estimate based on Bales's rigorous definition of what constitutes slavery. The British organization Anti-Slavery International estimates that there are two hundred million slaves in the world today (Norman C. Macht and Mary Hull, *The History of Slavery* [San Diego: Lucent Books, 1997], 88).

44. Brock and Thistlethwaite, *Casting Stones*, 121.

45. Bales, *Disposable People*, 9.

46. Ibid., 3-4.

47. Ibid., 239.

48. Delores S. Williams, *Sisters in the Wilderness: The Challenge of Womanist God-Talk* (Maryknoll, N.Y.: Orbis Books, 1993), 132.

49. James Walvin, *Slavery and the Slave Trade: A Short Illustrated History* (Jackson: University Press of Mississippi, 1983), 31.

50. Loewen, *Lies My Teacher Told Me*, 159.

51. Carolyn Egan and Linda Gardner, "Racism, Women's Health, and Reproductive Freedom," in *Scratching the Surface: Canadian Anti-Racist Feminist Thought*, ed. Enakshi Dua and Angela Robertson (Toronto: Women's Press, 1999), 295-307.

52. Christianson, *With Liberty for Some*, 281; Katie Monagle, "The Death Penalty," *Scholastic Update* 125 (September 1992): 13.

53. Nancy Folbre and the Center for Popular Economics, *The New Field Guide to the U.S. Economy* (New York: New Press, 1995), 8.15.

54. James Heintz, Nancy Folbre, and the Center for Popular Economics, *The Ultimate Field Guide to the U.S. Economy* (New York: New Press, 2000), 107.

55. Ibid., 133.

56. Folbre, *New Field Guide*, 7.11.

57. Barry M. Pritzker, *Native America Today: A Guide to Community Politics and Culture* (Santa Barbara: ABC-CLIO, 1999), 41.

58. Loewen, *Lies My Teacher Told Me*, 162.

59. Williams, *Sisters in the Wilderness*, 135.

60. June Jordan, "A Powerful Hatred," in *Affirmative Acts: Political Essays* (New York: Anchor, 1998), 86.

61. Dori S. Hutchinson, "The Journey towards Wellness," *The Journal of NAMI California* 11, no. 4 (2001): 7.

62. Hilda F. Besler and Charlotte I. Spungin, *Gay and Lesbian Students: Understanding Their Needs* (Washington, D.C.: Taylor & Francis, 1995), 49.

63. Julie K. Endersbe, *Homosexualtiy: What Does It Mean?* (Mankato, Minn.: Capstone Press, 2000), 39.

64. Folbre, *New Field Guide*, 5.9, 6.6.

65. For more on the SOA/WHISC, see Jack Nelson-Pallmeyer, *School of Assasins: The Case for Closing the School of the Americas and Changing U.S. Foreign Policy* (Maryknoll, N.Y.: Orbis Books, 1999).

66. This little quip from the common linguistic currency was used by a country singer in a now-famous song.

67. June Jordan, "Bosnia Betrayed," in *Affirmative Acts: Political Essays* (New York: Anchor, 1998), 55.

68. bell hooks, "A Revolution of Values," in *Teaching to Transgress: Education as the Practice of Freedom* (New York: Routledge, 1994), 28.

69. Dean Ritz, "Conquering Fibs," in *Defying Corporations, Defining Democracy: A Book of History and Strategy,* ed. Dean Ritz (New York: Apex, 2001), 105.

70. Korten, *When Corporations Rule the World,* 145.

71. hooks, "Revolution of Values," 29.

72. Vandana Shiva, "The Violence of Globalization: India Pushes Back," in *Global Uprising: Confronting the Tyrannies of the 21st Century,* ed. Neva Welton and Linda Wolf (Gabriola Island, B.C.: New Society, 2001), 170-71.

73. *Squeegee.* An Interactive Theatre Event Created & Performed by Street-Involved Youth, Headlines Theatre, Vancouver, B.C., May 19-23, 1999.

74. Ched Myers, *Who Will Roll Away the Stone?: Discipleship Queries for First World Christians* (Maryknoll, N.Y.: Orbis Books, 1994), 46.

75. Excerpted from the *UNESCO Slave Route Project, Conference Document* (London: Pan African Healing Foundation, September 8, 1998), 1.

76. When the word *Egyptian* refers to biblical characters it is capitalized; when it refers to first-world readers I use lower case.

CHAPTER 5

EGYPT THE LAND

1. Zora Neale Hurston, *Moses: Man of the Mountain* (J. B. Lippincott, 1939; reprint, Urbana and Chicago: University of Illinois Press, 1984), 13.

2. Robert Allen Warrior, "A Native American Perspective: Canaanites, Cowboys and Indians," in *Voices from the Margins: Interpreting the Bible in the Third World,* ed. R. S. Sugirtharajah (Maryknoll, N.Y.: Orbis Books, 1991), 293.

3. Leanne Logan, Geert Cole, Damien Simonis, and Scott Wayne, *Egypt: A Lonely Planet Travel Survival Kit* (Victoria, Australia: Lonely Planet, 1996), 28.

4. Guillemette Andreu, *Egypt in the Age of the Pyramids,* trans. David Lorton (Ithaca, N.Y.: Cornell University Press, 1997), 125-28.

5. Hecataeus of Miletus in the sixth century B.C.E. was the first to do so.

6. Herbert B. Huffman, "Egypt," in *Harper's Bible Dictionary,* ed. Paul Achtemeier, with the Society of Biblical Literature (San Francisco: Harper & Row, 1985), 248.

7. Andreu, *Egypt,* 118.

8. Joseph Kaster, *Wings of the Falcon: Life and Thought of Ancient Egypt,* trans. Joseph Kaster (New York: Holt, Rinehart & Winston, 1968), 232.

9. Walter Brueggemann, *The Land* (Philadelphia: Fortress Press, 1977), 3.

10. Jeanie Wylie-Kellermann, "Sounding the Jubal," *The Witness* 80, no. 1 (January-February 1997): 5.

11. William H. C. Propp, *Exodus 1-18: A New Translation with Introduction and Commentary* (New York: Doubleday, 1999), 347.

12. Greta Hort, "The Plagues of Egypt," 1957, 1958, in Nahum M. Sarna, *Exploring Exodus: The Heritage of Biblical Israel* (New York: Schocken Books, 1986), 70-73.

13. Terence Fretheim, *Exodus* (Louisville: Westminster/John Knox Press, 1991), 117.

14. Logan et al., *Egypt,* 30.

15. Propp, *Exodus 1-18,* 348; Kaster, *Wings of the Falcon,* 259.

16. Fretheim, *Exodus,* 113.

17. Propp, *Exodus 1-18,* 349.

18. George Pixley, *On Exodus: A Liberation Perspective,* trans. Robert Barr (Mary-knoll, N.Y.: Orbis Books, 1987), 45.

19. Ibid., 350.

20. Ibid., 328.

21. Ibid., 350.

22. Ibid., 332.

23. Compare Moses' affliction (Exod. 4:6), which is limited and immediately reversed, with the extensive and longer-lasting affliction of Miriam in Numbers 12.

24. Propp, *Exodus 1-18,* 351.

25. Nahum M. Sarna, *Exploring Exodus: The Heritage of Biblical Israel* (New York: Schocken Books, 1986), 70.

26. Ivone Gebara, *Longing for Running Water: Ecofeminism and Liberation* (Min-neapolis: Fortress Press, 1999), 2.

27. Judith Plaskow, "Anti-Judaism in Feminist Christian Interpretation," in *A Feminist Introduction,* vol. 1 of *Searching the Scriptures,* ed. Elisabeth Schüssler Fiorenza (New York: Crossroad, 1995), 119.

28. Godfrey Ashby, *Go Out and Meet God: A Commentary on the Book of Exodus* (Grand Rapids, Mich.: Eerdmans, 1998), 50; Fretheim, *Exodus,* 140.

29. Pamela Philipose, "Women Act: Women and Environmental Protection in India," in *Healing the Wounds: The Promise of Ecofeminism,* ed. Judith Plant (Toronto: Between the Lines, 1989), 71-72.

30. In 1989, Union Carbide and the Indian government negotiated a settlement of $470 million, but as of the year 2000 the corporation has paid only $3,000 to each family of the dead and $600 to the injured. See www.bhopal.net.

31. Ward Morhouse, "Unfinished Business: Bhopal Ten Years After," in *Defying Corporations, Defining Democracy: A Book of History and Strategy,* ed. Dean Ritz (New York: Apex, 2001), 18-19.

32. William Holladay, *A Concise Hebrew and Aramaic Lexicon of the Old Testament* (Grand Rapids: Eerdmans, 1988), 212.

33. Anthony R. Ceresko, *Introduction to the Old Testament: A Liberation Perspective* (Maryknoll, N.Y.: Orbis Books, 1992), 97.

34. "Wood and stone" appearing together as in the vessels that were filled with blood may be a reference to idol worship. See Umberto Cassuto, *A Commentary on the Book of Exodus,* trans. Israel Abrahams (Jerusalem: Magnes Press, 1967), 99.

35. Martha Shelley, *Haggadah: A Celebration of Freedom* (San Francisco: aunt lute books, 1998), 22-23.

36. Marylin Waring, *If Women Counted: A New Feminist Economics* (San Fran-cisco: Harper & Row, 1988), 15.

37. Sylvia Federici, "Reproduction and Feminist Struggle in the New International Division of Labor," in *Women, Development, and the Labor of Reproduction: Issues of Struggles and Movements,* ed. Mariarosa Dalla Costa and G. Dalla Costa (Lawrenceville, N.J.: Africa World Press, 1998), 1.

38. Denise Nadeau and Laurel Dykstra, "Jubilaction: Engaging with a Feminist Jubilee in a Multi-faith and Secular Context," in *Jubilee Wealth and the Market: Share the Wealth,* ed. John Miheve (Toronto: Canadian Ecumenical Jubilee Initiative, 1999), 97.

39. Pixley, *On Exodus,* 45.

40. Food & Agriculture Organization of the United Nations, "Evaluation of Food & Nutrition Situation in Iraq," in *The Impact of Sanctions on Iraq: The Children Are Dying* (New York: World View Forum, 1996), 11-73.

41. Chuck Quilty, "Looming Crisis Caps Decade of Genocide in Iraq," *The Catholic Radical* (Rock Island, Ill., Summer 2000): 1.

42. For more on the U'Wa and their struggle, see Abby Reyes, "Por Vida: In Solidarity with the U'Wa People," in *Global Uprising: Confronting the Tyrannies of the 21ˢᵗ Century*, ed. Neva Welton and Linda Wolf (Gabriola Island, B.C.: New Society, 2001), 125-30.

43. C. David Coats, *Old MacDonald's Factory Farm* (New York: Continuum, 1989), 87.

44. Mary Lee Kerr and Bob Hall, "Chickens Come Home to Roost," *The Progressive* (January 1992): 29.

45. Christopher D. Cook, "Fowl Trouble," *Harper's,* August 1999, 78.

46. Ibid.

47. Jim Montavalli, "Dr. Robert Bullard: Some People Don't Have the Complexion for Protection," *E* (July-August 1998): 10.

48. Nancy Folbre and the Center for Popular Economics, *The New Field Guide to the U.S. Economy* (New York: New Press, 1995), 8.15.

49. Jim Montavalli, "When Green Means Stop," *E* (July-August 1998): 4.

50. David Korten, *When Corporations Rule the World,* 2nd ed. (San Francisco: Berrett-Koehler, 2001), 91.

51. Desert Rat, "When the Tear Gas Fills the Sky: The Washing Machine Song," on *International Incident: With Desert Rat,* Desert Rat Records, 2000, Tacoma, Wash.

52. Fretheim, *Exodus,* 108.

53. Beth Lawrence, "Amphibian Alarm: Just Where Have All the Frogs Gone?" *Smithsonian* 23, no. 7 (October 1992): 115.

CHAPTER 6
PHARAOH

1. Zora Neale Hurston, *Moses: Man of the Mountain* (Urbana and Chicago: University of Illinois Press, 1984), 15.

2. Alan Gardiner, *Egypt of the Pharaohs* (Oxford: Clarendon, 1961), 52.

3. As there were only three women monarchs of Egypt and only Hatshepsut claimed the title pharaoh, I have used the male pronoun for pharaoh (Erik Hornung, *History of Ancient Egypt: An Introduction,* trans. David Lorton [Ithaca, N.Y.: Cornell University Press, 1999], 83; Pierre Montet, *Lives of the Pharaohs* [Cleveland: World Publishing Company, 1958], 81). I capitalize the first letter of the word *pharaoh* only when it is used as a proper noun referring to one of the pharaohs of Exodus or a specific pharaoh of Egypt.

4. Henri Frankfort, *Kingship and the Gods: A Study of Ancient Near Eastern Religion as the Integration of Society and Nature* (Chicago: University of Chicago Press, 1978), 7.

5. Guillemette Andreu, *Egypt in the Age of the Pyramids*, trans. David Lorton (Ithaca, N.Y.: Cornell University Press, 1997), 13.

6. John H. Hayes and J. Maxwell Miller, *Israelite and Judean History* (Philadelphia: Westminster Press, 1990), 153; Nahum M. Sarna, *Exploring Exodus: The Heritage of Biblical Israel* (New York: Schocken Books, 1986), 19.

7. Sarna, *Exploring Exodus,* 20.

8. Hurston, *Moses: Man of the Mountain,* 11.

9. Nahum M. Sarna, general editor, *The Jewish Publication Society Torah Commentary: Exodus* (Philadelphia: Jewish Publication Society, 1991), 5.

10. Ibid.

11. Based on Meir Sternberg's argument that "Hebrews" is a derisive term used by others to refer to the Israelites, I avoid the word unless it is in a quotation, or used as

here, in just such a derogatory way (Meir Sternberg, *Hebrews between Cultures: Group Portraits and National Literature* [Bloomington: Indiana University Press, 1998]).

12. In the earliest texts 1:22 reads "every boy you shall throw into the Nile." Some *midrashim* have it that in his zeal to destroy Israel, Pharaoh had even Egyptian infants killed.

13. J. Gerald Janzen, *Exodus* (Louisville: Westminster/John Knox, 1997), 18.

14. Walter Brueggemann, "Pharoah as Vassal: A Study of a Political Metaphor," *Catholic Biblical Quarterly* 57 (1995): 46 n. 53.

15. Terence Fretheim, *Exodus* (Louisville: Westminster/John Knox, 1991), 29.

16. We have discussed genocide and our complicity in its modern manifestations in chapter 4, and we will discuss it further in chapter 9; however, the central exodus tradition focuses on forced labor and not on genocide (Michael Walzer, *Exodus and Revolution* [New York: Basic Books, 1985], 27).

17. Sarna, *Exploring Exodus*, 65.

18. Kevin Bales, *Disposable People: New Slavery in the Global Economy* (Berkeley: University of California Press, 1999), 154.

19. Sarna, *Exploring Exodus*, 23.

20. Ibid.

21. *Englishman's Hebrew and Chaldee Concordance of the Old Testament* (London: Samuel Bagster & Sons, Ltd., 1890), 632.

22. Wes Howard-Brook and Anthony Gwyther, *Unveiling Empire: Reading Revelation Then and Now* (Maryknoll, N.Y.: Orbis Books, 1999), 164.

23. Louis Ginzberg, *The Legends of the Jews*, vol. 3, *Moses in the Wilderness*, trans. Paul Radin (Philadelphia: Jewish Publication Society of America, 1909-38), 299.

24. George Pixley, *On Exodus: A Liberation Perspective*, trans. Robert Barr (Maryknoll, N.Y.: Orbis Books, 1987), 32.

25. Fretheim, *Exodus*, 107.

26. Randall Bailey, "And They Shall Know That I Am YHWH: The P Recasting of the Plague Narratives in Exodus 7-11," *Journal of the Interdenominational Theological Center* 22 (Fall 1994): 7-9.

27. Umberto Cassuto, *A Commentary on the Book of Exodus*, trans. Israel Abrahams (Jerusalem: Magnes Press, 1967), 99.

28. Brueggemann, "Pharoah as Vassal."

29. Ibid.

30. Although Moses' humility is remarked upon in the text (Num. 12:3), his pride is evident through his actions.

31. Hurston, *Moses: Man of the Mountain*, 207.

32. Walzer, *Exodus and Revolution*, 24.

33. Tim Cole, *Selling the Holocaust: From Auschwitz to Schindler, How History Is Bought and Sold* (New York: Routledge, 1922), 70-71.

34. David Korten, *When Corporations Rule the World*, 2nd ed. (San Francisco: Berrett-Koehler, 2001), 115.

35. Mary Zepernick, "Man Corporate On Top of the World," in *Defying Corporations, Defining Democracy: A Book of History and Strategy*, ed. Dean Ritz (New York: Apex, 2001), 74. Zepernick points out the added irony that the eulogist Andrew Young had been a protégé of Martin Luther King.

36. David Bacon, "The Real Thing—Murders at Coke," *Dispatcher* [Newspaper of the International Longshore & Warehouse Union], November 2001.

37. Korten, *When Corporations Rule*, 298.

38. Brevard Childs, *The Book of Exodus: A Critical Commentary* (Philadelphia: Westminster Press, 1974), 170.

39. These translations are from Everett Fox, *Now These Are the Names: A New English Rendition of the Book of Exodus* (New York: Schocken Books, 1986).

40. Notice here that one of the issues in translation is monotheism: whether YHWH is the first or only god.

41. William Holladay, *A Concise Hebrew and Aramaic Lexicon of the Old Testament* (Grand Rapids: Eerdmans, 1988), 171-72.

42. I have attempted to avoid confusing the modern English use of heart with the ancient Hebrew, but it is both difficult and tempting.

43. *Kabed,* which appears five times in reference to Pharaoh's heart, also appears five times in reference to the ardor of the plagues (Fox, *Now These Are the Names,* 45).

44. Holladay, *Hebrew and Aramaic Lexicon,* 171-72, 99, 150.

45. Howard W. Stone, *Depression & Hope: New Insights for Pastoral Counseling* (Minneapolis: Fortress Press, 1998), xi.

46. Carter Heyward, "The Body of Christa: Hope for the World," in *Staying Power* (Cleveland: Pilgrim Press, 1995), 122.

47. Ched Myers, *Who Will Roll Away the Stone?: Discipleship Queries for First World Christians* (Maryknoll, N.Y.: Orbis Books, 1994), xxvii.

48. This particular quotation is taken from an exchange between a white middle-class student and June Jordan, African American poet and political essayist. The defense is quite telling as the white woman goes on to use her nobody status to absolve herself from any commitment to race and class justice (June Jordan, quoted in M. Shawn Copeland, "Toward a Critical Christian Feminist Theology of Solidarity," in *Women and Theology,* ed. Mary Ann Hinsdale and Phyllis H. Kaminski [Maryknoll, N.Y.: Orbis Books, 1994], 19).

49. Michael Lerner, *Surplus Powerlessness: The Psychodynamics of Everyday Life and the Psychology of Individual Social Transformation* (Amherst, N.Y.: Humanities Press, 1991). I owe to Walter Wink the idea that powerlessness is always a spiritual disorder; see Walter Wink, *Engaging the Powers: Discernment and Resistance in a World of Domination* (Minneapolis: Fortress Press, 1992), 203.

50. *Fourth world* is a term used by some First Nations leaders and activists to speak about themselves as a distinct and impoverished "world" living inside developed nations.

51. Dorothee Sölle, *Stations of the Cross: A Latin American Pilgrimage* (Minneapolis: Fortress Press, 1993), 109.

52. Adbusters, *Days of Resistance Calendar: 2001* (Vancouver: Adbusters Media Foundation, 2000), 5.

53. Rosemary Radford Ruether, "What Are the Inter-connections between the Impoverishment of Earth and the Impoverishment of People?," roundtable in the *Great Minds/Great Questions* series, sponsored by the Whidbey Institute, Plymouth Congregational Church, Seattle, December 11, 1998.

54. Myers, *Who Will Roll Away the Stone?,* 46.

55. James Heintz, Nancy Folbre, and the Center for Popular Economics, *The Ultimate Field Guide to the U.S. Economy* (New York: New Press, 2000), 102.

56. Korten, *When Corporations Rule,* 163.

57. Robert McAfee Brown, *Unexpected News: Reading the Bible with Third World Eyes* (Philadelphia: Westminster Press, 1984), 43.

58. Alice Miller, quoted in Myers, *Who Will Roll Away the Stone?,* 90.

CHAPTER 7
VIOLENCE, DESTRUCTION, HATRED, AND JUDGMENT

1. Walter Brueggemann, *Theology of the Old Testament: Testimony, Dispute, Advocacy* (Minneapolis: Fortress Press, 1997), 381.

2. Nahum M. Sarna, *Exploring Exodus: The Heritage of Biblical Israel* (New York: Schocken Books, 1986), 71 n. 6.

3. Egyptian and early Assyrian chariots carried two warriors; Hittite and later Assyrian chariots carried three. The Hebrew word *shalish*, translated "officers" in the NRSV, might also be translated "third," which may indicate that the Israelites used or were familiar with three-person chariots (J. W. Wevers, "Chariots," in *Interpreter's Dictionary of the Bible*, vol. 1 [Nashville: Abingdon Press, 1962], 1:552-54).

4. Henri Frankfort, *Kingship and the Gods: A Study of Ancient Near Eastern Religion as the Integration of Society and Nature* (Chicago: University of Chicago Press, 1978), 8, fig. 9.

5. Ibid., 10.

6. This is an example of the portrayal of Solomon as another pharaoh.

7. Translation of Everett Fox, *Now These Are the Names: A New English Rendition of the Book of Exodus* (New York: Schocken Books, 1986), 82.

8. Judith Plaskow, *Standing Again at Sinai: Judaism from a Feminist Perspective* (San Francisco: HarperSanFrancisco, 1991), 131.

9. William H. C. Propp, *Exodus 1-18: A New Translation with Introduction and Commentary* (New York: Doubleday, 1999), 354.

10. Terence Fretheim, "Some Reflections on Brueggemann's God," in *God in the Fray: A Tribute to Walter Brueggemann*, ed. Tod Linafelt and Timothy Beal (Minneapolis: Fortress Press, 1998), 25.

11. Mark S. Smith, *The Early History of God: YHWH and the Other Deities in Ancient Israel* (San Francisco: Harper & Row, 1990), 49-55, 94-96. For an explanation of the Ashera-Ashtoreth connection, see also Jacob Rabinowitz, *The Faces of God: Canaanite Mythology as Hebrew Theology* (Woodstock, Conn.: Spring Publications, 1998), 83 n. 43.

12. Smith, *Early History of God,* 163.

13. Patrick D. Miller, Jr., "God the Warrior: A Problem in Biblical Interpretation and Apologetics," *Interpretation* 19 (1965): 39.

14. Smith, *Early History of God,* 115-17; Isaiah 66:15 is another such reference, as is the woman clothed with the sun in Revelation 12:1.

15. Norma Rosen, "Bitiah: Memoir of a Tyrant's Daughter," in *Biblical Women Unbound* (Philadelphia: Jewish Publication Society, 1996), 4.

16. Nancy C. Lee, "Genocide's Lament: Moses, Pharaoh's Daughter, and the Former Yugoslavia," in *God in the Fray: A Tribute to Walter Brueggemann*, ed. Tod Linafelt and Timothy Beal (Minneapolis: Fortress Press, 1998), 76.

17. Susan Niditch, *War in the Hebrew Bible: A Study of the Ethics of Violence* (New York: Oxford University Press, 1993), 150.

18. Louis Ginzberg, quoted in Lee, "Genocide's Lament," 80.

19. J. Severino Croatto, *Exodus: A Hermeneutics of Freedom* (Maryknoll, N.Y.: Orbis Books, 1981), 30.

20. Josiah Young, "Exodus as a Paradigm for Black Theology," in *Exodus, a Lasting Paradigm*, ed. Bas van Iersel and Anton Weiler (Edinburgh: T & T Clark, 1987), 99.

21. Ibid., 95.

22. Renita J. Weems, "The Hebrew Women Are Not Like the Egyptian Women: The Ideology of Race, Gender, and Sexual Reproduction in Exodus 1," *Semeia* 59 (1992): 31.

23. Croatto, *Exodus*, 29-30.

24. Terence Fretheim, *Exodus* (Louisville: Westminster/John Knox, 1991), 19; Walter Brueggemann, "Pharoah as Vassal: A Study of a Political Metaphor," *Catholic Biblical Quarterly* 57 (1995): 28.

25. Martin Luther King, Jr., "The Death of Evil upon the Seashore," in *Strength to Love* (New York: Harper & Row, 1963), 71-81. This is a sermon preached in the Cathedral of St. John the Divine, in New York City, May 17, 1956, the second anniversary of the Supreme Court decision that declared segregated schooling unconstitutional.

26. Margaret Eletta Guider, *Daughters of Rahab: Prostitution and the Church of Liberation in Brazil* (Minneapolis: Fortress Press, 1995), 171.

27. Delores S. Williams, *Sisters in the Wilderness: The Challenge of Womanist God-Talk* (Maryknoll, N.Y.: Orbis Books, 1993), 150.

28. Robert Allen Warrior, "A Native American Perspective: Canaanites, Cowboys and Indians," in *Voices from the Margins: Interpreting the Bible in the Third World*, ed. R. S. Sugirtharajah (Maryknoll, N.Y.: Orbis Books, 1991), 289.

29. Croatto, *Exodus*, 29.

30. Williams, *Sisters in the Wilderness*, 151.

31. Martha Ann Kirk, *Celebrations of Women's Bible Stories: Tears, Milk, and Honey* (Kansas City, Mo.: Sheed & Ward, 1987), 12.

32. Denise Nadeau and Laurel Dykstra, "Jubilaction: Engaging with a Feminist Jubilee in a Multi-faith and Secular Context," in *Jubilee Wealth and the Market: Share the Wealth*, ed. John Miheve (Toronto: Canadian Ecumenical Jubilee Initiative, 1999), 88-89.

33. This has led to controversies about atonement, and some feminists reject the idea that Jesus died for the sins of humanity.

34. In the prophets there are images of God's violence as rape and sexual abuse; these passages especially demand protest and examination.

35. Plaskow, *Standing Again at Sinai*, 131.

36. Ibid., 132.

37. Rita Nakashima Brock, "And a Little Child Will Lead Us," in *Christianity, Patriarchy and Abuse: A Feminist Critique*, ed. Joanne Carlson Brown and Carole R. Bohn (New York: Pilgrim Press, 1989), 59.

38. Phyllis Trible, *Texts of Terror: Literary-Feminist Readings of Biblical Narratives* (Philadelphia: Fortress Press, 1984), 2.

39. Bruce A. Stevens, "Jesus the Divine Warrior," *Expository Times* 94, no. 11 (1983): 326-29; idem, "The Divine Warrior in the Gospel of Mark," *Biblische Zeitschrift* 31, no. 1 (1987): 109.

40. Croatto, *Exodus*, 30.

41. Two Hebrew words for chariot are used; both share a common root: *rekeb* appears nine times, and *merkabah* once (Exod. 14:25).

42. Martin Luther King Jr., quoted in Stephen Oates, *Let the Trumpet Sound: The Life of Martin Luther King, Jr.* (New York: New American Library, 1982), 84.

43. Williams, *Sisters in the Wilderness*, 151.

44. Jon Levenson, *Sinai and Zion: An Entry into the Jewish Bible* (San Francisco: HarperSanFrancisco, 1985), 23.

45. Audre Lorde, "A Litany for Survival," in *The Black Unicorn* (New York: Norton, 1978), 31.

46. Katie Monagle, "The Death Penalty," *Scholastic Update* 125 (September 1992): 13-14.

47. "Blacks Imprisoned in USA Tops South Africa Figure," *Jet*, January 28, 1991: 8.

48. David Love, "Justice System Discriminates against Black and Latino Youth," Knight Ridder/Tribune News Service, May 3, 2000.

49. Willa Boesak, *God's Wrathful Children: Political Oppression and Christian Ethics* (Grand Rapids: Eerdmans, 1995), 177.

50. From the Mernaptha Stela, in Sarna, *Exploring Exodus*, 11.

51. Jerome Miller, "Habitat for Inhumanity," *Utne Reader* 71 (September/October 1995): 87-88.

52. Boesak, *God's Wrathful Children*, 117.

53. Ibid., xv. Although they are very distant in starting point and conclusion, these political liberation theologians are strikingly similar to feminist liberation theologians

Carlson and Brown in their insistence that the agents of violence not be protected by god-language (Joanne Carlson and Rebecca Brown, "Introduction," in *Christianity, Patriarchy and Abuse: A Feminist Critique,* ed. Joanne Carlson Brown and Carole R. Bohn [New York: Pilgrim Press, 1989]).

54. Matthews, quoted in Boesak, *God's Wrathful Children,* 68.

55. Gutiérrez, quoted in Boesak, *God's Wrathful Children,* 182.

56. bell hooks, "killing rage," in *Killing Rage: Ending Racism* (New York: Henry Holt & Co., 1995), 20.

57. Robert Goss, *Jesus Acted Up: A Gay and Lesbian Manifesto* (San Francisco: HarperSanFrancisco, 1993), 145.

58. Arthur Solomon, *Eating Bitterness: A Vision beyond the Prison Walls: Poems and Essays of Arthur Solomon* (Toronto: NC Press, 1994), 76-77.

59. hooks, "killing rage," 12.

60. Josiah Young, "Exodus as a Paradigm for Black Theology," 99.

61. Brueggemann, "Pharoah as Vassal," 38.

62. Ibid., 36.

63. James H. Cone, *God of the Oppressed* (Maryknoll, N.Y.: Orbis Books, 1997), 59.

64. Warrior, "Native American Perspective ," 292.

CHAPTER 8

PHARAOH'S DAUGHTER, DAUGHTER OF GOD

1. Norma Rosen, "Bitiah: Memoir of a Tyrant's Daughter," in *Biblical Women Unbound* (Philadelphia: Jewish Publication Society, 1996), 166.

2. Jopie Siebert-Hommes, "But if She be a Daughter . . . She May Live!" in *A Feminist Companion to Exodus to Deuteronomy,* ed. Athalya Brenner (Sheffield: Sheffield Academic Press, 1994), 71.

3. Everett Fox, *Now These Are the Names: A New English Rendition of the Book of Exodus* (New York: Schocken Books, 1986), 21.

4. Cheryl Exum, "You Shall Let Every Daughter Live: A Study of Exodus 1:8-2:10," in *A Feminist Companion to Exodus to Deuteronomy,* ed. Athalya Brenner (Sheffield: Sheffield Academic Press, 1994), 56.

5. Nahum M. Sarna, *Exploring Exodus: The Heritage of Biblical Israel* (New York: Schocken Books, 1986), 32.

6. Exum, "You Shall Let Every Daughter Live," 57.

7. James S. Ackerman, "The Literary Context of the Moses Birth Story (Exodus 1-2), in *Literary Interpretations of Biblical Narratives,* ed. Kenneth R. R. Gros Louis, with James S. Ackerman and Thayer S. Warshaw (New York: Abingdon Press, 1974), 86, also 93-94.

8. Yair Zakovitch, "A Study of Precise and Partial Derivations in Biblical Etymology," *Journal for the Study of the Old Testament* 15 (1980): 31-50.

9. Martin Noth, *Exodus,* Old Testament Library (Philadelphia: Westminster Press, 1962), 26.

10. This would have been the most important question in Egypt, because it was through the queen's daughters that a man could make claim to the Egyptian throne (Barbara Watterson, *Women in Ancient Egypt* [New York: St. Martin's Press, 1991], 21-22).

11. Sarna, *Exploring Exodus,* 31.

12. Watterson, *Women in Ancient Egypt,* 21-31.

13. John Baines and Jaromir Malek, *Atlas of Ancient Egypt* (New York: Facts on File, 1980), 204.

14. William H. C. Propp, *Exodus 1-18: A New Translation with Introduction and Commentary* (New York: Doubleday, 1999), 150.

15. Watterson, *Women in Ancient Egypt*, 28.

16. Propp, *Exodus 1-18*, 156.

17. Brevard Childs, "The Birth of Moses," *Journal of Biblical Literature* 84 (1965): 112; Frederick Knobloch, "Adoption," *Anchor Bible Dictionary*, ed. David Noel Freedman (New York: Doubleday, 1992), 1:76-79.

18. Baines and Malek, *Atlas of Ancient Egypt*, 36, 43.

19. Childs, "Birth of Moses," 111.

20. Baines and Malek, *Atlas of Ancient Egypt*, 205.

21. Propp, *Exodus 1-18*, 156-57.

22. Ibid., 145.

23. Ibid., 150.

24. With the mounting evidence that the historical Miriam was a wilderness leader, it is unlikely that this girl is the wilderness figure. For more on Miriam as priest and wilderness leader and on the water motif, see Rita Burns, *Has the LORD Spoken Only through Moses? A Study of the Biblical Portrait of Miriam* (Atlanta: Scholars Press, 1987).

25. The mother does appear again in the genealogy as Jochebed (Exod. 6:20).

26. Historically it is unlikely that there was such a figure, as Egyptians were very reluctant to have daughters marry out, believing that women carried the divine spark that made the pharaoh a god (Watterson, *Women in Ancient Egypt*, 21).

27. Fox, *Now These Are the Names*, 4.

28. Quoted in Propp, *Exodus 1-18*, 156.

29. Quoted in ibid., 155.

30. Louis Ginzberg, *The Legends of the Jews*, vol. 2, *From Joseph to the Exodus*, trans. Henrietta Szold (Philadelphia: Jewish Publication Society of America, 1909-38), 270.

31. The collections of midrashic texts are independent of one another and thus contradictory. Bithiah is said to have feigned pregnancy but also to have described the infant's unusual discovery and adoption to her father. On the eve of the plague against the firstborn, she comes to Moses with Pharaoh, pleading for the life of her brother. Despite her close alliance with Pharaoh she is believed to have made the exodus, for she marries Miriam's husband, Caleb, after Miriam's death (Rosen, "Bitiah," 165, 166; Ginzberg, *The Legends of the Jews*, vol. 2, *From Joseph to the Exodus*, 270).

32. Cheryl Exum, *Plotted, Painted and Shot: Cultural Representations of Biblical Women* (Sheffield: Sheffield Academic Press, 1996), 89.

33. Elisabeth Schüssler Fiorenza, *Bread Not Stone: The Challenge of Feminist Biblical Interpretation* (Boston: Beacon Press, 1985), 15.

34. I have been using the term "hermeneutic of invention" for quite some time, thinking I had borrowed it; but when I went to name my source I could find none. Martha Ann Kirk describes Elisabeth Schüssler Fiorenza's fourth hermeneutic as one of ritualization and celebration, which comes close to my use of the term (Martha Ann Kirk, *Celebrations of Women's Bible Stories: Tears, Milk, and Honey* [Kansas City, Mo.: Sheed & Ward, 1987], 1). I understand a hermeneutic of "creative actualization" as making our stories concrete in the real world. This is doing political praxis; "hermeneutics of invention" involves creative exploration of texts, it does not necessarily include praxis.

35. Monique Wittig, *Les Guerilleries* (Boston: Beacon Press, 1971), 89.

36. Rosen, "Bitiah," 159, 163.

37. Ibid., 154.

38. Patricia Williams, "In Search of Pharaoh's Daughter," in *Out of the Garden: Women Writers on the Bible*, ed. Christina Buchmann and Celina Spiegel (New York: Fawcett Columbine, 1994), 56.

39. Ibid., 58.

40. Nancy C. Lee, "Genocide's Lament: Moses, Pharaoh's Daughter, and the Former Yugoslavia," in *God in the Fray: A Tribute to Walter Brueggemann,* ed. Tod Linafelt and Timothy K. Beal (Minneapolis: Fortress Press, 1998), 72.

41. Ibid., 74.

42. Ibid., 68.

43. Rosen, "Bitiah," 157.

44. Williams, "In Search of Pharaoh's Daughter," 63.

45. Delores S. Williams, *Sisters in the Wilderness: The Challenge of Womanist God-Talk* (Maryknoll, N.Y.: Orbis Books, 1993), 132.

46. Morris Jeff, Jr., quoted in Rita J. Simon, Howard Altstein, and Marygold Melli, *The Case for Transracial Adoption* (Washington, D.C.: American University Press, 1994), 41.

47. Sylvia Federici, "Reproduction and Feminist Struggle in the New International Division of Labor," in *Women, Development, and the Labor of Reproduction: Issues of Struggles and Movements,* ed. Mariarosa Dalla Costa and G. Dalla Costa (Lawrenceville, N.J.: Africa World Press), 47-81.

48. Rosen, "Bitiah," 151.

CHAPTER 9

SHIPHRAH AND PUAH

1. Renita J. Weems, "The Hebrew Women Are Not Like the Egyptian Women: The Ideology of Race, Gender, and Sexual Reproduction in Exodus 1," *Semeia* 59 (1992): 29.

2. Everett Fox, *Now These Are the Names: A New English Rendition of the Book of Exodus* (New York: Schocken Books, 1986), 13.

3. Brevard Childs, *The Book of Exodus: A Critical Commentary* (Philadelphia: Westminster Press, 1974), 16.

4. Ellen Frankel, *The Five Books of Miriam: A Woman's Commentary on the Torah* (San Francisco: HarperSanFrancisco, 1998).

5. Fox, *Now These Are the Names,* 12-14.

6. After Exum, with my own modifications; the language seems stilted in order to convey the repetition of words in the Hebrew (Cheryl Exum, "You Shall Let Every Daughter Live: A Study of Exodus 1.8-2.10," in *A Feminist Companion to Exodus to Deuteronomy,* ed. Athalya Brenner [Sheffield: Sheffield Academic Press, 1994], 47).

7. Ibid.

8. The statement is rendered with an exclamation point in English, after Siebert-Hommes, to convey emphasis (Jopie Siebert-Hommes, "But if She Be a Daughter . . . She May Live!" in *A Feminist Companion to Exodus to Deuteronomy,* ed. Athalya Brenner [Sheffield: Sheffield Academic Press, 1994], 74).

9. Ibid., 67.

10. Ibid., 66.

11. Nahum M. Sarna, *Exploring Exodus: The Heritage of Biblical Israel* (New York: Schocken Books, 1986), 24.

12. William H. C. Propp, *Exodus 1-18: A New Translation with Introduction and Commentary* (New York: Doubleday, 1999), 139.

13. Childs, *Book of Exodus,* 20; Martin Noth, *Exodus,* Old Testament Library (Philadelphia: Westminster Press, 1962), 23.

14. Ibid., 5.

15. Noth, *Exodus,* 19.

16. Propp, *Exodus 1-18,* 139.

17. Childs, *Book of Exodus,* 12.

18. Weems, "Hebrew Women," 29.

19. Ibid., 28.

20. Propp, *Exodus 1-18,* 140; Fox, *Now These Are the Names,* 15.

21. Weems, "Hebrew Women," 32-33.

22. Childs, *Book of Exodus,* 23.

23. Although biblical men like Abraham, Isaac, and Jacob also lie in situations of power imbalance, there are fewer of them and lying is only one of many strategies they use.

24. Exum, "You Shall Let Every Daughter Live," 49.

25. Richard J. Clifford, *The Wisdom Literature* (Nashville: Abingdon Press, 1998), 47.

26. Rita Burns, *Exodus, Leviticus, Numbers, With Excursuses on Feast, Ritual and Typology* (Wilmington, Del.: Glazier, 1983), 30.

27. Louis Ginzberg, *The Legends of the Jews,* vol. 3, *Moses in the Wilderness,* trans. Paul Radin (Philadelphia: Jewish Publication Society of America, 1909-38), 257, 264.

28. Daniel Berrigan, "Prophecy," in *And the Risen Bread: Selected Poems 1957-1997* (New York: Fordham University Press, 1998), 230.

29. Childs, *Book of Exodus,* 17.

30. Weems, "Hebrew Women," 32.

31. David Daube, *Civil Disobedience in Antiquity* (Edinburgh: Edinburgh University Press, 1972), 5 (emphasis added).

32. Ched Myers, "By What Authority: The Bible and Civil Disobedience," *Sojourners* 23 (May 1984): 11.

33. Daube, *Civil Disobedience in Antiquity,* 82; Daniel was set in sixth-century B.C.E. Babylon, but was actually written as resistance literature during the bloody reign of Antiochus IV Epiphanes in the second century B.C.E.

34. Gandhi, quoted in John Dear, *The Sacrament of Civil Disobedience* (Baltimore, Md.: Fortkamp, 1994), 39.

35. John Dominic Crossan, *The Historical Jesus: The Life of a Mediterranean Jewish Peasant* (San Francisco: HarperSanFrancisco, 1991), 171.

36. Rita Nakashima Brock, *Journeys by Heart: A Christology of Erotic Power* (New York: Crossroad, 1995), 105.

37. Daniel Stevick, quoted in Dear, *Sacrament of Civil Disobedience,* 91.

38. Dear, *Sacrament of Civil Disobedience,* xx.

39. Ibid., 14.

40. After an extensive search I could not find a credible source for this precise quotation, although it is often used. The idea is certainly in keeping with Rabbi Heschel's thoughts on making prayer active.

41. Dear, *Sacrament of Civil Disobedience,* 147.

42. Childs, *Book of Exodus,* 17.

43. Howard Troxler, "It's Time to Look at the Debt Never Paid," *St. Petersburg Times* [Florida], February 21, 2001. See www.sptimes.com.

44. Martin Luther King, Jr., "Letter from Birmingham City Jail," in *Nonviolence in America: A Documentary History,* rev. ed., ed. Staughton Lynd and Alice Lynd (Maryknoll, N.Y.: Orbis Books, 1995), 254-67.

CHAPTER 10

OTHER EGYPTIANS

1. Randall C. Bailey, "And They Shall Know that I Am YHWH: The P Recasting of the Plague Narratives in Exodus 7-11," *Journal of the Interdenominational Theological Center* 22 (Fall 1994): 14-15.

2. Randall C. Bailey, "Is That Any Name for a Nice Hebrew Boy? Exodus 2:1-10:

The De-Africanization of an Israelite Hero," in *The Recovery of Black Presence,* ed. Randall C. Bailey and Jacquelyn Grant (Nashville: Abingdon Press, 1995), 25-36.

3. Zora Neale Hurston seems also to have considered the possibility of Moses as an Egyptian. She makes the story of Moses' rescue by Pharaoh's daughter into a fabrication imagined by the infant's sister (*Moses: Man of the Mountain* [J. B. Lippincott, 1939; reprint, Urbana: University of Illinois Press, 1984], 40-51).

4. Bailey, "Is That Any Name," 26.

5. William H. C. Propp, *Exodus 1-18: A New Translation with Introduction and Commentary* (New York: Doubleday, 1999), 229-31.

6. M. Shawn Copeland, "Towards a Critical Christian Feminist Theology of Solidarity," in *Women and Theology,* ed. Mary Ann Hinsdale and Phyllis H. Kaminski (Maryknoll, N.Y.: Orbis Books, 1994), 23.

7. Bailey, "Is That Any Name," 36.

8. I have used Fox's translation here because it highlights the contrast between Egypt and the wilderness, death and life.

9. George Pixley, *On Exodus: A Liberation Perspective,* trans. Robert Barr (Maryknoll, N.Y.: Orbis Books, 1987), 52.

10. Ibid.

11. bell hooks, "Introduction," *Where We Stand: Class Matters* (New York: Routledge, 2000), 5.

12. William Holladay, *A Concise Hebrew and Aramaic Lexicon of the Old Testament* (Grand Rapids: Eerdmans, 1988), 244. The appearance of the word in 3:22 may be a pun with 3:8, where the verb appears in another form meaning "rescue" to describe what YHWH will do for Israel.

13. George Wesley Coats, "Despoiling the Egyptians," *Vetus Testamentum* 18 (1968): 450-57.

14. Kensington Welfare Rights Union, "The Rich Man's House," adapted from "The Enemy's Gate," on Anne Feeney, *Have You Been to Jail for Justice* (Nashville: Anne Feeney, 2000), Track 9.

15. Michael Walzer, *Exodus and Revolution* (New York: Basic Books, 1985), 26.

16. Julian Morgenstern, "The Despoiling of the Egyptians," *Journal of Biblical Literature* 68, no. 1 (1949): 1-28. The rest of Morgenstern's argument is that the event was definitely a despoiling but that this aspect was secondary to that of a ritual courtship dance, integral to the Passover and the worship in the wilderness for which Moses negotiated.

17. Perhaps the directive that each household too small for a whole lamb share with its closest neighbor (12:4) included Egyptian neighbors.

18. The King James Version reads *"borrowed."*

19. J. Gerald Janzen, *Exodus* (Louisville: Westminster/John Knox, 1997), 36-37.

20. For critiques of modern Jubilee interpretations and of the Jubilee texts themselves, see the following, all in *Jubilee Wealth and the Market: Share the Wealth,* ed. John Miheve (Toronto: Canadian Ecumenical Jubilee Initiative, 1999): Denise Nadeau and Laurel Dykstra, "Jubilaction: Engaging with a Feminist Jubilee in a Multi-faith and Secular Context," 77-111; Puleny Lenka-Bula, "Jubilee at the Turn of the 21st Century and the African Woman," 113-27; Jubilee South, "Towards a New Jubilee Covenant: A Contribution from the Jubilee South," 129-36.

21. It is a sobering truth about the power of the structures they oppose that the various modern Jubilee movements have been very successful in raising public awareness, and in North–South collaboration, but have had very little concrete success in actual debt cancellation.

22. Holladay, *Hebrew and Aramaic Lexicon,* 130.

23. A first-century C.E. Aramaic translation: Robert R. Stieglitz, "The Lowdown on the Riffraff," *Bible Review* 15 (August 1999): 54.

24. Propp, *Exodus 1-18*, 357.

25. Pixley, *On Exodus*, 67.

26. Pinchas Lapide, "Exodus in the Jewish Tradition," in *Exodus, a Lasting Paradigm*, ed. Bas van Iersel and Anton Weiler (Edinburgh: T & T Clark, 1987), 49.

27. Jon Levenson, quoted in Walter Brueggemann, "Pharoah as Vassal: A Study of a Political Metaphor," *Catholic Biblical Quarterly* 57 (1995): 29-31.

28. Jon Levenson, "Exodus and Liberation," *Horizons in Biblical Theology* 13 (1991): 139 n. 16. Of the passages cited by Levenson to make this point, only Leviticus 24:10-13 indicates a person of mixed-Israelite heritage; the others concern people of other nations, and while some passages exclude aliens or condemn interactions with them, all passages indicate that such interactions occurred.

29. George Pixley, *Historia de Israel de la Perspectiva de los Pobres: Israel, Desde su Fundación Revolucionaria Hasta su Fin Revolucionario (1220a.c.-135 d.c.)*, 2nd ed., (Mexico City: Palabra Ediciones, 1993), 16.

30. Rita Burns, *Exodus, Leviticus, Numbers, with Excursuses on Feast, Ritual and Typology* (Wilmington, Del.: Glazier, 1983), 99.

31. Stieglitz, "Lowdown on the Riffraff," 54 n. 1.

32. Louis Ginzberg, *The Legends of the Jews*, vol. 2, *From Joseph to the Exodus*, trans. Henrietta Szold (Philadelphia: Jewish Publication Society of America, 1909-38), 270.

33. bell hooks, "Being Rich," in *Where We Stand*, 77.

CHAPTER 11

SETTING THE PEOPLE FREE

1. Tom F. Driver, *Christ in a Changing World: Toward an Ethical Christology* (New York: Crossroad, 1981), 4.

2. Gregory Baum, "Exodus Politics," in *Exodus, a Lasting Paradigm*, ed. Bas van Iersel and Anton Weiler (Edinburgh: T & T Clark, 1987), 113.

3. Jon Sobrino and Juan Hernandez Pico, *Theology of Christian Solidarity* (Maryknoll, N.Y.: Orbis Books, 1985), 10; Ada María Isasi-Díaz, "Solidarity and Love of Neighbor in the 1980's," in *Feminist Theological Ethics: A Reader*, ed. Lois K. Daly (Philadelphia: Westminster/John Knox, 1994), 78.

4. M. Shawn Copeland, "Toward a Critical Christian Feminist Theology of Solidarity," in *Women and Theology*, ed. Mary Ann Hinsdale and Phyllis H. Kaminski (Maryknoll, N.Y.: Orbis Books, 1994), 3.

5. James Cone discussed control and paternalism (*God of the Oppressed* [Maryknoll, N.Y.: Orbis Books, 1997], 218-25); Isasi-Díaz, charity ("Solidarity and Love," 78); Maria Lugones, exercise of authority (Lugones, quoted in Toinette Eugene, "On 'Difference' and the Dream of Pluralist Feminism," *Journal of Feminist Studies in Religion* 8 [1992]: 98); and Ched Myers, control, paternalism, and charity (*Who Will Roll Away the Stone?: Discipleship Queries for First World Christians* [Maryknoll, N.Y.: Orbis Books, 1994], 78).

6. Isasi-Díaz, "Solidarity and Love," 78.

7. Copeland, "Toward a Critical Christian Feminist Theology of Solidarity," 23.

8. Ibid. Copeland is describing dynamics between white women and women of color.

9. Ibid., 25.

10. Although Canadians are stereotypically self-deprecating about our nation, we are still arrogant about our first-world way of life.

11. Carter Heyward, "Passion," in *Our Passion for Justice: Images of Power, Sexuality, and Liberation* (New York: Pilgrim Press, 1984), 19.

12. Coleen Fulmer, "Passionate God," in Martha Ann Kirk, *Celebrations of Women's Bible Stories: Tears, Milk, and Honey* (Kansas City: Sheed & Ward, 1987), 102.

13. In using the term "vigilance," it is important to remember the horror of Southern "vigilance committees," white gangs who lynched blacks and terrorized white abolitionists during and after the American Civil War.

14. These precepts come from the Christian, Protestant background of twelve-step programs that grew out of the evangelical Oxford movement. This connection works well for some Christians, but the fact that this is virtually the only recovery model available is a serious problem for people of other faiths. See Rebecca Farnsway, ed., *Twelve-Step Horror Stories* (Tucson: See Sharp Press, 2000).

15. Hans Christian Andersen, "The Emperor's New Clothes," in *Michael Hague's Favorite Hans Christian Andersen Fairy Tales* (New York: Holt, Rinehart, and Winston, 1981), 111-12.

16. Wes Howard-Brook and Anthony Gwyther, *Unveiling Empire: Reading Revelation Then and Now* (Maryknoll, N.Y.: Orbis Books, 1999), 122.

17. "Babylon Is Fallen," a traditional hymn first published with a tune by William E. Chute in 1878, was long used in the "shape note" singing tradition in the United States (and sometimes Chute's native Nova Scotia). For the history of William Chute, the Elastic Millennium Choir credits David Warren Steel of the University of Mississippi.

18. Dorothy Day, *The Long Loneliness: The Autobiography of Dorothy Day* (New York: Harper & Brothers, 1952), 286.

19. John O'Brien, *Theology and the Option for the Poor* (Collegeville, Minn.: Liturgical Press, 1992), 24.

20. Syracuse Cultural Workers, "Mission Statement," Dept. 712, PO Box 6367, Syracuse, NY 13217. www.syrculturalworkers.org.

21. Bread and Puppet, "The WHY CHEAP ART? Manifesto" (Glover, Vt.: Bread and Puppet, 1984).

22. An excellent example of solidarity and alliance building is the School of the Americas Watch affinity groups that took part in protests at the April 2000 meeting of the World Bank and International Monetary Fund. See Bruce Triggs, "Globalizing the SOA Watch," in *The Global Activist Manual: Local Ways to Change the World*, ed. Mike Prokosh and Laura Raymond (New York: Nation Books/Thunder's Mouth, 2002), 49.

23. The Independent Media Center network that began during the buildup to Seattle's 1999 WTO demonstrations, is one example: www.indymedia.org.

24. Leonardo Boff, quoted in Dan Cohn-Sherbok, *Exodus: An Agenda for Jewish-Christian Dialogue* (London: Bellew, 1992), 77.

BIBLIOGRAPHY

Ackerman, James S. "The Literary Context of the Moses Birth Story (Exodus 1-2)." In *Literary Interpretations of Biblical Narratives,* ed. Kenneth R. R. Gros Louis, with James S. Ackerman and Thayer S. Warshaw, 74-119. New York: Abingdon Press, 1974.

Achtemeier, Paul, ed. *Harper's Bible Dictionary.* San Francisco: HarperSanFrancisco, 1996.

Adams, Carol J. "Toward a Feminist Theology of Religion and the State." In *Violence against Women and Children: A Theological Sourcebook,* ed. Carol J. Adams and Marie Fortune, 15-35. New York: Continuum, 1995.

Adams, Howard. *A Tortured People: The Politics of Colonization.* Penticton, B.C.: Theytus Books, 1995.

Adar, Margo, and Sharon Howell. "The Subjective Side of Power." In *Healing the Wounds: The Promise of Ecofeminism,* ed. Judith Plant, 219-26. Toronto: Between the Lines, 1989.

Adbusters. *Days of Resistance Calendar: 2001.* Vancouver: Adbusters Media Foundation, 2000.

Alfaro, Juan. "God Protects and Liberates the Poor—O.T." In *Option for the Poor: Challenge to the Rich Countries,* ed. Leonardo Elizondo and Virgil Elizondo, 27-35. Edinburgh: T & T Clark, 1986.

Allison, Dorothy. *Two or Three Things I Know for Sure.* New York: Dutton, 1995.

Andersen, Hans Christian. "The Emperor's New Clothes." In *Michael Hague's Favorite Han Christian Andersen Fairy Tales,* 111-12. New York: Holt, Rinehart, and Winston, 1981.

Andreu, Guillemette. *Egypt in the Age of the Pyramids.* Translated by David Lorton. Ithaca, N.Y.: Cornell University Press, 1997.

Anzaldua, Gloria. *Borderlands/La Frontera: The New Mestiza.* San Francisco: Spinsters/aunt lute books, 1987.

Ashby, Godfrey. *Go Out and Meet God: A Commentary on the Book of Exodus.* Grand Rapids: Eerdmans, 1998.

Bacon, David. "The Real Thing—Murders at Coke." *Dispatcher* [Newspaper of the International Longshore & Warehouse Union]. November 2001.

Bailey, Randall C. "Africans in Old Testament Poetry and Narratives." In *Stony the Road We Trod: African American Biblical Interpretation,* ed. Cain Hope Felder, 165-84. Minneapolis: Fortress Press, 1991.

———. "And They Shall Know That I Am YHWH: The P Recasting of the Plague Narratives in Exodus 7-11." *Journal of the Interdenominational Theological Center* 22 (Fall 1994): 1-17.

———. "Beyond Identification: The Use of Africans in Old Testament Poetry and Narratives." In *Stony the Road We Trod: African American Biblical Interpretation,* ed. Cain Hope Felder, 165-84. Minneapolis: Fortress Press, 1991.

———. "The Danger of Ignoring One's Own Cultural Bias in Interpreting the Text." In *The Bible and Post-colonialism,* ed. R. S. Sugirtharajah, 66-90. Sheffield: Sheffield Academic Press, 1998.

———. "Is That Any Name for a Nice Hebrew Boy? Exodus 2:1-10: The De-Africanization of an Israelite Hero." In *The Recovery of Black Presence*, ed. Randall C. Bailey and Jacquelyn Grant, 25-36. Nashville: Abingdon Press, 1995.

Baines, John, and Jaromir Malek. *Atlas of Ancient Egypt.* New York: Facts on File, 1980.

Bales, Kevin. *Disposable People: New Slavery in the Global Economy.* Berkeley: University of California Press, 1999.

Baly, Denis. "Red Sea." In *Harper's Bible Dictionary,* ed. Paul Achtemeier, 858. San Francisco: HarperSanFrancisco, 1996.

Baum, Gregory. "Exodus Politics." In *Exodus, a Lasting Paradigm*, ed. Bas van Iersel and Anton Weiler, 109-17. Edinburgh: T & T Clark, 1987.

Bergen, Doris L. *Twisted Cross: The German Christian Movement in the Third Reich.* Chapel Hill: University of North Carolina Press, 1996.

Berrigan, Daniel. "Prophecy." In *And the Risen Bread: Selected Poems 1957-1997.* New York: Fordham University Press, 1998.

Berrill, Kevin T. "Anti-Gay Violence and Victimization in the United States: An Overview." In *Hate Crimes: Confronting Violence against Lesbians and Gay Men,* ed. Gregory M. Herek and Kevin T. Berrill, 19-24. Newbury Park, Calif.: Sage Publications, 1992.

Besler, Hilda F., and Charlotte I. Spungin. *Gay and Lesbian Students: Understanding Their Needs.* Washington, D.C.: Taylor & Francis, 1995.

"Blacks Imprisoned in USA Tops South Africa Figure." *Jet,* January 28, 1991: 8.

Boesak, Willa. *God's Wrathful Children: Political Oppression and Christian Ethics.* Grand Rapids: Eerdmans, 1995.

Boff, Leonardo. *When Theology Listens to the Poor.* San Francisco: Harper & Row, 1988.

Boff, Leonardo, and Clodovis Boff. *Introducing Liberation Theology.* Maryknoll, N.Y.: Orbis Books, 1987.

Borg, Marcus J. *Meeting Jesus Again for the First Time: The Historical Jesus and the Heart of Contemporary Faith.* San Francisco: HarperSanFrancisco, 1994.

Boys Don't Cry: The Brandon Teena Story. Twentieth Century Fox, 1999. Beverly Hills, California.

Bread and Puppet. "The WHY CHEAP ART? Manifesto." Glover, Vt.: Bread and Puppet, 1984.

Brecher, Jeremy, Tim Costello, and Brendan Smith. *Globalization from Below: The Power of Solidarity.* Cambridge, Mass.: South End Press, 2000.

Brenner, Claudia. "Survivor's Story: Eight Bullets." In *Hate Crimes: Confronting Violence against Lesbians and Gay Men,* ed. Gregory M. Herek and Kevin T. Berrill, 11-15. Newbury Park, Calif.: Sage Publications, 1992.

Brock, Rita Nakashima. "And a Little Child Will Lead Us." In *Christianity, Patriarchy and Abuse: A Feminist Critique,* ed. Joanne Carlson Brown and Carole R. Bohn, 42-61. New York: Pilgrim Press, 1989.

———. *Journeys by Heart: A Christology of Erotic Power.* New York: Crossroad, 1995.

Brock, Rita Nakashima, and Susan Brooks Thistlethwaite. *Casting Stones: Prostitution and Liberation in Asia and the United States.* Minneapolis: Fortress Press, 1996.

Brown, Robert McAfee. *Unexpected News: Reading the Bible with Third World Eyes.* Philadelphia: Westminster Press, 1984.

Brueggemann, Walter. *The Land.* Philadelphia: Fortress Press, 1977.

———. "Pharoah as Vassal: A Study of a Political Metaphor." *Catholic Biblical Quarterly* 57 (1995): 27-51.

———. *Theology of the Old Testament: Testimony, Dispute, Advocacy.* Minneapolis: Fortress Press, 1997.

Burns, Rita. "The Book of Exodus." In *Exodus, a Lasting Paradigm*, ed. Bas van Iersel and Anton Weiler, 11-21. Edinburgh: T & T Clark, 1987.

————. *Exodus, Leviticus, Numbers, With Excursuses on Feast, Ritual and Typology.* Wilmington, Del.: Glazier, 1983.

————. *Has the* LORD *Spoken Only through Moses? A Study of the Biblical Portrait of Miriam.* Atlanta: Scholars Press, 1987.

Casey, Jay. "The Exodus Theme in the Book of Revelation against the Background of the New Testament." In *Exodus, a Lasting Paradigm,* ed. Bas van Iersel and Anton Weiler, 34-43. Edinburgh: T & T Clark, 1987.

Cassuto, Umberto. *A Commentary on the Book of Exodus.* Translated by Israel Abrahams. Jerusalem: Magnes Press, 1967.

Ceresko, Anthony R. *Introduction to the Old Testament: A Liberation Perspective.* Maryknoll, N.Y.: Orbis Books, 1992.

Cheek, Alison. "Shifting the Paradigm: Feminist Bible Study." In *Searching the Scriptures.* Volume 1, *A Feminist Introduction,* ed. Elisabeth Schüssler Fiorenza, 338-50. New York: Crossroad, 1993.

Childs, Brevard. "The Birth of Moses." *Journal of Biblical Literature* 84 (1965): 109-22.

————. *The Book of Exodus: A Critical Commentary.* Philadelphia: Westminster Press, 1974.

Chittister, Joan. "Heart of Flesh: A Feminist Spirituality for Women and Men." Keynote address at Call to Action National Conference, Detroit, Michigan, November 15, 1997.

Christensen, Duane L., and Jo Milgrom. "Encountering the Exodus Story Through Handmade Midrash." In *Experiencing the Exodus from Egypt,* ed. Duane L. Christensen, 3-36. Berkeley: BIBAL Press, 1988.

Christianson, Scott. *With Liberty for Some: 500 Years of Imprisonment in America.* Boston: Northeastern University Press, 1998.

Clifford, Richard J. "Exodus." In *The New Jerome Biblical Commentary,* ed. Raymond E. Brown, Joseph A. Fitzmyer, and Roland E. Murphy, 45. Englewood Cliffs, N.J.: Prentice Hall, 1990.

————. *The Wisdom Literature.* Nashville: Abingdon Press, 1998.

Clise, Michele Durkson. *Stop the Violence Please.* Seattle: University of Washington Press, 1994.

Coats, C. David. *Old MacDonald's Factory Farm.* New York: Continuum, 1989.

Coats, George Wesley. "Despoiling the Egyptians." *Vetus Testamentum* 18 (1968): 450-57.

Cohn-Sherbok, Dan. *Exodus: An Agenda for Jewish-Christian Dialogue.* London: Bellew, 1992.

Cole, Tim. *Selling the Holocaust: From Auschwitz to Schindler, How History Is Bought and Sold.* New York: Routledge, 1922.

Cone, James. *A Black Theology of Liberation.* 20th anniversary edition. Maryknoll, N.Y.: Orbis Books, 1990.

————. *God of the Oppressed.* Maryknoll, N.Y.: Orbis Books, 1997.

————. *Martin & Malcolm & America: A Dream or a Nightmare.* Maryknoll, N.Y.: Orbis Books, 1991.

Cook, Christopher D. "Fowl Trouble." *Harper's,* August 1999, 78-79.

Copeland, M. Shawn. "Toward a Critical Christian Feminist Theology of Solidarity." In *Women and Theology,* ed. Mary Ann Hinsdale and Phyllis H. Kaminski, 3-38. Maryknoll, N.Y.: Orbis Books, 1994.

Croatto, J. Severino. *Exodus: A Hermeneutics of Freedom.* Maryknoll, N.Y.: Orbis Books, 1981.

————. "The Socio-Historical and Hermeneutical Relevance of the Exodus." In *Exodus, a Lasting Paradigm,* ed. Bas van Iersel and Anton Weiler, 25-133. Edinburgh: T & T Clark, 1987.

Cross, Frank Moore. *Canaanite Myth and Hebrew Epic.* Cambridge, Mass.: Harvard University Press, 1973.

Crossan, John Dominic. *The Historical Jesus: The Life of a Mediterranean Jewish Peasant.* San Francisco: HarperSanFrancisco, 1991.

Dalla Costa, Mariarosa, and G. Dalla Costa, eds. *Women, Development, and the Labor of Reproduction: Issues of Struggles and Movements.* Lawrenceville, N.J.: Africa World Press, 1998.

Daube, David. *Civil Disobedience in Antiquity.* Edinburgh: Edinburgh University Press, 1972.

David, Rosalie. *Handbook to Life in Ancient Egypt.* New York: Facts on File, 1998.

Davis, Mike. "Hell Factories in the Field." *The Nation,* February 20, 1995, 229.

Davis, John J. *Moses and the Gods of Egypt: Studies in the Book of Exodus.* Grand Rapids: Baker Book House, 1985.

Day, Dorothy. *The Long Loneliness: The Autobiography of Dorothy Day.* New York: Harper & Brothers, 1952.

Dear, John. *The Sacrament of Civil Disobedience.* Baltimore, Md.: Fortkamp, 1994.

Desert Rat. "When the Tear Gas Fills the Sky: The Washing Machine Song." On *International Incident: With Desert Rat.* Desert Rat Records, 2000, Tacoma, Washington.

Dixon, Christa K. *Negro Spirituals from Bible to Folksong.* Philadelphia: Fortress Press, 1976.

Driver, Tom F. *Christ in a Changing World: Toward an Ethical Christology.* New York: Crossroad, 1981.

DuBois, W. E. B. "Of the Black Belt." In *The Souls of Black Folk: Essays and Sketches.* Greenwich, Conn.: Fawcett, 1961.

Egan, Carolyn, and Linda Gardner. "Racism, Women's Health and Reproductive Freedom." In *Scratching the Surface: Canadian Anti-Racist Feminist Thought,* ed. Enakshi Dua and Angela Robertson, 295-307. Toronto: Women's Press, 1999.

Endersbe, Julie K. *Homosexuality: What Does It Mean?* Mankato, Minn.: Capstone Press, 2000.

Englishman's Hebrew and Chaldee Concordance of the Old Testament. London: Samuel Bagster & Sons Ltd., 1890.

Eugene, Toinette. "On 'Difference' and the Dream of Pluralist Feminism." *Journal of Feminist Studies in Religion* 8 (1992): 91-122.

Exum, Cheryl. *Plotted, Painted and Shot: Cultural Representations of Biblical Women.* Sheffield: Sheffield Academic Press, 1996.

———. "You Shall Let Every Daughter Live: A Study of Exodus 1.8-2.10." In *A Feminist Companion to Exodus to Deuteronomy,* ed. Athalya Brenner, 37-61. Sheffield: Sheffield Academic Press, 1994.

Farnsway, Rebecca, ed. *Twelve-Step Horror Stories.* Tucson: See Sharp Press, 2000.

Federici, Sylvia. "Reproduction and Feminist Struggle in the New International Division of Labor." In *Women, Development, and the Labor of Reproduction: Issues of Struggles and Movements,* ed. Mariarosa Dalla Costa and G. Dalla Costa. Lawrenceville, N.J.: Africa World Press, 1998.

Feld, Merle. *A Spiritual Life: A Jewish Feminist Journey.* New York: State University of New York Press, 1999.

Felder, Cain Hope. "Introduction." In *Stony the Road We Trod: African American Biblical Interpretation,* ed. Cain Hope Felder, 1-14. Minneapolis: Fortress Press, 1991.

Folbre, Nancy, and the Center for Popular Economics. *The New Field Guide to the U.S. Economy.* New York: New Press, 1995.

Food & Agriculture Organization of the United Nations. "Evaluation of Food & Nutrition Situation in Iraq." In *The Impact of Sanctions on Iraq: The Children Are Dying,* 11-73. New York: World View Forum, 1996.

Fox, Everett. *The Five Books of Moses: Genesis, Exodus, Leviticus, Numbers, Deuter-onomy: A New Translation with Introduction, Commentary, and Notes.* New York: Schocken Books, 1997.

———. *Now These Are the Names: A New English Rendition of the Book of Exodus.* New York: Schocken Books, 1986.

Frankel, Ellen. *The Five Books of Miriam: A Woman's Commentary on the Torah.* San Francisco: HarperSanFrancisco, 1998.

Frankfort, Henri. *Kingship and the Gods: A Study of Ancient Near Eastern Religion as the Integration of Society and Nature.* Chicago: University of Chicago Press, 1978.

Fretheim, Terence. *Exodus.* Louisville: Westminster/John Knox Press, 1991.

———. "Some Reflections on Brueggemann's God." In *God in the Fray: A Tribute to Walter Brueggemann,* ed. Tod F. Linafelt and Timothy Beal, 24-37. Minneapolis: Fortress Press, 1998.

Fulmer, Coleen. "Passionate God." In *Celebrations of Women's Bible Stories: Tears, Milk, and Honey,* ed. Martha Ann Kirk. Kansas City: Sheed & Ward, 1987.

Gardiner, Alan. *Egypt of the Pharaohs.* Oxford: Clarendon, 1961.

Gebara, Ivone. *Longing for Running Water: Ecofeminism and Liberation.* Minneapolis: Fortress Press, 1999.

Ginzberg, Louis. *The Legends of the Jews.* Vol. 2, *From Joseph to the Exodus.* Trans-lated by Henrietta Szold. Philadelphia: Jewish Publication Society of America, 1909-38.

———. *The Legends of the Jews.* Vol. 3, *Moses in the Wilderness.* Translated by Paul Radin. Philadelphia: Jewish Publication Society of America, 1909-38.

Goldberg, Eve, and Linda Evans. *The Prison Industrial Complex and the Global Econ-omy.* San Francisco: Agit Press, 1998.

Goss, Robert. *Jesus Acted Up: A Gay and Lesbian Manifesto.* San Francisco: Harper-SanFrancisco, 1993.

Gottwald, Norman K. "The Exodus as Event and Process: Test Case in the Biblical Grounding of Liberation Theology." In *The Future of Liberation Theology: Essays in Honor of Gustavo Gutiérrez,* ed. Marc H. Ellis and Otto Maduro, 250-71. Maryknoll, N.Y.: Orbis Books, 1989.

Granke, Lynn. "Canada after the Massacre." In *Women, Violence and Non-Violent Change,* ed. Aruna Gnanadason, Musimbi Kanyoro, and Lucia Ann McSpadden, 81-87. Geneva: WCC Publications, 1996.

Greinacher, Norbert. "Liberation Theology in the 'First World'?" In *Option for the Poor: Challenge to the Rich Countries,* ed. Leonardo Elizondo and Virgil Eli-zondo, 81-90. Edinburgh: T & T Clark, 1986.

Guider, Margaret Eletta. *Daughters of Rahab: Prostitution and the Church of Libera-tion in Brazil.* Minneapolis: Fortress Press, 1995.

Gutiérrez, Gustavo. *A Theology of Liberation: History, Politics and Salvation.* Mary-knoll, N.Y.: Orbis Books, 1973.

Hayes, John H., and J. Maxwell Miller. *Israelite and Judean History.* Philadelphia: West-minster Press, 1990.

Heintz, James, Nancy Folbre, and the Center for Popular Economics. *The Ultimate Field Guide to the U.S. Economy.* New York: New Press, 2000.

Heyward, Carter. "The Body of Christa: Hope for the World." In *Staying Power.* Cleve-land: Pilgrim Press, 1995.

———. "Passion." In *Our Passion for Justice: Images of Power, Sexuality, and Liberation.* New York: Pilgrim Press, 1984.

Hodgson, Jim. "A Collaboration against Hatred: Churches Meet to Seek Peace in Chiapas." *Sojourners* 27, no. 1 (January-February 1998): 11.

Holladay, William. *A Concise Hebrew and Aramaic Lexicon of the Old Testament.* Grand Rapids: Eerdmans, 1988.

hooks, bell. "Being Rich." In *Where We Stand: Class Matters,* 70-79. New York: Routledge, 2000.

hooks, bell. "Introduction." In *Where We Stand: Class Matters,* 1-9. New York: Routledge, 2000.

———. "killing rage." In *Killing Rage, Ending Racism,* 8-20. New York: Henry Holt & Co., 1995.

———. "A Revolution of Values." In *Teaching to Transgress: Education as the Practice of Freedom.* New York: Routledge, 1994.

———. *Yearning; Race, Gender, and Cultural politics.* Boston: South End, 1990.

Hornung, Erik. *History of Ancient Egypt: An Introduction.* Translated by David Lorton. Ithaca, N.Y.: Cornell University Press, 1999.

Howard-Brook, Wes. "Reading for/about Our Lives: Politics, Poetics and Personhood in the Fourth Gospel." Presented to the Meeting of the Johannine Literature Section of the Society of Biblical Literature Annual Meeting in New Orleans, 25 November 1996.

Howard-Brook, Wes, and Anthony Gwyther. *Unveiling Empire: Reading Revelation Then and Now.* Maryknoll, N.Y.: Orbis Books, 1999.

Huesman, John. "Exodus." In *Jerome Biblical Commentary,* ed. Raymond E. Brown, Joseph A. Fitzmyer, and Roland E. Murphy, 47-66. Englewood Cliffs, N.J.: Prentice Hall, 1968.

Huffman, Herbert B. "Egypt." In *Harper's Bible Dictionary,* ed. Paul Achtemeier, with the Society of Biblical Literature, 248. San Francisco: Harper & Row, 1985.

Hurston, Zora Neale. *Moses: Man of the Mountain.* J. B. Lippincott, 1939. Reprint, Urbana and Chicago: University of Illinois Press, 1984.

Hutchinson, Dori S. "The Journey towards Wellness." *The Journal of NAMI California* 11, no. 4 (2001): 7-8.

Isasi-Díaz, Ada María. "Solidarity and Love of Neighbor in the 1980's." In *Feminist Theological Ethics: A Reader,* ed. Lois K. Daly, 77-87. Philadelphia: Westminster/John Knox Press, 1994.

Janzen, J. Gerald. *Exodus.* Louisville: Westminster/John Knox Press, 1997.

John, Cresy, et al. "An Asian Feminist Perspective: The Exodus Story (Exodus 1.8-22. 2.1-10)." In *Voices from the Margins: Interpreting the Bible in the Third World,* ed. R. S. Sugirtharajah, 255-66. Maryknoll, N.Y.: Orbis Books, 1995.

Jordan, June. "Bosnia Betrayed." In *Affirmative Acts: Political Essays,* 55-58. New York: Anchor, 1998.

———. "A Powerful Hatred." In *Affirmative Acts: Political Essays,* 82-89. New York: Anchor, 1998.

Jubilee South. "Towards a New Jubilee Covenant: A Contribution from the Jubilee South." In *Jubilee Wealth and the Market: Share the Wealth,* ed. John Miheve, 129-36. Toronto: Canadian Ecumenical Jubilee Initiative, 1999.

Justification for the Abolition of the Prison Industrial Complex—Forty Acres and a Mule: An Educational Guide for White People of Conscience." Pamphlet from conference entitled "Critical Resistance: Beyond the Prison Industrial Complex," held at University of California, Berkeley, California, September 25-27, 1998.

Kaster, Joseph. *Wings of the Falcon: Life and Thought of Ancient Egypt.* Translated by Joseph Kaster. New York: Holt, Rinehart & Winston, 1968.

Kensington Welfare Rights Union. "The Rich Man's House." Adapted from "The Enemy's Gate." On Anne Feeney, *Have You Been to Jail for Justice,* Track 9. Anne Feeney, 2000, Nashville, Tennessee.

Kerr, Mary Lee, and Bob Hall. "Chickens Come Home to Roost." *The Progressive*, January 1992, 29.

King, Martin Luther, Jr. "The Death of Evil upon the Seashore." In *Strength to Love*, 71-81. New York: Harper & Row, 1963.

———. "Letter from Birmingham City Jail." In *Nonviolence in America: A Documentary History*. Revised edition, ed. Staughton Lynd and Alice Lynd, 254-67. Maryknoll, N.Y.: Orbis Books, 1995.

Kirk, Martha Ann. *Celebrations of Women's Bible Stories: Tears, Milk, and Honey*. Kansas City, Mo.: Sheed & Ward, 1987.

Knobloch, Frederick. "Adoption." In *Anchor Bible Dictionary*, ed. David Noel Freedman, 1:76-79. New York: Doubleday, 1992.

Korten, David. *When Corporations Rule the World*. 2nd ed. San Francisco: Berrett-Koehler, 2001.

Kwok Pui-lan. *Discovering the Bible in the Non-Biblical World*. Maryknoll, N.Y.: Orbis Books, 1997.

Lapide, Pinchas. "Exodus in the Jewish Tradition." In *Exodus, a Lasting Paradigm*, ed. Bas van Iersel and Anton Weiler, 47-55. Edinburgh: T & T Clark, 1987.

Lawrence, Beth. "Amphibian Alarm: Just Where Have All the Frogs Gone?" *Smithsonian* 23, no. 7 (October 1992): 113-20.

Lee, Nancy C. "Genocide's Lament: Moses, Pharaoh's Daughter, and the Former Yugoslavia." In *God in the Fray: A Tribute to Walter Brueggemann*, ed. Tod Linafelt and Timothy K. Beal, 66-82. Minneapolis: Fortress Press, 1998.

Lenka-Bula, Puleny. "Jubilee at the Turn of the 21st Century and the African Woman." In *Jubilee Wealth and the Market: Share the Wealth*, ed. John Miheve, 113-27. Toronto: Canadian Ecumenical Jubilee Initiative, 1999.

Lerner, Michael. "Editorial," *Tikkun*, March/April 1999, 6.

———. *Surplus Powerlessness: The Psychodynamics of Everyday Life*. Amherst, N.Y.: Humanities Press, 1991.

Levenson, Jon. "Exodus and Liberation." *Horizons in Biblical Theology* 13 (1991): 139-74.

———. *Sinai and Zion: An Entry into the Jewish Bible*. San Francisco: HarperSanFrancisco, 1985.

Loewen, James W. *Lies My Teacher Told Me: Everything Your American History Textbook Got Wrong*. New York: New Press, 1995.

Loffreda, Beth. *Losing Matt Shepard: Life and Politics in the Aftermath of Anti-Gay Murder*. New York: Columbia University Press, 2000.

Logan, Leanne, Geert Cole, Damien Simonis, and Scott Wayne. *Egypt: A Lonely Planet Travel Survival Kit*. Victoria, Australia: Lonely Planet, 1996.

Lorde, Audre. "A Litany for Survival." In *The Black Unicorn*. New York: Norton, 1978.

———. *Sister Outsider*. Trumansburg, N.Y.: Crossing Press, 1984.

Love, David. "Justice System Discriminates against Black and Latino Youth." Knight Ridder/Tribune News Service, May 3, 2000.

Macht, Norman C., and Mary Hull. *The History of Slavery*. San Diego: Lucent Books, 1997.

McCutcheon, John. "You Gotta Know When to Move." On *What It's Like*, Rounder Records, Cambridge, Mass., 1990. Published by Appalsongs (ASCAP), 1987.

Metzger, Bruce M. "Sortes Biblicae." In *The Oxford Companion to the Bible*, ed. Bruce Metzger and Michael D. Coogan, 714-15. New York: Oxford University Press, 1993.

Meyers, Carol. *Discovering Eve: Ancient Israelite Women in Context*. New York: Oxford University Press, 1988.

———. "Miriam the Musician." In *A Feminist Companion to Exodus to Deuteronomy*, ed. Athalya Brenner, 207-30. Sheffield: Sheffield Academic Press, 2001.

Miller, Jerome. "Habitat for Inhumanity." *Utne Reader* 71 (September/October 1995): 87-88.

Miller, Patrick D., Jr. "God the Warrior: A Problem in Biblical Interpretation and Apologetics." *Interpretation* 19 (1965): 39-46.

Mollenkott, Virginia Ramey. *The Divine Feminine: The Biblical Imagery of God as Female.* New York: Crossroad, 1983.

Monagle, Katie. "The Death Penalty." *Scholastic Update,* September 1992, 13-15.

Montet, Pierre. *Lives of the Pharaohs.* Cleveland: World Publishing Company, 1958.

Montavalli, Jim. "Dr. Robert Bullard: Some People Don't Have the Complexion for Protection." *E,* July-August 1998, 10.

———. "When Green Means Stop." *E,* July-August 1998, 4.

Morgenstern, Julian. "The Despoiling of the Egyptians." *Journal of Biblical Literature* 68, no. 1 (1949): 1-28.

Morhouse, Ward. "Unfinished Business: Bhopal Ten Years After." In *Defying Corporations, Defining Democracy: A Book of History and Strategy,* ed. Dean Ritz, 18-19. New York: Apex, 2001.

Morris, Jane Anne. "Help! I've Been Colonized and I Can't Get Up." In *Defying Corporations, Defining Democracy: A Book of History and Strategy,* ed. Dean Ritz, 8-12. New York: Apex, 2001.

———. "Strip Corporations of Their Cloaking Device." In *Defying Corporations, Defining Democracy: A Book of History and Strategy,* ed. Dean Ritz, 263-64. New York: Apex, 2001.

Myers, Ched. "By What Authority: The Bible and Civil Disobedience." *Sojourners* 23 (May 1984): 11.

———. *Who Will Roll Away the Stone?: Discipleship Queries for First World Christians.* Maryknoll, N.Y.: Orbis Books, 1994.

Nadeau, Denise, and Laurel Dykstra. "Jubilaction: Engaging with a Feminist Jubilee in a Multi-faith and Secular Context." In *Jubilee Wealth and the Market: Share the Wealth,* ed. John Miheve, 77-111. Toronto: Canadian Ecumenical Jubilee Initiative, 1999.

Nelson-Pallmeyer, Jack. *School of Assassins: The Case for Closing the School of the Americas and Changing U.S. Foreign Policy.* Maryknoll, N.Y.: Orbis Books, 1999.

Newton, John. "Analysis of Programmatic Texts of Exodus Movements." In *Exodus, a Lasting Paradigm,* ed. Bas van Iersel and Anton Weiler, 56-62. Edinburgh: T & T Clark, 1987.

Niditch, Susan. *War in the Hebrew Bible: A Study of the Ethics of Violence.* New York: Oxford University Press, 1993.

Noth, Martin. *Exodus.* Old Testament Library. Philadelphia: Westminster Press, 1962.

Oates, Stephen. *Let the Trumpet Sound: The Life of Martin Luther King Jr.* New York: New American Library, 1982.

O'Brien, John. *Theology and the Option for the Poor.* Collegeville, Minn.: Liturgical Press, 1992.

Parenti, Michael. *Land of Idols: Political Mythology in America.* New York: St. Martin's Press, 1994.

Philipose, Pamela. "Women Act: Women and Environmental Protection in India." In *Healing the Wounds: The Promise of Ecofeminism,* ed. Judith Plant, 67-75. Toronto: Between the Lines, 1989.

Pixley, George. *On Exodus: A Liberation Perspective.* Translated by Robert Barr. Maryknoll, N.Y.: Orbis Books, 1987.

———. *Historía de Israel de la Perspectiva de los Pobres: Israel, Desde su Fundación Revolucionaria Hasta su Fin Revolucionario (1220a.c.-135 d.c.).* 2nd ed. Mexico City: Palabra Ediciones, 1993.

Plaskow, Judith. "Anti-Judaism in Feminist Christian Interpretation." In *A Feminist*

Introduction, vol. 1 of *Searching the Scriptures*, ed. Elisabeth Schüssler Fiorenza, 117-29. New York: Crossroad, 1995.

———. *Standing Again at Sinai: Judaism from a Feminist Perspective*. San Francisco, HarperSanFrancisco, 1991.

Pritzker, Barry M. *Native America Today: A Guide to Community Politics and Culture*. Santa Barbara: ABC-CLIO, 1999.

Propp, William H. C. *Exodus 1-18: A New Translation with Introduction and Commentary*. New York: Doubleday, 1999.

Quilty, Chuck. "Looming Crisis Caps Decade of Genocide in Iraq." *The Catholic Radical* [Rock Island, Ill.], Summer 2000, 1, 6.

Rabinowitz, Jacob. *The Faces of God: Canaanite Mythology as Hebrew Theology*. Woodstock, Conn.: Spring Publications, 1998.

Reyes, Abby. "Por Vida: In Solidarity with the U'Wa People." In *Global Uprising: Confronting the Tyrannies of the 21st Century*, ed. Neva Welton and Linda Wolf, 125-30. Gabriola Island, B.C.: New Society, 2001.

Ritz, Dean. "Conquering Fibs." In *Defying Corporations, Defining Democracy: A Book of History and Strategy*, ed. Dean Ritz, 105. New York: Apex, 2001.

Roberts, James Deotis. *A Black Political Theology*. Philadelphia: Westminster Press, 1974.

———. *Liberation and Reconciliation: A Black Theology*. Maryknoll, N.Y.: Orbis Books, 1994.

Rosen, Norma. "Bitiah: Memoir of a Tyrant's Daughter." In *Biblical Women Unbound*. Philadelphia: Jewish Publication Society, 1996.

Ruether, Rosemary Radford. "What Are the Inter-connections between the Impoverishment of Earth and the Impoverishment of People?" Roundtable in the Great Minds/Great Questions Series, sponsored by the Whidbey Institute, Plymouth Congregational Church, Seattle, December 11, 1998.

Sarna, Nahum M. *Exploring Exodus: The Heritage of Biblical Israel*. New York: Schocken Books, 1986.

———, general editor. *The Jewish Publication Society Torah Commentary: Exodus*. Philadelphia: Jewish Publication Society, 1991.

Scanlon, Jennifer. "Educating the Living, Remembering the Dead: The Montreal Massacre as Metaphor." *Feminist Teacher* 8 (1994): 75-80.

Scheer, Christopher. "'Illegals' Made Slaves to Fashion," *The Nation*, September 11, 1995, 237.

Schneider, Susan. *Jewish and Female: Choices and Changes in Our Lives Today*. New York: Simon & Schuster, 1984.

Schüssler Fiorenza, Elisabeth. *Bread Not Stone: The Challenge of Feminist Biblical Interpretation*. Boston: Beacon Press, 1985.

Segovia, Fernando F., and Mary Ann Tolbert, eds. *Reading from This Place*. Minneapolis: Fortress Press, 1995.

Setel, Drorah O'Donnell. "Exodus." In *The Women's Bible Commentary*, ed. Carol Newsom and Sharon Ringe, 26-35. Louisville, Ky.: Westminster/John Knox Press, 1992.

Shannon, David T. "'An Antebellum Sermon': A Resource for an African American Hermeneutic." In *Stony the Road We Trod: African American Biblical Interpretation*, ed. Cain Hope Felder, 98-123. Minneapolis: Fortress Press, 1991.

Shelley, Martha. *Haggadah: A Celebration of Freedom*. San Francisco: aunt lute books, 1998.

Shiva, Vandana. "The Violence of Globalization: India Pushes Back." In *Global Uprising: Confronting the Tyrannies of the 21st Century*, ed. Neva Welton and Linda Wolf, 170-71. Gabriola Island, BC: New Society, 2001.

Siebert-Hommes, Jopie. "But if She Be a Daughter . . . She May Live!" In *A Feminist Companion to Exodus to Deuteronomy*, ed. Athalya Brenner, 62-74. Sheffield: Sheffield Academic Press, 1994.

Simon, Rita J., Howard Altstein, and Marygold Melli. *The Case for Transracial Adoption*. Washington, D.C.: American University Press, 1994.

Smith, Mark S. *The Early History of God: YHWH and the Other Deities in Ancient Israel*. San Francisco: Harper & Row, 1990.

Sobrino, Jon, and Juan Hernandez Pico. *Theology of Christian Solidarity*. Maryknoll, N.Y.: Orbis Books, 1985.

Sölle, Dorothee. *Stations of the Cross: A Latin American Pilgrimage*. Minneapolis: Fortress Press, 1993.

———. "Tears of Creation." In *A Feminist in Need of Names for God*. Lecture, Episcopal Divinity School, Cambridge, Mass., November 13, 1996.

Solomon, Arthur. "My Relations: O Canada." In *Eating Bitterness: A Vision Beyond the Prison Walls: Poems and Essays of Arthur Solomon*. Toronto: NC Press, 1994.

Squeegee. An Interactive Theatre Event Created & Performed by Street-Involved Youth. Program, Headlines Theatre, Vancouver, B.C., May 19-23, 1999.

Sternberg, Meir. *Hebrews between Cultures: Group Portraits and National Literature*. Bloominton: Indiana University Press, 1998.

Stevens, Bruce A. "The Divine Warrior in the Gospel of Mark." *Biblische Zeitschrift* 31, no. 1 (1987): 101-10.

———. "Jesus the Divine Warrior." *Expository Times* 94, no. 11 (1983): 326-29.

Stevenson, Winona. "Colonialism and First Nations Women in Canada." In *Scratching the Surface: Canadian Anti-Racist Feminist Thought*, ed. Enakshi Dua and Angela Robertson, 49-80. Toronto: Women's Press, 1999.

Stieglitz, Robert R. "The Lowdown on the Riffraff." *Bible Review* 15 (August 1999): 30-33, 54.

Stone, Howard W. *Depression & Hope: New Insights for Pastoral Counseling*. Minneapolis: Fortress Press, 1998.

Syracuse Cultural Workers. "Mission Statement." Syracuse Cultural Workers, Dept. 712, PO Box 6367, Syracuse, NY 13217. www.syrculturalworkers.org.

Tolbert, Mary Ann. "The Politics and Poetics of Location." In *Reading from This Place*, ed. Fernando F. Segovia and Mary Ann Tolbert, 305-18. Minneapolis: Fortress Press, 1995.

———. "Reading for Liberation." In *Reading from This Place*, ed. Fernando F. Segovia and Mary Ann Tolbert, 263-318. Minneapolis: Fortress Press, 1995.

Tracy, David. *The Analogical Imagination: Christian Theology and the Culture of Pluralism*. New York: Crossroad, 1986.

———. "Exodus: Theological Reflection." In *Exodus, a Lasting Paradigm*, ed. Bas van Iersel and Anton Weiler, 118-24. Edinburgh: T & T Clark, 1987.

Trible, Phyllis. *Texts of Terror: Literary-Feminist Readings of Biblical Narratives*. Philadelphia: Fortress Press, 1984.

Triggs, Bruce. "Globalizing SOA Watch." In *The Global Activist Manual: Local Ways to Change the World*, ed. Mike Prokosch and Laura Raymond, 48-53. New York: Nation Books/Thunder's Mouth, 2002.

Troxler, Howard. "It's Time to Look at the Debt Never Paid." *St. Petersburg Times* [Florida]. February 21, 2001, www.sptimes.com.

Tucker, Susan. *Telling Memories among Southern Women Domestic Workers and Their Employers in the Segregated South*. New York: Schocken Books, 1988.

UNESCO Slave Route Project, Conference Document. London: Pan African Healing Foundation, September 8, 1998.

The Union Haggadah Home Service for the Passover. Cincinnati: Central Conference of American Rabbis, 1923.

Vervenne, Marc. *Studies in the Book of Exodus: Redaction, Reception, Interpretation.* Leuven: Leuven University Press, 1996.

Voran, Marilyn. *Add Justice to Your Shopping List.* Kitchener, Ont.: Herald Press, 1986.

Walker, Alice. *In Search of Our Mothers' Gardens: Womanist Prose.* San Diego: Harcourt Brace Jovanovich, 1983.

Walvin, James. *Slavery and the Slave Trade: A Short Illustrated History.* Jackson: University Press of Mississippi, 1983.

Walzer, Michael. *Exodus and Revolution.* New York: Basic Books, 1985.

———. "Exodus and the Theory of Holy War." *Harvard Theological Review* 61 (1968): 1-14.

Waring, Marylin. *If Women Counted: A New Feminist Economics.* San Francisco: Harper & Row, 1988.

Warrior, Robert Allen. "A Native American Perspective: Canaanites, Cowboys and Indians." In *Voices from the Margins: Interpreting the Bible in the Third World,* ed. R. S. Sugirtharajah, 287-95. Maryknoll, N.Y.: Orbis Books, 1991.

Watterson, Barbara. *Women in Ancient Egypt.* New York: St. Martin's Press, 1991.

Weems, Renita J. "The Hebrew Women Are Not Like the Egyptian Women: The Ideology of Race, Gender, and Sexual Reproduction in Exodus 1." *Semeia* 59 (1992): 25-41.

———. "A Mistress, a Maid, and No Mercy (Hagar and Sarah)." In *Just a Sister Away: A Womanist Vision of Women's Relationships in the Bible,* 1-21. San Diego: LuraMedia, 1988.

Wevers, J. W. "Chariots." In *Interpreter's Dictionary of the Bible,* 1:552-54. Nashville: Abingdon Press, 1962.

Williams, Delores. *Sisters in the Wilderness: The Challenge of Womanist God-Talk.* Maryknoll, N.Y.: Orbis Books, 1993.

Williams, Patricia. "In Search of Pharaoh's Daughter." In *Out of the Garden: Women Writers on the Bible,* ed. Christina Buchmann and Celina Spiegel, 54-71. New York: Fawcett Columbine, 1994.

Wilson, Robert. "The Hardening of Pharaoh's Heart." *The Catholic Biblical Quarterly* 41, (1979): 18-36.

Wink, Walter. *Engaging the Powers: Discernment and Resistance in a World of Domination.* Minneapolis: Fortress Press, 1992.

Wittig, Monique. *Les Guerilleres.* Boston: Beacon Press, 1971.

Wood, Ellen Meiksins. "Labor, Class, and State in Global Capitalism." In *Rising from the Ashes? Labor in the Age of "Global" Capitalism,* ed. Ellen Meiksins Wood, Peter Meiksins, and Michael Yates, 3-16. New York: Monthly Review Press, 1998.

Wylie-Kellermann, Jeanie. "Sounding the Jubal." *The Witness* 80, no. 1 (January-February 1997): 5.

Young, Josiah. "Exodus as a Paradigm for Black Theology." In *Exodus, a Lasting Paradigm,* ed. Bas van Iersel and Anton Weiler, 93-99. Edinburgh: T & T Clark, 1987.

Young, Robert. *Young's Analytical Concordance to the Bible.* Grand Rapids: Eerdmans, 1970.

Zakovitch, Yair. "A Study of Precise and Partial Derivations in Biblical Etymology." *Journal for the Study of the Old Testament* 15 (1980): 31-50.

Zepernick, Mary. "Man Corporate on Top of the World." In *Defying Corporations, Defining Democracy: A Book of History and Strategy,* ed. Dean Ritz, 74-75. New York: Apex, 2001.

INDEX

African American biblical appropriation: liberation tradition of, 45; survival/quality of life tradition of, 45; *see also* black liberation theology

African Americans: and genocide, 71-75

Albright, William Foxwell: on story of Joshua, 7

Alfaro, Juan, 57; on God as liberating, 33

alliances, building, 210-11

Anzaldua, Gloria, 51

anti-Judaism, Christian, 30

apocalyptic literature, 204-5

atonement, 230n. 33

Augustine, St.: and theology of holy war, 29

Babel, Tower of, 112

Bailey, Randall: on depiction of African nations in Hebrew Bible, 58; on Moses' Egyptian identity, 179-82

base communities: as model of church, 31-32; repression of, 32

Baum, Gregory: on commitment to liberation, 197

Berrigan, Daniel: on civil disobedience, 172

Bible: authorship of, 9-13; dating of material in, 11-12; historical criti-

cism and, 19; as historical memory of poor, 20-21; and history, 4-9; and liberation theology, 20-21; as literature, 13-19; names of books of, 22; negative aspects of, 3; and patriarchy, 21; reading of, 3, 60; and religious conservatism, 3; reverence for, 60; as rich heritage, 20, 59-60; as sacred story, 19-21; source criticism and, 10-13; translations of, 22-23

biblical criticism: modern, 3-21

biblical interpretation: influenced by social location, xi-xii; and hermeneutical privilege of poor, 32; and hermeneutics of suspicion, 32; historical criticism and, 19; identification as issue in, 38; literary criticism and, 13-19; reading texts wrong, 52; source criticism and, 10-13

black liberation theology, 34-37, 42-46; as race-based, 35; and story of Hagar, 42-46; *see also* African American biblical appropriation

blood: plague of, 86

Boesak, Willa: on structural violence, 141-42

Boff, Leonardo: on Exodus, 33; on repression of base communities, 32; on various levels of theology, 34

Bohn, Carol: on God as violent, 135-36

Borg, Marcus: on Exodus, 52; on macro-story, 27

brick making, 111

Bright, John: on story of Joshua, 7

Brock, Rita Nakashima: on God as violent, 135-36

Brown, Joanne Carlson: on God as violent, 135-36

Brown, Robert McAfee: on exodus story, 57, 126

Brueggemann, Walter: on land, 81; on plague narratives, 114, 143-44; on violence, 128

Burns, Rita: on people of exodus, 190

Canaanites: story of, and Native American liberation theology, 47-49

Cannon, Katie, 37

capitalism, global, 198: structures of, 127; *see also* corporations; globalization

chariots: as symbol of empire and conquest, 129-32

chiasm, 17-18, 147-48, 165

Childs, Brevard: and outline of Exodus, 25-26; on story of midwives, 177

Christianity: origin of, as Jewish resistance movement, 29, 30; separation of spiritual and political in, 124-25

church: savior/liberator model of, 42

civil disobedience: in Bible, 173-75; of Jesus, 174-75; modern, 175-78; as sacrament, 176-77; story of Shiphrah and Puah and, 168-72; strategies of, 175

colonialism: classical model of, 63-64; and disparity of wealth between nations, 65

community, 205-6

Cone, James, 34, 36, 37; on Exodus-Sinai tradition, 34, 45

conquest: chariots as symbol of, 129-32; violence and, 128-29

context: biblical, of story of Pharaoh's daughter, 151-52; extra-biblical, of story of Pharaoh's daughter, 152-55; see also social location

conversion, 200-201

corporations: deceitfulness of, 76-77; and exploitation, 64-65; and FTAA, 103; above the law, 92-93, 125-26; and NAFTA, 103; wealth and power of, 64

Croatto, José Severino: on exodus paradigm and liberation theology, 33; on justice, 133; on systemic injustice and rage, 142; on violence, 133-34, 136-37

Crusades: and exodus theology, 29

D. See Deuteronomist source

Daly, Mary: on God as violent, 135-36

Daniel, book of: as charter of civil disobedience, 173

Daube, David: on civil disobedience, 173

daughter of Pharaoh, 146-62; as princess, 157-59; story of, 147-49; three feminist portraits of, 155-61

Day, Dorothy, 205-6

Dear, John: on civil disobedience, 176

deceit, 75-78

depression, 120-22

Deuteronomist source, 11

drowning: of Egyptians, 89-90

DuBois, W. E. B.: on penal system as slavery, 68

E. See Elohist source

earth, connection with, 206-7

ecofeminist theology, 90-97; see also environment; feminism

ecology: see environment

education, 211-13

Egypt: in Bible, 58-59; as empire, 57-78; Hebrew word for, 58; history of, 4-8, 57-58, 105-6, 149-51; 167-68; identification with, 51-53, 59-63, 196; land of, 79-104; pharaohs of, 105-10

Egyptian religion, 96-97; and plague narratives, 113-14

Egyptian society: clothing and jewelry in, 185-89; midwifery in, 167; pictured in book of Exodus, 5, 149-51

Egyptians: in exodus story, 62, 183-91; giving jewelry and clothes to Israelites, 185-89; Moses as, 179-83

Elohist source, 10-11

empire, 197-98: characteristics of, 63-64, 196; chariots as symbol of, 129-32; and Egypt, 57-78, 196; and exploitation, 65-68; Pharaoh as personification of, 116; Pharaoh as symbol of faults of, 115

English language: reading Bible in, 22-24

environment: of Egypt, 79-82; and plague narratives, 93-94; toxic waste and, 101-3; see also ecofeminism

exodus, the: 5-6, 24-29; as act of civil disobedience, 173; and Christian history, 29; holistic approach to, 46; as macro-story, 27; mixed multitude in, 189-91; as theme in Bible, 27-28; as theme in history, 29-31

Exodus, book of, xiii-xv, 24-37; and history of Egypt and Israel, 4-9; liberation readings of, 37; major themes of, 24; outline of, 24-26; as paradigmatic text for black theologians, 35; plague narratives in, 82-91; and preferential option for poor, 33; reading as Israel, 22-38; revelatory nature of, 36; setting of, 5; story of, 24-26;

violence in, 128-45;
women absent from,
91-92
Exodus International, 31
exodus paradigm: and
black theology, 35;
and liberation theol-
ogy, 33; and marginal-
ization of women, 42;
as obstacle to Native
American liberation
theology, 47
exploitation: of children,
70, 102; corporations
and, 64-65; of
resources, 101-3;
violence of, 65-68
Exum, Cheryl: on story of
Pharaoh's daughter,
154

Feld, Merle: "We All
Stood Together," 12-
13, 23
feminism: and empire,
xiii; *see also* ecofemi-
nism; women
firstborn, death of: plague
of, 89
first world: Christians,
197-213; despair,
120-22; economic
exploitation by, 65-68;
identification with
Egypt in, 51-53, 59-
63; perspective of, xiii;
reading Exodus in, 50-
53; supported by slav-
ery, 69-70
Fox, Everett: on nature of
biblical texts, 13
free market: effect of, on
poor, 76
Free Trade Agreement of
the Americas (FTAA),
103
Fretheim, Terence: ecological reading of plagues
of, 89, 103-4
FTAA. *See* Free Trade
Agreement of the
Americas

fundamentalism: and bib-
lical interpretation, 3
G-8: demonstrations
against, 189
Gabara, Ivone: on
ecofeminism, 90
Gandhi: on nonviolence,
174
Genesis, book of: story of
Hagar in, 43-46
genocide, 71-75: and his-
tory of North Amer-
ica, 71; resistance to,
166; U.N. definition
of, 71, 158-59
global capitalism: collu-
sion with, 196;
described by Marx,
221n.17; and empire,
65; resistance to, 204;
see also colonialism;
corporations; exploita-
tion; globalization
globalization, 197; corporations and, 64; and
poor, 32, 120
God: as angry, 139-41;
names of, in Bible, 9-
10; violence of, 135-
36, 196, 230n.34
Goss, Robert: on anger,
142
Gottwald, Norman: on
origins of Israel in
Palestine, 7
Guider, Margaret: critique
of liberation reading
of Exodus, 38-42; on
Exodus and liberation
theology, 32; and her-
meneutic of suspicion,
39; on the poor, 49-50;
on violence, 134-35
Gutiérrez, Gustavo: on
Exodus and liberation
theology, 33; on his-
torical praxis, 34; on
systemic injustice, 142
Gwyther, Anthony: on

apocalypse, 205; on
empire, 63-64

Hagar: as counter story
to exodus, 44; and
hermeneutics of suspi-
cion, 45; story of, 43-
46
heart: first-world, 119-27;
hard, 117-18; as
metaphor, 119-27; sig-
nificance of, 118-19
Hennacy, Ammon: and
civil disobedience, 175
hermeneutical privilege of
poor, 32
hermeneutic of identification-ascertainment, 46
hermeneutics of suspicion,
32, 155; applied by
Delores Williams, 45;
applied by Margaret
Guider, 39
Heschel, Abraham
Joshua: and civil dis-
obedience, 176
Heyward, Carter, 202
Hort, Greta: on the
plagues, 85
Howard-Brook, Wes: on
apocalypse, 205; on
empire, 63-64
humility, 201
Hurston, Zora Neale: on
Egypt, 79; on Pharaoh,
105, 107-8, 115

identification, xiv; of
black slaves with
Hebrew slaves, 34-35;
with Egypt, 51-53, 59-
63, 196; with election,
22-37; of indigenous
people with Canaan-
ites, 47-49; as issue in
biblical interpretation,
38; of poor with Israel,
32; excluding black
women, 46
Imperial Food fire, 101-2

individualism, 61, 123-25
Inez de la Cruz, Juana, 39
International Monetary
    Fund, 125-26; demon-
    strations against, 189;
    as structure of global
    capitalism, 127
Iraq: U.S.-backed sanc-
    tions against, 99-100
Israel: ancient history of,
    5-9; archaeology and,
    6-9; monarchy and, 8-
    9; urbanization in, 8
Israelites: agricultural life
    of, 8; exodus of, 24-26

J. See Jahwist source
Jägerstätter, Franz: and
    civil disobedience, 175
Jahwist source (J), 10
Jeff, Morris, Jr.: on race
    and adoption, 158-59
Jesus: and exodus tradi-
    tion, 29; as new
    Moses, 29; and non-
    violent civil disobedi-
    ence, 174
Jordan, June: on genocide,
    73
Joshua, book of: story of
    Rahab in, 39-42
Jubilee 2000 movement,
    188-89

King, Martin Luther, Jr.:
    on drowning of Egyp-
    tian army, 134; and
    image of exodus, 31;
    and nonviolence, 174;
    on violence, 66-67,
    138

Latin America: base com-
    munities in, 31-32; lib-
    eration theology of,
    31-34; readings of
    Exodus in, 32-34
Lee, Nancy: on daughter
    of Pharaoh, 156-57
Legend of Sargon: birth

narrative of, and story
    of birth of Moses,
    153-55
Lerner, Michael: rejecting
    image of God as vio-
    lent, 136; on surplus
    powerlessness, 121-22
Levenson, Jon: on archae-
    ology, 5
liberation: as communal
    experience, 34
liberation theology: and
    Bible, 20-21; black,
    34-37, 42-46; chal-
    lenging notion of Jesus
    as savior, 199; com-
    parison of black and
    Latin American, 35-
    37; critiques of, 38-50;
    and hermeneutics of
    suspicion, 39; Latin
    American, 31-34;
    Native American, 46-
    49; and preferential
    option for poor, 33
liturgy, public, 207-8
Lorde, Audre, 51
lying and deceit, 75-78;
    Shiphrah and Puah as
    liars, 168; woman in
    scripture as liars, 168

macro-story: exodus as,
    27
Matthews, Z. K., 142,
    143
Mendenhall, George: on
    origins of Israel in
    Palestine, 7
meritocracy: and individu-
    alism, 124
Mernaptha (pharaoh):
    stele of, 5-6, 106
midwives: as liars, 168;
    nationality of, 163-64;
    story of, and civil dis-
    obedience, 168-75
Miriam, Song of, 11-12,
    18, 89; as oldest refer-
    ence to exodus, 26-27
misappropriation: of exo-

dus story, 30-31; of
    oppressed people's
    story, 30
Morgenstern, Julian, 187
Morris, Jane Anne: on
    corporations, 64
Moses: nationality of,
    179-83; parallels with
    Pharaoh, 114-15; story
    of, 110-13, 179-83;
    story of birth of, 152-
    55
Murphy, Roland: on bibli-
    cal interpretation, 19
Myers, Ched, 78

NAFTA. See North Amer-
    ican Free Trade Agree-
    ment
Native American libera-
    tion theology, 46-49
Native Americans: and
    genocide, 71-75
Nevada Desert Experi-
    ence: and civil disobe-
    dience, 176
North American Free
    Trade Agreement
    (NAFTA), 103
Noth, Martin: theory of
    migratory infiltration
    of, 6-7
numerology, 17-18

oppressed: solidarity with,
    34
oppression: dividing
    humankind, 50; expe-
    rienced by African
    Americans, 35; global-
    ization and, 32; of
    indigenous peoples,
    47-49

P. See Priestly source
Pan African Healing
    Foundation, 78
passion: meaning of, 202
Passover: and rereading of
    story of exodus, 28
Passover Haggadah, 21,

28; and plague narratives, 82-83, 87
patriarchy: and Bible, 21
Pentateuch: sources of, 10-11
Pharaoh: and brick making, 112-13; daughter of, 146-62; hardness of heart of, 99, 105-27; officials of, 183-84; parallels with Moses, 114-15; as personification of empire, 116; and plagues, 113-14; portrait of, in Exodus, 106-10, 115-16; as symbol of faults of empire, 115
pharaohs: cosmic qualities of, 106; of Egypt, 105-10; modern, 116-17
Pixley, George: on mixed multitude, 190; on officials of Pharaoh, 183-84
plague narrative: in book of Exodus, 82-91; ecofeminist reading of, 91-97; and Egyptian religion, 96-97, 113-14; environment and, 93-94; modern parallels to, 97-104; relating struggle between YHWH and Pharaoh, 113-14; women absent from, 91-92, 98-99
Plaskow, Judith: on ecofeminism and Judaism, 90; on God as warrior, 135-36; on Torah, 20
Plowshares: and civil disobedience, 176
poor: Bible as historical memory of, 20-21; corporations and, 64; effect of free market on, 76; preferential option for, 33, 49-50; reading Bible, 32

postmodern paralysis, 51-52
poultry: farming in U.S., 101-3; and Imperial Food fire, 101-2
Priestly source, 11
prison industrial complex, 222n. 39; and slavery, 68-70
privilege, xiv; and violence, 65-68
proof-texting, 4
Propp, William: on plagues, 86
Protestant Reformation: and exodus theology, 29
Puah. See Shiphrah and Puah

race: and exploitation of environment, 102-3
racism: historical roots of, in North America, 123; and reproduction, 169-70
radical discipleship movement, xiii
Rahab: story of, examined by Margaret Guider, 39-42
Ramses II (pharaoh), 5, 106, 150
Ramses III (pharaoh), 150
religious conservatism, 3
reproduction: racism and, 169-70
Roberts, James Deotis, 36, 37
Rosen, Norma: on Midrash, 132; on Pharaoh's daughter, 146, 155-56, 158-59; rejecting image of God as violent, 136
Rothman, Stanley: on values of Western society, 63
Ruether, Rosemary Radford: on our lack of interaction with environment, 121-22

Ruíz, Bishop: on scripture and social reality, 20, 32

Sabbath economics, 188-89
salvation, 199
Sarah: and Hagar, story of, 43-46
School of the Americas Watch: and civil disobedience, 176
Schüssler Fiorenza, Elisabeth: on fourfold feminist hermeneutical process, 155
see, judge, and act: and Latin American base communities, 31-32
separation: of spiritual and political, 124-25
Seti I (pharaoh), 5, 106
Shelley, Martha, 97-98, 104
Shepard, Matthew, 51
Shiphrah and Puah, 5, 163-78; as liars, 168; significance of names of, 167
Shiva, Vandana: on globalization, 77
Siebert-Hommes, Jopie: on midwives in Exodus, 166; on women in Exodus, 147
sin, corporate, 199
slavery: children and, 70; in Egypt, 68; and empire, 68-70; and exodus paradigm, 43-46; and forced labor today, 68-70; penal system as, 68-69; as taught in school, 222n. 35
Sobrino, Jon: on oppression, 50
social location: and biblical interpretation, xi-xii; see also context
solidarity, 199-200: with oppressed, 34, 198

Sölle, Dorothee: on despair, 121
Solomon, Arthur, 46-47, 142-43
spirituality, privatized, 123-25; substituting for political engagement, 126-27

Tate, James, 51
Teena, Brandon, 51, 220n. 37
Tolbert, Mary Anne: on categories of critical analysis, xv-xvi; on privilege, 53
trade, international: effect of, on poor, 76
Trible, Phyllis, 63; on God as warrior, 136
triumphalism, spiritual, 124
Tubman, Harriet, 29
twelve: significance of, 147

Union Carbide: pesticide leak in Bhopal, India, 92-93
U.S. Army School of the Americas. See Western Hemispheric Institute for International Security Co-operation (WHISC), 74

values, traditional, 125-26; global implications of, 125-26
Vanunu, Mordechai: and civil disobedience, 175
violence: in Exodus, 128-45, 196; and genocide, 128; of God, 131-37; institutionalized, 128-

29; against oppressors, 137-38; and rage, 141-43; structural, 138-39

Walker, Alice: and womanist theology, 42-43
Walzer, Michael: on exodus, 31, 58
Warrior, Robert Allen: and use of biblical texts, xiii, 145; critique of liberation reading of Exodus of, 46-50; on land as unheard voice, 79; and Native American liberation theology, 46-50; on violence, 134-35
wealth, corporate, 116-17
Weems, Renita, 37; on drowning of Egyptians, 133; on Shiphrah and Puah, 163; on story of midwives, 170, 173
Wellhausen, Julius: Documentary Hypothesis of, 10
Western Hemispheric Institute for International Security Co-operation, 74
WHISC. See Western Hemispheric Institute for International Security Co-operation, 74
Williams, Delores, 37; critique of liberation reading of Exodus of, 38; on genocide, 72-73; and hermeneutic of suspicion, 45-46; on the poor, 49-50; on violence, 134-35, 138; and womanist theol-

ogy, 42-46, 49
Williams, Patricia: on Pharaoh's daughter as woman of privilege, 155-56
womanist theology, 42-46; hermeneutic of identification-ascertainment, 46
women: absent from book of Exodus and plague narratives, 91-92, 95, 98-99; in Egypt, 150; and exodus paradigm, 42; marginalization of, 42; in scripture as liars, 168; twelve mentioned in Exodus, 147
Woolman, John, 174
World Bank, 125; demonstrations against, 189; as structure of global capitalism, 127
World Trade Organization (WTO): protests against, 122-23, 189; as structure of global capitalism, 127
Wright, G. Ernest: on story of Joshua, 7
Wright, Rebecca, 51
WTO. See World Trade Organization

YHWH: chariots and, 131; and nonhuman world in plague narratives, 95-96; as warrior, 130-32, 196
Young, Josiah: on Exodus, 133; on judgment of the oppressors, 143

Also of Interest

Saint Francis

Marie Dennis

Art by John August Swanson

ISBN 1-57075-412-8

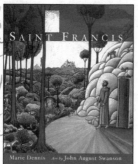

Through inspiring words and soul-enriching art, here is the story of Francis of Assisi. His life of reaching out and caring for others is a model for all people today.

Disturbing the Peace

The Story of Father Roy Bourgeois

James Hodge and Linda Cooper Hodge

ISBN 1-57075-434-9

The inspiring story of a prophetic priest in his campaign for peace and justice.

Please support your local bookstore, or call 1-800-258-5838.
For a free catalogue, please write us at
Orbis Books, Box 308
Maryknoll NY 10545-0302
Or visit our website at www.orbisbooks.com

Thank you for reading *Set Them Free*.
We hope you enjoyed it.